EUROPE
PHRASEBOOK

Europe phrasebook
3rd edition – February 2001

Published by
Lonely Planet Publications Pty Ltd, ABN 36 005 607 983
90 Maribyrnong St, Footscray, Victoria 3011, Australia

Lonely Planet Offices
Australia Locked Bag 1, Footscray, Victoria 3011
USA 150 Linden St, Oakland CA 94607
UK 10a Spring Place, London NW5 3BH
France 1 rue du Dahomey, 75011 Paris

Cover illustration
Not Another Friggin' Busker by Patrick Marris

ISBN 1 86450 224 X

text © Lonely Planet Publications Pty Ltd 2001
cover illustration © Lonely Planet Publications Pty Ltd 2001

Printed by The Bookmaker International Ltd
Printed in China

About the Authors

Mikel Morris wrote and updated the chapter on **Basque**. He's the author of the comprehensive dictionary *Morris Student Plus Euskara-Ingelesa English-Basque hiztegia*. He lives in Zarautz, Gipuzkoa, where he's the owner and director of a language school and publishing house.

Mar Cruz Piñol, who updated **Catalan**, is a native speaker of both Catalan and Castilian (Spanish). She's currently a lecturer in Spanish Philology at the University of Barcelona, where she's completing her doctoral thesis on the use of the Internet in teaching Spanish as a foreign language. This chapter was developed from Lonely Planet's *Spanish phrasebook* by Allison Jones and Izaskun Arretxe.

Eric den Hertog updated the **Dutch** chapter. A native Dutchman born and bred in Haarlem, Eric currently works as a management consultant and enjoys travelling. This chapter was developed from a chapter of Lonely Planet's *Western Europe phrasebook* written by Rob van Driesum.

French was updated by **Michael Janes**. Michael lives in London and has spent most of his life as a lexicographer, working mainly on French-English dictionaries. He's the author of several bilingual dictionaries, and has contributed to many English dictionaries and reference books. Michael has degrees in French from Bristol and London Universities, and a doctorate in linguistics from the University of Paris. This chapter was based on Lonely Planet's *French phrasebook* by Marie-Hélène Girard and Anny Monet.

German was updated by **Gunter Mühl**. From Hannover, Germany, Gunter teaches German at the University of Canterbury in Christchurch, New Zealand, and works as a freelance translator. This chapter was based on Lonely Planet's *German phrasebook*, written by Franziska Buck and Anke Munderloh.

Markella Calimassia, who wrote the chapter on **Greek**, grew up in Athens. After completing a BSc in genetics followed by a PhD at the Royal Botanic Gardens in London, she worked in Greece, Denmark, and England translating, editing and teaching modern Greek and English.

Francesco Cavallaro updated **Italian**. He was born in Sicily and grew up in Melbourne. He has a PhD in Italian linguistics and has taught Italian Studies at various universities in Australia, including the University of Melbourne and The University of Sydney. He is now an ESL Lecturer at Singapore Polytechnic. This chapter was developed from Lonely Planet's *Italian phrasebook*, written by Maurice Riverso and revised by Mirna Cicioni.

Maltese was updated by **Alexander Spiteri**. He is Head of Department of Maltese in a private school, and member of the Institute of Linguistics at the University of Malta. He lectures in Maltese methodology and Maltese for special purposes. Maltese was based on a chapter from Lonely Planet's *Mediterranean phrasebook* written by Albert Mashall.

Portuguese was written by **Clara Vitorino**, who has worked as a translator in Lisbon and is completing a PhD on 17th century Portuguese Literature. It was co-authored by Paula Fassman, Stephanie Gettelfinger and Audrey Un, from **AmeriConsulta**, Lda., a Lisbon-based company providing educational, translating and editing services.

Dr Rob Ó Maolalaigh wrote and updated the chapter on **Scottish Gaelic**. He also updated the **Irish** chapter, written by Dr Seán Ó Riain and published in Lonely Planet's *Western Europe phrasebook*. Rob was born in Dublin but now lives in Scotland where he lectures in the Department of Celtic, University of Edinburgh, where he is director of the Centre for Irish Studies.

The **Spanish** chapter was written by Allison Jones and Izaskun Arretxe, and further updated by **Allison Jones**. Allison has travelled and studied extensively in Spain, and works in the publishing industry.

Jim and Perihan Masters, co-authors of the Turkish chapter, are a husband and wife team, living on the Aegean Coast of Turkey. They sponsor the MSNBC Learning Practical Turkish Website.

Richard Crowe wrote and updated the Welsh chapter. He lives in Cardiff, and has worked as an assistant-editor on the University of Wales' Dictionary of the Welsh Language. He's now employed as a terminologist and senior translator at the National Assembly for Wales.

From the Authors

Mikel Morris is pleased that there might be some brave souls ready and willing to use Basque while visiting the country, thereby contributing to the perpetuation and prestige of the language. He gives his thanks to Txomin Arratibel and the Basque Translators' Association, EIZIE.

Mar Cruz Piñol gives many thanks to Laura Canós Antonino for sharing her knowledge of Catalan phonology and to her Australian friends Stewart King, Mike Rosel and Maureen Rosel.

Eric den Hertog is very grateful to his Australian girlfriend, Jacinta Noonan, whose many hours of assistance, and understanding of both English and Dutch, ensured the satisfactory completion of this project.

Markella Calimassia would like to thank her brother Georgios Callimassias, John Burke and her husband.

Francesco Cavallaro wishes to thank Peter D'onghia and all the editing staff at Lonely Planet for their assistance. The biggest thanks, however, is for Bee and Gianluca who make it all worthwhile.

Alexander Spiteri is grateful to Professor Albert J Borg, Chairman of the Institute of Linguistics, and Ms Edel Camilleri for assistance and encouragement in this project.

Clara Vitorino, **Paula Fassman**, **Stephanie Gettelfinger** and **Audrey Un** give their sincerest thanks to Paulo Fassman Correia and Wendy Graça, Inês Vitorino, Claudio Silva, António Pascoal, Kyle Oliveira and Dionisio Martínez. Gems all.

Jim Masters and Perihan Masters wish to thank their parents, children, sisters, brother, Taşkın Çalı and Jessica.

Richard Crowe is grateful to all those who've helped with this project, especially to all friends and colleagues in the University of Wales and the National Library of Wales.

From the Publisher
The talented Patrick Marris illustrated both the book and its cover. He still found time to design the book, together with Yukiyoshi Kamimura. Fabrice Rocher supervised layout and Fleur Goding proofed. Vicki Webb edited and wrote the introduction. Matt Anning, Karin Vidstrup Monk and Ingrid Seebus assisted with editing, while Natasha Velleley mapped out Europe. Sally Steward initiated the project, and Karin Vidstrup Monk and Peter D'Onghia rounded everyone up and supervised.

CONTENTS

INTRODUCTION

Some of the most rewarding things about travelling through western Europe is the rich variety of cuisine, customs, architecture and history. The flipside of course is that you'll encounter a number of very different languages. From Athens to Lisbon and up to Belfast, you may hear more than 14 languages from six different language groups.

Many European languages, including English, belong to what's known as the 'Indo-European' language family. This group of languages is believed to have originally developed from one language spoken thousands of years ago. Luckily for English-speakers, all but one use Roman script.

The Romance languages – Catalan, French, Italian, Portuguese and Spanish – all developed from Vulgar Latin, which spread throughout western Europe with the rule of the Roman Empire. The freedom with which English has borrowed Latin-based vocabulary means you'll quickly recognise many words from these languages.

DID YOU KNOW ...

- The **Union flag** has a circle of 12 gold stars on a blue background – 12 being a number representing wholeness.
- The **EU anthem** is the *Ode to Joy* from Beethoven's Ninth Symphony.
- **Europe Day**, 9 May, commemorates the 1950 declaration by French Foreign Minister Robert Schuman, regarded as marking the creation of the European Union.

EUROPE

Basque Country

Catalunya

NORWAY

Atlantic Ocean

NORTHERN IRELAND

SCOTLAND

Edinburgh

SWEDEN

North Sea

Belfast

IRELAND

BRITAIN

DENMARK

Dublin

WALES

NETHERLANDS

ENGLAND

Cardiff

Amsterdam

CHANNEL ISLANDS

Brussels

Berlin

GERMANY

BELGIUM

LUXEMBOURG

Paris

Luxembourg

CZECH REP.

FRANCE

LIECHTENSTEIN

Bern

Vienna

SWITZERLAND

AUSTRIA

Bay of Biscay

SLOVENIA

SAN MARINO

CROATIA

Andorra la Vella

MONACO

ITALY

PORTUGAL

CORSICA

Rome

Adriatic Sea

Lisbon

Madrid

ANDORRA

SPAIN

SARDINIA

Tyrrhenian Sea

Mediterranean Sea

SICILY

Valletta

MALTA

MOROCCO

ALGERIA

TUNISIA

LIBYA

0   250   500 km
0   150   300 mi

Map   13

INTRODUCTION

Irish, Scottish Gaelic and Welsh are all Celtic languages, spoken in the UK since before the Anglo-Saxon invasion. The use of these languages plays an important part in reclaiming the cultural heritage of Scotland, Wales and Ireland.

The Germanic languages Dutch and German have many similarities in pronunciation and vocabulary, and being related to English, you'll have a head-start with many familiar words.

Greek, the language of the *Iliad* and the *Odyssey*, forms a single branch of the Indo-European language family . It uses Greek script.

Maltese, thought to be an Arabic language, has over time been influenced by the Romance languages, and is the only form of Arabic to use Roman script.

Turkish is part of the Altaic language family, which includes languages spoken from the Balkan Peninsula to north-east Asia. Arabic script was replaced by Roman script in the early 1900s.

Finally, Basque is a bit of a linguistic enigma. It has no known relation to other European languages – or to any other recorded language – and is thought to be the only language to survive the Roman invasion of Europe.

This book provides the basics to get you around from day-to-day, while getting to know people on the way. In countries where English is spoken widely, trying a few words in the local tradi-tional language will make you especially welcome, whether at the pub, eating out or when asking directions.

MONEY TALKS

Euros bank notes and coins are in circulation as of E-Day, 1 January 2002.

The euro's symbol (€) was inspired by the Greek letter epsilon (ε) – Greece being the cradle of Euro-pean civilisation and ε being the first letter of the word 'Europe'. The parallel lines stand for the stability of the currency. It's abbreviated as 'EUR'.

INTRODUCTION

HOW TO USE THIS PHRASEBOOK
Transliterations
Simplified tranliterations have been provided in blue throughout this book. Italics is used to indicate where to place stress in a word.

Polite Forms
When a language has polite and informal forms of the singular pronoun 'you', the polite form has been used in most cases. However, you will come across the informal form of 'you' in some phrases, such as those for talking with children.

ALL IN THE NEIGHBOURHOOD

The *European Economic Community* was founded by the Treaty of Rome in 1957, later developing into the *European Community*, then *European Union (EU)*. At the turn of the century, member states included Austria, Belgium, Britain, Denmark, Finland, France, Germany, Greece, Ireland, Italy, Luxembourg, the Netherlands, Portugal, Spain and Sweden.

Major EU organisations include:

• *Council of Ministers*
  made up of government ministers from member states. Votes on major decisions and shares legislative and budgetary power with Parliament.

• *European Commission*
  the largest of the Union's institutions, responsible for daily government. Initiates legislation, manages the EU budget, and negotiates trade and cooperation agreements.

• *European Parliament*
  represents the people of member states, with powers similar to those of national parliaments, with legislative and budgetary powers

INTRODUCTION

Arthur or Martha?

When there are both masculine and feminine forms of a word, this is indicated in either of two ways, with the masculine form always appearing first:

- with a slash separating the masculine and feminine endings of a word:

  nurse   een-fer-*mee-ye*-re/ah   *infermiere/a*

- when the distinction between masculine and feminine is more complex, each word is given in full, separated with a slash:

  writer   skreet-*tree*-che/   *scrittrice/*
                  screet-*to*-re   *scrittore*

An explanation of gender as used in each language can be found at the beginning of every chapter.

Finally

Don't be concerned if you feel you can't memorise words. You'll find the most essential words and phrases in the Quick Reference section at the start of each chapter. You could also try tagging a few pages for other key phrases, or use the notes pages to write your own reminders.

ABBREVIATIONS USED IN THIS BOOK

f	feminine	pl	plural
inf	informal	pol	polite
m	masculine	sg	singular

BASQUE

BASQUE

QUICK REFERENCE

Hi!	*kai*-sho!	Kaixo!
Goodbye.	a-*goorr*	Agur.
How are you?	sair mo-*doos*?	Zer moduz?
Fine, and you?	*on*-gee e-tah *soo*?	Ongi, eta zu?
Excuse me.	barr-*kah*-too	Barkatu.
Please.	me-*se*-des	Mesedez.
Thank you.	es-*ke*-rree-*kahs*-ko	Eskerrik asko.
You're welcome.	es o-*rre*-gah-teek	Ez horregatik.
I'd like a ...	... nai noo-*ke*	... nahi nuke.
Cheers!	*to*-pah!	Topa!

Where's the toilet, please?
ko-*moo*-nah non dah-*go*?   Komuna non dago?

I don't understand.
es toot oo-*lairr*-tzen   Ez dut ulertzen.

Do you speak English?
een-*ge*-le-ses bah ahl
dah-kee-*soo*?   Ingelesez ba al dakizu?

Do you have any rooms available?
bah ahl doo-*soo* ge-lah
lee-bre-reek?   Ba al duzu gela librerik?

How much is this?
ow *sen*-baht dah?   Hau zenbat da?

How do I get to ...?
non-deek *yo*-ah-ten
dah ...-(e)rah?   Nondik joaten da ...-(e)ra?

On the left.	es-*kairr*-tah-rah	Ezkerrean.
On the right.	es-*koo*-bee-ahn	Eskubian.
Straight on.	*soo*-sen/*soo*-se-ne-ahn	Zuzen/Zuzenean.

1	baht	bat	6	say	sei
2	bee	bi	7	*sahs*-pee	zazpi
3	*ee*-roo	hiru	8	*sorr*-tzee	zortzi
4	low	lau	9	be-*de*-rah-tzee	bederatzi
5	bost	bost	10	*ah*-mahrr	hamar

BASQUE

No one quite knows the origin of Basque, but that hasn't stopped some eccentrics from declaring that it's related to the Sioux language, to Japanese, even to the language of the Atlanteans. The most interesting, and plausible, theory is that Basque is the lone survivor of a family of languages which extended across Europe, but which were ultimately wiped out and supplanted by such Indo-European invaders as the Celts, Germanic tribes and the Romans. There are those who try to link extinct languages such as those of the Etruscans and Picts to this supposedly defunct language family. Even in recent times, some linguists have called this ancient family of languages 'Basque-Caucasian', implying that Basque may be ultimately related, albeit distantly so, to such languages as Georgian or Chechen. Nevertheless, the ultimate answer to the enigma of where the Basque language actually came from remains lost in the distant hazes of Europe's prehistoric past.

Over the past millennia, Basque has intermingled with the languages of its invaders and neighbours, and this is reflected in its vocabulary. The Basque number system, like that of the Celts, is based on scores and even the name for twenty, *hogei*, is similar to the Welsh word for twenty, 'ugain'. Basque borrowed words directly from Latin and, unlike the Romance languages, it has kept these words more or less as they were. In more recent times, Basque has borrowed heavily from the Gascon dialect of Provençal, Spanish, French, and now even English.

Basque is spoken by up to 800,000 people throughout seven provinces, which are divided into three basic political entities – the Basque Autonomous Community (BAC); Navarre; and Iparralde (aka the French Basque Country). Though the only communities where Basque is the primary language are smaller towns, its use is increasing in larger cities, especially among young people.

Centuries of neglect and marginalisation, combined with two centuries of French republicanism and 40 years of Spanish fascism, pushed Basque to the brink of extinction. Nevertheless, the situation has improved greatly since it was declared an official language along with Spanish in 1979 in the BAC and Navarre. Basque still lacks official recognition of any kind in France.

Today, most children in the BAC are now taught in Basque, there is a Basque TV channel, and dozens of local municipal channels which feature the language either prominently or exclusively. There are Basque-language rock bands, rap singers, and some software packages have Basque versions. Basque is going from strength to strength, and the fruits of a generation educated in Basque, the first in history, will be readily apparent in the years to come.

While speaking Spanish in the Basque-speaking towns might be expected from a foreigner, those foreigners who make an attempt to speak Basque will be warmly received as someone struggling to communicate in one of the most ancient languages of Europe.

PRONUNCIATION

Basque pronunciation doesn't pose many problems for the English speaker who can roll their 'r's fairly well. The stress in Basque is generally on the second-last syllable.

Letters not described here are pronounced as they are in English.

Vowels

a	ah	as the 'a' in 'father', but shorter
e	e	as the 'e' in 'bet';
	ai	sometimes as the 'y' in 'sky'
i	ee	as the 'i' in 'marine'
o	o	as the 'o' in 'hot'
u	oo	as the 'u' in 'flute'

Vowel Combinations

ai	ai	as the 'y' in 'sky'
au	ow	as the 'ow' in 'cow'

Consonants

g	g	as the 'g' in 'game'; never as the 'g' in 'gentle'
h		silent in the Spanish Basque Country (in the French Basque Country, pronounced as the 'h' in 'horse')
j	y	as the 'y' in 'yes' (in parts of the Basque Country around Donostia-San Sebastian, it's pronounced as the 'ch' in Scottish 'loch')
in	ny	as the 'ny' in 'canyon'. This sound is written as ñ in Spanish.
r	rr	trilled at the end of a word;
	r	elsewhere, as the 'tt' in 'butter' when pronounced quickly
rr	rr	trilled
x	sh	as 'sh' as in 'ship'
tx	ch	as the 'ch' in 'cheese'
ts	chy	like the 'ch' in 'cheese', but softer. Even some Basque-speakers confuse this sound with *tx*.
tz	tz	as the 'tz' in 'Ritz'
z	s	as the 's' in 'sin'

BASQUE

PRONOUNS

SG			Pl		
I	nee(k)	*ni(k)*	**we**	goo(k)	*gu(k)*
you (inf)	ee(k)	*hi(k)*	**you**	soo-ek	*zuek*
you (pol)	soo(k)	*zu(k)*	**they**	be-rai-ek	*beraiek*
he/she/it	be-rah(k)	*bera(k)*			

GREETINGS & CIVILITIES
You Should Know

Hi!	*kai*-sho!	Kaixo!
Good morning.	e-goo-*non*	Egun on.
Good afternoon/ evening.	ah-*rrah*-chyahl-de *on*	Arratsalde on.
Good night.	gah-*bon*	Gabon.

BASQUE

How are you?	sair mo-*doos*?	*Zer moduz?*
What's up?	sair be-*rree*?	*Zer berri?*
Fine, and you?	*on*-gee e-tah *soo*?	*Ongi, eta zu?*
Fine, thanks.	*on*-gee,	*Ongi,*
	es-*ke*-rree-*kahs*-ko	*eskerrik asko.*
Excuse me.	barr-*kah*-too	*Barkatu.*
Please.	me-*se*-des	*Mesedez.*
Thank you.	es-*ke*-rree-*kahs*-ko	*Eskerrik asko.*
You're welcome.	es o-*rre*-gah-teek	*Ez horregatik.*
Goodbye.	a-*goorr*	*Agur.*
See you later.	*ge*-ro *ahrr*-te	*Gero arte.*
Take care.	*on*-do ee-*beel*-(y)ee	*Ondo ibili.*

Forms of Address

Mr Agirre	a-*gee*-rre *yow*-na	*Agirre jauna*
Mrs Agirre	a-*gee*-rre *ahn*-dre-ah	*Agirre andrea*
Hey!	ai-*soo*!	*Aizu!*

SMALL TALK
Meeting People

What's your name?
    sair ee-sen doo-*soo*?   *Zer izen duzu?*

My name's John.
    jon doot ee-*se*-nah   *John dut izena.*

I'd like to introduce you to ...
    ... owr-*kes*-too nai nee-soo-*ke*   *... aurkeztu nahi nizuke*

I'm pleased to meet you.
    pos-*gah*-rree-ah sait soo   *Pozgarria zait zu*
    e-*sah*-goo-tze-ah   *ezagutzea.*

I'm here on ...	*nah*-go e-*men*	*... nago hemen.*
business	ne-*go*-see-o-e-tahn	*negozioetan*
holidays	o-*porr*-e-tahn	*oporretan*
studying	ee-*kahs*-ten	*ikasten*

How long have you been here?
   noys-teek *sow*-de e-*men*?   *Noiztik zaude hemen?*
I've been here (three days).
   (*ee*-roo e-*goon*) dee-*rah*   *(Hiru egun) dira hemen*
   e-*men* nah-*go*-e-lah   *nagoela.*
How long are you here for?
   noys *ahrr*-te e-*gon* be-*ahrr*   *Noiz arte egon behar duzu*
   doo-soo e-*men*?   *hemen?*
We're here for (two weeks).
   (bee ahs-*te*) e-*gon*-go   *(Bi aste) egongo gara hemen.*
   gah-*rah* e-*men*

Nationalities

You'll find that some country names in Basque are similar to English. If your country isn't listed here, try saying it with Basque pronunciation and you might be understood.

Where are you from?   non-*go*-ah sah-*rah*?   *Nongoa zara?*

I'm from ...	... nais	... *naiz.*
Australia	ows-*trah*-lee-a-ko-ah	*Australiakoa*
Canada	kah-*nah*-dah-ko-ah	*Kanadakoa*
England	een-*gah*-lah-te-rra-ko-ah	*Ingalaterrakoa*
Ireland	eerr-*lahn*-dah-ko-ah	*Irlandakoa*
New Zealand	se-*lahn*-dah	*Zeelanda*
	be-*rree*-ko-a	*Berrikoa*
Scotland	es-*ko*-see-ah-ko-ah	*Eskoziakoa*
the US	es-*tah*-too ba-*too*-	*Estatu*
	e-tah-ko-ah	*Batuetakoa*
Wales	*gah*-les-ko-ah	*Galeskoa*

Where do you live?
   non *bee*-see sah-*rah*?   *Non bizi zara?*
I live in (Darwin).
   (dahr-*wee*-nen) bee-see nais   *(Darwin)-en bizi naiz.*

BASQUE

Occupations

What do you do?
   sairr-tah ah-*ree*-tzen sah-*rah*?   *Zertan aritzen zara?*

I'm (a/an) ...	...nais	... *naiz.*
artist	ahrr-*tees*-tah	*artista*
business person	en-*pre*-sah-ree-ah	*enpresaria*
doctor	me-*dee*-koo-ah	*medikua*
engineer	een-*yee*-ne-roo-ah	*injinerua*
journalist	kah-*se*-tah-ree-ah	*kazetaria*
lawyer	ah-*bo*-kah-too-ah	*abokatua*
musician	moo-*see*-kah-ree-ah	*musikaria*
nurse	e-*ree*-sai-nyah	*erizaina*
office worker	boo-*le*-gah-ree-ah	*bulegaria*
retired	e-*rre*-tee-rah-too-ah	*erretiratua*
secretary	ee-*dahs*-kah-ree-ah	*idazkaria*
student	ee-*kahs*-le-ah	*ikaslea*
unemployed	*lahn*-gah-be-ah	*langabea*
waiter	kah-*mah*-re-ro-ah	*kamareroa*

BASQUE LINGO

Euskal Herrian beti jai!		
e-oos-*kahl* e-*rree*-ahn	The Basque Country's	
be-tee yai!	always partying!	
Gora gu 'ta gutarrak!		
go-rah goo tah	Hurray for us!	
goo-tah-rrahk!		
Gero arte Bonaparte!		
ge-ro *ahrr*-te	See you later, alligator!	
bo-nah-*pahrr*-te!		
Agur Ben Hur!		
ah-*goorr* be-*noorr*!	In a while, crocodile!	

Family

Are you married?
es-*kon*-doo-ah ahl sah-*rah*?   *Ezkondua al zara?*

Do you have a girlfriend/boyfriend?
ahn-*dre*-gai-reek/   *Andregairik/*
se-*nahrr*-gai-reek   *senargairik*
bah ahl doo-*soo*?   *ba al duzu?*

How many children do you have?
sen-baht se-*me*-ah-lah-bah   *Zenbat seme-alaba*
dee-too-*soo*?   *dituzu?*

I'm ...   ... nais   ... *naiz.*
married   es-*kon*-doo-ah   *Ezkondua*
separated   bah-*nah*-too-ah   *Banatua*
single   es-*kon*-gah-be-ah   *Ezkongabea*
widowed   ah-*lahrr*-goo-nah   *Alarguna*

I have a partner.
bah-doot lah-*goo*-nah   *Badut laguna.*

BREAKING THE LANGUAGE BARRIER

Do you speak English?
een-*ge*-le-ses bah ahl   *Ingelesez ba al*
dah-kee-*soo*?   *dakizu?*

I know a little Basque.
e-*oos*-kah-rah ah-*poorr*   *Euskara apur bat*
baht bah-dah-*keet*   *badakit.*

I don't understand.
es toot oo-*lairr*-tzen   *Ez dut ulertzen.*

Could you speak
more slowly please?
po-*lee*-kee-ah-go eetz   *Polikiago hitz*
e-*geen*-go ahl doo-*soo*?   *egingo al duzu?*

Could you write
that down please?
ee-*dah*-tzee-ko ahl dee-dah-   *Idatziko al didazu hori,*
soo o-ree, me-se-des?   *mesedez?*

Could you speak in
Castillian, please?
   airr-dah-rahs e-*geen*-go
   ahl dee-*dah*-soo, me-*se*-des?

*Erdaraz egingo
al didazu mesedez?*

How do you say
(that in Basque)?
   no-lah e-*sah*-ten dah
   (*o*-ree e-oos-kah-*rahs*)?

*Nola esaten da
(hori euskaraz)?*

GETTING AROUND
Directions

Excuse me, can you help me please?
   bahrr-*kah*-too, lah-*goon*-doo-ko
   ahl dee-*dah*-soo, me-*se*-des?

*Barkatu, lagunduko
al didazu, mesedez?*

Where's the toilet, please?
   ko-*moo*-nah, non dah-*go*?

Komuna non dago?

How do I get to ...?
   non-deek *yo*-ah-ten
   dah ...(e)rah?

*Nondik joaten
da ... -(e)ra?*

I don't know.	es *tah*-keet	*Ez dakit.*
At the end.	ahs-*ke*-ne-ahn	*Azkenean.*
On the left.	es-*kairr*-tah-rah	*Ezkerrean.*
On the right.	es-*koo*-bee-ahn	*Eskubian.*
Straight on.	*soo*-sen/ *soo*-se-ne-ahn	*Zuzen/zuzenean.*
avenue	e-*torr*-bee-de-ah	*etorbidea*
square	*plah*-sah;	*plaza;*
	en-*pah*-rahn-tzah	*enparantza*
street	*kah*-le-ah	*kalea*

Bus

Does this bus go	ow-*to*-boos ow	*Autobus hau ba*
to the ...?	*bah* ahl *do*-ah ...?	*al doa ...?*
beach	on-*dahrr*-tzah-rah	*hondartzara*
city centre	ee-*ree* airr-*dee*-rah	*hiri-erdira*
station	geel-*to*-kee-rah	*geltokira*

Do you stop at ...?
  ...-(e)n gel-*dee*-tzen ahl sah-*rah*?   ... *(e)n gelditzen al zara?*
Where do I change for ...?
  non ahl-*dah*-too be-*ahrr*   *Non aldatu behar*
  doot ...(e)rah yo-ah-te-*ko*?   *dut ... (e)ra joateko?*
Could you let me know
when we get to ...?
  ah-*bee*-sah-too-ko ahl   *Abisatuko al*
  dee-*dah*-soo ...(e)rah   *didazu ...(e)ra*
  ee-*ree*-chyee-tah-ko-ahn?   *iritsitakoan?*

Taxi

Are you free?
  lee-bre ahl sow-*de*?   *Libre al zaude?*

Could you take	... e-*rah*-mahn-go	... *eramango*
me to the/this ...?	ahl now-*soo*?	*al nauzu?*
address	el-*bee*-de	*helbide*
	on-*ne*-tah-rah	*honetara*
airport	ai-*re*-porr-too-ah	*aireportura*
city centre	ee-*ree*-airr-dee-rah	*hiri-erdira*
railway station	tren-gel-to-kee-rah	*tren-geltokira*

BASQUE

SWITCHY-CHANGEY

Looking for that town on the map and can't find it?
Maybe the Spanish was painted out, or perhaps you
have an old map with the old, now unofficial Spanish
name. Here's some help.

Arrasate	Mondragon
Bilbo	Bilbao
Doneztebe	Santesteban
Donostia	San Sebastian
Hondarribia	Fuenterrabia
Iruñea (or *Iruña*)	Pamplona
Lizarra	Estella
Soraluze	Placencia de las Armas

BASQUE

How much is it to get to ...?

sen-baht kos-*tah*-tzen
dah ... (e)rah yo-ah-te-ah?

*Zenbat kostatzen
da ... (e)ra joatea?*

Here's fine, thank you.

e-men *on*-do dah,
es-*ke*-rreek *ahs*-ko

*Hemen ondo da,
eskerrik asko.*

How much do I owe you?

sen-baht sorr dee-*soot*?

Zenbat zor dizut?

SIGNS

EDARITEGIA	BAR
EMAN BIDEA	GIVE WAY
ERTZAINTZA	BASQUE POLICE
IRTEERA	EXIT
KONTUZ!	CAUTION!
LINEA	LINE
NORAKOA	DESTINATION
SARRERA	ENTRANCE
SARTZEA DEBEKATURIK	NO ENTRY
UDALTZAINGOA	MUNICIPAL POLICE

ACCOMMODATION
At the hotel

Do you have any rooms available?

bah ahl doo-*soo* ge-lah
lee-bre-reek?

Ba al duzu gela librerik?

I'd like a ...	... *ge*-lah nai doot	... *gela nahi dut.*
single room	ba-*ten*-tzah-ko	*batentzako*
double room	bee-*ren*-tzah-ko	*birentzako*

I want a room	... *doo*-en	... *duen gela*
with a ...	*ge*-lah nai doot	*nahi dut.*
bathroom	*ba*-nyoo-ge-lah baht	*bainugela bat*
double bed	*o*-e bee-*koy*-tzah	*ohe bikoitza*
shower	*doo*-chah	*dutxa*

How much is it per ...?	*sen*-baht dah ... bah-*koy*-tze-ko?	*Zenbat da ...* *bakoitzeko?*
night	gow	*gau*
person	pairr-*chyo*-nah	*pertsona*

Does it include breakfast?
go-*sah*-ree-ah *bahrr*-ne ahl dah? — *Gosaria barne al da?*

It's fine, I'll take it.
e-*dairr*-kee, *ahrr*-too e-*geen*-go doot — *Ederki, hartu egingo dut.*

I'm/We're leaving now.
bah-no-ah/ *bah*-go-ahs — *Banoa/Bagoaz.*

I'd like to pay the bill.
kon-*too*-ah orr-*dain*-doo nai doot — *Kontua ordaindu nahi dut.*

Requests & Complaints

The key for room (20) please.
(o-gay) *gah*-rren *ge*-lah-ko *geel*-tzah, me-*se*-des — *(Hogei) garren gelako giltza, mesedez.*

It's too ...	... dah	... *da.*
cold	*o*-tze-gee-ah	*hotzegia*
dark	ee-*lyoo*-ne-gee-ah	*ilunegia*
noisy	sah-*rah*-tah-chyoo-e-gee-ah	*zaratatsuegia*

Can I leave my backpack at reception until tonight?
mo-*chee*-lah ah-*rre*-rahn oos-*te*-reek bah ahl *dah*-go gowrr *gow*-e-ra ahrr-*te*? — *Motxila harreran uzterik ba al dago gaur gauera arte?*

Please, call a taxi for me.
me-*se*-des, day e-gee-o-soo *tahk*-see bah-*tee* — *Mesedez, dei egiozu taxi bati.*

BASQUE

AROUND TOWN
At the Post Office

Do you sell ...?	... *sahl*-tzen ahl doo-*soo*?	... *saltzen al duzu*?
envelopes	*so*-bre-reek	*sobrerik*
pens	bo-*lee*-grah-fo-reek	*boligraforik*
postcards	pos-*tah*-leek	*postalik*

Telephone

Hello. (making a call)	ai-*soo*?	*Aizu*?
Hello. (answering a call)	bai, e-*sahn*?	*Bai, esan*?
Could I speak to John?	yon *orr* ahl dah-*go*?	*Jon hor al dago*?
Who's calling?	*no*-ren pahrr-*tes*?	*Noren partez*?
It's ...	... nais	... *naiz*.

Just a minute, I'll put him on.
> ee-*chah*-ron, o-*rain*-che *Itxaron, oraintxe*
> yah-*rree*-ko *dah* *jarriko da*.

I'm sorry he's not here just now.
> bahr-*kah*-too, *bah*-nyah *Barkatu, baina*
> *oo*-ne o-*ne*-tahn es tah-*go* *une honetan ez dago*.

What time will he be back?
> sairr *orr*-doo-tahn *Zer ordutan*
> ee-*tzoo*-lee-ko *dah*? *itzuliko da*?

INTERESTS & ENTERTAINMENT
Sightseeing

Where's the ...?	non dah-*go* ...?	*Non dago* ...?
bus station	ow-*to*-boos gel-*to*-kee-a	*autobus- geltokia*
city centre	ee-*ree* airr-*dee*-ah	*hiri-erdia*
old part of town	*ahl*-de *sah*-rrah	*alde zaharra*
tourist information office	too-*rees*-mo boo-*le*-go-ah	*turismo -bulegoa*
train station	tren gel-*to*-kee-ah	*tren-geltokia*

WRITING ON THE WALL

The Basque Country is thoroughly politicised and this is reflected by its graffiti. Here's a sample:

Amnistia Osoa!	Total Amnesty!
Askatasuna!	Freedom!
... askatu!	Free ...!
Bakea orain!	Peace Now!
Gora ...!	Long Live ...!
Herriak ez du barkatuko!	The people shall never forgive!
... herria zurekin!	..., the people are with you!
Intsumisioa!	No Military Service!
... kanpora!	... go home!
Nuklearrik ez!	No nukes!
Presoak kalera!	Free the prisoners!

BASQUE

Going Out

Even though you'll understand very little, if anything, it's interesting to see a *bertsolari* in action. A *bertsolari* ad-libs poetry, complete with rhyme and meter, to a particular tune.

I feel like going to a ...	... *bah*-te-rah yo-*ah*-te-ko go-*go*-ah dow-*kaht*	... *batera joateko gogoa daukat*
bar	tah-*bairr*-nah	*taberna*
concert	kon-*tzairr*-too	*kontzertu*
nightclub	dees-*ko*-te-kah	*diskoteka*
restaurant	yah-*te*-che	*jatetxe*
theatre	ahn-*tzo*-kee	*antzoki*

What are you doing this ...?	gowrr ... o-*ne*-tahn sairr e-*geen* be-*ahrr* doo-*soo*?	*Gaur ... honetan zer egin behar duzu?*
evening	ah-*rrah*-chyahl-de-ahn	*arratsaldean*
weekend	ahs-*te*-boo-roo	*asteburu*

Would you like to go for a meal?

non-bait yahn nai ahl se-noo-*ke*?	*Nonbait jan nahi al zenuke?*

Not at the moment, thanks.

o-*rain* es, es-*ke*-rreek ahs-*ko*	*Orain ez, eskerrik asko.*

I'm sorry, I can't.

bahrr-*kah*-too, *bah*-nyah e-*seen* doot	*Barkatu, baina ezin dut.*

Sure!	e-*dairr*-kee!	*Ederki!*
Yes, that'd be great!	bai, o-*ree*-she!	*Bai horixe!*

Sports & Interests

With Basques, soccer is king, and other sports such as basketball and rugby are also widely played. Basque handball, aka *pilota* or *pelota*, is quite famous around the world, and a variant of it, *jai-alai*, is well known in the US. Basques also take to folk sports such as wood-chopping, stone lifting, and ox-drawn stone dragging. These sports all involve heavy betting.

What do you do in your spare time?

sairr e-*gee*-ten *doo*-soo *lee*-bre sow-de-ne-*an*?	*Zer egiten duzu libre zaudenean?*

Do you like sport?

kee-*ro*-lahk ah-*chye*-geen dee-too-*soo*?	*Kirolak atsegin dituzu?*

Yes, very much.	bai, *o*-so	*Bai, oso.*
Not, not at all.	es, *bah*-te-re es	*Ez, batere ez.*

Do you feel like going for a swim?

ee-*ge*-ree-an e-*geen* nai
ahl doo-*soo*?

*Igerian egin nahi
al duzu?*

Do you want to go
hiking this weekend?

men-dee-rah yo-*ahn* nai
ahl doo-*soo* ahs-*te*-boo-roo
o-ne-*tahn*?

*Mendira joan nahi
al duzu asteburu
honetan?*

Would you like to go to a
football match?

foo-bol pahrr-*tee*-doo
bah-te-rah yo-*ahn* nai
ahl doo-*soo*?

*Futbol-partidu
batera joan nahi
al duzu?*

Would you like to see a
wood-chopping contest?

ais-*kol*-ah-poos-too baht
ee-*koo*-see nai ahl doo-*soo*?

*Aizkol-apustu bat
ikusi nahi al duzu?*

Hurray for Real/Athletic!

ow-pah e-*rre*-ah-lah!/
aht-*le*-teek!

*Aupa Erreala/
Athletic!*

BASQUE

Festivals & Saint's Days

Every town and village has its own patron saint's day celebrated
with festivities, fairs, or in the case of the very smallest places,
erromeriak, 'town picnics'.

The better known festivals include *San Roke* festival in Gernika
(16 August), San Antolin Festival in Lekeitio (2 September), *San
Inazio* in Azpeitia (31 July), *Our Lady of Guadalupe* in Hondarribia
(9 September), and the folkloric *Basque Festival* in Zarautz (9
September).

The Basque Country is well known for its *txistu*, 'flutes', which
are as sweet sounding as they are austere. Basque music is also
characterised by *trikitixa*, 'accordion music', played at every festival
and accompanied by dances such as the *zortziko* and the *arin-arin*.

BASQUE

Aberri Eguna
'Day of the Basque Homeland'. Coincides with Easter and has heavy political overtones.

Amabirjina Zuria
Vitoria-Gasteiz, August 4-9

Aste Nagusia
held in Donostia-San Sebastian during August, and is followed by another celebration in Bilbao

Ihauteriak
carnaval, held in February. The most famous are in Tolosa, Azpeitia and Lantz.

San Fermin
this festival held on 7 July in *Iruñea*, 'Pamplona', is world famous

San Sebastian Eguna
St Sebastian Day is celebrated on 20 January in Donostia-San Sebastian

Happy Birthday!	so-*ree*-o-nahk!	*Zorionak!*
	(lit: good fortunes)	
Merry Christmas!	e-*goo*-be-rree on	*Eguberri On!*
Happy New Year!	*oorr*-te *be*-rree on!	*Urte Berri On!*
Good luck!	*sorr*-te on!	*Zorte on!*
Congratulations!		
so-*ree*-o-nak!/		*Zorionak!/*
be-*hon*-day-soo-lah!		*Bejondeizula!*

IN THE COUNTRY

Camping

Can I camp here?
bah ahl *dow*-kaht e-*men*
kan-*pah*-tze-reek?

*Ba al daukat hemen
kanpatzerik?*

Is there a campsite nearby?
bah ahl *dah*-go *kahn*-pee-nyeek
e-men een-*goo*-roo-ahn?

*Ba al dago kanpinik
hemen inguruan?*

FOOD

Cheers!	*to*-pah!	*Topa!*
Bon appetit!	on e-*geen*!	*On egin!*
Waiter!	ai-*soo*!	*Aizu!*

BASQUE

Main Meals

bakailaoa	bah-*kai*-lyow-ah	cod
bakailuz beteak	bah-*kai*-lyow-ahs be-te-ahk	with cod
barazkiak	ba-*rahs*-kee-ahk	vegetables
entsalada	en-*chyah*-lah-dah	salad
errusiar entsalada	e-*rroo*-see-ahrr en-*chyah*-lah-dah	potato salad with mayonnaise
eskalopea	es-*kah*-lo-pe-ah	crumbed fillet
esparragoak	es-*pah*-rrah-go-ahk	asparagus
frijituak	free-*hee*-too-ahk	fritters
kakotxak	kah-*ko*-chahk	the area around the neck of a fish, considered to be the best part
legatza	le-*gah*-tzah	hake
patata frijituak	pah-*tah*-tah free-*hee*-too-ahk	chips (French fries)
piper muturtxodunak	*pee*-per moo-*toorr*-cho-doo-nahk	fine red pimento peppers
saiheskiak	sai-*es*-kee-ahk	ribs
txirlak	*cheerr*-lahk	clams
txuleta	choo-*le*-tah	steak

xapoa	*shah*-po-ah	angler
xerra	*she*-rrah	chop
xipiroiak	shee-*pee*-roy-ahk	squid

Desserts

flana	*flah*-nah	creme caramel
etxeko kopa	e-che-ko *ko*-pah	ice-cream dessert
gazta	*gahs*-tah	cheese
izozkia	ee-*sos*-kee-ah	ice cream
mamia	mah-*mee*-ah	sheep's milk curds (don't be put off by the name, it's great)
menbrilua	mem-*bree*-lyoo-ah	quince jelly
natilak	nah-*tee*-lyahk	custard
trufa tarta	*troo*-fah *tahrr*-tah	chocolate truffle cake
whisky tarta	*wees*-kee *tahrr*-tah	whisky-flavoured ice-cream cake

Drinks

I'd like a ...	... nai noo-*ke*	... *nahi nuke*.
black coffee	*kah*-fe *oo*-chyah	*kafe hutsa*
coffee with a dash of milk	*kah*-fe e-*bah*-kee-ah	*kafe ebakia*
white coffee	kah-*fes*-ne-ah	*kafesnea*
water	*oo*-rah	*ura*
mineral water	oor mee-*ne*-rah-lah	*ur minerala*
beer	ga-*rah*-garr-do-ah	*garagardoa*
draught beer	*kah*-nyah baht	*kaina bat*
bottle of wine	bo-*tee*-lyah baht arr-*do*-ah	*botila bat ardoa*
red wine	*ahr*-do *bel*-tzah	*ardo beltza*
rosé	*ahr*-do *go*-rree-ah	*ardo gorria*

BASQUE

SHOPPING

Where's the nearest ...?	non *dah*-go ... oorr-*bee*-lye-nah?	*Non dago ... hurbilena?*
bookshop	lee-*boo*-roo-te-gee-reek	*liburutegirik*
camera shop	ahrr-*gahs*-kee-den-dah-reek	*argazki-dendarik*
department store	e-*ros*-te-che-reek	*erostetxerik*
drycleaners	teen-*dah*-te-gee-reek	*tindategirik*
greengrocers	froo-*tah*-den-dah-reek	*frutadendarik*
market	mairr-*kah*-too-reek	*merkaturik*
newsagency	kee-*os*-ko-reek	*kioskorik*
supermarket	soo-*pairr*-mairr-kah-too-reek	*supermerkaturik*
tobacconist	es-*tahn*-ko-reek	*estankorik*
travel agency	bee-*dai* ah-gen-tzee-ah-reek	*bidai-age ntziarik*

BASQUE

I'm just looking.
be-*gee*-rah *nah*-go bah-*kah*-rreek
Begira nago bakarrik.

I'd like to buy ...
... e-*ro*-see nai noo-ke
... erosi nahi nuke.

How much is this?
ow *sen*-baht dah?
Hau zenbat da?

Could you write the price down?
ah-*poon*-too-ko ahl dee-*dah*-soo pre-*see*-o-ah?
Apuntatuko al didazu prezioa?

Can I look at it?
be-*gee*-rah-too-ko ahl dee-*ot*?
Begiratuko al diot?

Do you have anything cheaper?
e-*sairr* mairr-*ke*-ah-go-reek ahl doo-*soo*?
Ezer merkeagorik al duzu?

I'll buy it.
 ahrr-too-ko doot   *Hartuko dut.*
Do you accept credit cards?
 kre-*dee*-too chahrr-*te*-leek   *Kreditu-txartelik*
 o-*nahrr*-tzen ahl doo-*soo*?   *onartzen al duzu?*
Can I have a receipt?
 e-*rre*-see-bo-ah e-*mahn*-go   *Errezibua emango*
 ahl dee-dah-*soo*?   *al didazu?*

TIME & DATES
Days

Monday	ahs-*te*-le-nah	*astelehena* (lit: week first)
Tuesday	ahs-*te*-ahrr-*te*-ah	*asteartea* (lit: week middle)
Wednesday	ahs-*te*-ahs-ke-nah	*asteazkena* (lit: week-end)
Thursday	os-*te*-goo-nah	*osteguna* (lit: Ortzi's day)
Friday	os-*tee*-rah-lah	*ostirala*
Saturday	lah-*roon*-bah-tah	*larunbata*
Sunday	ee-*gahn*-de-ah	*igandea* (lit: resurrection)

In Biscay, in the north-west of Basque Country, days of the week have different names:

Monday	*astelehena*
Tuesday	*martitzena* (Mars' day)
Wednesday	*eguastena*
Thursday	*eguena*
Friday	*barikoa* (lit: without meat day)
Saturday	*zapatua*
Sunday	*domeka* (lit: Lord's day)

BASQUE

Months

January	oorr-*tah*-rri-lyah	*urtarrila* (lit: year month)
February	o-*chyai*-lyah	*otsaila* (lit: wolf month)
March	mahrr-*cho*-ah	*martxoa*
April	ah-*pee*-ree-lyah	*apirila*
May	mai-*ah*-tzah	*maiatza*
June	e-*kai*-nyah	*ekaina* (lit: storm month)
July	oos-*tai*-lyah	*uztaila* (lit: crop month)
August	ah-*boos*-too-ah	*abuztua*
September	ee-*rai*-lyah	*iraila* (lit: fern month)
October	*oo*-rree-ah	*urria* (lit: scarcity)
November	ah-*sah*-ro-ah	*azaroa* (lit: sowing time)
December	ah-*ben*-doo-ah	*abendua* (lit: advent)

day after tomorrow	*e*-tzee	*etzi*
day before yesterday	e-*re*-ne-goon	*herenegun*
today	gowrr	*gaur*
tomorrow	*bee*-ahrr	*bihar*
yesterday	*ah*-tzo	*atzo*

BASQUE

NUMBERS

Basques count in scores, a habit some believe came from contact with Celtic peoples. Thus, all the numbers you really need to know are one to twenty. For example, 99 is quite literally four-twenty and nineteen.

1	baht	*bat*
2	bee	*bi*
3	*ee*-roo	*hiru*
4	low	*lau*
5	bost	*bost*
6	say	*sei*
7	*sahs*-pee	*zazpi*
8	*sorr*-tzee	*zortzi*
9	be-*de*-rah-tzee	*bederatzi*
10	*ah*-mahrr	*hamar*
11	ah-*mai*-kah	*hamaika*

12	ah-*mah*-bee	*hamabi*
13	ah-*mai*-roo	*hamairu*
14	ah-*mah*-low	*hamalau*
15	ah-*mah*-bost	*hamabost*
16	ah-*mah*-say	*hamasei*
17	ah-*mah*-sahs-pee	*hamazazpi*
18	ah-*mah*-sorr-tzee	*hamazortzi*
19	e-*me*-re-tzee	*hemeretzi*
20	*o*-gay	*hogei*
21	*o*-gay-tah baht	*hogeita bat*
30	*o*-gay-tah-mahrr	*hogeita hamar*
40	*be*-rro-gay	*berrogei* (lit. re-twenty)
50	*be*-rro-gay-tah-mahrr	*berrogeita hamar*
60	ee-*roo*-ro-gay	*hirurogei* (lit. 3 twenty)
70	ee-*roo*-ro-gay-tah-mahr	*hirurogeita hamar*
80	*low*-ro-gay	*laurogei* (lit. 4 twenty)
90	*low*-ro-gay-tah-mahrr	*laurogeita hamar*
100	*e*-oon	*ehun*
200	be-*rre*-oon	*berrehun* (lit: re-hundred)
300	ee-roo-*re*-oon	*hirurehun*
400	low-*re*-oon	*laurehun*
1000	*mee*-lyah	*mila*
one million	mee-*lyoy*	*miloi*

BASQUE

EMERGENCIES

Phrases to use in emergencies can be found in the Spanish chapter, page 483.

CATALAN

QUICK REFERENCE

Hello!	oh-luh!	*Hola!*
Goodbye.	uh-*the*-oo (see-*ah*-oo)!	*Adéu (siau)!*
How are you?	kohm uhs-*tahs*?	*Com estàs?*
I'm pleased to meet you.	uhn-kuhn-*tah*-thuh	*Encantada.*
Yes./No.	see/no	*Sí./No.*
Excuse me.	puhr-*tho*-nee	*Perdoni.*
Sorry.	oo sen-too	*Ho sento.*
Please.	sees-*plah*-oo	*Sisplau.*
Thank you.	*grah*-see-uhs	*Gràcies.*
You're welcome.	duh rrehs	*De res.*
I (don't) understand.	(no) oo uhn-*teng*	*(No) ho entenc.*
Do you speak English?	pahr-luh uhn-gles?	*Parla anglès?*
Bon apetit!	bohn proo-*feet*!	*Bonprofit!*
I'd like a ... ticket.	bool-*dree*-uh oom bee-*lyeht* ...	*Voldria un bitllet ...*
one-way	duh-*nah*-thuh	*d'anada*
return	duh-*nah* ee toor-*nah*	*d'anar i tornar*

Do you have any rooms available?
ee *ah*-bee-tuh-see-ons lyee-oo-ruhs?   *Hi ha habitacions lliures?*

Where's the toilet, please?
on son uhls luh-*bah*-boos?   *On son els lavabos?*

On the left.	uh luhs-*keh*-rruh	*A l'esquerra.*
On the right.	uh luh dreh-tuh	*A la dreta.*
Straight on.	tot rrehk-tuh	*Tot recte.*

1	oon(-uh)	*un(a)*	6	sees	*sis*
2	dos/doo-uhs	*dos/dues*	7	seht	*set*
3	trehs	*tres*	8	boo-eet	*vuit*
4	koo-*ah*-truh	*quatre*	9	noh-oo	*nou*
5	seenk	*cinc*	10	deh-oo	*deu*

CATALAN

CATALAN

Catalan is one of the nine Romance languages, and is recognised as an official language by the UN as the principal language of Andorra. It's spoken by up to 10 million people in the north-east of Spain, a territory that comprises Catalonia proper, coastal Valencia and the Balearic Islands (Majorca, Minorca and Ibiza).

Outside Spain, Catalan is also spoken in Andorra, the south of France and the town of Alguer, Alghero, in Sardinia. In north-east Spain, Catalan is an official language alongside Castilian Spanish. It's taught in schools and widely spoken. Catalan's rich cultural heritage has produced painters like Dalí, architects like Gaudí and great writers like Mercè Rodoreda.

Despite the fact that almost all Catalan speakers from Spain also speak Castilian Spanish, they usually appreciate visitors attempting to communicate, even in rudimentary fashion, in Catalan.

GENDER

In Catalan, some nouns may be either masculine or feminine in gender. In this chapter, when there's a choice between a masculine and feminine form of a word, they are separated by a slash, with the masculine form given first:

musician (m/f) moo-zeek/moo-zee-kuh   *músic/música*

PRONUNCIATION

Catalan sounds aren't hard for English-speakers to pronounce.
Stress normally falls on the second-last syllable.

Vowels

Vowels vary according to whether they're in stressed or in
unstressed syllables.

a	ah	stressed, as the 'a' in 'father';
	uh	unstressed, as the 'a' in 'sofa'
e	e	stressed, as the 'e' in 'pet';
	eh	stressed, as the 'e' in 'merry';
	uh	unstressed, as the 'e' in 'open'
i	ee	as the 'i' in 'marine'
o	o	stressed, as the 'o' in 'hot';
	oh	stressed, sometimes as the 'o' in 'port'
	oo	unstressed, as the 'oo' in 'zoo'
u	oo	silent between *g* and *e/i* and between *q* and *e/i*; elsewhere, as the 'u' in 'flute'

DOUBLE DOTS

A vowel marked by two overdots (ï), indicates that vowel
sound should be pronounced as a separate syllable.

ensaïmada   **en-suh-ee-mah-duh**   sweet pastry

Consonants

Letters not described here are pronounced as they are in English.

b	p	at the end of a word, as the 'p' in 'pot';
	b	elsewhere, as the 'b' in 'bat'
c	k	as the 'c' in 'cat' before *a*, *o*, and *u*;
	s	as the 'c' in 'celery' before *e* and *i*
ç	s	as the 'c' in 'celery'
d	t	at the end of a word, as the 't' in 'tiger';
	th	between vowels, as the 'th' in 'other';
	d	elsewhere as the 'd' in 'bad'

CATALAN

g	g	as the 'g' in 'game' at the start of a word and before *a*, *o* and *u*;
	zh	as the 's' in 'pleasure' before *e* and *i*;
	ch	as the 'ch' in 'cheese' in the suffix *-ig*
h		silent
j	zh	as the 's' in 'pleasure'
ll	ly	as the 'lli' in 'million'
l.l	l	as the 'l' in 'like' (not pronounced as *ll*)
ñ	ny	as the 'ny' in 'canyon'
q(u)	k	as the 'k' in 'king'
r	r	as the 'r' in 'rat' in the middle of a word;
	rr	trilled at the start of a word;
		usually silent at the end of a word
rr	rr	trilled
s	z	in the middle of a word and before a vowel, as the 'z' in 'zebra';
	s	elsewhere, as the 's' in 'sin'
tx	ch	as the 'ch' in 'cheese'
v	b	as the 'b' in 'beer'
x	ks	mostly as the 'x' in 'taxi';
	sh	sometimes as the 'sh' in 'shiver'

CATALAN

PRONOUNS		
SG		
I	zhoh	*jo*
you (inf)	too	*tu*
you (pol)	boos-*teh*	*vostè*
he	ely	*ell*
she	ely-uh	*ella*
PL		
we	noo-*zahl*-truhs	*nosaltres*
you	boo-*zahl*-truhs	*vosaltres*
they (m)	elys	*ells*
they (f)	ely-uhs	*elles*

CATALAN

GREETINGS & CIVILITIES
You Should Know

Hello!	*oh*-luh!	*Hola!*
Goodbye.	uh-*the*-oo (see-*ah*-oo)!	*Adéu (siau)!*
Good morning.	bohn *dee*-uh	*Bon dia.*
Good afternoon.	*boh*-nuh *tahr*-thuh	*Bona tarda.*
Good evening.	bohm *bes*-pruh	*Bon vespre.*
Goodnight.	*boh*-nuh neet	*Bona nit.*
See you later.	feenz *ah*-ruh	*Fins ara.*
How are you?	kohm uhs-*tahs*?	*Com estàs?*
(Very) well.	(mol) be	*(Molt) bé.*
Yes./No.	see/no	*Sí./No.*
Excuse me.	puhr-*tho*-nee	*Perdoni.*
May I?	pook?	*Puc?*
Sorry. (excuse/	oo *sen*-too;	*Ho sento;*
forgive me)	puhr-*tho*-nee	*Perdoni.*
Please.	sees-*plah*-oo	*Sisplau.*
Thank you.	*grah*-see-uhs	*Gràcies.*
Many thanks.	*mol*-tuhs *grah*-see-uhs	*Moltes gràcies.*
You're welcome.	duh rrehs	*De res.*

Forms of Address

Madam/Mrs	suh-*nyo*-ruh	*Senyora*
Sir/Mr	suh-*nyo*	*Senyor*
mate	koo-*leh*-guh	*Collega*

SMALL TALK
Meeting People

What's your name?
   kohm uhs *thee*-oo?   *Com es diu?*
My name's ...
   uhm deek ...   *Em dic ...*
I'd like to introduce you to ...
   bool-*dree*-uh pruh-zuhn-
   tahr-tuh ah ...   *Voldria presentar-te a ...*

I'm pleased to meet you.
   uhn-kuhn-*tah*-thuh   *Encantada.*

I'm (m/f) (Irish).
   sok (eer-luhn-*dehs*/   *Sóc (irlandès/irlandesa).*
   eer-luhn-*deh*-zuh)

I live in (Darwin).
   beesk uh (*dahr*-oo-een)   *Visc a (Darwin).*

Where do you live?   om *bee*-oos?   *On vius?*
Where are you from?   don ets?   *D'on ets?*

I'm here ...   sok uh-*kee* ...   *Sóc aquí ...*
   on business   duh bee-*aht*-zhuh   *de viatge de*
                   thuh nuh-*goh*-sees   *negocis*
   on holiday   duh buh-*kahn*-suhs   *de vacances*
   studying   uhs-too-thee-*ahnt*   *estudiant*

Occupations

What do you do?
   uh keht duh-*thee*-kuhs?   *A què et dediques?*

I'm (a/an) ...   sok ...   *Sóc ...*
   artist   uhr-*tees*-tuh   *artista*
   business person   koo-muhr-see-*ahn*   *comerciant*
   doctor   *met*-zhuh/   *metge/*
                   muht-*zheh*-suh   *metgessa*
   engineer   uhn-zhee-*nye*/   *enginyer/*
                   uhn-zhee-*nye*-ruh   *enginyera*
   musician   moo-zeek/   *músic/*
                   moo-zee-kuh   *música*
   nurse   een-fuhr-*me*/   *infermer/*
                   een-fuhr-*me*-ruh   *infermera*
   office worker   oo-fee-see-*nee*-stuh   *oficinista*
   student   uhs-too-thee-*ahn*   *estudiant*
   teacher   proo-fuh-*so*/   *professor/*
                   proo-fuh-*so*-ruh   *professora*
   waiter   kuhm-*bre*/   *cambrer/*
                   kuhm-*bre*-ruh   *cambrera*

CATALAN

I'm ...	uhs-*teek* ...	*Estic ...*
retired	zhoo-bee-*laht*/	*jubilat/*
	zhoo-bee-*lah*-thu	*jubilada*
unemployed	uh-luh-*toor*	*a l'atur*

Family

Do you have a girlfriend/boyfriend?
tens shee-*koh*-tuh/shee-*koht*?   *Tens xicota/xicot?*

How many children do you have?
koo-*ahns* feelys tens?   *Quants fills tens?*

I'm single.
sok sool-*te*-ruh   *Sóc soltera.*

I have a partner.
teeng puh-*reh*-lyuh   *Tinc parella.*

BREAKING THE LANGUAGE BARRIER

Do you speak English?
pahr-luh uhn-*glehs*?   *Parla anglès?*

Could you speak in Castillian please?
poht puhr-*lah* kuhs-tuh-*lyah*   *Pot parlar castellà*
sees-*plah*-oo?   *sisplau?*

I (don't) understand.
(no) oo uhn-*teng*   *(No) ho entenc.*

Could you speak more slowly please?
poht puhr-*lah* mez uh pohk   *Pot parlar més a poc*
uh pohk sees-*plah*-oo?   *a poc sisplau?*

Could you repeat that?
poht rruh-puh-*tee*-roo?   *Pot repetir-ho?*

Could you write that down please?
poht uhs-kree-*oo*-ruh-oo,   *Pot escriure-ho,*
sees-*plah*-oo?   *sisplau?*

How do you say ...?
kohm uhz *thee*-oo ...?   *Com es diu ...?*

What's this called in Catalan?
kohm uhz *thee*-oo uh-*shoh*   *Com es diu això*
uhn kuh-tuh-*lah*?   *en català?*

CATALAN

PAPERWORK

adreça	address
carnet de conduir	drivers licence
carnet d'identitat	identification
data de naixement	date of birth
edat	age
estat civil	marital status
lloc de naixement	place of birth
nacionalitat	nationality
nom i cognom	name & surname
passaport	passport
sexe	sex
visat	visa

GETTING AROUND
Directions

Excuse me, can you help me please?
puhr-*tho*-nee, uhm poht
uh-zhoo-*thah*? *Perdoni, em pot ajudar?*

Where's the toilet, please?
on son uhls luh-*bah*-boos? *On son els lavabos?*

On the left.	uh luhs-*keh*-rruh	*A l'esquerra.*
On the right.	uh luh *dreh*-tuh	*A la dreta.*
Straight on.	tot *rrehk*-tuh	*Tot recte.*
At the end.	uhl fons	*Al fons.*

avenue	uh-been-*goo*-thuh	*avinguda*
square	*plah*-suh	*plaça*
street	kuh-*rre*	*carrer*

Buying Tickets

Do I need to book?
e thuh fe *oo*-nuh rruh-*zer*-buh? *He de fer una reserva?*

I'd like to book a seat to ...
bool-*dree*-uh rruh-zuhr-*bah*
oon suh-ee-*en* puhr uh ... *Voldria reservar un seient per a ...*

CATALAN

CATALAN

I'd like ...	bool-*dree*-uh ...	*Voldria ...*
a one-way ticket	oom bee-*lyeht* duh-*nah*-thuh	*un bitllet d'anada*
a return ticket	oom bee-*lyeht* duh-*nah* ee toor-*nah*	*un bitllet d'anar i tornar*
two tickets	dos bee-*lyehts*	*dos bitllets*

Is there a discount for ...?	ee *ahl*-goon duhs-*kom*-tuh puhr uh ...?	*Hi ha algun descompte per a ...?*
children	nehns	*nens*
pensioners	puhn-see-oo-*nees*-tuhs	*pensionistes*
students	uhs-too-thee-*ahns*	*estudiants*

Bus

Does this bus go to the ...?	uh-*keht* uh-oo-too-*booz* bah ...?	*Aquest autobús va a ...?*
beach	luh *plaht*-zhuh	*la platja*
city centre	uhl *sen*-truh thuh luh see-oo-*taht*	*el centre de la ciutat*
station	luhs-tuh-see-*o*	*l'estació*

Do you stop at ...?	*pah*-ruh ...?	*Para a ...?*

Train & Metro

Which line takes me to ...?
    kee-nuh *lee*-nee-uh-*gah*-foo puhr uh ...?   *Quina línia agafo per a ...?*

Where do I change for ...?
    on e thuh fe truhnz-*bor* puhr uh ...?   *On he de fer transbord per a ...?*

Could you let me know when we get to ...?
    poht uh-bee-*zahr*-muh koo-*ahn* uh-*rree-behm* uh ...?   *Pot avisar-me quan arribem a ...?*

Taxi

Are you free?
uhs-*tah* lyee-*oo*-ruh?   *Està lliure?*

How much is it to go to ...?
koo-*ahm* bahl uh-*nah* ...?   *Quant val anar a ...?*

How much do I owe you?
koo-*ahn* es?   *Quant és?*

Please take me to ...	sees-*plah*-oo, doo-*geem* uh ...	*Sisplau, dugui'm a ...*
this address	uh-*kehs*-tuh uh-*dre*-suh	*aquesta adreça*
the airport	lah-e-roo-*pohrt*	*l'aeroport*
the railway station	luhs-tuh-see-*o* thuh *trehns*	*l'estació de trens*

Here's fine, thanks.
uh-*kee* zhuh buh be, *grah*-see-uhs   *Aquí ja va bé, gràcies.*

SIGNS

ENTRADA	ENTRANCE
INFORMACIO	INFORMATION
NO TOCAR	DO NOT TOUCH
OBERT/TANCAT	OPEN/CLOSED
PENSIÓ (P)	GUESTHOUSE
PROHIBIT ...	NO ...
ACAMPAR	CAMPING
ENTRAR	ENTRY
FER FOTOS	PHOTOGRAPHY
FUMAR	SMOKING
RESERVAT	RESERVED
SERVEIS	TOILETS
SORTIDA	EXIT

CATALAN

ACCOMMODATION
At the Hotel

Do you have any rooms available?
ee *ah*-bee-tuh-see-ons lyee-*oo*-ruhs?	*Hi ha habitacions lliures?*

I'd like ...	bool-*dree*-uh ...	*Voldria ...*
a single room	oo-nuh-bee-tuh-see-*o* een-dee-bee-thoo-*ahl*	*una habitació individual*
a double room	oo-nuh-bee-tuh-see-*o* *tho*-pluh	*una habitació doble*
to share a dorm	koom-puhr-*tee* oon door-mee-*toh*-ree	*compartir un dormitori*

I want a room with a ...	boo-ee *oo*-nuh-bee-tuh-see-*o* uhm ...	*Vull una habitació amb ...*
bathroom	*kahm*-bruh thuh bahny	*cambra de bany*
double bed	lyeet duh muh-tree-*moh*-nee	*llit de matrimoni*

How much is it per night/person?
koo-*ahm* bahl puhr neet/ puhr-*so*-nuh?	*Quant val per nit/ persona?*

It's fine, I'll take it.
duh-*kohrt*, muh luh ke-thoo	*D'acord, me la quedo.*

The key for room (17) please.
luh *klah*-oo-puhr uh luh-bee-tuh-see-*o* (dee-*seht*), sees-*plah*-oo	*La clauper a l'habitació (disset), sisplau.*

I'd like to pay the bill.
bool-*dree*-uh puh-*gah* uhl *kom*-tuh	*Voldria pagar el compte.*

Please call a taxi for me.
poht troo-*kah* oon *tahk*-see puhr mee, sees-*plah*-oo?	*Pot trucar un taxi per mi, sisplau?*

CATALAN

Requests & Complaints

I don't like this room.
    no muh-*grah*-thuh-*kehs*-
    tuh-bee-tuh-see-*o*

*No m'agrada aquesta
habitació.*

Can I change to another dormitory?
    poht kuhm-bee-*ahr*-muh
    thuh-bee-tuh-see-*o*?

*Pot canviar-me
d'habitació?*

Can I leave my backpack at
reception until tonight?
    pook duh-*shah* luh *me*-buh
    moo-*chee*-lyuh luh rre-suhp-
    see-*o* feenz uh-*kehs*-tuh neet?

*Puc deixar la meva
motxilla a la recepció
fins aquesta nit?*

AROUND TOWN
At the Post Office

I'd like to send a ...
    bool-*dree*-uh
    uhm-bee-*ah* ...

Voldria enviar ...

  letter
    oo-nuh *kahr*-tuh
  parcel
    oom puh-*ket*

  una carta
  un paquet

I'd like some stamps.
    bool-*dree*-uh suh-*zhelys*

Voldria segells.

How much is it to send this to ...?
    koo-*ahm* bahl uhm-bee-*ah*
    uh-*shoh* uh ...?

*Quant val enviar
això a ...?*

Where's the poste restante section?
    on es luh *lyees*-tuh thuh
    koo-*rreh*-oos?

*On és la llista de
correus?*

Is there any mail for me?
    ee ah koo-*rreh*-oo puhr
    uh mee?

*Hi ha correu per
a mi?*

CATALAN

CATALAN

Telephone

I want to ring (Australia).
　boo-ee troo-*kah* uh
　(a-oos-*trah*-lee-uh)   *Vull trucar a*
    (Austràlia).
I want to make a reverse-charge
(collect) phone call.
　bool-*dree*-uh fe *oo*-nuh troo-*kah*-   *Voldria fer una trucada*
　thuh thuh koo-bruh-*men*   *de cobrament*
　uh thuhs-tee-nuh-see-*o*   *a destinació.*
The number is ...
　uhl *noo*-muh-roo es ...   *El número és ...*
Hello! (making a call)   *oh*-luh!   *Hola!*
Hello! (answering a call)   *dee*-gee?   *Digui?*
Can I speak to (Roger)?
　kuh ee ah (uhn roo-*zhe*)?   *Que hi ha (en Roger)?*
It's (Nœria).
　duh (luh *noo*-ree-uh)   *De (la Núria).*

At the Bank

I want to exchange	bool-*dree*-uh	*Voldria canviar ...*
some ...	kuhm-bee-*ah* ...	
money	thee-*nes*	*diners*
travellers cheques	chehks thuh	*txecs de viatge*
	bee-*aht*-zhuh	

I want to change (dollars) into
pessetes/Euros.
　boo-ee kuhm-bee-*ah* (*doh*-luhrs)   *Vull canviar (dòlars)*
　uhm puh-*she*-tuhs/*ehoo*-rooss   *en pessetes/euros.*
What's the exchange rate?
　uh kohm uhs-*tah* uhl *kahm*-bee?   *A com està el canvi?*
What's your commission?
　koo-*ahn* koh-bruhn duh   *Quant cobren de*
　koo-mee-see-*o*?   *comissió?*
Please write it down.
　moo poht uhs-kree-*oo*-ruh   *M'ho pot escriure*
　sees-*plah*-oo?   *sisplau?*

INTERESTS & ENTERTAINMENT
Sightseeing

I'm looking for a/the ...	uhs-*teek* boos-*kahn* ...	*Estic buscant ...*
city centre	uhl *sen*-truh thuh luh see-oo-*taht*	*el centre de la ciutat*
police	luh poo-lee-*see*-uh	*la policia*
post office	koo-*rreh*-oos	*correus*
public toilet	uhls luh-*bah*-boos *poo*-pleeks	*els lavabos públics*
restaurant	oon rruhs-tuh-oo-*rahn*	*un restaurant*
telephone centre	luh suhn-*trahl* tuh-luh-*foh*-nee-kuh	*la central telefònica*
tourist information office	loo-fee-*see*-nuh thuh too-*rees*-muh	*l'oficina de turisme*

CATALAN

Going Out

What are you doing this evening?
keh fahz uh-*kehs*-tuh neet? — *Què fas aquesta nit?*

What are you doing this weekend?
keh fahs uh-*keht* kahp duh suhm-*mah*-nuh? — *Què fas aquest cap de setmana?*

Would you like to go for a ...	bohls buh-*nee* ah fe ...?	*Vols venir a fer ...?*
drink	*oo*-nuh *ko*-puh	*una copa*
meal	uh soo-*pah*	*a sopar*

I feel like going to ...
    teeng *gah*-nuhz thuh-*nah* ...   *Tinc ganes d'anar ...*
What's on at the cinema tonight?
    kee-nuh puh-*lee*-koo-luh   *Quina pel·lícula*
    fahn uhl *see*-nuh   *fan al cine*
    uh-*keh*-stuh neet?   *aquesta nit?*
Are there any tickets for ...?
    ee ah uhn-*trah*-thuhs puhr ...?   *Hi ha entrades per ...?*
Is it in English?
    ez uhn uhn-*glehs*?   *És en anglès?*
Hope to see you again soon.
    uhs-*pe*-roo beh-*oo*-ruht uh-bee-*aht*   *Espero veure't aviat.*
I'll give you a call.
    zhaht troo-kuh-*re*   *Ja et trucaré.*

Sports & Interests

What do you do in your spare time?
    keh fahs uhn uhl *te*-oo tems   *Què fas en el teu temps*
    lyee-*oo*-ruh?   *lliure?*
What do you like doing?
    keh tuh-*grah*-thuh fe?   *Què t'agrada fer?*
Do you like sport?
    tuh-*grah*-thuhn uhlz   *T'agraden els esports?*
    uhs-*pohrts*?
Yes, very much.
    muhn-*kahn*-tuhn   *M'encanten.*
No, not at all.
    no muh-*grah*-thuhn zhens   *No m'agraden gens.*
Do you feel like (going for a swim)?
    uht be thuh goost   *Et ve de gust (nedar)?*
    (nuh-*thah*)?
Yes, that'd be great.
    uhm be mol duh goost   *Em ve molt de gust.*
Not at the moment, thanks.
    no *grah*-see-uhs, *ah*-ruh no   *No gràcies, ara no.*

Festivals

Día de Sant Jordi (St George Day, 23 April)
the nation's patron saint is honoured through the tradition of
giving a rose or a book as a gift

La Diada (Catalan Independence Day, 11 September)
every village, town or neighbourhood goes into festival mode
at least one day a year to celebrate its local saint with a *festa
major*, 'grand festival'. The emphasis is on local customs, music and dancing, and you'll probably encounter some of the
following traditions:

sardanes   suhr-*thah*-nuhs
Catalan national dance

castellers   kuhs-tuh-*lyes*
human towers. Neighbourhoods or villages compete for the
honour of building the most impressive tower.

nans i gegants   nahnz ee zhuh-*gahns*
a procession of people wearing huge papier mache painted heads
or riding inside painted wooden giants

correfoc   ko-rruh-*fohk*
a popular event at which *dracs* and *dimonis* (people dressed as
giant dragons and devils) chase spectators along the street breath-
ing fireworks

cercavila   sehr-kuh-*bee*-luh
groups of local residents roaming around the neighbourhood
dressed up for a festival day

Happy Christmas!	bohn nuh-*thahl!*	*Bon nadal!*
Happy New Year!	bohn ahny noh-oo!	*Bon any nou!*
Happy birthday!	puhr molz ahnys!	*Per molts anys!*
Happy saint's day!	puhr molz ahnys!	*Per molts anys!*
Congratulations!	fuh-lee-see-*tahts!*	*Felicitats!*
Good luck!	*boh*-nuh sohrt!	*Bona sort!*

CATALAN

FOOD

breakfast	uhz-moor-*zah*	*esmorzar*
lunch	dee-*nah*	*dinar*
dinner	soo-*pah*	*sopar*

Bon apetit!   bohn proo-*feet*!   *Bon profit!*

I'm vegetarian. (m/f)
    sok buh-zhuh-tuh-ree-*ah*/   *Sóc vegetarià/*
    buh-zhuh-tuh-ree-*ah*-nuh   *vegetariana.*

Typical Meals

allioli
    garlic sauce
calçots
    shallots, usually served braised with an almond dipping sauce.
    A seasonal delicacy.
escalivada
    roasted red peppers and eggplant in olive oil
escudella i carn d'olla
    a Christmas dish of soup and meatballs
fuet
    a thin pork sausage, native to Catalunya
mongetes seques i butifarra
    haricot beans with thick pork sausage
pa amb tomàquet (i pernil)
    crusty bread rubbed with ripe tomatoes, garlic and olive oil
    and often topped with cured ham

Desserts

coca
    a dense cake, especially popular during St Joan (John) celebra-
    tions, when it's decorated with candied peel or pine nuts
crema catalana
    a light creme caramel with a burnt toffee sauce
ensaïmada mallorquina
    a sweet Mallorcan pastry
mel i mató
    a dessert of curd cheese with honey

CATALAN

Non-Alcoholic Drinks

almond drink	oor-*shah*-tuh	orxata
fruit juice	sook	suc
soft drinks	rruh-*frehsks*	refrescs
...water	ah-ee-goo-uh...	aigua ...
mineral	mee-nuh-*rahl*	mineral
tap	ah-ee-goo-uh thuh luh-*sheh*-tuh	de l'aixeta
black coffee	kuh-*feh* sohl	cafè sol
long black	*do*-pluh	doble
iced coffee	kuh-*feh* zhuh-*laht*	cafè gelat
decaffeinated coffee	kuh-*feh* thuhs-kuh-fuh-ee-*naht*	cafè descafeinat
tea	teh	te
coffee with ...	kuh-*feh* ...	cafè ...
liqueur	kuh-ruh-*hee*-lyoo (see-guh-*lo*)	carajillo (cigaló in north Catalunya)
a little milk	tuh-*lyaht*	tallat
milk	ùhm lyet	amb llet
milk and liqueur	tree-*fah*-zeek	trifàsic

Alcoholic Drinks

What will you have?
   keh *boh*-luhn *pren*-druh?   *Què volen prendre?*
It's on me.
   pah-goo zhoh   *Pago jo.*
Cheers!
   suh-loot (ee *fohr*-suhlkuh-*noot*)!   *Salut (i força al canut!)*

I'll have a/an ...	uhm be thuh goost ...	*Em ve de gust ...*
beer	*oo*-nuh suhr-*beh*-zuh	una cervesa
champagne	oon *kah*-buh	un cava
muscatel	moos-kuh-*tely*	moscatell
ratafia (liqueur)	rruh-tuh-*fee*-uh	ratafia
rum	oon rrom	un rom
whisky	oon oo-*ees*-kee	un whisky

glass of ... wine	oom bee ...	*un vi ...*
red	*neh*-gruh	*negre*
rosé	rroo-*zaht*	*rosat*
sparkling	thuh-*goo*-lyuh	*d'agulla*
white	blahnk	*blanc*

SHOPPING

Where's the	on es lah/uhl ... mes	*On és la/el ... més*
nearest ...?	proo-*pe*-ruh/proo-*pe*?	*propera/proper?*
bookshop	lyee-bruh-*ree*-uh	*llibreria*
camera shop	boo-*tee*-guh thuh *fo*-toos	*botiga de fotos*
chemist (pharmacy)	fuhr-*mah*-see-uh	*farmàcia*
department store	grahnz muh-guht-*zehms*	*grans magatzems*
greengrocer	boo-*tee*-guh thuh buhr-*thoo*-ruhs	*botiga de verdures*
fruitshop	froo-ee-tuh-*ree*-uh	*fruiteria*
launderette	boo-guh-thuh-*ree*-uh	*bugaderia*
market	muhr-*kaht*	*mercat*
newsagency	kee-*ohsk*	*quiosc*
supermarket	soo-puhr-muhr-*kaht*	*supermercat*
travel agency	uh-*zhehn*-see-uh thuh bee-*aht*-zhuhs	*agència de viatges*

I'm just looking.
    noo-*mes* uhs-*teek* mee-*rahn*   *Només estic mirant.*
I'd like to buy ...
    bool-*dree*-uh koom-*prah* ...   *Voldria comprar ...*
I'll buy it.
    lah/uhl *kom*-proo   *La/el compro.*
Do you accept credit cards?
    uhk-*sep*-tuhn tuhr-*zheh*-tuhz   *Accepten targetes de crèdit?*
    thuh *kreh*-theet?
Can I have a receipt?
    poo-*dree*-uh thoo-*nahr*-muh   *Podria donar-me un rebut?*
    oon rruh-*boot*?

Essential Groceries

Do you sell ...?	beh-nuhn ...?	Venen ...?
bread	pah	pa
condoms	pruh-zuhr-buh-tee-oos	preservatius
sanitary napkins	koom-preh-zuhs	compreses
shampoo	shuhm-poo	xampú
soap	suh-bo	sabó
sunscreen	kre-muh soo-lahr	crema solar
tampons	tuhm-pons	tampons
tissues	moo-kuh-thoz thuh puh-pe	mocadors de paper
toilet paper	puh-pe ee-zhee-eh-neek	paper higiènic
toothbrush	rruhs-pahly duh thens	raspall de dents
toothpaste	pah-stuh thuh thens	pasta de dents

CATUNYA'S EMPIRE

As a result of Catalunya's role in the Reconquista in the middle ages, the Catalan language (català) is also the first language of most people in the Balearic Islands and nearly half those in Valencia, areas that were taken from the Muslims by Catalunya in the 13th century.

Catalan is also spoken on a narrow strip of Aragón bordering Catalunya, and in the French district of Roussillon. Farther afield, residents of the town of Alghero in Sardinia (L'Alguer in Catalan) speak Catalan, a remnant of Catalunya's medieval empire. It's also the national language of Andorra in the Pyrenees, and an official language of the United Nations.

In 1998, Catalunya passed the Ley de la Lengua, seeking to enshrine the use of the language in all official activities and promote its use in everyday life.

CATALAN

TIME & DATES
Time

One thing to remember when asking about times in Catalan –
minutes past and to the hour are referred to as being before the
next hour.

half past two
   dos koo-*ahrts* deh trehs   *dos quarts de tres*
                                      (lit: two quarters to three)

twenty past nine
   oon koo-*ahrt* ee   *un quart i cinc de deu*
   seenk deh *deh*-oo   (lit: one quarter and five minutes
                                        to ten)

ten to five
   trehs koo-*ahrts* ee   *tres quarts i cinc de cinc*
   seenk deh seenk   (lit: three quarters and five minutes
                                        to five)

Days

Monday	dee-*lyoons*	*dilluns*
Tuesday	dee-*mahrs*	*dimarts*
Wednesday	dee-*me*-kruhs	*dimecres*
Thursday	dee-*zhoh*-oos	*dijous*
Friday	dee-*behn*-druhs	*divendres*
Saturday	dee-*sahp*-tuh	*dissabte*
Sunday	dee-oo-*men*-zhuh	*diumenge*

Months

January	zhuh-*ne*	*gener*
February	fuh-*bre*	*febrer*
March	mahrs	*març*
April	uh-*breel*	*abril*
May	mahch	*maig*
June	zhoony	*juny*
July	zhoo-lee-*ohl*	*juliol*
August	uh-*gost*	*agost*
September	suh-*tem*-bruh	*setembre*
October	ook-*too*-bruh	*octubre*
November	noo-*bem*-bruh	*novembre*
December	duh-*zem*-bruh	*desembre*

Seasons

spring	pree-muh-*beh*-ruh	*Primavera*
summer	uhs-*tee*-oo	*Estiu*
autumn	tuhr-*tho*	*Tardor*
winter	ee-*behrn*	*Hivern*

NUMBERS

0	*zeh*-roo	*zero*
1	*oon*(-uh)	*un(a)*
2	dos/*doo*-uhs	*dos/dues*
3	trehs	*tres*
4	koo-*ah*-truh	*quatre*
5	seenk	*cinc*
6	sees	*sis*
7	seht	*set*
8	boo-*eet*	*vuit*
9	*noh*-oo	*nou*
10	*deh*-oo	*deu*
11	*on*-zuh	*onze*
12	*dot*-zuh	*dotze*
13	*tret*-zuh	*tretze*

CATALAN

14	kuh-*tor*-zuh	*catorze*
15	*keen*-zuh	*quinze*
16	*seht*-zuh	*setze*
17	dee-*seht*	*disset*
18	dee-boo-*eet*	*divuit*
19	dee-*noh*-oo	*dinou*
20	been	*vint*
30	*trehn*-tuh	*trenta*
40	koo-*rahn*-tuh	*quaranta*
50	seen-koo-*ahn*-tuh	*cinquanta*
60	suh-*shahn*-tuh	*seixanta*
70	suh-*than*-tuh	*setanta*
80	boo-ee-*than*-tuh	*vuitanta*
90	noo-*rahn*-tuh	*noranta*
100	sen	*cent*
1000	meel	*mil*

CATALAN

DUTCH

QUICK REFERENCE

Hello.	dahkh/hah-*loh*	Dag./Hallo.
Well, thanks.	khut, dahnk ü	Goed, dank u.
Goodbye.	dahkh	Dag.
Yes./No.	yaa/nay	Ja./Nee.
Please.	ahls-tü-*bleeft*	Alstublieft.
Thank you.	dahnk ü (wehl)	Dank u (wel).
You're welcome.	khayn dahnk	Geen dank.
Excuse me.	pahr-*don*	Pardon.
Sorry.	*so*-ree	Sorry.

I'd like a ... ticket.	ik wil khraakh ...	Ik wil graag ...
one-way	ern *ehng*-ker-ler-reys	een enkele reis
return	ern rer-*tur*	een retour

Do you have any rooms available?
  hayft ü *kaa*-mers vrey?   Heeft u kamers vrij?

How much is it?
  hoo-vayl kost heht?   Hoeveel kost het?

How are you?
  hoo khaat hehtmeht ü?   Hoe gaat het met u?

I (don't) understand.
  ik ber-*khreyp* heht (neet)   Ik begrijp het (niet).

Do you speak English?
  spraykt ü *ehng*-erls?   Spreekt u Engels?

Where are the toilets?
  waar zeyn de twah-*leht*-tern?   Waar zijn de toiletten?

Where's ...?	waar is ...?	Waar is ...?
Turn left/right.	khaa links/rehkhts	Ga links/rechts.
Go straight ahead	khaa rehkht-*dor*	Ga rechtdoor.

1	ayn	*één*	6	zehs	zes
2	tway	*twee*	7	*zay*-vern	zeven
3	dree	*drie*	8	ahkht	acht
4	veer	*vier*	9	*nay*-khern	negen
5	veyf	*vijf*	10	teen	tien

DUTCH

DUTCH

Most English speakers use the term 'Dutch' to describe the language spoken in the Netherlands, and 'Flemish' for that spoken in the northern half of Belgium and a tiny north-western corner of France. Both are, in fact, the same language, the correct term for which is *Nederlands*, Netherlandic, a West Germanic language that's spoken by about 25 million people worldwide.

The differences between Dutch and Flemish are similar to those between British and North American English – despite some differences they're very much the same language, with a shared literature.

When travelling in the Netherlands and Flemish-speaking Belgium, you'll find that virtually everyone speaks English to some degree. Don't let that put you off. Like almost anywhere else in the world, an effort to speak the local tongue will always be met with goodwill. If people still insist on speaking English, it's because they want to ease communication rather than deny you the chance of speaking their language.

GENDER

Netherlandic nouns have three genders – masculine, feminine and neuter.

When talking about people, you'll often find both masculine and feminine versions of a word.

| student (m/f) | stü-*dehnt*/ | student/ |
| | stü-*dehnt*-er | studente |

These versions are rendered in the text here with the masculine form first.

When a noun is preceded by the definite article 'the', masculine and feminine forms take the article *de*, pronounced *der*, while neutral forms use *het* or *ert*. The indefinite article 'a/an' is *een/ern*.

PRONUNCIATION
Vowels

Single vowels are fairly straightforward, with long and short sounds for each vowel. Compound vowels are a little more complicated.

Short Vowels

a	ah	as the 'u' in 'cut'
e	eh	as the 'e' in 'bet';
	er	as the 'e' in 'her'
i	i	as the 'i' in 'in'
o	o	as the 'o' in 'hot'
u	er	as the 'e' in 'her'

Long Vowels

a/aa	aa	as the 'a' in 'father'
e/ee	ey	as the 'ey' in 'hey'
i	ee	as the 'i' in 'marine'
o/oo	oh	as the 'o' in 'note'
u/uu	ü	like the ü in German 'über' as the 'u' in june, but with the tongue pushed foward

Vowel Combinations

au	ow	as the 'ow' in 'cow', but pronounced with lips rounded
ei	ey	as the 'ey' in 'hey'
eu	er	as the 'e' in 'open' + the 'u' in 'put'
ie	ee	as the 'ie' in 'thief'
ij	ey	as the 'ey' in 'hey'
oe	oo	as the 'oo' in 'zoo';
	u	sometimes as the 'u' in 'put'
ou	ow	as the 'ow' in 'cow', but pronounced with lips rounded
ui	er	there's no equivalent in English, but like the the 'e' in 'her' + the 'a' in 'ago'

DUTCH

Consonants

ch	kh	as the 'ch' in Scottish 'loch'
g	kh	usually as the 'ch' in Scottish 'loch';
	zh	sometimes as the 's' in 'pleasure'
j	y	as the 'y' in 'yes';
	zh	occasionally, as the 's' in 'pleasure';
	j	sometimes as the 'j' in 'jam'
r	r	as the 'r' in 'rat', often produced at the back of the throat
s	s	usually as the 's' in 'sin';
	zh	sometimes as the 's' in 'pleasure'
v	f	at the start of a word, as the 'f' in 'fox';
	v	elsewhere, as the 'v' in 'velvet'
w	w	at the end of a word, as the 'w' in 'water';
	v	elsewhere, as the 'v' in 'velvet'

KEEP YOURSELF NICE

The second person pronoun 'you' has both polite (*u*) and informal (*je*) versions (see page 70). In this chapter, only the polite form is given.

GREETINGS & CIVILITIES
You Should Know

Hello.	dahkh/hah-*loh*	*Dag./Hallo.*
Good morning.	*khu*-der *mor*-khern	*Goedemorgen.*
Good afternoon.	*khu*-der *mid*-dahkh	*Goedemiddag.*
Good evening.	*khu*-dern *aa*-vont	*Goedenavond.*
Good night.	*khu*-der nahkht	*Goedenacht.*
How are you?	hoo khaat hehtmeht ü?	*Hoe gaat het met u?*
Well, thanks.	khut, dahnk ü	*Goed, dank u.*
Goodbye.	dahkh	*Dag.*
Yes./No.	yaa/ney	*Ja./Nee.*
Excuse me.	pahr-*don*	*Pardon.*

DUTCH

Sorry. (excuse/ forgive me)	*so*-ree	*Sorry.*
Please.	ahls-tü-*bleeft*	*Alstublieft.*
Thank you.	dahnk ü (wehl)	*Dank u (wel).*
Many thanks.	veyl dahnk	*Veel dank.*
May I?	mahkh ik?	*Mag ik?*
That's fine.	daht is khud.	*Dat is goed.*
You're welcome.	kheyn dahnk	*Geen dank.*

Forms of Address

Netherlandic has both a formal and an informal version of the pronoun 'you'. The formal is *u* (pronounced ü); the informal is *je* (pronounced yer).

Netherlandic has become less formal in recent years, and *u* is no longer commonly used to address people of the same age, let alone younger people, whether you know them or not. But people who are older, especially if you don't know them, should still be addressed with *u*. Flemish tends to be slightly more formal than Dutch.

PRONOUNS		
SG		
I	ik	*ik*
you (inf)	yer	*je*
you (pol)	ü	*u*
he	hey	*hij*
she	zey/zer	*zij/ze*
it	heht	*het*
PL		
we	vey	*wij*
you	yoo-lee	*jullie*
they	zey/zer	*zij/ze*

DUTCH

Madam/Mrs	mer-*vrow*	*Mevrouw (Mevr)*
Sir/Mr	mer-*near*	*Meneer (Mr)*
Miss	yer-*frow*	*Juffrouw*
companion (m/f)	*reys*-kher-noht/	*reisgenoot/*
	reys-kher-noht-er	*reisgenote*
friend (m/f)	*vreent*/vreend-*in*	*vriend/vriendin*

SMALL TALK
Meeting People

What's your name?	hoo heyt ü?	*Hoe heet u?*
My name's ...	ik heyt ...	*Ik heet ...*
I'd like to introduce you to ...		
mahkh ik ü *vor*-stehl-lern		*Mag ik u voorstellen*
aan ...		*aan ...*
I'm pleased to meet you.		
aan-kher-naam		*Aangenaam.*

Nationalities

If your country isn't listed here, try saying it in English, as many country names have a similar pronunciation in Dutch.

| Where are you from? | | |
| waar komt ü vahn-*daan?* | | *Waar komt u vandaan?* |

I'm from ...	ik kom ert ...	*Ik kom uit ...*
Australia	ow-*straa*-lee-yer	*Australië*
Belgium	*behl*-khee-yer	*België*
Canada	*kah*-nah-dah	*Canada*
Flanders	*vlaan*-der-ern	*Vlaanderen*
the Netherlands	*ney*-der-lahnt	*Nederland*
New Zealand	new *zee*-lahnd	*Nieuw Zeeland*
the UK	ert ver-*een*-ikht	*het Verenigd*
	koh-ningk-reyk	*Koninkrijk*
the US	der ver-*een*-ikh-der	*de Verenigde*
	staat-ern	*Staten*

DUTCH

Occupations

What (work) do you do?

waht *dut* ü (vor wehrk)?   *Wat doet u (voor werk)?*

I'm a/an ...   ik behn ern ...   *Ik ben een ...*

artist	*kern*-ster-naar	*kunstenaar*
business person	zaa-*kern*-mahn/	*zakenman/*
	zaa-*kern*-vrow	*zakenvrouw*
doctor	*dok*-ter	*dokter*
engineer	in-*zhehn*-yer	*ingenieur*
farmer	buer	*boer*
journalist	zhoor-nah-*list/*	*journalist/*
	zhoor-nah-*list*-er	*journaliste*
labourer	*ahr*-bey-der/	*arbeider/*
	ahr-beyd-ster	*arbeidster*
lawyer	aht-voh-*kaat/*	*advocaat/*
	aht-voh-*kaat*-er	*advocate*
mechanic	mon-*ter*	*monteur*
nurse	ver-*pley*-kher/	*verpleger/*
	ver-*pleykh*-ster	*verpleegster*
office worker	kahn-*tor*-wehr-ker	*kantoorwerker*
scientist	*wey*-tern-skhahp-per	*wetenschapper*
student	stü-*dehnt/*	*student*
	stü-*dehnt*-er	*studente*
teacher	*lear*-aar/lear-aar-ehs	*leraar/lerares*
waiter	*oh*-ber/	*ober/*
	sehr-*vear*-ster	*serveerster*
writer	*skhrey*-ver/	*schrijver/*
	skhreyf-ster	*schrijfster*

Religion

What religion are you?

waht is üw *khots*-deenst?   *Wat is uw godsdienst?*

I'm not religious.

ik behn neet rey-lee-*khee*-ers   *Ik ben niet religieus.*

I'm ...	ik behn ...	*Ik ben ...*
Buddhist	bu-*dist*	*boeddhist*
Catholic	kah-toh-*leek*	*katholiek*
Christian	*kris*-tern	*christen*
Hindu	*hin*-doo	*hindoe*
Jewish	yohts	*joods*
Muslim	*mos*-lim	*moslim*

Family

Are you married?
behnt ü kher-*trowt*?   *Bent u getrouwd?*

I'm single/married.
ik behn on-kher-*trowt*/   *Ik ben ongetrouwd/*
kher-*trowt*   *getrouwd.*

How many children do you have?
hoo-veyl *kin*-der-ern heyft ü?   *Hoeveel kinderen heeft u?*

I don't have any children.
ik hehp kheyn *kin*-der-ern   *Ik heb geen kinderen.*

I have a daughter/son.
ik hehp ern *dokh*-ter/zohn   *Ik heb een dochter/zoon.*

Do you have a boyfriend/girlfriend?
heyft ü ern vreend/vreend-*in*?   *Heeft u een vriend/vriendin?*

How many brothers and sisters
do you have?
hoo-veyl bruers ehn   *Hoeveel broers en*
zer-sters heyft ü?   *zusters heeft u?*

brother	bruer	*broer*
daughter	*dokh*-ter	*dochter*
family	faa-*mee*-lee	*familie*
father	vaa-der	*vader*
grandfather	*khroht*-vaa-der	*grootvader*
grandmother	*khroht*-mu-der	*grootmoeder*
husband	mahn	*man*
mother	mu-der	*moeder*
sister	zer-ster	*zuster*
son	zohn	*zoon*
wife	vrow	*vrouw*

DUTCH

Kids' Talk

Note that the informal form of the pronoun 'you', *je*, is used in this section (see Forms of Address, page 70).

How old are you?	hoo owd ben yer?	*Hoe oud ben je?*
His/Her name is ...	zeyn/haar naam is ...	*Zijn/haar naam is ...*

When's your birthday?
  wah-*near* is joweh
  ver-*jaar*-dahkh?   *Wanneer is jouw verjaardag?*

Do you have your own room?
  hehb yer ern *ey*-khern *kaa*-mer?   *Heb je een eigen kamer?*

I share my room.
  ik deyl meyn kaamer   *Ik deel mijn kamer.*

I have my own room.
  ik hehb meyn *ey*-khern kaamer   *Ik heb mijn eigen kamer.*

What are your favourite hobbies?
  waht zeyn jow faa-vo-*ree*-teh
  hob-bees?   *Wat zijn jouw favoriete hobbies?*

collecting things	*ding*-ern ver-zaa-meh-*lern*	*dingen verzamelen*
making things	*ding*-ern *maa*-kern	*dingen maken*
playing outside	*ber*-tern *spey*-lern	*buiten spelen*
sports	sport	*sport*
video games	*vi*-di-oh *spel*-ern	*video spellen*
watching TV	tey-*vey* *gey*-kern	*TV kijken*

Do you have any pets?
  hehb yer *hers*-dear-ern?   *Heb je huisdieren?*

We have a ...	wey *hehb*-ern ern ...	*Wij hebben een ...*
budgie	*khraas*-paar-keet	*grasparkiet*
canary	kah-*naar*-ree	*kanarie*
cat	kaht	*kat*
dog	hont	*hond*
guinea pig	*kaar*-vee-aar	*cavia*
hamster	*hahm*-ster	*hamster*
rabbit	koh-*neyn*	*konijn*

Feelings

How are you?
 hoo *khaat* heht meht ü?   *Hoe gaat het met u?*

What's up?   waht is ehr?   *Wat is er?*

I'm ...   ik behn ...   *Ik ben ...*
 angry   bohs   *boos*
 grateful   *dahngk*-baar   *dankbaar*
 happy   bley   *blij*
 lonely   *eyn*-zaam   *eenzaam*
 sad   ver-*dreet*-tikh   *verdrietig*
 sleepy   *slaa*-per-erkh   *slaperig*
 tired   moo   *moe*

I'm ...   ik ...   *Ik ...*
 cold   hehb heht kowd   *heb het koud*
 hot   hehb heht waarm   *heb het warm*
 in a hurry   hehb haast   *heb haast*
 right   hehb *kher*-leyk   *heb gelijk*
 sorry   hehb speyt   *heb spijt*
 (un)well   behn neet *lehk*-ker   *ben niet lekker*
 worried   maak meh *zor*-khern   *maak me zorgen*

Useful Phrases

Just a minute.   ern *oh*-khern-blik-yer   *Een ogenblikje.*
Wait!   wahkht!   *Wacht!*
Good luck!   (veyl) sük-*sehs!*   *(Veel) succes!*
It's (not) important.
 heht is (neet) ber-*lahng*-reyk   *Het is (niet) belangrijk.*
It's (not) possible.
 heht is (neet) *moh*-kher-lerk   *Het is (niet) mogelijk.*

BREAKING THE LANGUAGE BARRIER

Do you speak English?
   spreykt ü *ehng*-erls?   *Spreekt u Engels?*
Does anyone speak English?
   spreykt *ee*-mahnt *ehng*-erls?   *Spreekt iemand Engels?*
I speak a little Netherlandic.
   ik spreyk ern *bey*-tyer   *Ik spreek een beetje*
   ney-der-lahnts   *Nederlands.*
I don't speak ...
   ik spreyk kheyn ...   *Ik spreek geen ...*
I (don't) understand.
   ik ber-*khreyp* heht (neet)   *Ik begrijp het (niet).*
Could you speak slowly please?
   kernt ü ahls-tü-*bleeft*   *Kunt u alstublieft*
   lahng-zaamer *sprey*-kern?   *langzamer spreken?*
Could you repeat that?
   kernt ü daht hehr-*haa*-lern?   *Kunt u dat herhalen?*
How do you say ...?
   hoo zehkht mehn ...?   *Hoe zegt men ...?*
What does ... mean?
   waht ber-*tey*-kernt ...?   *Wat betekent ...?*

SIGNS

INGANG	ENTRANCE
GERESERVEERD	RESERVED
GESLOTEN	CLOSED
INLICHTINGEN	INFORMATION
KOUD	COLD
NOODUITGANG	EMERGENCY EXIT
RICHTING	THIS WAY TO
TOILETTEN	TOILETS
HEREN/MANNEN	MEN
DAMES/VROUWEN	WOMEN
UITGANG	EXIT
VERBODEN ...	NO ...
TOEGANG	ENTRY
TE ROKEN	SMOKING

DUTCH

PAPERWORK

(achter)naam	(sur)name
adres	address
beroep	profession
geboortebewijs	birth certificate
geboortedatum	date of birth
geboorteplaats	place of birth
geslacht	sex
godsdienst	religion
handtekening	signature
huwelijkse staat	marital status
leeftijd	age
legitimatie	identification
nationaliteit	nationality
reden voor bezoek	reason for visit
rijbewijs	driving licence
paspoort(nummer)	passport (number)
toeristenkaart	tourist card
visum	visa

GETTING AROUND
Directions

Where's ...?	waar is ...?	*Waar is ...?*
How do I get to ...?	hoo kom ik in ...?	*Hoe kom ik in ...?*
Is it far from/near here?		
	is heht vehr/dikht-*bey*?	*Is het ver/dichtbij?*
Can you show me (on the map)?		
	kernt ü heht (op der kaart)	*Kunt u het (op de kaart)*
	aan-*wey*-zern?	*aanwijzen?*
Go straight ahead.	khaa rehkht-*dor*	*Ga rechtdoor.*
Turn left/	khaa links-*ahf*/	*Ga linksaf/*
right at the ...	rehkhts-ahf bey ...	*rechtsaf bij ...*
next corner	der *vol*-khern-*dehr* huk	*de volgende hoek*
traffic lights	heht *stop*-likht	*het stoplicht*

behind	*ahkh*-ter	*achter*
far	vehr	*ver*
in front of	vor	*voor*
near	dikht-bey	*dichtbij*
opposite	tey-khern-*oh*-ver	*tegenover*

Buying Tickets

Where can I buy a ticket?
> waar kahn ik ern *kaart*-yer
> koh-pern?

*Waar kan ik een
kaartje kopen?*

I want to go to ...
> ik vil naar ... khaan

Ik wil naar ... gaan.

I'd like to book a seat to ...
> ik wil khraakh ern plaats
> rey-zehr-*vear*-ern naar ...

*Ik wil graag een plaats
reserveren naar ...*

I'd like ...	ik wil khraakh ...	*Ik wil graag ...*
a one-way ticket	ern *ehng*-ker-ler-reys	*een enkele reis*
a return ticket	ern rer-*tur*	*een retour*
two tickets	twey *kaar*-tyers	*twee kaartjes*
a student's fare	ern stü-*dehn*-tern-tah-*reef*	*een studententarief*
a child's fare	ern *kin*-der	*een kinderkorting*
a pensioner's fare	sehs-*tikh* plers kor-ting	*een 60+ korting*
1st class	*ear*-ster *klahs*	*eerste klas*
2nd class	*twey*-der *klahs*	*tweede klas*

Can I get a stand-by ticket?
> kahn ik ern stand-by
> ticket *krey*-khern?

*Kan ik een stand-by
ticket krijgen?*

Bus & Tram

Where's the bus/tram stop?
> waar is der *bers*-hahl-ter?

Waar is de bushalte?

Which bus goes to ...?
> *wehl*-ker bers khaat naar ...?

Welke bus gaat naar ...?

Does this bus go to ...?
    khaat *dey*-zer bers naar ...?   *Gaat deze bus naar ...?*
How often do buses pass by?
    hoo vaak komt der bers?   *Hoe vaak komt de bus?*
Could you let me know when we get to ...?
    kernt ü mer *laa*-tern   *Kunt u me laten weten*
    wey-tern wah-*near* wer in   *wanneer we in*
    ... *aan*-ko-mern?   *... aankomen?*
I want to get off!
    ik vil *ert*-stahp-pern!   *Ik wil uitstappen!*

What time's the ... bus?	hoo laat is der ... bers?	*Hoe laat is de ... bus?*
first	*ear*-ster	*eerste*
last	*laat*-ster	*laatste*
next	*vol*-khern-der	*volgende*

Train & Metro

Is this the right platform for ...?
    is dit heht *yer*-ster pehr-*ron*   *Is dit het juiste perron*
    vor ...?   *voor ...?*
How long will it be delayed?
    hoo-*lahng* is heht ver-*traakht?*   *Hoelang is het vertraagd?*
Which line takes me to ...?
    wehl-ker leyn brehngt   *Welke lijn brengt*
    mer naar ...?   *me naar ...?*
What's the next station?
    waht is het *vol*-khern-der   *Wat is het volgende*
    staht-*shon?*   *station?*

express	*snehl*-treyn	*sneltrein*
local	*stop*-treyn	*stoptrein*
sleeping car	*slaap*-waa-khon	*slaapwagon*

Taxi

Can you take me to ...?
kernt ü mey naar ...
brehng-ern?

How much is it to go to ...?
hoo-*veyl* kost heht naar ...?

The next corner, please.
der *vol*-khern-der huk,
ahls-tü-*bleeft*

The next street to the left/right.
der *vol*-khern-der straat
links/rehkhts

Please slow down.
reyt ahls-tü-*bleeft*
lahng-zaam-er

Please wait here.
wahkht heer ahls-tü-*bleeft*

Here's fine, thanks.
heer is khud, dahnk ü

Stop here!   stop heer!

Kunt u mij naar ...
brengen?

Hoeveel kost het naar ...?

De volgende hoek,
alstublieft.

De volgende straat
links/rechts.

Rijd alstublieft
langzamer.

Wacht hier alstublieft.

Hier is goed, dank u
Stop hier!

THEY MAY SAY ...

pahs-sah-*zheers* mu-tern ...	Passengers must ...
oh-ver-stahp-pern	change trains
naar pehr-*ron* ner-mer ...	go to platform number ...
der treyn ver-*trehkt* vahn pehr-*ron* ...	The train leaves from platform ...
der treyn is ver-*traakht*/ *ahf*-kher-lahst	The train is delayed/ cancelled.
ehr is ern ver-*traakh*-ing vahn ... ür	There's a delay of ... hours.
heht is vol	It's full.

DUTCH

Useful Phrases

Is it a direct route?
    is heht ern rehkht-streyk-ser   *Is het een rechtstreekse*
    ver-*bin*-ding?   *verbinding?*
Is this seat taken?
    is dey-zer plaats ber-*zeht*?   *Is deze plaats bezet?*
I want to get off at ...
    ik vil *ert*-stahp-pern bey ...   *Ik wil uitstappen bij ...*

What time does the ...	hoo laat ver-*trehkt*/	*Hoe laat vertrekt/*
leave/arrive?	ah-ree-*veart* der ...?	*arriveert de ...?*
boat	boht	*boot*
bus	bers	*bus*
train	treyn	*trein*
tram	trehm	*tram*

Car & Bicycle

Where can I hire a car/bicycle?
    waar kahn ik ern *oh*-toh/   *Waar kan ik een auto/fiets*
    feets *hü*-rern?   *huren?*

daily/weekly
    pehr dahkh/weyk   *per dag/week*

Where's the next petrol station?
    waar is heht *vol*-khern-der   *Waar is het volgende*
    behn-zee-ner-staht-*shon*?   *benzinestation?*

DUTCH

Please check the oil and water.
   kon-tro-*lear* ahls-tü-*bleeft*
   oh-lee ehn *waa*-ter

*Controleer alstublieft
olie en water.*

How long can I park here?
   hoo-lahng kahn ik heer
   pahr-*kear*-ern?

*Hoelang kan ik hier
parkeren?*

Does this road lead to ...?
   khaat *dey*-zer wehkh naar ...?

Gaat deze weg naar ...?

I have a flat tyre.
   ik hehp ern *lehk*-ker bahnt

Ik heb een lekke band.

It's not working.
   heht wehrkt neet

Het werkt niet.

air	lerkht	*lucht*
battery	*ahk*-kü	*accu*
brakes	*rehm*-mern	*remmen*
clutch	*kop*-per-ling	*koppeling*
drivers licence	*rey*-ber-weys	*rijbewijs*
engine	*moh*-tor	*motor*
lights	*likh*-tern	*lichten*
oil	*oh*-lee	*olie*
puncture	lehk-ker *bahnt*	*lekke band*
radiator	raa-dee-*yaa*-tor	*radiator*
road map	*wey*-khern-kaart	*wegenkaart*
tyres	*bahn*-dern	*banden*
windscreen	*vor*-rert	*voorruit*

ACCOMMODATION
At the Hotel

Do you have any rooms available?
heyft ü *kaa*-mers vrey?   *Heeft u kamers vrij?*

I'd like (a) ...	*ik* wil khraakh (ern) ...	*Ik wil graag (een) ...*
single room	eyn-pehr-*sohns*-kaa-mer	*eenpersoons kamer*
double room	twey-per-*sohns*-kaa-mer	*tweepersoons kamer*
to share a dorm	ern beht op ern *slaap*-zaal	*een bed op een slaapzaal*

We want a room with a ...	vey vil-ern ern kaa-mer meht ...	*Wij willen een kamer met ...*
bathroom	*baht*-kaa-mer	*badkamer*
shower	dush	*douche*

How much is it per night/person?
hoo-veyl is heht pehr nahkht/per-*sohn*?   *Hoeveel is het per nacht/persoon?*

Can I see it?
kahn ik heht zeen?   *Kan ik het zien?*

It's fine, I'll take it.
heht is khud, ik neym heht   *Het is goed, ik neem het.*

Where's the bathroom?
waar is der *baht*-kaa-mer?   *Waar is de badkamer?*

Is there hot water all day?
is ehr der hey-ler dahkh wahrm *waa*-ter?   *Is er de hele dag warm water?*

I'd like to pay the bill.
ik wil khraakh *ahf*-rey-ker-nern   *Ik wil graag afrekenen.*

I'm/We're leaving now.
ik ver-*trehk*/wey ver-*trehk*-kern nü   *Ik vertrek/wij vertrekken nu.*

(See also Camping, page 91.)

DUTCH

Requests & Complaints

Can I use the telephone?
kahn ik der tey-ler-*fohn*
kher-*brer*-kern?

Kan ik de telefoon gebruiken?

Do you have a safe where
I can leave my valuables?
heyft ü ern klers waar ik
meyn *waar*-der-vol-ler
sper-lern kahn *laa*-tern?

Heeft u een kluis waar ik mijn waardevolle spullen kan laten?

Please change the sheets.
ver-*skhohn* ahls-tü-*bleeft*
der laa-kerns

Verschoon alstublieft de lakens.

Is there somewhere to wash clothes?
is ehr ehr-kherns om
klear-ern ter *wahs*-sern?

Is er ergens om kleren te wassen?

I can't open/close the window.
ik kahn heht raam neet
oh-pern/dikht dun

Ik kan het raam niet open/dicht doen.

I've locked myself out of my room.
ik hehp mer-zehlf
ber-tern-kher-sloh-tern

Ik heb mezelf buiten-gesloten.

The toilet won't flush.
der wey-*sey*/heht twah-*leht*
trehkt neet dor

De WC/het toilet trekt niet door.

Useful Words

bathroom	*baht*-kaa-mer	*badkamer*
bed	beht	*bed*
blanket	*dey*-kern	*deken*
fan	vehn-tee-*laa*-tor	*ventilator*
key	*sler*-terl	*sleutel*
lift (elevator)	lift	*lift*
sheet	*laa*-kern	*laken*
shower	dush	*douche*
toilet	wey-*sey*/twah-*leht*	*WC/toilet*

| towel | *hahn*-duk | *handdoek* |
| window | raam | *raam* |

... water	*... waa*-ter	*...water*
hot	wahrm	*warm*
cold	kowt	*koud*

AROUND TOWN
At the Post Office

I'd like to send	ik wil khraakh ern	*Ik wil graag een*
a/an ...	... ver-*stü*-rern	*... versturen.*
aerogram	*lerkht*-post-blaht	*luchtpostblad*
letter	breef	*brief*
parcel	pah-*keht*	*pakket*
postcard	*breef*-kaart	*briefkaart*
telegram	tey-ler-*khrahm*	*telegram*

I'd like some stamps.

| ik wil khraakh waht *post*-zey-kherls | *Ik wil graag wat postzegels.* |

How much does it cost to send this to ...?

| *hoo*-veyl kost heht om dit naar ... ter *stü*-rern? | *Hoeveel kost het om dit naar ...te sturen?* |

airmail	*lerkht*-post	*luchtpost*
envelope	ahn-ver-*lop*	*envelop*
mail box	*bree*-vern-bers	*brievenbus*
parcel	pah-*keht*	*pakket*
registered mail	*aan*-kher-tey-kernt	*aangetekend*
surface mail	*zey*-post	*zeepost*

DUTCH

Telephone

I want to ring ...	ik vil ... *beh*-lern	*Ik wil ... bellen.*
The number is ...	heht *ner*-mer is ...	*Het nummer is ...*

How much does a three-minute
call cost?
    hoo-veyl kost ern kher-*sprehk*   *Hoeveel kost een gesprek*
    vahn dree mee-*nü*-tern?   *van drie minuten?*
How much does each extra
minute cost?
    hoo-veyl kost *ee*-der-er   *Hoeveel kost iedere*
    mee-*nüt ehk*-straa?   *minuut extra?*
I'd like to speak to ...
    ik vil khraakh ... *sprey*-kern   *Ik wil graag ... spreken.*
I want to make a reverse-charge
(collect) phone call.
    ik vil ern ber-*taa*-ling   *Ik wil een betaling*
    ont-*vahng*-er kher-*sprehk*   *ontvanger gesprek.*
I've been cut off.
    ik behn *ahf*-kher-bro-kern   *Ik ben afgebroken.*
It's engaged.
    heht is ber-*zeht*   *Het is bezet.*

Internet

Is there an Internet cafe
around here?
    is ehr eyn *in*-tehr-neht   *Is er een internet*
    kah-*fey* in deh bürt?   *café in de buurt?*
I want to connect to the Internet.
    ik vil kheh-*brerk mah*-kehn   *Ik wil gebruck maken*
    fahn heht *in*-tehr-neht   *van het internet.*
I want to check my email.
    ik vil meyn *eh*-meyl   *Ik wil mijn email .*
    beh-*key*-kehn   *bekijken*

At the Bank

What's the exchange rate?
  waht is der *wis*-serl-kurs?   *Wat is de wisselkoers?*

I'd like to exchange   ik vil waht ...   *Ik wil wat ...*
some ...   *wis*-ser-lern   *wisselen.*
  money   khehlt   *geld*
  travellers cheques   *reys*-shehks   *reischeques*

How many Euros/guilders
per dollar?
  hoo-veyl e-ros/*kherl*-dern   *Hoeveel euros/gulden*
  pair *dol*-lahr?   *per dollar?*
Can I have money transferred
here from my bank?
  kahn ik khehlt vahn meyn   *Kan ik geld van mijn*
  bahnk *heer*-naar-too   *bank hiernaartoe*
  laa-tern *oh*-ver-maa-kern?   *laten overmaken?*
How long will it take?
  hoo-lahng dut heht   *Hoelang doet het erover?*
  ehr-*oh*-ver?
Has my money arrived yet?
  is meyn khehlt ahl   *Is mijn geld al*
  aan-kher-*koh*-mern?   *aangekomen?*

banknotes	*bahnk*-bil-jeht-tern	*bankbiljetten*
cashier	kahs-*seer*	*kassier*
coins	*mern*-tern	*munten*
credit card	krer-*deet*-kaart	*creditcard*
loose change	*wis*-serl-khehlt	*wisselgeld*

INTERESTS & ENTERTAINMENT
Sightseeing

What are the main attractions?
> waht zeyn der vor-*naam*-ster
> ber-zeens-*waar*-dikh-hey-dern?

*Wat zijn de voornaamste
bezienswaardigheden?*

How old is it?
> hoo owt is heht?

Hoe oud is het?

Can I take photographs?
> kahn ik *foh*-tohs *ney*-mern?

Kan ik foto's nemen?

What time does it open/close?
> hoo laat *oh*-pernt/slert heht?

Hoe laat opent/sluit het?

ancient	(zear) owt	(zeer) oud
archaeological	ahr-khey-oh-*loh*-khees	archeologisch
beach	strahnt	strand
bulb(s)	bol(-lern)	bol(len)
castle	kah-*steyl*, berkht	kasteel, burcht
cathedral	kah-tey-*draal*	kathedraal
church	kairk	kerk
city centre	heht sehn-*trerm*	het centrum
concert hall	kon-*sehrt*-kher-bow	concertgebouw
flower(s)	blum(-ern)	bloem(en)
library	bee-blee-oh-*teyk*	bibliotheek
main square	pleyn/*khroh*-ter *mahrkt*	plein/grote markt
market	mahrkt	markt
old city	ow-der staht	oude stad
opera house	*oh*-per-aa-kher-*bow*	operagebouw
palace	pah-*leys*	paleis
ruins	rü-*ee*-ner	ruïne
stadium	*staa*-dee-on	stadion
statues	*stahnt*-beyl-dern	standbeelden
tulip(s)	terlp(-ern)	tulp(en)
university	ü-nee-vehr-see-*teyt*	universiteit
windmill	*moh*-lern	molen
tourist infor-mation office	der *vey*-vey-vey	de VVV

Going Out

What's there to do in the evenings?
   waht vahlt ehr *saa*-vonts
   ter dun?
   *Wat valt er 's-avonds
   te doen?*

Are there any nightclubs?
   zeyn ehr *dis*-kohs?
   Zijn er disco's?

Are there places where you
can hear local music?
   zeyn ehr *plaat*-sern waar
   jer mü-*zeek* vahn der
   streyk kernt *hor*-ern?
   *Zijn er plaatsen waar
   je muziek van de
   streek kunt horen?*

How much is it to get in?
   hoo-veyl kost ahn-*trey*?
   Hoeveel kost entree?

Festivals

Bevrijdingsdag (Liberation Day, 5 May)
   marks the end of German occupation. Every five years it's a
   public holiday.

Dodenherdenking (Remembrance day, 4 May)
   Remembrance day for victims of World War II. The Queen
   lays a wreath at the National Monument on Dam Square in
   Amsterdam. Speeches are given, followed by the laying of more
   wreaths. At 8 pm, the country observes two minutes of silence.

Eerste Kerstdag & Tweede Kerstdag (Christmas Day & the second
   Christmas Day, 25 & 26 December)
   both days focus on religion and dinner spent with family.
   A second round of present the day after Christmas is becoming more and more common. Both days are usually regarded
   with equal importance.

DUTCH

Koninginnedag (Queen's Day, 30 April)

A popular public holiday. Amsterdam becomes one big party with street stalls, live music and lots of beer. The Queen makes a televised appearance in two towns.

Oudejaarsavond (New Year's Eve)

A big evening with parties everywhere. At midnight, the whole place seems to explode as everyone rushes outside to let off fireworks. The streets are full of people, smoke, explosions and noise.

Sinterklaas

officially falls on 6 December to honour St Nicholas, the patron saint of children. However, in practice it's celebrated the evening before, where the focus is on gift-giving. *Sinterklaas* comes from Spain with his helpers *Zwarte Pieten*, 'Black Peters', who throw sweets around and carry sacks in which to take away naughty children.

IN THE COUNTRY
Weather

What's the weather like?
   hoo is heht wear?   *Hoe is het weer?*

It's raining today.
   heht *rey*-kher vahn-daakh   *Het regent vandaag.*

It's snowing today.
   heht *sney*-wert vahn-daakh   *Het sneeuwt vandaag.*

It's ... today.	heht wear is vahn-*daakh* ...	*Het is vandaag* ...
cloudy	ber-*wolkt*	*bewolkt*
cold	kowt	*koud*
foggy	*mis*-terkh	*mistig*
hot	heyt	*heet*
sunny	*zon*-nerkh	*zonnig*
windy	*win*-der-erkh	*winderig*

DUTCH

Camping

Are we allowed to camp here?
  moh-khern vey heer
  kahm-*pehr*-ern?

*Mogen wij hier
kamperen?*

Is there a campsite nearby?
  is ehr ern *kehm*-ping
  dikht-*bey*?

*Is er een camping
dichtbij?*

can opener	*blik*-oh-per-ner	*blikopener*
compass	kom-*pahs*	*kompas*
firewood	*brahnt*-howt	*brandhout*
gas cartridge	*khahs*-paa-trohn	*gaspatroon*
mattress	maa-*trahs*	*matras*
penknife	*zahk*-mehs	*zakmes*
rope	tow	*touw*
tent	tehnt	*tent*
tent pegs	*haa*-ring-ern	*haringen*
torch (flashlight)	*zahk*-lahmp	*zaklamp*
sleeping bag	*slaap*-zahk	*slaapzak*
stove	*brahn*-der	*brander*
water bottle	*vehlt*-flehs	*veldfles*

FOOD

Depending on the region, the main meal of the day is eaten either
in the evening or at midday.

breakfast	*ont*-beyt	*ontbijt*
lunch	*mid*-daakh-ey-tehn	*middageten*
dinner	*dee*-ney	*diner*

DUTCH

Vegetarian Meals

I'm a vegetarian.

ik behn vey-kher-*taa*-ree-yer		*Ik ben vegetariër.*

I don't eat ...	ik eyt kheyn ...	*Ik eet geen ...*
chicken	kip	*kip*
fish	vis	*vis*
ham	hahm	*ham*

Staple Foods

bread (pumpernickel, rye bread or black bread, usually eaten with cheese or herring)	ro-kheh-brohd	*roggebrood*
eggs	ey-eh-rern	*eieren*
fruit	frerkh-tern	*vruchten*
herring (usually eaten raw with chopped onions)	haa-ring	*haring*
meat (salted)	pey-kehl-vleys	*pekelvlees*
pastry (meat or fish)	pahs-tey	*pastei*
potatoes	aar-dah-peh-lern	*aardappelen*
seafood	fis-geh-rekh-tern	*visgerechten*
vegetables	groon-teh	*groente*

MENU DECODER

Breakfast & Lunch

beschuit
  Dutch crisp bread, eaten with cheese, *hagelslag* or
  gestampte muisjes (see *muisjes*)

hagelslag
  fine, vermicelli-like strands of chocolate or coloured aniseed
  sugar; a hit with kids

halve maantjes
  croissants

havermoutpap
  oatmeal porridge

(ontbijt)koek
  Dutch honey cake

leverworst
  liver sausage

muisjes
  sugar-coated aniseed. *Gestampte muisjes* are ground
  muisjes

rookvlees
  smoked beef, thinly sliced

soep	soup
groente	vegetable
ossestaart	oxtail
schildpad	turtle

theeworst
  (lit: tea-sausage) spiced and smoked, light-pink
  liver-sausage

uitsmijter
  sliced bread with cold meat (usually ham or thinly sliced
  roasted beef), covered with fried eggs and a garnish such
  as pickles

Main Meals

biefstuk tartaar
  raw minced beef with egg and spices

blinde vink
  beef or veal wrapped in bacon, fried

groene haring
fresh, raw herring, untreated apart from being cleaned and kept on ice. Don't dismiss it until you've tried it.

lekkerbekje
fried fish fillet

meerval
freshwater catfish

nieuwe haring
'new' herring, fresh and mild-flavoured, in theory the first herring of the season. A favourite at fish stalls.

osseworst
ox sausage, spiced and smoked

rolmops
pickled herring wrapped around gherkin and/or onion

zeewolf
saltwater catfish

zoute haring
salted herring, kipper

Desserts

aardbeien met slagroom
strawberries with whipped cream

bokkepoot
(lit: billy-goat leg) a biscuit with a sweet filling. Covered with almond slivers, with both ends dipped in chocolate.

boterletter, boterstaaf
pastry with soft marzipan filling

flensjes
thin pancakes

moorkop
large cream-puff with chocolate icing

oliebol
dough fritter with currants, served with caster sugar. Popular New Year's treat.

poffertjes
a mound of tiny round pancakes, served with caster sugar

vlaai, Limburgse vlaai
tangy fruit pie on bread-dough base

wentelteefjes
stale bread soaked in egg, milk and cinnamon, then fried and served with sugar

DUTCH

Non-Alcoholic Drinks

water (with ice)	*vaa*-ter (meht eys)	*water (met ijs)*
chocolate milk	*zhoh*-koh-mehl	*Chocomel*
coffee	*kof*-fee	*koffie*
juice	sahp	*sap*
freshly squeezed	fehrs kher-*pehrst*	*vers geperst*
orange juice	zhü der-o-*ronzh*	*jus d'orange*
tea	tey	*thee*
with milk	meht mehlk	*met melk*
with lemon	meht *sit*-run	*met citroen*

Alcoholic Drinks

Beerenburg
 a herbal *genever* from Friesland
genever (also spelled *jenever*)
 Dutch gin based on juniper berries, drunk neat and chilled
 from small glasses. *Jonge*, 'young', is smooth and relatively easy
 to drink, while *oude*, 'old', has a strong juniper flavour and
 can be an acquired taste.
lambic
 popular Belgian beer. Varieties include *gueuze*, which is
 sour, and the sweet *kriek* and *framboise*, which are cherry
 and raspberry flavoured respectively.
sneeuwwitje
 (lit: Snow White) 50/50 lemonade and beer
trappist
 dark and often very strong Belgian beer, drunk from goblets.
 Originally brewed by Trappist monks. There are countless brands
 and varieties graded by alcohol content, such as *dubbel* and *tripel*.

beer	beer	*bier*
brandy	vee-er	*vieux*
lager	pils	*pils*
... wine	veyn	*... wijn*
house	hers	*huis*
red	rohd	*rood*
white	wit	*wit*

DUTCH

AT THE MARKET

DUTCH

Basics

bread	*broht*	brood
butter	*boh*-ter	boter
cereal	ont-*beyt*-graa-nern	ontbÿtgranen
cheese	kaas	kaas
chocolate	zhoh-koh-*laa*(-der)	chocola(de)
eggs	*ey*-er-rern	eieren
flour	meyl	meel
honey	*hoh*-ning	honing
margarine	mahr-zhaa-*ree*-ner	margarine
milk	mehlk	melk
olive oil	oh-*ley*-foh-lee	olÿfolie
pasta	*pahs*-tah	pasta
rice	reyst	rÿst
sugar	ser-ker	suiker
yogurt	*yo*-khert	yoghurt
(mineral) water	(mee-ner-aal) *waa*-ter	(mineraal)water

Meat & Poultry

beef	*rernd*-vleys	rundvlees
chicken	kip	kip
ham	hahm	ham
lamb	*lahms*-vleys	lamsvlees
meat	fleys	vlees
pork	*fahr*-kehns-vleys	varkensvlees
salted meat	pey-kehl-vleys	pekelvlees
sausage	vorst	worst
turkey	kahl-*kun*	kalkoen
veal	*kahlfs*-vleys	kalfsvlees

Vegetables

beans	*boh*-nern	bonen
beetroot	*roh*-der beet	rode biet
cabbage	khol	kool
carrot	*vor*-tehl	wortel
cauliflower	*blum*-kohl	bloemkool
cucumber	kom-*kom*-mer	komkommer
lettuce	slaa	sla
mushrooms	*zhahm*-pi-nons	champignons
onion	er	ui

AT THE MARKET

peas	*ehrw*-tern	erwten
potatoes	*aar*-dahp-peh-lern	aardappelen
spinach	spi-*naa*-zee	spinazie
string beans	*sney*-boh-nern	snÿbonen
tomato	toh-*maat*	tomaat
vegetables	*khrun*-ter	groente
zucchini	kur-*zheht*	courgette

Seafood

fish	vis	vis
herring	*haa*-ring	haring
lobster	krayft	kreeft
mussels	*mos*-seh-lern	mosselen
shrimp	khahr-*naa*-lern	garnalen

Pulses

broad beans	*tern*-boh-nern	tuinbonen
butter beans	*khey*-ler	gele sperziebonen
	spehr-zee-boh-nern	
split peas	spli-*tehrw*-tern	spliterwten
lentils	*lin*-zern	linzen

Fruit

apple	*ahp*-pehl	appel
apricot	ahb-*ree*-kohs	abrikoos
banana	bah-*naan*	banaan
cherries	*kher*-sern	kersen
fruit	*frerkh*-tern	vruchten
lemon	sit-*run*	citroen
orange	*see*-naa-sahp-pehl	sinaasappel
peach	*pehr*-zik	perzik
plum	prerm	pruim
strawberries	*aard*-bey-ern	aardbeien

Spices & Condiments

garlic	*knof*-lohk	knoflook
mayonnaise	mey-o-*neys*	mayonaise
mustard	*mos*-terd	mosterd
pepper	*pey*-per	peper
salt	zowt	zout

SHOPPING

baker	*vaar*-me *bah*-ker	*warme bakker*
barber	*bahr*-beer	*barbier*
clothing store	*kley*-ding-zaak	*kledingzaak*
delicatessan	de-li-kaa-*tehs*-sern-*ving*-kerl	*delicatessenwinkel*
greengrocer	*khrun*-ter-bur	*groenteboer*
hairdresser	*kahp*-per	*kapper*
late-night store	*aa*-vont-ving-kerl	*avondwinkel*
shoe repairs	*skhun*-maa-ker	*schoenmaker*
travel agency	*reys*-bü-roh	*reisbureau*

How much is it?   *hoo*-veyl kost heht?   *Hoeveel kost het?*

Do you accept credit cards?
    ahk-sehp-*teart* ü   *Accepteert u*
    krer-*deet*-kaar-tern?   *kredietkaarten?*

Essential Groceries

batteries	bah-ter-*rey*-ern	*batterijen*
bread	broht	*brood*
butter	*boh*-ter	*boter*
cheese	kaas	*kaas*
chocolate	zhoh-koh-*laa*(-der)	*chocola(de)*
coffee	*ko*-fee	*koffie*
gas cartridge	*khahs*-paa-trohn	*gaspatroon*
matches	*lü*-see-fehrs	*lucifers*
milk	mehlk	*melk*
mineral water	mee-ner-aal-*waa*-ter/spaa	*mineraalwater/spa*
fruit	frert/ *frerkh*-tern	*fruit/ vruchten*
soap	zeyp	*zeep*
sausage	vorst	*worst*
sugar	*ser*-ker	*suiker*
tea	tey	*thee*
toilet paper	wey-*sey*-pah-*peer*	*WC-papier*
toothpaste	*tahnt*-pahs-taa	*tandpasta*
washing powder	*wahs*-pu-der	*waspoeder*
yogurt	*yo*-khert	*yoghurt*

Souvenirs

clogs	*klomp*-ern	*klompen*
diamonds	dee-aa-*mahn*-tern	*diamanten*
Delft blue (pottery)	dehlfts-blow	*Delfts blauw*
earrings	*or*-behl-lern	*oorbellen*
handicraft	*hahnt*-wehrk	*handwerk*
necklace	*hahls*-keht-ting	*halsketting*
pottery	*aar*-der-wehrk	*aardewerk*
rug	kleyt	*kleed*

Clothing

boots	*laar*-zehn	*laarzen*
clothing	*kley*-ding	*kleding*
coat	yahs	*jas*
gloves	hahnt-*skhu*-nern	*handschoenen*
hat	hut	*hoed*
jacket	*yahs*-yer	*jasje*
jumper (sweater)	trer	*trui*
raincoat	*rey*-khehn-yahs	*regenjas*
scarf	zhaal	*sjaal*
shoes	*skhu*-nern	*schoenen*
trousers	bruk	*broek*
umbrella	paa-raa-*plü*	*paraplu*

Materials

brass	*meh*-sing	*messing*
cotton	kah-*tun*	*katoen*
gold	khowt	*goud*
leather	lear	*leer*
linen	*lin*-ern	*linnen*
satin	sah-*teyn*	*satijn*
silk	*zey*-der	*zijde*
silver	*zil*-vehr	*zilver*
velvet	veh-*lurs*	*velours*
wool	wohl	*wol*

DUTCH

Colours

black	zvahrt	*zwart*
blue	blow	*blauw*
brown	brern	*bruin*
dark	*dong*-ker	*donker*
green	khrun	*groen*
grey	khreys	*grijs*
light	likht	*licht*
orange	oh-*ron*-yer	*oranje*
pink	*roh*-zeh	*roze*
purple	paas	*paars*
red	rohd	*rood*
turquoise	ter-*koys*	*turkoois*
white	vit	*wit*
yellow	kheyl	*geel*

Toiletries

condoms	kon-*dohms*	*condooms*
hairbrush	*bor*-sterl	*borstel*
razor (blade)	*skhear*-mehs	*scheermes*
razor (electric)	*skhear*-ahp-pah-raat	*scheerapparaat*
sanitary napkins	*maant*-ver-bahnd	*maandverband*
shaving cream	*skhear*-zeyp	*scheerzeep*
soap	zeyp	*zeep*
sunscreen	*zon*-ner-brahnt-oh-lee	*zonnebrandolie*
tampons	tahm-*pons*	*tampons*
tissues	*tis*-yoos	*tissues*
toothbrush	*tahn*-dern-bor-sterl	*tandenborstel*

Stationery & Publications

crayons	veht kreyt	*vet krijt*
envelope	on-ver-lohp	*envelop*
ink	ingkt	*inkt*
map	kaart	*kaart*
paper	pa-*peer*	*papier*
pen	pehn	*pen*
pencil	*pot*-loht	*potlood*
rubber	kherm	*gum*
scissors	skhaar	*schaar*
writing paper	*skhreyf*-paa-peer	*schrijfpapier*
English-language ...	*ehng*-is-*taal*-likh-er ...	*Engelstalige ...*
newspaper	krahnt	*krant*
novel	roh-*mahn*	*roman*

Photography

How much is it to process this film?
> *hoo*-veyl kost heht om
> dey-zer film ter
> ont-*wik*-ker-lern?

> *Hoeveel kost het om*
> *deze film te*
> *ontwikkelen?*

When will it be ready?
> *wahn*-near is heht klaar?

> *Wanneer is het klaar?*

I'd like a film for this camera.
> ik vil khraag film vor
> dey-zer *kaa*-mer-aa

> *Ik wil graag film voor*
> *deze kamera.*

B&W	zvahrt-vit	*zwart-wit*
camera	*kaa*-mer-aa	*kamera*
colour (film)	*kler*(-ern-film)	*kleur(enfilm)*
film	film	*film*
flash	flits	*flits*
light meter	*likht*-mey-ter	*lichtmeter*

DUTCH

Smoking

A packet of cigarettes, please.		
ern *pahk*-yer see-khaar-*eht*-tern, ahls-tü-*bleeft*		*Een pakje sigaretten, alstublieft.*
Do you have a light?		
heyft ü ern *vür*-tyer?		*Heeft u een vuurtje?*
Do you mind if I smoke?		
fint ü heht ehrkh ahls ik rohk?		*Vindt u het erg als ik rook?*
Please don't smoke here.		
rohk heer ahls-tü-bleeft neet		*Rook hier alstublieft niet.*

cigarettes	see-khaar-*eht*-tern	*sigaretten*
cigarette papers	vluee	*vloei*
filtered	meht *fil*-ter	*met filter*
lighter	*aan*-stey-ker	*aansteker*
matches	*lü*-see-fehrs	*lucifers*
menthol	*men*-tol	*menthol*
pipe	peyp	*pijp*

Sizes & Comparisons

Enough!	kher-*nukh!*	*Genoeg!*
big	khroht	*groot*
double	*der*-berl	*dubbel*
a dozen	ern doh-zeyn	*een dozijn*
few	*wey*-nikh-er	*weinige*
less	*min*-der	*minder*
a little (amount)	ern *bey*-tyer	*een beetje*
many	*vey*-ler	*vele*
more	mear	*meer*
much	veyl	*veel*
once	eyns/ *eyn*-maal	*eens/eenmaal*
a pair	ern paar	*een paar*
percent	pro-*sehnt*	*procent*
small	kleyn	*klein*
some	*som*-mer-kher	*sommige*
too much	ter-*veyl*	*teveel*
twice	*twey*-maal	*tweemaal*

HEALTH

Parts of the Body

My ... hurts.	meyn ... dut peyn	*Mijn ... doet pijn.*
back	rerkh	*rug*
chest	borst	*borst*
ear	or	*oor*
eye	ohkh	*oog*
foot	vut	*voet*
hand	hahnt	*hand*
head	hohft	*hoofd*
leg	beyn	*been*
mouth	mont	*mond*
neck	nehk	*nek*
nose	ners	*neus*
skin	hert	*huid*
stomach	maakh	*maag*
teeth	*tahn*-dern	*tanden*

Ailments

I'm sick.	ik behn zeek	*Ik ben ziek.*
I have (a/an) ...	ik hehp ...	*Ik heb ...*
burn	ern ver-*brahn*-ding	*een verbranding*
cold	ern ver-*kowd*-heyt	*een verkoudheid*
constipation	ver-*stop*-ping	*verstopping*
sore throat	ern zear-er keyl	*een zere keel*
diarrhoea	dee-ah-*rey*	*diarree*
fever	korts	*koorts*
headache	*hohft*-peyn	*hoofdpijn*
indigestion	in-dee-*khehs*-tee	*indigestie*
infection	ern ont-*stey*-king	*een ontsteking*
influenza	khreep	*griep*
itch	yerk	*jeuk*
sprain	ern ver-*ster*-king	*een verstuiking*
sunburn	*zon*-ner-brahnt	*zonnebrand*
temperature	korts	*koorts*
venereal disease	ern ver-*near*-ee-ser zeek-ter	*een venerische ziekte*

I have low/high blood pressure.
  ik hehp *hoh*-kher/*laa*-kher *blut*-drerk — *Ik heb hoge/lage bloeddruk.*

I feel nauseous.
  ik behn *mis*-ser-lerk — *Ik ben misselijk.*

Useful Words & Phrases

Where's a/the ...?	waar is ...?	*Waar is ...?*
chemist	der droh-*khist*	*de drogist*
dentist	der *tahnt*-ahrts	*de tandarts*
doctor	der *dok*-ter	*de dokter*
hospital	het *zee*-kern-hers	*het ziekenhuis*

I feel better/worse.
  ik vool mer *bey*-ter/*slehkh*-ter — *Ik voel me beter/slechter.*

At the Chemist

I need medication for ...
  ik hehp mey-dee-*sey*-nern noh-derkh vor ... — *Ik heb medicijnen nodig voor ...*

antiseptic	ahn-tee-*sehp*-tees	*antiseptisch*
Band-Aids	*pleys*-ters	*pleisters*
bandage	fer-*bahnt*	*verband*
cough lozenge	*hust*-pahs-tille	*hoestpastille*
cough syrup	*hust*-si-rup	*hoestsiroop*
laxative	laak-*sear*-mid-dehl	*laxeermiddel*
sleeping tablet	*slaap*-tahb-leht	*slaaptablet*

At the Dentist

I have a toothache (molars/incisors).
  ik hehp *kees*-peyn/*tahnt*-peyn — *Ik heb kiespijn/tandpijn.*

I've lost a filling.
  ik behn ern *ver*-ling ver-*lor*-ern — *Ik ben een vulling verloren.*

I've broken a tooth.
  ik hehp ern tahnt
  kher-*broh*-kern

Ik heb een tand
gebroken.

I don't want it extracted.
  ik vil neet daht heht
  kher-*trok*-kern wort

Ik wil niet dat het
getrokken word.

Please give me an anaesthetic.
  kheyf mer ahls-tü-*bleeft*
  ern ver-*doh*-ving

Geef me alstublieft
een verdoving.

TIME & DATES
Days

Monday	*maan*-dahkh	maandag
Tuesday	*dins*-dahkh	dinsdag
Wednesday	*vuns*-dahkh	woensdag
Thursday	*don*-der-dahkh	donderdag
Friday	*vrey*-dahkh	vrijdag
Saturday	*zaa*-ter-dahkh	zaterdag
Sunday	*zon*-dahkh	zondag

Months

January	jah-nü-*aa*-ree	januari
February	fey-brü-*aa*-ree	februari
March	maart	maart
April	ah-*pril*	april
May	mey	mei
June	*yü*-nee	juni
July	*yü*-lee	juli
August	ow-*khers*-ters	augustus
September	sehp-*tehm*-ber	september
October	ok-*toh*-ber	oktober
November	noh-*vehm*-ber	november
December	dey-*sehm*-ber	december

DUTCH

Seasons

spring	*lehn*-ter/ *vor*-yaar	*lente/voorjaar*
summer	*zoh*-mer	*zomer*
autumn	hehrfst/ *naa*-yaar	*herfst/najaar*
winter	*win*-ter	*winter*

Present

now	nü	*nu*
today	vahn-*daakh*	*vandaag*
this morning	vahn-*okh*-ternt	*vanochtend*
tonight	vahn-*aa*-vont	*vanavond*
this week/	dey-zer weyk/	*deze week/*
year	dit yaar	*dit jaar*

Past

yesterday	*khis*-ter-ern	*gisteren*
last night	*khis*-ter-ern-*aa*-vont	*gisterenavond*
yesterday morning	*khis*-ter-ern-*mor*-khern	*gisterenmorgen*
day before yesterday	ear-*khis*-ter-ern	*eergisteren*
last week/year	*vor*-i-kher *weyk/*	*vorige week/vorig*
	vor-ikh *yaar*	*jaar*

Future

tomorrow	*mor*-khern	*morgen*
tomorrow morning	*mor*-khern-*okh*-ternt	*morgenochtend*
tomorrow	*mor*-khern-*mid*-dahkh/	*morgenmiddag/*
afternoon/evening	*mor*-khern-*aa*-vont	*morgenavond*
day after tomorrow	*oh*-ver-*mor*-khern	*overmorgen*
next week	*vol*-khern-der *weyk*	*volgende week*
next year	*vol*-khernd *yaar*	*volgend jaar*

During the Day

afternoon	*mid*-dahkh	*middag*
dawn	*daa*-khe-*raat*	*dageraad*

day	dahkh	dag
early	vrukh	vroeg
late	laat	laat
midnight	mid-der-*nahkht*	middernacht
morning	*okh*-ternt	ochtend
night	nahkht	nacht
noon	twaalf ür *smid*-dahkhs	twaalf uur
		's-middags
sunrise	zons-*op*-khahng	zonsopgang
sunset	zons-*on*-der-khahng	zonsondergang

NUMBERS & AMOUNTS

0	nerl	nul
1	eyn	één
2	twey	twee
3	dree	drie
4	veer	vier
5	veyf	vijf
6	zehs	zes
7	*zey*-vern	zeven
8	ahkht	acht
9	*ney*-khern	negen
10	teen	tien
11	elf	elf
12	twaalf	twaalf
13	*dehr*-teen	dertien
14	*vear*-teen	veertien
15	*veyf*-teen	vijftien

DUTCH

16	*zehs*-teen	*zestien*
17	*zey*-vern-teen	*zeventien*
18	*ahkh*-teen	*achttien*
19	*ney*-khern-teen	*negentien*
20	*tvin*-terkh	*twintig*
30	*dehr*-terkh	*dertig*
40	*vear*-terkh	*veertig*
50	*veyf*-terkh	*vijftig*
60	*zehs*-terkh	*zestig*
70	*zey*-vern-terkh	*zeventig*
80	*tahkh*-terkh	*tachtig*
90	*ney*-khern-terkh	*negentig*
100	*hon*-dert	*honderd*
1000	*der*-zernt	*duizend*
one million	eyn mil-*yun*	*één miljoen*

ABBREVIATIONS

ANWB	Dutch motoring federation
BTW	VAT (value-added tax)
BV	Pty (private company)
M/Mevr	Mr/Mrs/Ms
NV	Ltd/Inc
TCB	Belgian Motoring Club
-str/-weg/-pl	St/Rd/Sq
v.Chr./n.Chr.	AD/BC
VVV	Dutch tourist information

DUTCH

EMERGENCIES

Help!	help!	*Help!*
Go away!	khaa wehkh!	*Ga weg!*
Thief!	deef!	*Dief!*
I'll call the police!	ik rup der	*Ik roep de politie!*
	poh-*leet*-see!	
I'm ill.	ik behn zeek	*Ik ben ziek.*

It's an emergency!
  heht is ern *noht*-kher-vahl!   *Het is een noodgeval!*
There's been an accident!
  ehr is ern *on*-kher-lerk   *Er is een ongeluk*
  kher-*bert*!   *gebeurd!*
Call a doctor!
  haal ern dok-ter!   *Haal een dokter!*
Call an ambulance!
  haal ern zee-kern-oh-toh!   *Haal een ziekenauto!*
Call the police!
  haal der poh-leet-see!   *Haal de politie!*
Where's the police station?
  waar is heht poh-leet-   *Waar is het politie*
  see-bü-roh?   *bureau?*
I've been raped.
  ik behn aan-kher-rahnd   *Ik ben aangerand.*
I've been robbed!
  ik behn ber-rohft!   *Ik ben beroofd!*
I'm lost.
  ik behn der wehkh kweyt   *Ik ben de weg kwijt.*
Could you help me please?
  kernt ü mey ahls-tü-*bleeft*   *Kunt u mij alstublieft*
  hehl-pern?   *helpen?*
Could I use the telephone?
  zow ik *moh*-khern *behl*-lern?   *Zou ik mogen bellen?*

Dealing With the Police

My ... was stolen.	meyn ... is kher-*stoh*-lern!	*Mijn ... is gestolen!*
I've lost my ...	ik behn meyn ... *ver*-lor-ern	*Ik ben mijn ... verloren.*
bags	*tahs*-sern	*tassen*
handbag	*hahnd*-tahs	*handtas*
money	khehlt	*geld*
travellers cheques	*reys*-shehks	*reis cheques*
passport	*pahs*-port	*paspoort*
I want to contact my ...	ik wil kon-*tahkt* op-ney-mern meht meyn ...	*Ik wil kontakt opnemen met mijn*
embassy	ahm-bah-*saa*-der	*ambassade*
consulate	kon-sü-*laat*	*consulaat*

DUTCH

FRENCH

FRENCH

QUICK REFERENCE

Hello.	bō-zhoor	Bonjour.
Goodbye.	oh-re-vwahr; sah-lü	Au revoir; Salut.
Yes./No.	wee/nō	Oui./Non.
Sorry; Excuse me.	pahr-dō	Pardon.
Please.	seel voo pleh	S'il vous plaît.
Thank you (very much).	mehr-see boh-koo	Merci (beaucoup).
You're welcome.	zhe voo zã-pree	Je vous en prie.
I'd like a ...	zhe voo-drei ...	Je voudrais ...
room	oon shabr	une chambre
ticket	ē bee-yay	un billet
one-way	ah-lay sepl	aller simple
return	ah-lay ei rer-toor	aller et retour
Where is ...?	oo ei ...?	Où est ...?

Turn left/right.
    too-nay ah gohsh/drwaht   Tournez à gauche/droite.
Go straight ahead.
    kon-tin-yoo-eh too drwah   Continuez tout droit.
I (don't) understand.
    zhe (ne) kō-prã (pah)   Je (ne) comprends (pas).
Do you speak English?
    voo pahr-lay ã-gleh?   Vous parlez anglais?
Where are the toilets?
    oo sō lay twah-leht?   Où sont les toilettes?
How much is it?
    seh kō-byē?   C'est combien?
What time is it?
    kehl err ei teel?   Quelle heure est-il?

1	ē	un	6	sees	six
2	der	deux	7	seht	sept
3	trwah	trois	8	weet	huit
4	kahtr	quatre	9	nerf	neuf
5	sēk	cinq	10	dees	dix

FRENCH

French is one of the Romance languages, which means that it's descended from Latin. In France itself, there are over 50 million French speakers, and it's an official language in Belgium, Switzerland and Luxembourg. Being able to speak some French will broaden your travel experience and ensure that you're treated with appreciation.

French began to emerge as a distinct language in the 9th century AD. When Paris became the capital of France in the 12th century, the dialect of the Parisian region, Francien, spread, to the detriment of the Provençal language in the south and other regional dialects.

The edict of Villers-Cotterets, issued by François I in 1539, made the use of French compulsory for official documents. During the French Rennaissance in the 16th century, efforts were made to enrich and dignify the national tongue. This involved coining words from Greek and Latin roots, and the adoption of etymological spellings, which later reformers haven't been able to rationalise.

GENDER

Some nouns in French may have both masculine and feminine forms. A feminine noun is often formed by adding -e to the end of the masculine form of the noun. In this chapter, the masculine form of a word appears first. The feminine ending is separated by a slash:

a friend (m/f)   un/e ami/e

This indicates that the masculine form is *un ami* and the feminine form is *une amie*. In cases where the feminine is more complicated than adding an -e to the masculine form, both forms of the word appear in full, masculine first:

waiter (m/f)   *le serveur/la serveuse*

FRENCH

During the 17th century, the poet Malherbe and the grammarian Vaugelas, a founding member of the French Academy, *l'Académie française*, were influential in a movement to 'purify' the language and codify its usage, establishing norms which have, to a large extent, remained in force.

The Academy, established in 1635, has preserved its purist stand by opposing the introduction of English words such as 'sandwich', 'weekend', 'shopping' and 'record'. However, you'll hear much of this 'franglais' on your travels. From the 17th to the 19th century, French was the foremost international language, though it's now been overshadowed by English. It remains one of the official languages at the United Nations and UNESCO.

PRONUNCIATION
Vowels

a	ah	as the 'u' in cup
e	e	as the 'e' in 'open';
	eh	as the 'e' in 'merry', but slightly longer
é	ay	as the 'e' in 'bed', but slightly longer
è	eh	as the 'e' in 'merry', but slightly longer
i	ee	as the 'i' in 'marine'
o	o	as the 'o' in 'hot';
	oh	as the 'o' in 'spoke'
u	ü	to make this sound, purse your lips as if you were saying 'oo', but make the sound 'ee'

Vowel Combinations

ai	ay	as the 'e' in 'bed'
au	oh	as the 'o' in 'port'
eau	oh	as the 'o' in 'port'
eu	er	as the 'e' in the 'her', but shorter
ie	yay	as the 'ie' in 'pier'
oi	wah	as the 'w' in 'water' + the 'a' in 'father'
ou	oo	as the 'oo' in 'book';
ui	wee	as the 'wee' in 'week'

Nasal Vowels

When pronouncing nasal vowels, the breath escapes partly through the nose and partly through the mouth. The three nasal vowels in French occur where a syllable ends in a single *n*, *m* or *nt* – the last consonants aren't pronounced, but indicate the nasalisation of the preceding vowel.

on/om	ō	as the 'o' in 'long'
in/im/ain/aim/ ein/eim/un	ē	between the 'a' in 'ant' and the 'ai' in 'ain't'
an/am/en/em	ā	as the 'en' in 'encore'
ien	yē	as the 'y' in 'yellow' + the 'a' in 'bang'

Consonants

These are generally pronounced as in English, with a few exceptions. Consonants at the end of a word aren't pronounced, unless they run on to the following word (see Liaison, page).

c	k	as the 'c' in 'cat' before *a*, *o* and *u*;
	s	as the 'c' in 'celery' before *e*, *i* and *y*
ç	s	as the 'c' in 'celery'
g	g	as the 'g' in 'game' before *a*, *o* and *u*
	zh	as the 's' in 'pleasure' before *e* and *i*
h		silent
j	zh	as the 's' in 'pleasure'
l	l	pronounced with the tip of the tongue touching the back of the upper front teeth
q	k	as the 'k' in 'king'
r	r	the standard *r* of Parisian French is pronounced deep in the throat. It's produced by moving the bulk of the tongue backwards while the tip of the tongue rests behind the lower front teeth. It's quite similar to the noise made by some people before spitting, but with much less friction.
s	z	between vowels, as the 'z' in 'zoo';
	s	elsewhere, as the 's' in 'sin'

FRENCH

Liaison

French consonants are only pronounced at the end of a word when the following word begins with a vowel or a silent *h*. This 'running-on' of a sound is called 'liaison'. Thus, the sentence *il est artiste*, 'he's an artist', sounds like eel-eh tahr-teest.

s, x	z	as the 'z' in 'zoo'		
		you have	voo zah-vay	*vous avez*
		the eyes	lay-zyer	*les yeux*
d	t	as the 't' in 'tame'		
		big animal	grã-tah-nee-mahl	*grand animal*

PRONOUNS					
SG			**PL**		
I	zhe	*je*	we	noo	*nous*
you (inf)	tü	*tu*	you (pol)	voo	*vous*
he/it (m)	eel	*il*	they	eel/ehl	*ils/elles*
she/it (f)	ehl	*elle*			

Stress

Stress in French is much weaker than in English. The final syllable of a word is lengthened, and each syllable should be pronounced with approximately equal stress.

GREETINGS & CIVILITIES
You Should Know

Hello. (pol)	bõ-zhoor	*Bonjour.*
Hello. (inf)	sah-lü	*Salut.*
Good morning/ afternoon.	bõ-zhoor	*Bonjour.*
Good evening/night.	bõ-swahr	*Bonsoir.*
How are you?	ko-mã tah-lay voo?	*Comment allez-vous?*
Well, thanks.	byẽ mehr-see	*Bien, merci.*

FRENCH

Not bad.	sah vah	*Ça va.*
And you?	ay voo?	*Et vous?*
Goodbye. (pol)	oh-re-vwahr; sah-lü	*Au revoir; Salut.*
Goodbye. (inf)	chah-oh	*Tchao.*
See you.	ah byē toh	*A bientôt.*
Yes./Yeah.	wee/weh	*Oui./Ouais.*
No.	nō	*Non.*
Excuse me.	ehk-skü-zay mwah	*Excusez-moi.*
May I?	zhe per?	*Je peux?*
Sorry; Excuse me.	pahr-dō	*Pardon.*
Please.	seel voo pleh	*S'il vous plaît.*
Thank you (very much).	mehr-see boh-koo	*Merci (beaucoup).*
You're welcome.	zhe voo zā-pree	*Je vous en prie.*

Forms of Address

If in doubt as to whether to use *Madame* or *Mademoiselle*, stick to *Madame*.

Madam/Mrs	mah dahm	*Madame (Mme)*
Sir/Mr	mer-syer	*Monsieur (M)*
Ms/Miss	mah-dwah-zehl	*Mademoiselle (Mlle)*

SMALL TALK
Meeting People

What's your name?
   ko-mā voo zah-play voo?   *Comment vous appelez-vous?*

My name's ...
   zhe mah-pehl   *Je m'appelle ...*

I'm a friend (m/f) of ...
   zhe swee zē/zü nah-mee de ...   *Je suis un/e ami/e de ...*

I'd like to introduce you to ...
   zhe voo pray-zāt ...   *Je vous présente ...*

Pleased to meet you (m/f).
   ā-shā-tay   *Enchanté/e.*

FRENCH

I'm here ...	zhe swee zee-see poor ...	*Je suis ici pour ...*
on a holiday	lay vah-kās	*les vacances*
on business	le trah-vahy	*le travail*
to study	la zay-tüd	*les études*

Nationalities

You'll find that many country names in French are similar to those in English. If your country isn't listed here, try saying it in English and you'll most likely be understood, although remember that it will have French pronunciation.

Where are you from?
voo ve-nay doo?   *Vous venez d'où?*

I'm from ...	zhe vyē ...	*Je viens ...*
Australia	doh-strah-lee	*d'Australie*
Africa	dah-freek	*d'Afrique*
Canada	dü kah-nah-dah	*du Canada*
England	dā-gle-tehr	*d'Angleterre*
Ireland	deer-lād	*d'Irlande*
Scotland	day-kos	*d'Écosse*
the USA	day zay-tah-zü-nee	*des États-Unis*
Wales	dü pay de gahl	*du pays de Galles*

Occupations

What (work) do you do?
voo feht kwah kom may-tyay?   *Vous faites quoi comme métier?*

I'm (a/an) ...	zhe swee ...	*Je suis ...*
artist	ē/ü nahr-teest	*un/e artiste*
business person	ē nom/ün fahm dah-fehr	*un homme/une femme d'affaires*
chef	kwee-zee-nyay/ kwee-zee-nyehr	*cuisinier/cuisinière*
doctor	mehd-sē	*médecin*
engineer	ē-zhay-nyerr	*ingénieur*
homecarer	zom/fahm oh fwah-yay	*homme/femme au foyer*

journalist	zhoor-nah-leest	*journaliste*
lawyer	ah-vo-kah/	*avocat/*
	ah-vo-kaht	*avocate*
mechanic	may-kah-nees-yē/	*mécanicien/*
	may-kah-nees-yehn	*mécanicienne*
nurse	ē-feer-myay/	*infirmier/*
	ē-feer-myehr	*infirmière*
office worker	ã-plwah-yay	*employé/e*
	de bü-roh	*de bureau*
retired	re-tray-tay	*retraité/e*
scientist	syã-tee-feek	*scientifique*
teacher	pro-feh-serr	*professeur*
unemployed	shoh-merr/	*chômeur/*
	shoh-merz	*chômeuse*
waiter	sehr-verr/sehr-verz	*serveur/serveuse*
writer	ay-kree-vē	*écrivain*

FRENCH

Religion

What's your religion?
    kehl eh vo-tre re-lee-zhyõ?   *Quelle est votre religion?*

I'm (m/f) not religious.
    zhe ne swee pah krwah-yã/t   *Je ne suis pas croyant/e.*

I'm ...	zhe swee ...	*Je suis ...*
Buddhist	boo-deest	*bouddhiste*
Catholic	kah-to-leek	*catholique*
Christian	kray-tyē/tyehn	*chrétien/ne*
Hindu	ē-doo	*hindou/e*
Jewish	zhweef/zhweev	*juif/juive*
Musli	mü-zül-mã/-mahn	*musulman/e*
Protestant	pro-tehs-tã/t	*protestant/e*

FRENCH

Family

Are you married?
   voo zeht mah-ryay?   *Vous êtes marié/e?*
Do you have a boyfriend/girlfriend?
   voo zah-vay zē pe-tee-tah-mee/   *Vous avez un petit ami/*
   ün pe-tee-tah-mee?   *une petite amie?*
Do you have any children?
   voo zah-vay day zā-fā?   *Vous avez des enfants?*

I'm ...	zhe swee ...	*Je suis ...*
single	seh-lee-bah-tehr	*célibataire*
married	mah-ryay	*marié/e*
separated	say-pah-ray	*séparé/e*
divorced	dee-vor-say	*divorcé/e*
widowed	verf/verv	*veuf/veuve*

I have a partner.
   zhay ē/ü nah-mee   *J'ai un/e ami/e.*
I don't have any children.
   zhe nay pah dā-fā   *Je n'ai pas d'enfants.*
I have a daughter/son.
   zhay ün feey/ē fees   *J'ai une fille/un fils.*

baby	ē bay-bay	*un bébé*
boy	ē gahr-sō	*un garçon*
brother	ē frehr	*un frère*
children	day-zā-fā	*des enfants*
daughter	ün feey	*une fille*
family	ün fah-meey	*une famille*
father	ē pehr	*un père*
girl	ün feey	*une fille*
grandparents	day grā-pah-rā	*des grands-parents*
grandfather	ē grā-pehr	*un grand-père*
grandmother	ün grā-mehr	*une grand-mère*
husband	ē mah-ree/nay-poo	*un mari/époux*
mother	ün mehr	*une mère*
sister	ün serr	*une sœur*
son	ē fees	*un fils*
wife	ün fahm/ay-pooz	*une femme/épouse*

FRENCH

Feelings

I'm (m/f) sorry. (condolence)
   zhe swee day-zo-lay   *Je suis désolé/e.*
I'm (m/f) grateful.
   zhe voo swee re-ko-neh-sã/t   *Je vous suis reconnaissant/e.*

I'm ...	zhay ...	*J'ai ...*
Are you ...?	ah-vay voo ...?	*Avez-vous ...?*
cold	frwah	*froid*
hot	shoh	*chaud*
hungry	fẽ	*faim*
right	reh-zõ	*raison*
sleepy	so-mehy	*sommeil*
thirsty	swahf	*soif*

I'm ...	zhe swee ...	*Je suis ...*
Are you ...?	eht voo ...?	*Etes-vous ...?*
angry	fah-shay	*fâché/e*
happy	er rer/er-rerz	*heureux/heureuse*
in a hurry	pray-say	*pressé/e*
sad	treest	*triste*
tired	fah-tee-gay	*fatigué/e*
well	byẽ	*bien*

BREAKING THE LANGUAGE BARRIER

Do you speak English?
   voo pahr-lay ã-gleh?   *Vous parlez anglais?*
I speak a little ...
   zhe pahrl ẽ per de ...   *Je parle un peu l'île ...*
I (don't) understand.
   zhe (ne) kõ-prã (pah)   *Je (ne) comprends (pas).*
Could you speak more slowly?
   ehs-ke voo poo-ryay   *Est-ce que vous*
   pahr-lay plü lãt-mã?   *pourriez parler plus lentement?*
Could you repeat that, please?
   poo-vay-voo ray-pay-tay   *Pouvez-vous répéter,*
   seel voo pleh?   *s'il vous plaît?*

FRENCH

Can you spell that for me?
    voo poo-vay ay-play
    seel voo pleh?
	Vous pouvez épeler,
	s'il vous plaît?

How do you say ...? ko-mã tehs-kõ dee ...?	*Comment est-ce qu'on dit ...?*
What does ... mean? ke ver deer ...?	*Que veut dire ...?*

BODY LANGUAGE

French speakers are very tactile and expressive. For example, a man greeting one of his male friends or acquaintances would shake hands (even if they last met earlier the same day), and a woman would greet a female friend or acquaintance by a friendly *bisou*, kiss, on the cheek. When a man meets a female acquaintance, they shake hands, or if they know each other well, will usually kiss on the cheek.

The number of kisses given on each cheek varies according to regional custom – in Paris it's usually six kisses (three on each cheek). Numbers can range between a paltry single kiss per cheek in south-eastern parts of France, to four per cheek in the west of the country. Anything much beyond eight kisses in total tends to become a bit of a joke.

The French equivalent of giving someone the finger or putting up two fingers is the bold and expressive use of the whole arm. This is a gesture where you put your left hand on your right elbow and thrust the whole arm up. This is known as the *bras d'honneur*, 'arm of honour'.

FRENCH

SIGNS

ARRIVÉES	ARRIVALS
BANLIEUE	TRAINS TO SUBURBS
CÉDEZ LE PASSAGE	GIVE WAY
DÉPARTS	DEPARTURES
DÉVIATION	DETOUR
ENREGISTREMENT	CHECK-IN COUNTER
ENTRÉE INTERDITE	NO ENTRY
GARE	TRAIN STATION
GRANDES LIGNES	MAIN LINE TRAINS
GUICHET	TICKET OFFICE
OBJETS TROUVÉS	LOST & FOUND
SORTIE	WAY OUT
STATIONNEMENT INTERDIT	NO PARKING

PAPERWORK

bulletin de naissance	birth certificate
confession	religion
date de naissance	date of birth
lieu de naissance	place of birth
métier	profession
nom et prénom	name
permis de conduire	drivers licence
raison de voyage	reason for travel
études	study
travail	business
vacances	holiday
situation de famille	marital status

FRENCH

GETTING AROUND
Directions

Go straight ahead.
  kon-tin-yoo-eh too drwah — *Continuez tout droit.*
Cross the road.
  trav-ehr-say lah rü — *Traversez la rue.*

Turn left/right	too-nay ah gohsh/	*Tournez à gauche/*
at the next ...	drwaht oh	*droite au*
	proh-shuh ...	*prochain ...*
corner	kar-foor	*coin*
intersection	kwē	*carrefour*

behind	de-ree-ehr	*derrière*
in front of	de-vã	*devant*
far	loo-wã	*loin*
near (to)	preh de	*près de*
opposite	ã fuhs de	*en face de*

north	nor	*nord*
south	süd	*sud*
east	ehst	*est*
west	oo-est	*ouest*

Buying Tickets

I'd like to ... my	zhe voo-dreh ... mah	*Je voudrais ...*
reservation.	ray-zehr-vah-syō	*ma réservation.*
cancel	ah-nü-lay	*annuler*
change	shã-zhay	*changer*
confirm	kō-feer-may	*confirmer*

I'm a ...	zhe swee ...	*Je suis ...*
pensioner	re-tray-tay	*retraité/e*
student	zay-tü-dyã/t	*étudiant/e*

1st class	pre-myehr klahs	*première classe*
2nd class	zgōd/de-zyehm	*seconde/deuxième*
	klahs	*classe*

FRENCH

Bus & Tram

Where's the bus/tram stop?		
oo eh lah-reh doh-toh-büs/ der trahm-weh?		*Où est l'arrêt d'autobus/ de tramway?*
Which bus goes to ...?		
kehl büs vah ah ...?		*Quel bus va à ...?*
Does this bus go to ...?		
ehs-ke se büs vah ah ...?		*Est-ce que ce bus va à ...?*

What time's the ... bus?	le ... büs pahs ah kehl err?	*Le ... bus passe à quelle heure?*
first	pre-myay	*premier*
last	dehr-nyay	*dernier*
next	pro-shé	*prochain*

Do you stop at ...?		
ehs-ke voo voo zah-reh-tay ah ...?		*Est-ce que vous vous arrêtez à ...?*
Could you let me know when we get to ...?		
poo-vay voo me deer kã noo zah-ree-võ ah ...?		*Pouvez-vous me dire quand nous arrivons à ...?*
I want to get off!		
zhe ver day-sãdr!		*Je veux descendre!*

Metro

The underground network in Paris consists of two systems – the *Métro* and the *RER*. The *RER (Réseau Express Régional)* is a network of suburban services which passes through the city centre. There's one standard fare to anywhere on the Paris Metro. Tickets are normally bought in a *carnet*, a packet of 10.

Which line goes to ...?	
kehl leeny vah ah ...?	*Quelle ligne va à ...?*
Is this the line to ...?	
ehs-ker seht leeny vah ah ...?	*Est-ce que cette ligne va à ...?*
What's the next stop?	
kehl eh lah pro-shehn stah-syõ?	*Quelle est la prochaine station?*

FRENCH

Train

France's train network is operated by the *SNCF (Société Nationale des Chemins de Fer)*. The high-speed train is the *TGV (Train à Grande Vitesse)*. Before boarding any train, you must validate your ticket in one of the orange *composteurs* which you'll find somewhere between the ticket office and the platform.

Where's the nearest train station?
    oo eh lah gahr lah plü prosh?   *Où est la gare la plus proche?*
Is this the right platform for ...?
    seh le bõ keh poor ...?   *C'est le bon quai pour ...?*
How long will it be delayed?
    eel oh-rah kõ-byē de re-tahr?   *Il aura combien de retard?*
Is that seat taken?
    ehs-ke seht plahs eh   *Est-ce que cette place est*
    to-kü-pay?   *occupée?*

THEY MAY SAY ...

ler trē ah ...   The train is ...
   dü rer-tahr   delayed
   ay-tay ah-nü-lay   cancelled

---

dining car	le vah-gõ rehs-toh-rã	*le wagon-restaurant*
express	rah-peed	*rapide*
left-luggage	kõ-seeny	*consigne*
lockers	oto-mah-teek	*automatique*
local	lo-kahl	*local*
platform	le keh	*le quai*
sleeping car	ē vah-gõ lee	*un wagon-lit*

FRENCH

Taxi

Are you free?
voo zeht leebr?   *Vous êtes libre?*

Please take me to ...
kō-dwee-zay mwah ah ...,   *Conduisez-moi à ...,*
seel voo pleh   *s'il vous plaît.*

How much does it cost to go to ...?
seh kō-byē poor ah-lay ah ...?   *C'est combien pour aller à ...?*

Does that include luggage?
lay bah-gazh sō kō-pree?   *Les bagages sont compris?*

Here's fine, thanks.
ee-see sah vah mehr-see   *Ici ça va, merci.*

The next corner, please.
oh pro-shē kwē de rü   *Au prochain coin de rue,*
seel voo pleh   *s'il vous plaît.*

Straight on!
kō-tee-nway!   *Continuez!*

The next street to the left/right.
lah pro-shehn rü ah   *La prochaine rue à*
gohsh/drwaht   *gauche/droite.*

Stop here, please!
ah-reh-tay voo ee-see   *Arrêtez-vous ici,*
seel voo pleh!   *s'il vous plaît!*

Please wait here.
ah-tā-day ee-see seel voo pleh   *Attendez ici, s'il vous plaît.*

Car

I'd like to rent a small/large car.
zhe voo-drah lway ün pe-teet/   *Je voudrais louer une petite/*
grohs vwah-tür   *grosse voiture.*

How much is it daily/weekly?
kehl eh le tah-reef pahr   *Quel est le tarif par jour/par*
zhoor/pahr se-mehn?   *semaine?*

Does that include insurance/mileage?
ehs-ke lah-sü-rās/le kee-lo-   *Est-ce que l'assurance/le*
may-trahzh eh kō-pree/z?   *kilométrage est compris/e?*

FRENCH

Where's the next petrol
(gas) station?
    oo eh lah pro-shehn
    stah-syō sehr-vees?   *Où est la prochaine
                     station service?*
Is this the road to ...?
    seh lah root poor ...?   *C'est la route pour ...?*

air	le kō-pray-serr	*le compresseur*
battery	ün bah-tree	*une batterie*
brakes	lay frē	*les freins*
clutch	lā-breh-yahzh	*l'embrayage*
diesel	dyay-zehl	*diesel*
drivers licence	le pehr-mee de kō-dweer	*le permis de conduire*
engine	le mo-terr	*le moteur*
indicator	le kleeny-o-tā	*le clignotant*
leaded	kee kō-tyē dü plō	*qui contient du plomb*
lights	lay fahr	*les phares*
main road	lah grād root	*la grande route*
petrol (gas)	leh-sās	*l'essence*
radiator	le rah-dyah-terr	*le radiateur*
regular (premium)	(petrol) nor-mahl	*normale*
repairs	day ray-pah-rahs-yō	*des réparations*
speed limit	lah lee-mee-tahs-yō de vee-tehs	*la limitation de vitesse*
super (petrol/gas)	sü-pehr	*super*
tollway	ün oh-toh-root ah pay-azh	*une autoroute à péage*
tyres	lay pner	*les pneus*
unleaded	sā plō	*sans plomb*
windscreen	le pahr-breez	*le pare-brise*

ACCOMMODATION
At the Hotel

We have a reservation.
  noo-zah-vō zün
  ray-zehr-vah-syō

*Nous avons une
réservation.*

How much is it per night/person?
  kehl eh le pree pahr
  nwee/pehr-son?

*Quel est le prix par
nuit/personne?*

Can I see it?
  zhe per lah vwahr?

Je peux la voir?

Is there hot water all day?
  eel yah de loh shohd
  pā-dā toot lah zhoor-nay?

*Il y a de l'eau chaude
pendant toute la journée?*

I'll take it.
  seh byē zhe lah prā

C'est bien, je la prends.

I'd like to pay the bill.
  zhe voo-dreh ray-glay (lah not)

Je voudrais régler (la note).

Can I leave my luggage here
until (tonight)?
  pweezh lay-say may bah-
  gahzh zhüs-kah (se swahr)?

*Puis-je laisser mes bagages
jusqu'à (ce soir)?*

Please call a taxi for me.
  ah-play mwah ē tahk-see
  seel voo pleh

*Appelez-moi un taxi, s'il vous
plaît.*

(See also Camping, page 136.)

Requests & Complaints

I need ...
  zhay be-zwē de ...

J'ai besoin de ...

Where's the bathroom?
  oo eh lah sahl de bē?

Où est la salle de bain?

The key for room (10) please.
  lah klay de lah shābr
  (dees) seel voo pleh

*La clé de la chambre (dix), s'il
vous plaît.*

FRENCH

Do you have a safe where I can
leave my valuables?

ehs-ke voo-zah-vay zē
kof-re-for poor day-poh-zay
may zob-zheh de vah-lerr?

*Est-ce que vous avez un
coffre-fort pour déposer mes
objets de valeur?*

Is there somewhere to wash clothes?

ehs-keel yah ē nā-drwah oo
ō per fehr lah lay-seev?

*Est-ce qu'il y a un endroit
où on peut faire la lessive?*

Can I use the telephone?

ehs-ke zhe per zü-tee-lee-
zay le tay-lay-fon?

*Est-ce que je peux utiliser le
téléphone?*

I've locked myself out of my room.

zhe me swee zā-fehr-may de-or

Je me suis enfermé.e dehors.

AROUND TOWN
At the Post Office

I'd like to send a(n) ...	zhe voo-dreh zā-vwah-yay ...	*Je voudrais envoyer ...*
aerogram	ē nah-ay-ro-grahm	*un aérogramme*
letter	ün lehtr	*une lettre*
parcel	ē ko-lee	*un colis*
postcard	ün kahrt pos-tahl	*une carte postale*

I'd like some stamps.

zhe voo-dreh day tēbr

Je voudrais des timbres.

Where's the poste restante section?

oo eh le sehr-vees de
post rehs-tāt?

*Où est le service de
poste restante?*

Is there any mail for ...?

yah-teel dü koo-ryay poor ...?

Y a-t-il du courrier pour ...?

air mail	pahr ah-vyō	*par avion*
envelope	ün ā-vlop	*une enveloppe*
express mail	pahr ehk-sprehs	*par express*
mail box	ün bwah toh lehtr	*une boîte aux lettres*
registered mail	ā re-ko-mā-day	*en recommandé*
surface mail	pahr vwah de tehr	*par voie de terre*

FRENCH

Telephone

Do you speak English?
  voo pahr-lay ā-gleh?   *Vous parlez anglais?*

I want to ring ...
  zhe voo-dreh zah-play ...   *Je voudrais appeler ...*

The number's ...
  le nü-may-roh eh ...   *Le numéro est ...*

I want to make a reverse-charge
(collect) call.
  zhe ver tay-lay-fo-nay ā   *Je veux téléphoner en*
  pay-say-vay   *PCV.*

I've been cut off.
  zhay ay-tay koo-pay   *J'ai été coupé.*

telephone card	ün tay-lay-kahrt	*une télécarte*
telephone book	ē nah-nwehr	*un annuaire du*
	dü tay-lay-fon	*téléphone*
telephone box	ün kah-been	*une cabine*
	tay-lay-fo-neek	*téléphonique*

Internet

Is there a local Internet cafe around here?
  ehs-ke keel-yah ē kah-fay   *Est-ce qu'il y a un café-*
  een-ter-neht dā lay ān-vee-rō?   *Internet dans les environs?*

I'd like to connect to the Internet.
  zhe day-zee-re me ko-nek-tehr   *Je désire me connecter à*
  ah een-ter-neht   *Internet.*

I'd like to check my email.
  zhe voo-dreh kon-sül-tehr   *Je voudrais consulter mon*
  mon koo-ree-ehr   *courrier électronique.*
  eh-lek-tro-neek

FRENCH

At the Bank

I want to exchange some ...	zhe ver shā-zhay ...	*Je veux changer ...*
money	de lahr-zhā	*de l'argent*
travellers cheques	day shehk de vwah-yahzh	*des chèques de voyage*

What's the exchange rate?
kehl eh le toh de shāzh? — *Quel est le taux de change?*

What's your commission?
kehl eh votrer ko-mee-syō? — *Quelle est votre commission?*

The ATM swallowed my credit card.
le gee-shay oh-to-mah-teek ah ah-vah-lay mah kahrt de kray-dee — *Le guichet automatique a avalé ma carte de crédit.*

Can I use my credit card to withdraw money?
poo-rehzh ü-tee-lee-zay mah kahrt de kray-dee poor re-tee-ray de lahr-zhā? — *Pourrais-je utiliser ma carte de crédit pour retirer de l'argent?*

Can I have money transferred here from my bank?
ehs-ke zhe per fehr ē veer-māde mō kōt ā bāk ee-see? — *Est-ce que je peux faire un virement de mon compte en banque ici?*

Has my money arrived?
ehs-ke mo nahr-zhā eh tah-ree-vay? — *Est-ce que mon argent est arrivé?*

credit card	ün kahrt de kray-dee; ün kahrt bler; ün kahrt bā-kehr	*une carte de crédit; une carte bleue; une carte bancaire*
exchange	lay-shāzh	*l'échange*
identification	ün pyehs dee-dā-tee-tay	*une pièce d'identité*
signature	lah see-nyah-tür	*la signature*
withdrawal	ē re-treh	*un retrait*

INTERESTS & ENTERTAINMENT
Sightseeing

Where's the tourist office?
oo eh lo-fees de too-reesm? *Où est l'office de tourisme?*

What are the main attractions?
kehl sõ lay zã-drwah lay
plü zē-tay-reh-sã? *Quels sont les endroits les plus intéressants?*

Is there an admission charge?
eel foh pay-yay lã-tray? *Il faut payer l'entrée?*

What's that?
kehs-ke seh? *Qu'est-ce que c'est?*

Can I take photographs?
zhe per prãdr day fo-toh? *Je peux prendre des photos?*

ancient	ã-teek	*antique*
archaeological	ahr-kay-o-lo-zheek	*archéologique*
bridge	ē põ	*un pont*
building	ē bah-tee-mã	*un bâtiment*
castle	ē shah-toh	*un château*
cathedral	ün kah-tay-drahl	*une cathédrale*
caves	day grot	*des grottes*
church	ün ay-gleez	*une église*
city walls	lay rã-pahr	*les remparts*
convent	ē koo-vã	*un couvent*
main square	ün plahs sã-trahl	*une place centrale*
market	ē mahr-shay	*un marché*
monastery	ē mo-nahs-tehr	*un monastère*
monument	ē mo-nü-mã	*un monument*
museum	ē mü-zay	*un musée*
old city	lah vyehy veel	*la vieille ville*
palace	ē pah-leh	*un palais*
park	ē pahrk	*un parc*
parliament	le pahr-le-mã	*le parlement*
opera house	(le tay-ahtr de) lo-pay-rah	*(le théâtre de) l'opéra*
ruins	day rween	*des ruines*
statues	day stah-tü	*des statues*
zoo	ē zoh	*un zoo*

FRENCH

Going Out

In Paris, you'll find information on cultural events, music, theatre, films, exhibitions and festivals in two weekly publications – *Pariscope* and *L'Officiel des Spectacles*. They're available from most newsstands.

I'd like to go to a/the ...	zhe voo-dreh zah-lay ...	*Je voudrais aller ...*
cinema	oh see-nay-mah	*au cinéma*
concert	ah ē kō-sehr	*à un concert*
disco	ā bwaht	*en boîte*
restaurant	dā zē rehs-toh(-rā)	*dans un restau(rant)*
theatre	oh tay-ahtr	*au théâtre*

What are you doing tonight/
this weekend?
   ke feh tü se swahr/   *Que fais-tu ce soir/*
   wee-kehnd?   *week-end?*
Do you want to go dancing?
   see noo-zah-lyō dā-say?   *Si nous allions danser?*
I'd love to come.
   zhe vyē-dreh ah-vehk   *Je viendrai avec plaisir.*
   play-zeer

bar	ē bahr	*un bar*
concert	ē kō-sehr	*un concert*
dance floor	lah peest (de dās)	*la piste (de danse)*
gig	ē kō-sehr	*un concert*
nightclub	ün dees-ko-tehk/ bwaht	*une discothèque/ boîte*
to go clubbing	sor-teer ā bwaht	*sortir en boîte*
party; night out	ün swah-ray	*une soirée*
performance	ē spehk-tahkl	*un spectacle*
show	ē shoh	*un show*
ticket office	ē gee-shay	*un guichet*

FRENCH

Sports & Interests

An enthusiast or fan of a sport, hobby or particular interest is called un *amateur*.

What do you do in your spare time?
ke feh tü pā-dā tay lwah-zeer? *Que fais-tu pendant tes loisirs?*

Do you play ...?	voo feht ...?	*Vous faites ...?*
Do you like ...?	ehm tü ...?	*Aimes-tu ...?*
I like ...	zhehm ...	*J'aime ...*
I don't like ...	zhe nehm pah ...	*Je n'aime pas ...*
art	lahr	*l'art*
chess	lay-zay-shehk	*les échecs*
cycling	le see-kleesm	*le cyclisme*
dancing	lah dãs	*la danse*
going to the beach	ah-lay ah lah plahzh	*aller à la plage*
good food	lah bon kwee-zeen	*la bonne cuisine*
football	le foot-bohl	*le football*
hiking	lah mahrsh	*la marche*
gardening	le zhahr-dee-nahzh	*le jardinage*
going out	sor-teer	*sortir*
films	le see-nay-mah	*le cinéma*
music	lah mü-zeek	*la musique*
reading	leer	*lire*
skiing	le skee	*le ski*
swimming	lah nah-tah-syō	*la natation*
tennis	le tay-nees	*le tennis*
travelling	vwah-yah-zhay	*voyager*

Festivals

Some French villages hold festivals to honour anything from a local saint to the year's garlic crop.

Epiphany
> on January 6 people eat *la galette des Rois*, a round, flat cake made of puff pastry. The one who finds *la fève*, 'the charm', hidden in the cake is crowned king or queen. Everybody says *Vive le Roi* or *Vive la Reine!*, 'God save the King or Queen!'.

FRENCH

Noël

Christmas is celebrated traditionally in France, with a Christmas tree, presents and turkey. In Alsace, *le Père Fouettard*, 'the Bogeyman', comes to see if the children are well behaved.

| Christmas Day | le zhoor de no-ehl | *le jour de Noël* |
| Christmas Eve | lah vehy de no-ehl | *la veille de Noël* |

Saint Nicholas Day

on 6 December, Saint Nicholas gives gingerbread to the children. In Alsace, *le Père Fouettard*, 'Hans Trapp', accompanies Saint Nicholas and threatens to take naughty children away in his sack. In the north of France, people play practical jokes on their friends.

IN THE COUNTRY
Weather

It's fine today.

	eel feh boh oh-zhoor-dwee	*Il fait beau aujourd'hui.*
It's ...	eel feh ...	*Il fait ...*
Will it be ...	ehs-keel fe-rah ...	*Est-ce qu'il fera*
tomorrow?	de-mē?	*... demain?*
cold	frwah	*froid*
hot	shoh	*chaud*
sunny	boh	*beau*
windy	dü vā	*du vent*

It's cloudy.	le tā eh koo-vehr	*Le temps est couvert.*
It's raining.	eel pler	*Il pleut.*
It's snowing.	eel nehzh	*Il neige.*

Camping

Is there a campsite nearby?

	ehs-keel yah ē kā-peeng preh dee-see?	*Est-ce qu'il y a un camping près d'ici?*

Can we camp here?

	ehs-kõ per kā-pay ee-see?	*Est-ce qu'on peut camper ici?*

FRENCH

Where can I hire a tent?
  oo pweezh loo-ay ün tăt?   *Où puis-je louer une tente?*

can opener	loo-vrer-bwaht	*l'ouvre-boîtes*
firewood	dü bwah de shoh-fahzh	*du bois de chauffage*
gas cartridge	ün kahr-toosh de gahz	*une cartouche de gaz*
hammock	le ah-mahk	*le hamac*
mallet	le mah-yay	*le maillet*
mattress	le mah-tlah	*le matelas*
penknife	le kah-neef	*le canif*
rope	lah kord	*la corde*
sleeping bag	le sahk de koo-shahzh	*le sac de couchage*
stove	le ray-shoh	*le réchaud*
tent	lah tăt	*la tente*
tent pegs	lay pee-keh de tăt	*les piquets de tente*
torch (flashlight)	lah lăp de posh	*la lampe de poche*
water bottle	lah goord	*la gourde*

FOOD

Service is usually included in the bill, but if you pay cash you should leave coins. And don't call the waiter *garçon* – this is only done in the movies! Just say: seel voo pleh (*s'il vous plaît*).

breakfast	le pe-tee day-zher-nay	*le petit déjeuner*
lunch	le day-zher-nay	*le déjeuner*
dinner	le dee-nay	*le dîner*

Vegetarian Meals

I'm (m/f) a vegetarian.
  zhe swee vay-zhay-tah-ryē/ vay-zhay-tah-ryehn   *Je suis végétarien/ végétarienne.*

FRENCH

I don't eat ...	zhe ne māzh pah de ...	*Je ne mange pas de ...*
beef	berf	*bœuf*
chicken	poo-lay	*poulet*
fish	pwah-sō	*poisson*
ham	zhā-bō	*jambon*
seafood	frwee de mehr	*fruits de mer*

Staple Foods & Condiments

fish	pwah-sō	*du poisson*
fruit	day frwee	*des fruits*
gherkins	day kor-nee-shō	*des cornichons*
honey	dü myehl	*du miel*
liver/farmhouse pâté	dü pah-tay de fwah/ kā-pahny	*du pâté de foie/ campagne*
mayonnaise	de lah meh-yo-nehz	*de la mayonnaise*
meat	de lah vyād	*de la viande*
mustard	de lah moo-tahrd	*de la moutarde*
oil	de lweel	*de l'huile*
parsley	dü pehr-see	*du persil*
potato	day pom de tehr	*des pommes de terre*
salt	dü sehl	*du sel*
sugar	dü sükr	*du sucre*
vegetables	day lay-güm	*des légumes*
vinegar	dü vee-nehgr	*du vinaigre*

Breakfast Menu

bread	dü pē	*du pain*
butter	dü berr	*du beurre*
cereal	day say-ray-ahl	*des céréales*
croissant	ē krwah-sō	*un croissant*
jam	de lah kō-fee-tür	*de la confiture*
... eggs	day-zer ...	*des œufs ...*
fried	sür le plah	*sur le plat*
hard-boiled	dür	*durs*
poached	po-shay	*pochés*
scrambled	broo-yay	*brouillés*
soft-boiled	ah lah kok	*à la coque*

FRENCH

MENU DECODER

Starters & Snacks
boudin antillais en feuille de chêne et
pommes de terres en robe des champs
   West-Indian sausage with lettuce and potatoes in their jackets
concombre à la crème-ciboulette
   cucumber with cream and chives

une crêpe ...   thin pancake with ...
   à la confiture   jam
   au citron   lemon
   au miel   honey
   au sucre   sugar

fromage blanc battu aux fines herbes
   cream cheese blended with sweet herbs
méli-mélo de légumes vapeur
   mixed steamed vegetables
salade de tomates avec basilic huile vierge
   tomato salad with basil and virgin olive oil
sushi de poisson cru sur lit de soja croquantraw
   fish sushi on a bed of crunchy soya bean sprouts

Main Meals
flamiche au Maroilles   Maroilles cheese pie
lapin aux pruneaux   rabbit with prunes
bäckaoffa/baekehoffe
   Alsatian stew, made with potatoes, vegetables and meat
   marinated in white wine (Alsace)
brochette de volailles au citron
   poultry kebab with lemon
choucroute
   cabbage with pork, potatoes and sauerkraut (Alsace)
cotriade
   fillet of fish with seafood and a saffron sauce
demi-cannette rôtie avec pommes château
   half a roast duckling with potatoes sauteed in butter
émincé de haddock fumé avec pommes mousseline
   slivers of smoked haddock with balls of mashed
   potato in a light pastry case

FRENCH

émincé de poulet mariné aux grains de coriandre en salade
  slivers of marinated chicken with coriander seeds and salad
entrecôte grillée avec sauce au bleu
  grilled rib steak with blue cheese sauce
filets de rascasse grillés aux tagliatelles safranées
  grilled fillets of scorpion fish with tagliatelli seasoned with saffron
fondue savoyarde
  cheese fondue (Lyon)
moelleux de porc au curry avec riz sauvage
  tender pork curry with wild rice
pissaladière
  bread dough with onion puree, anchovies and black olives
soupe au pistou
  vegetable soup with basil and garlic
tapenade
  capers, black olives, anchovies and tuna with lemon and olive oil

salade ...   *... salad*
   au bleu   blue cheese and walnut
   composée   mixed
   de crudités   raw vegetable
   d'endives   chicory
   multicolore au basilic   pepper, tomato, radish,
                    cucumber, egg, corn and basil

sole normande
  sole in a sauce of butter, onion, white wine, mushrooms,
  cider, calvados (apple brandy) and fresh cream (Normandy)

Desserts
charlotte
  custard and fruit in lining of almond fingers
clafoutis
  fruit tart, usually made with berries
île flottante crème vanille
  soft meringues floating on custard with vanilla cream
mousse au chocolat crème anglaise
  chocolate mousse with custard
poires Belle Hélène
  pears and ice cream in a chocolate sauce

FRENCH

Non-Alcoholic Drinks

freshly-squeezed orange juice	ün o-rǎzh pray-say	*une orange pressée*
(soya) milk	dü leh (de so-zhah)	*du lait (de soja)*
... water	de loh ...	*de l'eau ...*
mineral	mee-nay-rahl	*minérale*
tap	dü ro-bee-neh	*du robinet*
coffee	ē kah-fay ...	*un café ...*
with milk	oh leh	*au lait*
with cream	krehm	*crème*
decaffeinated	day-kah-fay-ee-nay	*décaféiné*
espresso	ehks-prehs	*express*
black coffee	ē nwahr	*un noir*
herbal tea	ün tee-zahn	*une tisane*
hot chocolate	ē sho-ko-lah shoh	*un chocolat chaud*
tea	ē tay	*un thé*

Alcoholic Drinks

I'd like a ...	zhe voo-dray ...	*Je voudrais ...*
beer	ün byehr	*une bière*
brandy	ē ko-nyahk	*un cognac*
cider	dü seedr	*du cidre*
martini	ē mahr-tee-nee	*un martini*
shandy	ē pah-nah-shay	*un panaché*
sparkling wine	dü moo-ser	*du mousseux*

You might want to try the following drinks which are common in France.

un kir	ē keer	blackcurrant liqueur and white wine
un kir royal	ē keer rwah-yahl	blackcurrant liqueur and champagne
un pastis	ē pahs-tees	aniseed liqueur served with water
un picon bière	ē pee-kō byehr	beer mixed with a sweet liqueur

AT THE MARKET

Basics

bread	dü pé	*du pain*
butter	dü berr	*du beurre*
cereal	day say-ray-ahl	*des céréales*
cheese	dü fro-mahzh	*du fromage*
chocolate	dü sho-ko-lah	*du chocolat*
croissant	ē krwah-sō	*un croissant*
eggs	day-zer	*des œufs*
flour	de lah fah-reen	*de la farine*
margarine	de lah mahr-gah-ree-ne	*de la margarine*
marmalde	de lah mahr-meh-lahd	*de la marmelade*
milk	dü lay	*du lait*
(olive) oil	de lweel (do-leev)	*de l'huile (d'olive)*
pasta	day paht	*des pâtes*
rice	dü ree	*du riz*
sugar	dü sükr	*du sucre*
(mineral) water	de loh (mee-nay-rahl)	*de l'eau (minérale)*
yogurt	dü yah-oort	*du yaourt*

Meat & Poultry

beef	dü berf	*du bœuf*
chicken	dü poo-lay	*du poulet*
ham	dü zhā-bō	*du jambon*
lamb	de lahn-yoh	*de l'agneau*
meat	de lah vyäd	*de la viande*
pork	dü por	*du porc*
sausage	de lah soh-sees	*de la saucisse*
turkey	de lah dahn-de	*de la dinde*
veal	dü voh	*du veau*

Vegetables

beetroot	de lah beh-trahv	*de la betterave*
cabbage	dü shoo	*du chou*
carrot	day kah-rot	*des carottes*
capsicum	dü pwah-vrō	*du poivron*
cauliflower	dü shoo-fler	*du chou-fleur*
celery	dü se-leh-ree	*du céleri*

AT THE MARKET

FRENCH

cucumber	dü kô-kô-bre	*du concombre*
eggplant	de loh-behr-zheen	*de l'aubergine*
green beans	day zah-ree-koh-vehr	*des haricots verts*
lettuce	de lah lay-tü	*de la laitue*
mushrooms	day shah-peen-yõ	*des champignons*
onion	day on-yõ	*des oignons*
peas	day pe-tee pwah	*des petits pois*
potato	day pom de tehr	*des pommes de terre*
spinach	day zeh-pee-nahr	*des épinards*
tomato	day to-maht	*des tomates*
vegetables	day lay-güm	*des légumes*
zucchini	day koor-zheht	*des courgettes*

Seafood

fish	dü pwah-sõ	*du poisson*
lobster	dü o-mahr	*du homard*
mussels	day mool	*des moules*
oysters	day zwee-tr	*des huîtres*
shrimp	day kre-veht greez	*des crevettes grises*

Pulses

broad beans	day fehv	*des fèves*
chickpeas	day pwah-sheesh	*des pois chiches*
lentils	day lã-tee-ye	*des lentilles*

Fruit

apple	pom	*pomme*
apricot	ah-bree-ko	*abricot*
banana	bah-nah-ne	*banane*
fruit	day frwee	*des fruits*
grapes	ray-zé	*raisins*
lemon	see-trõ	*citron*
orange	o-rahnzh	*orange*
peach	pehsh	*pêche*
pear	pwahr	*poire*
plum	prün	*prune*
strawberry	frayz	*fraises*

un pineau	ē pee-noh	cognac and grape juice
une suze	ün süz	fermented gentian
un muscat	ē müs-kah	muscatel wine
un porto	ē pohr-toh	port wine
un punch	ē pernch	punch

The main wine-growing regions of France are Alsace, Beaujolais, Bordeaux, Bourgogne, Champagne, Côte du Rhône, Jura, Languedoc, Loire, Provence and Savoie.

We'd like to try a local wine.
noo-zay-me-yō   *Nous aimerions*
goo-tay ē vē de payy   *goûter un vin de pays.*

red	roozh	*rouge*
sparkling	moo-ser	*mousseux*
sweet	de-mee-sehk	*demi-sec*
table wine	vē de tahbl;	*vin de table;*
	vē or-dee-nehr	*vin ordinaire*
very dry	brüt	*brut*
white	blā	*blanc*

SHOPPING

bakery	ün boo-lā-zhree	*une boulangerie*
cheese shop	ün fro-mah-zhree	*une fromagerie*
delicatessen	ün shahr-kü-tree	*une charcuterie*
fish shop	ün pwah-son-ree	*une poissonnerie*
greengrocer	ē mahr-shā der lay-güm	*un marchand de légumes*
market	ē mahr-shay	*un marché*
small grocer	ün ay-pees-ree	*une épicerie*

How much is it?
seh kō-byē?   *C'est combien?*
Can I pay by credit card?
ehs-ke zhe per pay-yay   *Est-ce que je peux payer*
ah-vehk mah kahrt de kray-dee? *avec ma carte de crédit?*

I'm just looking.
zhe re-gahrd   *Je regarde.*
Can you write down the price?
ehs-ke voo poo-vay   *Est-ce que vous pouvez*
zay-kreer le pree?   *écrire le prix?*
Can I have a receipt, please?
zhe per ah-vwah-rē re-sü   *Je peux avoir un reçu,*
seel voo pleh?   *s'il vous plaît?*

Essential Groceries

I'd like ...	zhe voo-dray ...	*Je voudrais ...*
batteries	day peel	*des piles*
bread	dü pē	*du pain*
butter	dü berr	*du beurre*
cheese	dü fro-mahzh	*du fromage*
chocolate	dü sho-ko-lah	*du chocolat*
coffee	dü kah-fay	*du café*
eggs	day zer	*des œufs*
flour	de lah fah-reen	*de la farine*
gas cylinder	ün boo-tehy de gahz	*une bouteille de gaz*
ham	dü zhā-bō	*du jambon*
honey	dü myehl	*du miel*
jam	de lah kō-fee-tür	*de la confiture*
matches	day zah-lü-meht	*des allumettes*
milk	dü leh	*du lait*
olive oil	de lweel do-leev	*de l'huile d'olive*
pepper	dü pwahvr	*du poivre*
salt	dü sehl	*du sel*
soap	dü sah-vō	*du savon*
sugar	dü sükr	*du sucre*
tea	dü tay	*du thé*
toilet paper	dü pah-pyay ee-zhyay-neek	*du papier hygiénique*
toothpaste	dü dā-tee-frees	*du dentifrice*
washing powder	de lah lay-seev	*de la lessive*
yogurt	dü yah-oort	*du yaourt*

FRENCH

Souvenirs

handicrafts	day zob-zheh ahr-tee-zah-noh	*des objets artisanaux*
jewellery	day bee-zhoo	*des bijoux*
embroidery	lah bro-dree	*la broderie*
lace	de lah dã-tehl	*de la dentelle*
miniature statue	ün stah-tweht	*une statuette*
necklace	ē ko-lyay	*un collier*
poster	ē pos-tehr	*un poster*
ring	ün bahg	*une bague*

Clothing

blouse	ē shmee-zyay	*un chemisier*
boots	day bot	*des bottes*
clothing	day veht-mã	*des vêtements*
coat	ē mã toh	*un manteau*
dress	ün rob	*une robe*
hat	ē shah-poh	*un chapeau*
jacket	ün vehst	*une veste*
jumper (sweater)	ē pü-lo-vehr	*un pull-over*
lingerie	de lah lē-zhree	*de la lingerie*
overalls	ün sah-lo-peht	*une salopette*
raincoat	ē nē-pehr-may-ahbl	*un imperméable*
shirt	ün shmeez	*une chemise*
shoes	day shoh-sür	*des chaussures*
skirt	ün zhüp	*une jupe*
socks	day shoh-seht	*des chaussettes*
stockings	day bah	*des bas*
swimsuit	ē mah-yoh de bē	*un maillot de bain*
T-shirt	ē tee-shert	*un T-shirt*
trousers	ē pã-tah-lõ	*un pantalon*
underwear	day soo veht-mã	*des sous-vêtements*

FRENCH

Materials

brass	ã kweevr	*en cuivre*
ceramic	ã say-rah-meek	*en céramique*
cotton	ã ko-tõ	*en coton*
glass	ã vehr	*en verre*
gold	ã nor	*en or*
handmade	feh ah lah mẽ	*fait à la main*
leather	ã kweer	*en cuir*
linen	ã lẽ	*en lin*
silk	ã swah	*en soie*
silver	ã nahr-zhã	*en argent*
wool	ã lehn	*en laine*

Colours

black	nwahr	*noir/e*
blue	bler	*bleu/e*
brown	brẽ/brün	*brun/e*
dark	fõ-say	*foncé/e*
green	vehr/t	*vert/e*
light	klehr	*clair/e*
pink	rohz	*rose*
purple	vyo-leh/t	*violet/te*
orange	o-rãzh	*orange*
red	roozh	*rouge*
white	blã/blãsh	*blanc/blanche*
yellow	zhohn	*jaune*

Toiletries

aftershave	ẽ nah-preh-rah-zahzh	*un après-rasage*
antiperspirant	ẽ day-o-do-rã	*un déodorant*
comb	ẽ pehny	*un peigne*
condoms	day pray-zehr-vah-teef	*des préservatifs*
deodorant	ẽ day-o-do-rã	*un déodorant*
hairbrush	ün bros ah shver	*une brosse à cheveux*
moisturiser	de lah krehm ee-drah-tãt	*de la crème hydratante*

FRENCH

razor	ē rah-zwahr	*un rasoir*
razor blades	day lahm de rah-zwahr	*des lames de rasoir*
sanitary napkins	day sehr-vyeht ee-zhyay-neek	*des serviettes hygiéniques*
shaving cream	de lah moos ah rah-zay	*de la mousse à raser*
scissors	day see-zoh	*des ciseaux*
shampoo	dü shā-pwē	*du shampooing*
sunscreen	de lah krehm ay-krã to-tahl	*de la crème écran total*
tampons	day tā-pō	*des tampons*
tissues	day moo-shwahr ã pah-pyay	*des mouchoirs en papier*
toothbrush	ün bros ah dā	*une brosse à dents*

Stationery & Publications

Where's the English-language section?
oo eh le reh-yō ā-gleh?	*Où est le rayon anglais?*

Do you have a copy of ...?
ehs-ke voo zah-vay ē nehg-zā-plehr de ...?	*Est-ce que vous avez un exemplaire de ...?*

Is there an English translation of this?
ehs-keel ehg-zeest ün trah-dük-syō ā-glehz de ser-see?	*Est-ce qu'il existe une traduction anglaise de ceci?*

dictionary	ē deek-syo-nehr	*un dictionnaire*
envelope	ün ā-vlop	*une enveloppe*
magazine	ē mah-gah-zeen	*un magazine*
newspaper	ē zhoor-nahl	*un journal*
(English-language)	(ã nā-gleh)	*(en anglais)*
paper	dü pah-pyay	*du papier*
pen	ē stee-loh	*un stylo*
stamps	day tēbr	*des timbres*
... map	ē plā ...	*un plan ...*
city	de lah veel	*de la ville*
underground	dü may-troh	*du métro*

FRENCH

Photography

How much is it to process this film?
seh kō byē poor day-vlo-pay se feelm?

C'est combien pour développer ce film?

When will it be ready?
kā-tehs-ke se-lah se-rah preh?

Quand est-ce que cela sera prêt?

I'd like a film for this camera.
zhe voo-dreh zün peh-lee-kül poor seh-tah-pah-rehy fo-toh

Je voudrais une pellicule pour cet appareil photo.

I'd like to have some passport photos taken.
zhe voo-dreh fehr day fo-toh dee-dā-tee-tay

Je voudrais faire des photos d'identité.

battery	day peel	*des piles*
B&W	nwahr ay blā	*noir et blanc*
colour	koo-lerr	*couleur*
camera	ē nah-pah-rehy fo-toh	*un appareil photo*
film	ün peh-lee-kül	*une pellicule*
film speed	ah-zah	*ASA*
flash	ē flahsh	*un flash*
lens	ē nob-zhehk-teef	*un objectif*
light meter	ē pohz-mehtr	*un posemètre*
slide film	ün peh-lee-kül dyah-poh	*une pellicule diapos*
video tape	ün bād vee-day-oh	*une bande vidéo*

FRENCH

Smoking

Tobacco can be bought at *un débit de tabac, bureau de tabac, un café-tabac* or *un bar-tabac.*

A packet of cigarettes, please.
 ē pah-keh de see-gah-reht   *Un paquet de cigarettes, s'il*
 seel voo pleh   *vous plaît.*
Are these cigarettes strong/mild?
 ehs-ke say see-gah-reht sō *Est-ce que ces cigarettes sont*
 fort/lay-zhehr?   *fortes/légères?*
Do you have a light?
 voo zah-vay dü fer?   *Vous avez du feu?*
Can I smoke here?
 ō per fü-may ee-see?   *On peut fumer ici?*
Can I have an ashtray?
 zhe per ah-vwah rē   *Je peux avoir un*
 sā-dree-yay?   *cendrier?*

cigarettes	day see-gah-reht	*des cigarettes*
cigarette papers	dü pah-pyay ah see-gah-reht	*du papier à cigarettes*
filtered	ah-vehk feeltr	*avec filtre*
lighter	ē bree-keh	*un briquet*
pipe	ün peep	*une pipe*
(pipe) tobacco	dü tah-bah (poor lah peep)	*du tabac (pour la pipe)*
roll-your-owns	day klop roo-lay ah lah mē	*des clopes roulées à la main*

Sizes & Comparisons

big(ger)	(plü) grā/d	*(plus) grand/e*
biggest	le/lah plü grā/d	*le/la plus grand/e*
enough	ah-say	*assez*
few	per	*peu*
least	le mwē(z)	*le moins*
less	mwē(z)	*moins*
a little bit	ē per	*un peu*
many	boh-koo	*beaucoup*

FRENCH

more	plü(z)	*plus*
most	le plü(z)	*le plus*
none	oh-kẽ/-kün	*aucun/e*
small(er)	(plü) pe-tee/t	*(plus) petit/e*
smallest	le/lah plü pe-tee/t	*le/la plus petit/e*
some	kehl-ke	*quelque(s)*
too much/many	troh	*trop*

HEALTH
Parts of the Body

My ... hurts.	zhay de lah doo-lerr dã ...	*J'ai de la douleur dans ...*
ankle	lah shveey	*la cheville*
arm	le brah	*le bras*
back	le doh	*le dos*
breast	le sẽ	*le sein*
chest	lah pwah-treen	*la poitrine*
ear	lo-rehy	*l'oreille*
eye	ler-y	*l'œil*
finger	le dwah	*le doigt*
foot	le-pyay	*le pied*
hand	lah mẽ	*la main*
head	lah teht	*la tête*
jaw	lah mah-shwahr	*la mâchoire*
knee	le zhnoo	*le genou*
leg	lah zhãb	*la jambe*
mouth	lah boosh	*la bouche*
muscle	le müskl	*le muscle*
nose	le nay	*le nez*
ribs	lay koht	*les côtes*
shoulder	lay-pohl	*l'épaule*
skin	lah poh	*la peau*
spine	lah ko-lon vehr-tay-brahl	*la colonne vertébrale*
stomach	lehs-to-mah	*l'estomac*
teeth	lay dã	*les dents*
testicles	lay tehs-tee-kül	*les testicules*
throat	lah gorzh	*la gorge*

FRENCH

Ailments

I'm sick.
zhe swee mah-lahd   *Je suis malade.*
I've been vomiting.
zhay vo-mee   *J'ai vomi.*
I have sunburn.
zhay pree ē koo de so-lehy   *J'ai pris un coup de soleil.*

I feel ...	zhay day ...	*J'ai des ...*
dizzy	vehr-teezh	*vertiges*
nauseous	noh-zay	*nausées*
shivery	free-sō	*frissons*

I have (a/an) ...	zhay ...	*J'ai ...*
allergy	ün ah-lehr-zhee	*une allergie*
bite (dog)	ün mor-sür	*une morsure*
(insect)	ün pee-kür	*une piqûre*
burn	ün brü-lür	*une brûlure*
cough	ün too	*une toux*
diarrhoea	lah dyah-ray	*la diarrhée*
earache	mahl oh-zo-rehy	*mal aux oreilles*
eczema	de lehg-zay-mah	*de l'eczéma.*
fever	de lah fyehvr	*de la fièvre*
headache	mahl ah lah teht	*mal à la tête*
hayfever	le rüm day fwē	*le rhume des foins*
indigestion	ün ē-dee-zhehs-tyō	*une indigestion*
inflammation	ün ē-flah-mah-syō	*une inflammation*
influenza	lah greep	*la grippe*
itch	ün day-mā-zheh-zō	*une démangeaison*
lump	ün gro-serr	*une grosseur*
pain	ün doo-lerr	*une douleur*
sore throat	mahl ah lah gorzh	*mal à la gorge*
stomachache	mahl oh vātr	*mal au ventre*
venereal disease	ün mah-lah-dee vay-nay-ryehn	*une maladie vénérienne*
worms	day vehr	*des vers*

FRENCH

Useful Words & Phrases

Where's a/the ...?	oo eh ...?	*Où est ...?*
chemist	le far-mah-syē	*le pharmacien*
dentist	le dã-teest	*le dentiste*
doctor	le mehd-sē	*le médecin*
hospital	loh-pee-tahl	*l'hôpital*

I'm allergic to ...	zhe swee zah-lehr-zheek ...	*Je suis allergique ...*
antibiotics	oh-zã-tee-byo-teek	*aux antibiotiques*
bees	oh-zah-behy	*aux abeilles*
dairy products	oh pro-dwee leh-tyay	*aux produits laitiers*
penicillin	ah lah pay-nee-see-leen	*à la pénicilline*

At the Chemist

Where's the nearest all-night chemist?
　　oo eh lah fahr-mah-see
　　de nwee lah plü prosh?　　*Où est la pharmacie de nuit la plus proche?*
I need medication for ...
　　zhay be-zwē dē may-dee-kah-mã poor ...　　*J'ai besoin d'un médicament pour ...*
Do I need a prescription for ...?
　　zhay be-zwē dün or-do-nãs poor ...?　　*J'ai besoin d'une ordonnance pour ...?*

FRENCH

antibiotics	day zã-tee-byo-teek	*des antibiotiques*
antiseptic	de lã-tee-sehp-teek	*de l'antiseptique*
aspirin	de lahs-pee-reen	*de l'aspirine*
bandage	ē bã-dahzh	*un bandage*
Band-Aid	ē pãs-mã (ah-day-zeef)	*un pansement (adhésif)*
contraceptives	ē kõ-trah-sehp-teef	*un contraceptif*
cough medicine	ün pahs-teey poor lah too	*une pastille pour la toux*
laxatives	day lahk-sah-teef	*des laxatifs*
painkillers	day kahl-mã	*des calmants*
vitamins	day vee-tah-meen	*des vitamines*

At the Dentist

I have a toothache.
zhay mahl oh dã — *J'ai mal aux dents.*

I've lost a filling.
zhay pehr-dü ē plõ-bahzh — *J'ai perdu un plombage.*

My gums hurt.
may-zhã-seev me fõ mahl — *Mes gencives me font mal.*

I don't want it extracted.
zhe ne ver pah ke
voo lah-rah-shyay — *Je ne veux pas que vous l'arrachiez.*

Please give me an anaesthetic.
soo-zah-nehs-tay-zee
seel voo pleh — *Sous anesthésie, s'il vous plaît.*

TIME & DATES
Time

What time is it?	kehl err ei teel?	*Quelle heure est-il?*
It's ... in the	eel ei ... err	*Il est ... heures.*
morning	dü mah-tē	*du matin*
afternoon	de la-preh mee-dee	*de l'après midi*
evening	dü swahr	*du soir*

(See page 157 for numbers.)

FRENCH

Days

Monday	lē-dee	*lundi*
Tuesday	mahr-dee	*mardi*
Wednesday	mehr-kre-dee	*mercredi*
Thursday	zher-dee	*jeudi*
Friday	vā-dre-dee	*vendredi*
Saturday	sahm-dee	*samedi*
Sunday	dee-māsh	*dimanche*

Months

January	zhā-vyay	*janvier*
February	fayv-reeyay	*février*
March	mahrs	*mars*
April	ah-vreel	*avril*
May	meh	*mai*
June	zhwē	*juin*
July	zhwee-yeh	*juillet*
August	oo(t)	*août*
September	sehp-tābr	*septembre*
October	ok-tobr	*octobre*
November	no-vābr	*novembre*
December	day-sābr	*décembre*

Seasons

spring	le prē-tā	*le printemps*
summer	lay-tay	*l'été*
autumn	loh-ton	*l'automne*
winter	lee-vehr	*l'hiver*

Present

right now	too de sweet	*tout de suite*
now	mē-tnā	*maintenant*
today	oh-zhoor-dwee	*aujourd'hui*
this morning	se mah-tē	*ce matin*
this afternoon	seh tah-preh-mee-dee	*cet après-midi*
tonight	se-swahr	*ce soir*
this week	seht se-mehn	*cette semaine*
this year	seht ah-nay	*cette année*

FRENCH

Past

half an hour ago	eel-yah ün de-mee-err	*il y a une demi-heure*
yesterday ...	ee-yehr ...	*hier ...*
morning	mah-tē	*matin*
afternoon	ah-preh-mee-dee	*après-midi*
last night/evening	ee-yehr swahr	*hier soir*
day before yesterday	ah-vah-tee-yehr	*avant-hier*
last week	lah se-mehn dehr-nyehr	*la semaine dernière*
last year	lah-nay dehr-nyehr	*l'année dernière*

Future

soon	byē-toh	*bientôt*
tomorrow ...	de-mē ...	*demain ...*
morning	mah-tē	*matin*
afternoon	ah-preh-mee-dee	*après-midi*
evening	swahr	*soir*
the day after tomorrow	ah-preh-de-mē	*après-demain*
next week	lah se-mehn pro-shehn	*la semaine prochaine*
next year	lah-nay pro-shehn	*l'année prochaine*

During the Day

afternoon	lah-preh-mee-dee	*l'après-midi*
dawn	lob/lo-ror	*l'aube/l'aurore*
day	le zhoor	*le jour*
evening	le swahr	*le soir*
midday	mee-dee	*midi*
midnight	mee-nwee	*minuit*
morning	le mah-tē	*le matin*
night	lah nwee	*la nuit*
sunrise	lob	*l'aube*
sunset	le koo-shay	*le coucher*
	dü so-lehy	*du soleil*

FRENCH

NUMBERS & AMOUNTS

0	zay-roh	*zéro*	18	dee-zweet	*dix-huit*
1	ē	*un*	19	deez-nerf	*dix-neuf*
2	der	*deux*	20	vē	*vingt*
3	trwah	*trois*	21	vē tay ē	*vingt et un*
4	kahtr	*quatre*	22	vē der	*vingt-deux*
5	sēk	*cinq*	30	trāt	*trente*
6	sees	*six*	40	kah-rāt	*quarante*
7	seht	*sept*	50	sē-kāt	*cinquante*
8	weet	*huit*	60	swah-sāt	*soixante*
9	nerf	*neuf*	70	swah-sāt-dees	*soixante-dix*
10	dees	*dix*			
11	ōz	*onze*	80	kah-trer-vē	*quatre-vingts*
12	dooz	*douze*			
13	trehz	*treize*	90	kah-trer-vē-dees	*quatre-vingt-dix*
14	kah-torz	*quatorze*			
15	kēz	*quinze*	100	sā	*cent*
16	sehz	*seize*	1000	meel	*mille*
17	dee-seht	*dix-sept*	one million	ē mee-lyō	*un million*

FRENCH

Useful Words

Enough!	ah-say!; sah sü-fee!	*Assez!; Ça suffit!*
double	doobl	*double*
a dozen	ün doo-zehn	*une douzaine*
few	per de	*peu de*
a few	kehl-ke	*quelques*
less	mwẽ	*moins*
a little	ē per	*un peu*
many	boh-koo de	*beaucoup de*
more	plü(z)	*plus*
once	ün fwah	*une fois*
a pair	ün pehr	*une paire*
percent	poor sã	*pour cent*
too much	troh	*trop*
twice	der fwah	*deux fois*

ABBREVIATIONS

h	*heure*	o'clock
HS	*hors service*	out of order
HT	*hors taxe*	no tax
PC	*parti communiste*	Communist Party
PS	*parti socialiste*	Socialist Party
RATP	*Régie autonome des transports parisiens*	Paris transport authority
SNCF	*Société nationale des Chemins de fer français*	French railways
TTC	*toutes taxes comprises*	tax included
TVA	*taxe à la valeur ajoutée*	value added tax
UE	*Union européenne*	European Union
VF	*version française*	film dubbed in French
VO	*version originale*	film with French subtitles

EMERGENCIES

Help!	oh skoor!	*Au secours!*
Go away!	ah-lay voo-zā!	*Allez-vous-en!*
Fire!	oh fer!	*Au feu!*
Thief!	oh vo-lerr!	*Au voleur!*

Call ...!	ah-play ...!	*Appelez ....!*
an ambulance	ün ā-bü-lās!	*une ambulance*
a doctor	ē mehd-sē!	*un médecin*
the police	lah po-lees!	*la police*

FRENCH

Where's the police station?
oo eh le ko-mee-sah-ryah   *Où est le commissariat*
de po-lees?   *de police?*

I've (m/f) been raped.
zhay ay-tay vyo-lay   *J'ai été violé/e.*

I have medical insurance.
zhay ün ah-sü-rās   *J'ai une assurance*
mah-lah-dee   *maladie.*

Could I use the telephone?
ehs-ke zhe poo-reh zü-tee-   *Est-ce que je pourrais*
lee-zay le tay-lay-fon?   *utiliser le téléphone?*

Where are the toilets?
oo sō lay twah-leht?   *Où sont les toilettes?*

Dealing with the Police

My ... was stolen.	ō mah vo-lay ...	*On m'a volé ...*
bags	may bah-gahzh	*mes bagages*
handbag	mō sah kah mē	*mon sac à main*
money	mo nahr-zhā	*mon argent*
travellers cheques	may shehk de	*mes chèques*
	vwah-yahzh	*de voyage*
passport	mō pahs-por	*mon passeport*

FRENCH

I'm (m/f) sorry. I apologise.
  zhe swee day-zo-lay.
  zhe mehk-sküz

Je suis désolé/e. Je m'excuse.

Can I call someone?
  zhe per ah-play kehl-kē?

Je peux appeler quelqu'un?

Can I pay an on-the-spot fine?
  zhe per pay-yay lah-mãd
  too de sweet?

*Je peux payer l'amende
tout de suite?*

I want to contact my
embassy/consulate.
  zhe ver kõ-tahk-tay
  mo-nã-bah-sahd/mõ
  kõ-sü-lah

*Je veux contacter
mon ambassade/
mon consulat.*

GERMAN

QUICK REFERENCE

GERMAN

Hello.	goo-ten taak	Guten Tag.
Goodbye.	owf *vee*-der-zeh-en	Auf Wiedersehen.
Yes./No.	yaa/nain	Ja./Nein.
Excuse me.	ent-*shul*-di-gung	Entschuldigung.
Sorry.	ent-*shul*-di-gung	Entschuldigung.
Please.	*bit*-te	Bitte.
Thank you.	*dahng*-ke	Danke.
You're welcome.	*bit*-te zair	Bitte sehr.
Where's ...?	vaw ist ...?	Wo ist ...?

I'd like a ... ticket.	ikh *merkh*-te ai-ne ...	Ich möchte eine ...
one-way	*ain*-fah-khe	einfache
	faar-kahr-teh	Fahrkarte
return	*rük*-faar-kahr-teh	Rückfahrkarte

I (don't) understand.
ikh fer-*shteh*-e
(üü-ber-howpt *nikhts*)
*Ich verstehe
(überhaupt nichts).*

Do you speak English?
shpre-khen zee *eng*-lish?
Sprechen Sie Englisch?

Go straight ahead.
geh-en zee ge-raa-de-*ows*
Gehen Sie geradeaus.

Turn left/right.
bee-gen zee *lingks/rekhts*
Biegen Sie links/rechts.

Do you have any rooms available?
haa-ben zee nokh
tsim-mer frai?
*Haben Sie noch
Zimmer frei?*

I'm looking for a public toilet.
ikh *zoo*-kheh ai-neh
erf-fehnt-li-kheh
to-ah-*leht*-teh
*Ich suche eine
öffentliche
Toilette.*

1	ains	*eins*	6	zeks	*sechs*
2	tsvai	*zwei*	7	zee-ben	*sieben*
3	drai	*drei*	8	ahkht	*acht*
4	feer	*vier*	9	noyn	*neun*
5	fünf	*fünf*	10	tsehn	*zehn*

It might be a surprise to know that German is, in fact, a close relative of English. English, German and Dutch are all known as West Germanic languages. This means that you know quite a few German words already – *Arm*, *Finger*, *Gold* – and you'll be able to figure out many others – such as *Mutter*, 'mother', *trinken*, 'to drink', *gut*, 'good'.

A primary reason why English and German have grown apart is that the Normans, on invading England in 1066, brought with them a large number of non-Germanic words. This caused English to have lots of synonyms, with the more basic word being Germanic, and the more literary or specialised one coming from French. For instance, the Germanic 'start' and 'green' as opposed to the French 'commence' and 'verdant'.

German is spoken throughout Germany and Austria, and in most of Switzerland. Although you may hear different dialects,

GENDER

Some German nouns can be either masculine or feminine. A feminine noun often looks like the masculine form, but with the suffix *-in* added to the end of the word. Where a word can be either masculine or feminine, in this chapter the feminine ending is separated with a slash.

secretary (m/f)   *Sekretär/in*

This indicates that the masculine form is *Sekretär* and the feminine form is *Sekretärin*.

In cases where the feminine is more complicated than adding *-in* to the masculine form, both forms of the word appear in full, masculine first:

nurse (m/f)   *Krankenpfleger/*
                         Krankenschwester

there's a strong tradition of a prescribed official language – *Hochdeutsch*, 'High German'. High German is used in this book and will always be understood. In some areas, English is so widely spoken that you mightn't have a chance to use German, even if you want to. However, as soon as you move out of the larger cities, especially in what was East Germany, the situation is totally different. *Gute Reise!*

FORMALITIES

German has both polite and informal forms of the second person pronoun 'you' – *Sie* (pol) and *du* (inf). In this chapter, only the polite form, *Sie*, is given.

PRONUNCIATION

German pronunciation is relatively straightforward. Each letter or combination of letters is pronounced consistently, so you can almost always tell how a word is pronounced by the way it's spelt.

Vowels

German vowels can be long or short. Some letters or letter combinations in the German alphabet don't exist in English – these are the vowels with an umlaut (*ä, ö, ü*). Keep in mind that these vowels are pronounced differently.

Short Vowels

a	ah	as the 'u' in 'cut'
ä	air	as the 'ai' in 'air', but shorter;
	e	as the 'e' in 'bet'
äh	air	as the 'ai' in 'air'
e	e	as the 'e' in 'bet'
i	i	as in 'hit'
o	o	as in 'hot'
ö	er	as the 'e' in 'her'
u	u	as the 'u' in 'pull'
ü/y	ü	as the 'i' in 'kiss', but with rounded lips

PRONOUNS

SG			PL		
I	ikh	*ich*	we	veer	*wir*
you (inf)	doo	*du*	you (inf)	eer	*ihr*
you (pol)	zee	*Sie*	you (pol)	zee	*Sie*
he	er	*er*	they	zee	*sie*
she	zee	*sie*			
it	es	*es*			

Long Vowels

A long vowel has the same sound quality as its short counterpart, but is pronounced longer. The spelling for long vowels is often indicated by an *h* after the vowel, or a doubling of the vowel, but not always. The vowel *i* is often lengthened by writing *ie*.

a, aa, ah	aa	as the 'a' in 'far'
e, ee, eh	eh	as the 'e' in 'egg', but longer
i, ie	ee	as the 'i' in 'marine'
o, oo, oh	aw	as the 'o' in 'for'
ö	er	as the 'e' in 'her', but longer
u, uh	oo	as the 'oo' in 'zoo', pronounced with very rounded lips
ü, üh	üü	as the 'i' in 'kiss', but with rounded lips

GERMAN

Vowel Combinations

au	ow	as the 'ow' in 'cow'
äu	oy	as the 'oy' in 'toy'
ei	ai	as the 'ai' in 'aisle'
eu	oy	as the 'oy' in 'toy'

Consonants

Most German consonants are similar to their English counterparts. One important difference is that *b*, *d* and *g* sound like 'p', 't' and 'k' respectively at the end of a word or syllable.

Letters that may be unfamiliar include the *ß* (a sharp 's') that may also be written as *ss* and is pronounced as the 's' in 'sin'. There are also *ch*-sounds which may be pronounced in two ways depending on what letters come before and after. After *a*, *o*, *u* and *au*, the *ch* is a guttural sound like the 'ch' in Scottish 'loch'. Everywhere else, *ch* is pronounced like the 'h' in 'huge'.

Only consonants and double consonants that differ from English are given here.

b, bb	p	at the end of a word or syllable, as the 'p' in 'pet';
	b	elsewhere, as the 'b' in 'bliss'
c	ts	normally as the 'ts' in 'lets';
	k	in some foreign words, as the 'k' in 'king'
ch	kh	after *a*, *o*, *u* or *au*, as the 'ch' in Scottish 'loch';
		elsewhere, as the 'h' in 'huge'
d, dd	t	at the end of a word or syllable, as the 't' in 'tang';
	d	elsewhere, as the 'd' in 'drink'
f, ff	f	as the 'f' in 'fun'
g, gg	g	as the 'g' in 'game'
g	k	at the end of a word or syllable, as the 'k' in 'king';
	kh	when part of the unit *ig*, as the 'h' in 'huge';
	zh	in some foreign words, as the 's' in 'pleasure'
h		silent following a vowel;
	h	elsewhere, as the 'h' in horse
j	y	as the 'y' in 'yes';
	zh	in some foreign words, as the 's' in 'treasure'
ng	ng	as the 'ng' in 'sing'
r, rr	r	slightly rolled at the back of the mouth
s	z	between two vowels, as the 'z' in 'zoo';
	s	elsewhere, as the 's' in 'sin'
ss, ß	s	as the 's' in 'sin'

GERMAN

v	f	mostly pronounced as the 'f' in 'fun';
	v	in words of Greek and Latin origin, as the 'v' in 'velvet'
w	v	as the 'v' in 'velvet'
z	ts	as the 'ts' in 'bets'

Letter Combinations

chs	ks	as the 'x' in 'fox'
ck	k	as the 'k' in 'king'
qu	kv	as the 'k' in 'king' + the 'v' in 'velvet'
sch	sh	as the 'sh' in 'ship'
sp/st	shp/sht	at the beginning of a word or syllable, the 's' is pronounced as the 'sh' in 'ship'
-tion	tsyawn	the 't' is pronounced as the 'ts' in 'bets'

GERMAN

Stress

Stress in German is very straightforward – the majority of German words are stressed on the first syllable. However, some prefixes aren't stressed, such as in the word *verstehen*, 'understand', which is stressed on *stehen*. Some foreign words, especially from Latin and Greek, are stressed on the last syllable (*Organisation*, *Appetit*).

GREETINGS & CIVILITIES
You Should Know

Hello.	goo-ten taak	*Guten Tag.*
Hi.	hah-*lo*	*Hallo.*
Goodbye.	owf *vee*-der-zeh-en	*Auf Wiedersehen.*
Bye.	tshüs	*Tschüss.*
Yes./No.	yaa/nain	*Ja./Nein.*
Excuse me.	ent-*shul*-di-gung	*Entschuldigung.*
May I?	dahrf ikh?	*Darf ich?*
Sorry. (excuse/ forgive me)	ent-*shul*-di-gung	*Entschuldigung.*
Please.	*bit*-te	*Bitte.*
Thank you.	*dahng*-ke	*Danke.*
Many thanks.	fee-len *dahngk*	*Vielen Dank.*
You're welcome.	*bit*-te zair	*Bitte sehr.*

Forms of Address

Frau (lit: Mrs), is regarded as a respectful form of address for women whether they're married or not. *Fräulein*, 'Miss', once used for young women, has become old-fashioned and is slowly disappearing from the spoken language.

companion/friend	froynt/ *froyn*-din	*Freund/in*
Gentlemen!	mai-ne *her*-ren	*Meine Herren!*
Ladies!	mai-ne *daa*-men	*Meine Damen!*
Mr/Mrs	her/frow	*Herr/Frau*

Often when addressing a professional person or someone of status, the person's title is used.

| Doctor ... | (frow) *dok*-tor ... | *(Frau) Doktor ...* |
| Professor ... | (frow) pro-*fes*-sor ... | *(Frau) Professor ...* |

SMALL TALK
Meeting People

When Germans ask *Wie geht es Ihnen?*, 'How are you?', they expect a more or less honest answer, depending on the level of intimacy. Unlike English, 'How are you?' is never used on its own as a form of greeting.

Good day.	*goo*-ten taak	*Guten Tag.*
Good morning.	*goo*-ten *mor*-gen	*Guten Morgen.*
Good afternoon.	*goo*-ten taak	*Guten Tag.*
Good evening.	*goo*-ten *aa*-bent	*Guten Abend.*
Goodnight.	*goo*-te nahkht	*Gute Nacht.*
How are you?	vee *geht* es ee-nen?	*Wie geht es Ihnen?*
Well, thanks.	dahng-ke, goot	*Danke, gut.*
Not too bad.	es *geht*	*Es geht.*
Not so good.	nikht zaw *goot*	*Nicht so gut.*
And you?	unt *ee*-nen?	*Und Ihnen?*
What's your name?	vee hai-sen *zee*?	*Wie heißen Sie?*
My name's ...	ikh *hai*-se ...	*Ich heiße ...*

I'm pleased to meet you.

    ahn-ge-nehm; zair er-*froyt*   *Angenehm; Sehr erfreut.*

GERMAN

Nationalities

You'll find that many country names in German are similar in English. Remember, though, that even if a word looks like the English equivalent, it will have a German pronunciation, for instance, *Japan*, is pronounced *yaa*-pahn).

Where are you from?
    vo-hair *kom*-men zee?   *Woher kommen Sie?*

I'm from ...	ikh *kom*-me ows ...	*Ich komme aus ...*
Australia	ows-*traa*-lyen	*Australien*
Canada	ka-na-da	*Kanada*
New Zealand	noy-*zeh*-lahnt	*Neuseeland*
the UK	dem fer-*ai*-nikh-ten	*dem Vereinigten*
	ker-nikh-raikh	*Königreich*
the US	den oo-es-*aa*	*den USA*

Occupations

What work do you do?
    ahls vahs *ahr*-bai-ten zee?   *Als was arbeiten Sie?*

I'm (a/an) ...	ikh bin ...	*Ich bin ...*
artist	*künst*-ler/in	*Künstler/in*
business	ge-*shefts*-mahn/	*Geschäftsmann/*
person	ge-*shefts*-frow	*Geschäftsfrau*
chef	kokh/ *ker*-khin	*Koch/Köchin*
doctor	ahrtst/ *erts*-tin	*Arzt/Ärztin*
engineer	in-zhen-*yerr*/in	*Ingenieur/in*
lawyer	*rekhts*-ahn-vahlt/	*Rechtsanwalt/*
	rekhts-ahn-vel-tin	*Rechtsanwältin*
nurse	*krahng*-ken-pfleh-ger/	*Krankenpfleger/*
	krahng-ken-shves-ter	*Krankenschwester*
office	bü-*raw-ahn*-ge-shtel-ter/	*Büroangestellter/*
worker	bü-*raw-ahn*-ge-shtel-te	*Büroangestellte*
retired	*rent*-ner/ *rent*-ne-rin	*Rentner/in*
student	shtu-*dent*/shtu-*den*-tin	*Student/in*
teacher	*lair*-rer/ *lair*-re-rin	*Lehrer/in*
unemployed	*ahr*-baits-laws	*arbeitslos*
waiter	*kel*-ner/ *kel*-ne-rin	*Kellner/in*

GERMAN

GERMAN

Religion

What's your religion?
vahs ist ee-re re-li-*gyawn*?   *Was ist Ihre Religion?*
I'm not religious.
ikh bin nikht re-li-*gyers*   *Ich bin nicht religiös.*

I'm ...	ikh bin ...	*Ich bin ...*
atheist	ah-te-*ist*/ ah-te-*is*-tin	*Atheist/in*
Buddhist	bu-*dist*/bu-*dis*-tin	*Buddhist/in*
Catholic	kah-*taw*-lish	*Katholisch*
Christian	krist/ *kris*-tin	*Christ/in*
Hindu	*hin*-doo	*Hindu*
Jewish	*yoo*-de/*yüü*-din	*Jude/Jüdin*
Muslim	*mos*-lem	*Moslem*

Family

I'd like to	dahrf ikh ee-nen	*Darf ich Ihnen ...*
introduce my ...	... *for*-shtel-len?	*vorstellen?*
boyfriend	mai-nen *froynt*	*meinen Freund*
daughter	mai-ne *tokh*-ter	*meine Tochter*
girlfriend	mai-ne *froyn*-din	*meine Freundin*
grandchildren	mai-ne *eng*-kel	*meine Enkel*
grandparents	mai-ne *graws*-el-tern	*meine Großeltern*
husband	mai-ne *mahn*	*meinen Mann*
parents	mai-ne *el*-tern	*meine Eltern*
son	mai-nen *zawn*	*meinen Sohn*
wife	mai-ne *frow*	*meine Frau*

Feelings

How are you feeling?
vee *füü*-len zee zikh?   *Wie fühlen Sie sich?*
What's up?
vahs ist *laws*?   *Was ist los?*
I (don't) like ...
... ge-*felt* meer (nikht)   *... gefällt mir (nicht).*

I'm ...	ikh bin ...	*Ich bin ...*
angry	*ber*-ze	*böse*
grateful	*dahngk*-baar	*dankbar*
happy	*glük*-likh	*glücklich*
lonely	*ain*-zaam	*einsam*
sad	*trow*-rikh	*traurig*
sleepy	*shlairf*-rikh	*schläfrig*
tired	*müü*-de	*müde*

I'm ...		
right	ikh haa-be *rekht*	*Ich habe recht.*
hot/cold	meer ist *hais/kahlt*	*Mir ist heiß/kalt.*
in a hurry	ikh haa-be es *ai*-likh	*Ich habe es eilig.*
sorry	es toot meer *lait*	*Es tut mir leid.*
worried	ikh mah-khe meer *zor*-gen	*Ich mache mir Sorgen.*

GERMAN

Useful Phrases

Sure.	klaar	*Klar!*
Just a minute.	ai-nen mo-*ment*	*Einen Moment!*
It's (not) important.	es ist (nikht) *vikh*-tikh	*Es ist (nicht) wichtig.*
It's (not) possible.	es ist (nikht) *merk*-likh	*Es ist (nicht) möglich.*
Wait!	*vahr*-ten zee maal	*Warten Sie mal!*
Good luck!	feel *glük*	*Viel Glück!*

BREAKING THE LANGUAGE BARRIER

Do you speak English?
shpre-khen zee *eng*-lish?   *Sprechen Sie Englisch?*

Does anyone here speak English?
shprikht heer   *Spricht hier*
yeh-mahnt *eng*-lish?   *jemand Englisch?*

I don't speak ...
ikh shpre-khe kain ...   *Ich spreche kein ...*

Do you understand?
fer-*shteh*-en zee mikh?   *Verstehen Sie mich?*

I understand.
ikh fer-*shteh*-e   *Ich verstehe.*

I don't understand anything at all.
ikh fer-shteh-e   *Ich verstehe*
üü-ber-howpt *nikhts*   *überhaupt nichts.*

Could you translate
that for me, please?
kern-ten zee meer dahs   *Könnten Sie mir das*
bit-te üü-ber-*zet*-tsen?   *bitte übersetzen?*

Could you speak more
slowly please?
kern-ten zee bit-te   *Könnten Sie bitte*
lahng-zah-mer shpre-khen?   *langsamer sprechen?*

Could you please write that down?
kern-ten zee dahs bit-te   *Könnten Sie das bitte*
owf-shrai-ben?   *aufschreiben?*

How do you pronounce this word?
vee *shprikht* mahn   *Wie spricht man*
dee-zes vort *ows*?   *dieses Wort aus?*

Could you repeat that?
kern-ten zee dahs bit-te   *Könnten Sie das bitte*
vee-der-*haw*-len?   *wiederholen?*

How do you say ... in German?
vahs haist ... owf *doytsh*?   *Was heißt ... auf deutsch?*

What does ... mean?
vahs be-*doy*-tet ...?   *Was bedeutet ...?*

BODY LANGUAGE

Germans can be quite reserved, so don't always expect a hearty welcome. When meeting someone for the first time people normally shake hands, and if they know each other well enough, might exchange kisses. This is regarded as perfectly normal between women and between women and men. Men usually avoid it, giving each other a pat on the shoulder instead.

GERMAN

PAPERWORK

Adresse	address
Alter	age
Ausweispapiere	identification
Beruf	profession
Einwanderung	immigration
Familienstand	marital status
Führerschein	drivers licence
Geburtsdatum	date of birth
Geburtsort	place of birth
Geburtsurkunde	birth certificate
Geschlecht	sex
Grenze	border
Name	name
Nationalität	nationality
Passnummer	passport number
(Reise)pass	passport
Religion	religion
Visum	visa
Zoll	customs

GERMAN

SIGNS

AUSGANG	EXIT
AUSKUNFT	INFORMATION
DAMEN/FRAUEN	WOMEN
EINGANG	ENTRANCE
EINTRITT FREI	FREE ADMISSION
GEÖFFNET	OPEN
GESCHLOSSEN	CLOSED
HEISS	HOT
HERREN/MÄNNER	MEN
KALT	COLD
KEIN ZUTRITT	NO ENTRY
NOTAUSGANG	EMERGENCY EXIT
RESERVIERT	RESERVED
TOILETTEN	TOILETS
RAUCHEN VERBOTEN	NO SMOKING

GETTING AROUND

Trains are the most common form of transport for long distances. There are some long-distance buses, but mostly buses only run within cities or connect rural areas with the nearest town. An alternative to trains are the special agencies called *Mitfahrzentralen* which arrange lifts. You'll find them in all large cities.

Directions

Excuse me, can you help me please?
ent-*shul*-di-gen zee,	*Entschuldigen Sie,*
kern-nen zee meer	*können Sie mir*
bit-te *hel*-fen?	*bitte helfen?*

Where's ...?	vaw ist ...?	*Wo ist ...?*
How do I get to the ...?	vee *kom*-me ikh ...?	*Wie komme ich ...?*
city centre	tsum *shtaht*-	*zum*
	tsen-trum	*Stadtzentrum*
metro (underground)	tsur *oo*-baan	*zur U-Bahn*
railway station	tsum *baan*-hawf	*zum Bahnhof*

Can you show me (on the map)?
 kern-nen zee es meer
 (owf der kahr-te) *tsai*-gen?
   Können Sie es mir
   (auf der Karte) zeigen?

Go straight ahead.
 geh-en zee ge-raa-de-*ows*
   Gehen Sie geradeaus.

In that direction.
 in *dee*-zer rikh-tung
   In dieser Richtung.

Turn left/right	bee-gen zee …	*Biegen Sie … links/*
at the …	*lingks/rekhts* ahp	*rechts ab.*
bottom	*un*-ten	*unten*
end	ahm *en*-de	*am Ende*
next corner	bai der nairkhs-ten *ek*-ke	*bei der nächsten Ecke*
top	*aw*-ben	*oben*
traffic lights	bai der *ahm*-pel	*bei der Ampel*

back	tsu-*rük*	*zurück*
behind	*hin*-ter	*hinter*
far	vait	*weit*
here	heer	*hier*
in front of	fawr	*vor*
near	*naa*-e	*nahe*
opposite	geh-gen-*üü*-ber	*gegenüber*

GERMAN

Buying Tickets

Where can I buy a ticket?
 vaw kahn ikh ai-ne
 faar-kahr-te kow-fen?
   Wo kann ich eine
   Fahrkarte kaufen?

I want to go to …
 ikh merkh-te naakh
 … faa-ren
   Ich möchte nach
   … fahren.

I'd like ...	ikh *merkh*-te ...	*Ich möchte ...*
a one-way ticket	ai-ne *ain*-fah-khe faar-kahr-te	*eine einfache Fahrkarte*
a return ticket	ai-ne *rük*-faar-kahr-teh	*eine Rückfahrkarte*
two tickets	tsvai *faar*-kahr-ten	*zwei Fahrkarten*

with ... concession	mit faar-prais-er-*mair*-si-gung füür ...	*mit Fahrpreiser-mäßigung für ...*
children's	*kin*-der	*Kinder*
pensioner	*rent*-ner	*Rentner*
student	shtu-*den*-ten	*Studenten*

| 1st class | *er*-ster klahs-se | *erster Klasse* |
| 2nd class | *tsvai*-ter klahs-se | *zweiter Klasse* |

GERMAN

Bus

Where do buses for ... stop?

| vaw hahl-ten dee bus-se naakh ...? | *Wo halten die Busse nach ...?* |

Which bus goes to ...?

| vel-kher bus fairt naakh ...? | *Welcher Bus fährt nach ...?* |

Does this bus go to ...?

| fairt *dee*-zer bus naakh ...? | *Fährt dieser Bus nach ...?* |

What time's the ... bus?	vahn fairt der ... bus?	*Wann fährt der ... Bus?*
first	*ers*-te	*erste*
last	*lets*-te	*letzte*
next	*nairkhs*-te	*nächste*

Could you let me know when we get to ...?

| kern-ten zee meer bit-te be-s*hait* zaa-gen, ven veer in ... *ahn*-kom-men? | *Könnten Sie mir bitte Bescheid sagen, wenn wir in ... ankommen?* |

I want to get off!

| ikh merkh-te *ows*-shtai-gen! | *Ich möchte aussteigen!* |

Metro

Where can I buy a ticket?
vaw kahn ikh ai-ne
faar-kahr-te kow-fen?

*Wo kann ich eine
Fahrkarte kaufen?*

Is there a ... ticket? gipt es ai-ne ... *Gibt es eine ...*
-faar-kahr-te? *-fahrkarte*

daily *taa*-ges *Tages*
weekly *vo*-khen *Wochen*

Which line takes me to ...?
vel-khe leen-ye fairt naakh ...? *Welche Linie fährt nach ...?*

Train

There are two extra-rapid trains
– the older IC (Inter City) and
the modern ICE (Inter City
Express). Both services only
stop in major cities and have
special fares. Normal speed
trains service the smaller cities.

> **THEY MAY SAY ...**
>
> er ist *ows*-ge-bukht
> It's full.

For the IC you have to pay a supplement in addition to the normal
ticket, for the ICE there are special tickets.

Is this the right platform
for the train to ...?
fairt der tsook naakh ... *Fährt der Zug nach ...*
owf *dee*-zem baan-shtaik ahp? *auf diesem Bahnsteig ab?*
Is this the train to ...?
ist *dahs* der tsook naakh ...? *Ist das der Zug nach ...?*
Does this train stop at ...?
helt *dee*-zer tsook in ...? *Hält dieser Zug in ...?*
Is the train from ... late?
haht der tsook ows ... *Hat der Zug aus ...*
fer-*shpair*-tung? *Verspätung?*
How long will it be delayed?
vee-feel fer-*shpair*-tung *Wieviel Verspätung*
virt air haa-ben? *wird er haben?*

GERMAN

Taxi

Are you free?
zint zee *frai*?   *Sind Sie frei?*

How much is it to go to ...?
vahs *kos*-tet es bis ...?   *Was kostet es bis ...?*

Can you take me to the/this ...?	kern-nen zee mikh ... bring-en?	*Können Sie mich ... bringen?*
airport	tsum *flook*-haa-fen	*zum Flughafen*
city centre	tsum *shtaht*-tsen-trum	*zum Stadtzentrum*
hotel	tsoo dee-zem haw-*tel*	*zu diesem Hotel*
railway station	tsum baan-hawf	*zum Bahnhof*
street	tsoo *dee*-zer shtraa-se	*zu dieser Straße*

Continue!
vai-ter!   *Weiter!*

Please slow down.
faa-ren zee bit-te
lahng-zah-mer   *Fahren Sie bitte langsamer.*

The next street to the left/right.
bee-gen zee ahn der
nairkhs-ten *ek*-ke
lingks/rekhts ahp   *Biegen Sie an der nächsten Ecke links/rechts ab.*

Here's fine, thanks.
hahl-ten zee bit-te *heer*   *Halten Sie bitte hier.*

Please stop at the next corner.
hahl-ten zee bit-te ahn
der *nairkhs*-ten *ek*-ke   *Halten Sie bitte an der nächsten Ecke.*

Stop here!
hahl-ten zee *heer*!   *Halten Sie hier!*

Please wait here.
bit-te vaar-ten zee *heer*   *Bitte warten Sie hier.*

GERMAN

Useful Phrases

What time does the ... leave?	vahn fairt ... ahp?	*Wann fährt ... ab?*
What time does the ... arrive?	vahn komt ... ahn?	*Wann kommt ... an?*
boat	dahs bawt	*das Boot*
bus	der bus	*der Bus*
train	der tsook	*der Zug*
tram	dee *shtraa*-sen-baan	*die Straßenbahn*
underground	dee *oo*-baan	*die U-Bahn*

Car

I'd like to hire a car.
ikh merkh-te ain *ow*-taw mee-ten

Ich möchte ein Auto mieten.

How much is it per day/week?
vee-feel *kos*-tet es praw taak/ *vo*-khe?

Wieviel kostet es pro Tag/Woche?

Does that include ...?	ist ... *in*-be-grif-fen?	*Ist ... inbegriffen?*
insurance	dee fer-*zikh*-e-rung	*die Versicherung*
mileage	dahs ki-lo-*meh*-ter-gelt	*das Kilometergeld*

Where's the next petrol station?
vaw ist dee nairkhs-te *tahngk*-shtel-le?

Wo ist die nächste Tankstelle?

I want ... litres of petrol (gas).
geh-ben zee meer ... lee-ter ben-*tseen*

Geben Sie mir ... Liter Benzin.

I need a mechanic.
ikh brow-khe ai-nen me-*khaa*-ni-ker

Ich brauche einen Mechaniker.

I have a flat tyre.
ikh haa-be ai-ne *pahn*-ne

Ich habe eine Panne.

GERMAN

air	*luft*	*Luft*
battery	bah-te-*ree*	*Batterie*
brakes	*brem*-zen	*Bremsen*
diesel	*dee*-zel	*Diesel*
engine	maw-*tor*	*Motor*
gear	gahng	*Gang*
ignition	*tsün*-dung	*Zündung*
indicator	*bling*-ker	*Blinker*
jack	*vaa*-gen-heh-ber	*Wagenheber*
lights	*shain*-ver-fer	*Scheinwerfer*
oil	erl	*Öl*
... petrol (gas)	... ben-*tseen*	*... Benzin*
leaded	fer-*blai*-tes	*verbleites*
unleaded	blai-*frai*-es	*bleifreies*
radiator	*küü*-ler	*Kühler*
(spare) tyre	(re-*zer*-ve-)*rai*-fen	*(Reserve)reifen*
windscreen	*vint*-shuts-shai-be	*Windschutzscheibe*

ACCOMMODATION
At the Hotel

Do you have any
rooms available?
  haa-ben zee nokh
  tsim-mer frai?
  *Haben Sie noch
  Zimmer frei?*

SIGNS	
AUSGEBUCHT	NO VACANCIES
FREI	AVAILABLE
VOLL	FULL
ZIMMER	ROOMS

I'd/We'd like ...	ikh merkh-te/	*Ich möchte/*
	veer merkh-ten ain ...	*Wir möchten ein ...*
a single room	*ain*-tsel-tsim-mer	*Einzelzimmer*
a double room	*dop*-pel-	*Doppelzimmer*
	tsim-mer	
to share a dorm	bet in ai-nem	*Bett in einem*
	shlaaf-zaal	*Schlafsaal*
a room with a	tsim-mer	*Zimmer*
bathroom	mit *baat*	*mit Bad*

How much is it per night/person?
vee-feel *kos*-tet es praw
nahkht/per-zawn?

Wieviel kostet es pro
Nacht/Person?

Can I see the room?
kahn ikh dahs
tsim-mer *zeh*-en?

Kann ich das
Zimmer sehen?

Where's the bathroom?
vaw ist dahs *baat*?

Wo ist das Bad?

Do you have a safe where
I can leave my valuables?
haa-ben zee ai-nen *sehf*,
in dehm ikh mai-ne
vert-zah-khen lahs-sen kahn?

Haben Sie einen Safe,
in dem ich meine
Wertsachen lassen kann?

I've locked myself out of my room.
ikh haa-be mikh ows mai-
nem *tsim*-mer *ows*-ge-shpert

Ich habe mich aus meinem
Zimmer ausgesperrt.

I'm/We are leaving now.
ikh *rai*-ze/veer *rai*-zen yetst *ahp*

Ich reise/Wir reisen jetzt ab.

I'd like to pay the bill.
kahn ikh bit-te dee
rekh-nung haa-ben?

Kann ich bitte die
Rechnung haben?

(Also see Camping, page 188-89.)

AROUND TOWN
At the Post Office

I'd like to send a(n) ...	ikh merkh-te ... zen-den	*Ich möchte ... senden.*
aerogram	ai-nen *luft*-post-laikht-breef	*einen Luftpost-leichtbrief*
fax	ain *fahks*	*ein Fax*
letter	ai-nen *breef*	*einen Brief*
parcel	ain pah-*keht*	*ein Paket*
postcard	ai-ne *post*-kahr-te	*eine Postkarte*
telegram	ain te-le-*grahm*	*ein Telegramm*

GERMAN

How much is the postage?		
	vee-feel kos-tet dahs *por*-to?	*Wieviel kostet das Porto?*
I'd like some stamps.		
	ikh *merkh*-te	*Ich möchte*
	breef-mahr-ken kow-fen	*Briefmarken kaufen.*
I'd like to have my mail forwarded.		
	ikh merkh-te mai-ne *post*	*Ich möchte meine Post*
	naakh-zen-den lahs-sen	*nachsenden lassen.*

airmail	*luft*-post	*Luftpost*
counter	*shahl*-ter	*Schalter*
destination	be-*shtim*-mungks-ort	*Bestimmungsort*
envelope	*um*-shlaak	*Umschlag*
mailbox	*breef*-kahs-ten	*Briefkasten*
parcel	pah-*keht*	*Paket*
post office box	*post*-fahkh	*Postfach*
poste restante	*post*-laa-gernt	*postlagernd*

Telephone

Where can I make a phone call?		
	vaw kahn ikh	*Wo kann ich*
	teh-le-fo-*nee*-ren?	*telefonieren?*
I want to make a		
long-distance call to ...		
	bit-te ain *fern*-ge-	*Bitte ein*
	shprairkh naakh ...	*Ferngespräch nach ...*
I want to make a		
reverse-charges (collect) call.		
	ikh *merkh*-te ain	*Ich möchte ein*
	er-ge-shprairkh	*R-Gespräch.*
The number is ...		
	dee *num*-mer ist ...	*Die Nummer ist ...*
It's engaged.		
	es ist be-*zetst*	*Es ist besetzt.*
I've been cut off.		
	ikh bin *un*-ter-bro-khen	*Ich bin unterbrochen*
	vor-den	*worden.*

I'd like to speak to (Mrs Schmidt).
ikh *merkh*-te (frow *shmit*)
shpre-khen

Ich möchte (Frau Schmidt) sprechen.

This is ...

heer ist ...

Hier ist ...

area code	fawr-vaal	Vorwahl
directory enquiries	teh-le-*fawn*-ows-kunft	Telefonauskunft
pay phone	*münts*-teh-le-fawn	Münztelefon
phone book	teh-le-*fawn*-bookh	Telefonbuch
phone box	teh-le-*fawn*-tsel-le	Telefonzelle
phonecard	teh-le-*fawn*-kahr-te	Telefonkarte
telephone	teh-le-*fawn*	Telefon

GERMAN

Internet

Is there a local Internet cafe?
gibt ehs ain in-tehr-neht
kah-fay in dehr *nair*-eh?

Gibt es ein Internet Café in der Nähe?

I want to connect to the Internet.
ikh *merkh*-te dahs in-
tehr-neht geh-*brow*-khehn

Ich möchte das Internet gebrauchen.

I'd like to send an email.
ikh mus ai-neh ee-mayl
ahb-shi-kehn

Ich muß eine E-mail abschicken.

At the Bank

I'd like to change some
travellers cheques.
ikh *merkh*-te rai-ze-sheks
ain-ler-zen

Ich möchte Reiseschecks einlösen.

I'd like to exchange some money.
ikh *merkh*-te gelt
um-tow-shen

Ich möchte Geld umtauschen.

What's the exchange rate?
vee ist der *vek*-sel-kurs?

Wie ist der Wechselkurs?

How much do I get for ...?
vee-feel be-*kom*-me ikh füür ...?

Wieviel bekomme ich für ...?

Can I have money transferred
here from my bank?

kahn ikh heer-hair *gelt*
fon mai-ner *bahngk*
ü-ber-*vai*-zen lahs-sen?

*Kann ich hierher Geld
von meiner Bank
überweisen lassen?*

amount	be-*traak*	*Betrag*
bank account	*bahngk*-kon-to	*Bankkonto*
cash	baar/ *baar*-gelt	*bar/Bargeld*
cashier (m/f)	kahs-*see*-rer/	*Kassierer/in*
	kahs-*see*-re-rin	
cheque	*shek*-kahr-te	*Scheckkarte*
coin/s	*mün*-tse/n	*Münze/n*
commission	ge-*büür*	*Gebühr*
credit card	kre-*deet*-kahr-te	*Kreditkarte*
currency	*vair*-rung	*Währung*
Euro	*oy*-roh	*Euro*
exchange	*gelt*-vek-sel	*Geldwechsel*
receipt	*kvit*-tung	*Quittung*
signature	*un*-ter-shrift	*Unterschrift*
transfer	ü-ber-*vai*-zung	*Überweisung*

INTERESTS & ENTERTAINMENT
Sightseeing

Do you have a guidebook/street map?

haa-ben zee ai-nen
rai-ze-füü-rer/ *shtaht*-plaan?

*Haben Sie einen
Reiseführer/Stadtplan?*

What are the main attractions?

vahs zint dee *howpt*-zeh-
ens-vür-dikh-kai-ten?

*Was sind die
Hauptsehenswürdigkeiten?*

What's that?

vahs ist *dahs*?

Was ist das?

Can I take photographs?

dahrf ikh faw-to-grah-*fee*-ren?

Darf ich fotografieren?

What time does it open/close?

vahn mahkht es *owf/tsoo*?

Wann macht es auf/zu?

castle	shlos	*Schloss*
cathedral	dawm	*Dom*
church	*kir*-khe	*Kirche*
fountain	*brun*-nen	*Brunnen*
harbour	*haa*-fen	*Hafen*
main square	*howpt*-plahts	*Hauptplatz*
monument	*dengk*-maal	*Denkmal*
museum	mu-*zeh*-um	*Museum*
old part of the city	*ahlt*-shtaht	*Altstadt*
palace	pah-*lahst*	*Palast*
ruins	ru-*ee*-nen	*Ruinen*
stadium	shtaa-di-*on*	*Stadion*
statues	shtaa-*tu*-en	*Statuen*
tomb	graap	*Grab*
tower	turm	*Turm*
zoo	*teer*-gahr-ten	*Tiergarten*

GERMAN

Going Out

What's there to do in the evenings?
vahs kahn mahn aa-bents
un-ter-*neh*-men?

*Was kann man abends
unternehmen?*

Is there a concert on tonight?
gipt es hoy-te aa-bent ain
kon-*tsert*?

*Gibt es heute abend ein
Konzert?*

What band is playing tonight?
vahs füür ai-ne *bent* shpeelt
hoy-te?

*Was für eine Band spielt
heute?*

Would you like to do something ...?	hahst doo lust, ... vahs tsoo un-ter-*neh*-men?	*Hast du Lust, ... was zu unternehmen?*
tonight	hoy-te aa-bent	*heute abend*
tomorrow	*mor*-gen	*morgen*
cinema	*kee*-no	*Kino*
concert	kon-*tsert*	*Konzert*
dancing	*tahn*-tsen	*tanzen*
club	*dis*-ko	*Disco*

party	*paa*-ti	*Party*
performance	*owf*-füü-rung	*Aufführung*
pub	*knai*-pe	*Kneipe*
restaurant	re-sto-*rö*	*Restaurant*
theatre	teh-*aa*-ter	*Theater*

Sports & Interests

What are your favourite hobbies?
    vahs zint dai-ne *ho*-bees?   *Was sind deine Hobbys?*

Do you like ...?	mer-gen zee ...?	*Mögen Sie ...?*
arts	kunst	*Kunst*
literature	li-te-rah-*toor*	*Literatur*
music	mu-*zeek*	*Musik*
sports	shport	*Sport*
travel	*rai*-zen	*Reisen*

Do you play/go ...?	shpee-len zee ...?	*Spielen Sie ...?*
basketball	*baas*-ket-bahl	*Basketball*
cycling	*raat*-shport	*Radsport*
diving	*tow*-khen	*Tauchen*
fencing	*fekh*-ten	*Fechten*
figure skating	*ais*-kunst-lowf	*Eiskunstlauf*
hang-gliding	*drah*-khen-flee-gen	*Drachenfliegen*
ice hockey	*ais*-hok-ki	*Eishockey*
ice skating	*ais*-low-fen	*Eislaufen*
kayaking	*kaa*-yahk-faa-ren	*Kajakfahren*
paragliding	*glait*-shirm-flee-gen	*Gleitschirmfliegen*
parachuting	*fahl*-shirm-shpring-en	*Fallschirmspringen*
rafting	*raaf*-ting	*Rafting*
rowing	*roo*-dern	*Rudern*
sailing	*zeh*-geln	*Segeln*
shuttlecock	*feh*-der-bahl	*Federball*
speed skating	*ais*-shnel-lowf	*Eisschnelllauf*
table tennis	*tish*-ten-nis	*Tischtennis*
volleyball	*vol*-li-bahl	*Volleyball*

GERMAN

Festivals

Karneval (northwest Germany); *Fasching* (south Germany)
the carnival starts at 11 minutes past 11 o'clock on 11 November and lasts until Ash Wednesday, *Aschermittwoch*. The main celebrations are held during the last week.

Maibäume (Maypole)
the erection of a Maypole in spring, either of tall fir or birch, is a 400-year-old tradition. The Maypole is decorated with colourful ribbons, and in rural regions a dance around the Maypole is held on 1 May.

Oktoberfest
held in Munich at the end of September to early October, this is Germany's biggest festival. It starts with a procession of beer brewers and their traditional horses and carts. The opening's highlight is the tapping of the first beer barrel by the mayor of Munich, who then shouts *O'zapft is!* 'the barrel is tapped'.

GERMAN

CHEERS!

Cheers!
  prawst!
  ain *praw*-zit der
  ge-*müüt*-likh-kait!
  oahns, tsvoa, ksuf-fah!

Prost!
Ein Prosit der Gemütlichkeit!
(lit: cheers on the friendliness!)
Oans, zwoa, Gsuffa!
(lit: one, two, booze!)

Weihnachten (Christmas)
Germany's most important celebration. The main celebration is on Christmas Eve. After traditional dishes of stuffed goose, *Weihnachtsgans* or Christmas carp, *Weihnachtskarpfen*, many people go to midnight Mass.

Merry Christmas!   *frer*-li-khe   *Fröhliche*
                     vai-nakh-ten!   *Weihnachten!*

GERMAN

IN THE COUNTRY
Weather

What's the weather like?

vee ist dahs *vet*-ter?		*Wie ist das Wetter?*

The weather's ... today.	dahs vet-ter ist hoy-te ...	*Das Wetter ist heute ...*
cloudy	*vol*-kikh	*wolkig*
cold	kahlt	*kalt*
fine	shern	*schön*
foggy	*neh*-blikh	*neblig*
frosty	*fros*-tikh	*frostig*
hot	hais	*heiß*
muggy	shvüül	*schwül*
stormy	*shtür*-mish	*stürmisch*
warm	vahrm	*warm*
windy	*vin*-dikh	*windig*

Camping

Am I/Are we allowed to camp here?

kahn ikh/kern-nen veer heer *tsel*-ten?	*Kann ich/Können wir hier zelten?*

Is there a campsite nearby?

gipt es in der nair-e ai-nen *kem*-ping-plahts?	*Gibt es in der Nähe einen Campingplatz?*

How much do you charge ...?	vee-feel be-*rekh*-nen zee ...?	*Wieviel berechnen Sie ...?*
per person	praw per-*zawn*	*pro Person*
for a tent	füür ain *tselt*	*für ein Zelt*

can opener	*daw*-zen-erf-ner	Dosenöffner
firewood	*bren*-holts	Brennholz
hammock	*heng*-e-maht-te	Hängematte
kettle	*kes*-sel	Kessel
matches	*shtraikh*-herl-tser	Streichhölzer
penknife	*tah*-shen-mes-ser	Taschenmesser
sleeping bag	*shlaaf*-zahk	Schlafsack
stove	hert	Herd
tent	tselt	Zelt
tent pegs	*tselt*-hair-ring-e	Zeltheringe
torch (flashlight)	*tah*-shen-lahm-pe	Taschenlampe

GERMAN

FOOD

breakfast	*früü*-shtük	Frühstück
lunch	*mit*-taak-es-sen	Mittagessen
dinner	*aa*-bent-es-sen	Abendessen

Vegetarian Meals

Do you serve vegetarian meals?
haa-ben zee owkh   *Haben Sie auch*
ve-ge-*taa*-ri-she kost?   *vegetarische Kost?*

I'm (m/f) a vegetarian.
ikh bin ve-ge-*taa*-ri-er/   *Ich bin Vegetarier/in.*
ve-ge-*taa*-ri-er-in

I'm (m/f) a vegan.
ikh bin maa-kro-   *Ich bin Makrobiotiker/in.*
bi-*aw*-ti-ker/in

I don't eat ...	ikh *es*-se ...	Ich esse ...
chicken	kain *hüün*-khen	kein Hühnchen
fish	kai-nen fish	keinen Fisch
meat	kain flaish	kein Fleisch
pork	kain	kein
	shvai-ne-flaish	Schweinefleisch

GERMAN

Staple Foods & Condiments

bread roll	*brert*-khen	*Brötchen*
cinnamon	tsimt	*Zimt*
cloves	*nel*-ken	*Nelken*
croissant	kro-ah-*sō*	*Croissant*
fish	fish	*Fisch*
fruit	*frükh*-te/awpst	*Früchte/Obst*
garlic	*knawp*-lowkh	*Knoblauch*
ham	*shing*-ken	*Schinken*
herbs	*kroy*-ter	*Kräuter*
meat	flaish	*Fleisch*
mustard	zenf	*Senf*
parsley	peh-ter-*zee*-lye	*Petersilie*
pepper	*pfef*-fer	*Pfeffer*
potatoes	kahr-*to*-feln	*Kartoffeln*
salt	zahlts	*Salz*
tomato sauce	to-maa-ten-*ket*-shahp	*Tomatenketchup*
vegetables	ge-*müü*-ze	*Gemüse*
vinegar	*es*-sikh	*Essig*

Breakfast Menu

cereal	tse-re-*aa*-li-en	*Zerealien*
honey	*haw*-nikh	*Honig*
jam	...-mahr-me-*laa*-de	*...-marmelade*
apricot	ah-pri-*kaw*-zen	*Aprikosen*
strawberry	*ert*-bair	*Erdbeer*
juice	*frukht*-zahft	*Fruchtsaft ...*
marmalade	o-rō-zhen-mahr-me-*laa*-de	*Orangenmarmelade*
muesli	*müüs*-li	*Müesli*
porridge	*haa*-fer-brai	*Haferbrei*
sausage	vurst	*Wurst*
boiled eggs	ge-*kokh*-te *ai*-er	*gekochte Eier*
fried eggs	*shpee*-gel-ai	*Spiegelei*
scrambled eggs	*rüür*-ai-er	*Rühreier*

MENU DECODER

Starters & Buffet Meals

Aufschnitt	*owf*-shnit	cold cuts
Bauernsuppe	*bow*-ern-zup-pe	'farmer's soup' (cabbage & sausage)
belegtes Brot	be-*lehk*-tes brawt	open sandwich
Brezel	*breh*-tsel	pretzel
Fleischbrühe	*flaish*-brüü-e	bouillon
Gemüsesuppe	ge-*müü*-ze-zup-pe	vegetable soup
geräucherte Forelle	ge-*roy*-kher-te fo-*rel*-le	smoked trout
geräucherter Lachs	ge-*roy*-kher-ter lahks	smoked salmon
geräucherter Schinken	ge-*roy*-kher-ter *shing*-ken	smoked ham
Linsensuppe	*lin*-zen-zup-pe	lentil soup
Pfannkuchen	*pfahn*-koo-khen	pancake
Rollmops	*rol*-mops	pickled herrings
Russische Eier	*rus*-si-she ai-er	eggs with mayonnaise
Zwiebelsuppe	*tsvee*-bel-zup-pe	onion soup
Wurst	vurst	sausage
Wurstplatte	*vurst*-plaht-te	cold cuts
Blutwurst	*bloot*-vurst	blood sausage
Bockwurst	*bok*-vurst	pork sausage
Bratwurst	*braat*-vurst	fried pork sausage
Leberwurst	*leh*-ber-vurst	liver sausage
Weißwurst	*vais*-vurst	veal sausage
Zwiebelwurst	*tsvee*-bel-vurst	liver-and-onion sausage

Main Dishes

Brathuhn	*braat*-hoon	roast chicken
Eintopf/Ragout	*ain*-topf/rah-*goo*	stew
Frikadelle	fri-kah-*del*-le	meatball
Hackbraten	*hahk*-braa-ten	meatloaf
Hasenpfeffer	*haa*-zen-pfef-fer	hare stew with mushroom and onion

GERMAN

GERMAN

Holsteiner Schnitzel	*hol*-shtai-ner *shnit*-tsel	veal schnitzel with fried egg, accompanied by seafood
Kohlroulade	kawl-ru-*laa*-de	cabbage leaves stuffed with minced meat
Königsberger Klopse	*ker*-nikhs-ber-ger *klop*-se	meatballs in a sour-cream-and-caper sauce
Labskaus	*lahps*-kows	thick meat-and-potato stew
Schlachtplatte	*shlahkht*-plaht-te	selection of pork and sausage
Schmorbraten	*shmawr*-braa-ten	beef pot roast
Schweinebraten	*shvai*-ne-braa-ten	roast pork
Wiener Schnitzel	*vee*-ner shnit-tsel	crumbed veal

Dessert & Pastries

Apfelstrudel	ahp-fel-*shtroo*-del	apple strudel
Cremespeise	*krehm*-shpai-ze	mousse
Gebäck	ge-*bek*	pastries
Kompott	kom-pot	stewed fruit
Königstorte	*ker*-nikhs-tor-te	rum-flavoured fruit cake
Kuchen	*koo*-khen	cake
Obstsalat	*awpst*-zah-laat	fruit salad
Schwarzwälder Kirschtorte	*shvahrts*-vel-der *kirsh*-tor-te	Black Forest cake (chocolate layer cake filled with cream and cherries)
Spekulatius	shpe-ku-*laa*-tsi-us	almond biscuits
Torte	*tor*-te	layer cake
Nürnberger Lebkuchen	*nürn*-ber-ger *lehp*-koo-khen	spicy biscuits with chocolate, nuts, fruit peel and honey

Non-Alcoholic Drinks

malt beer	*mahlts*-beer	*Malzbier*
mineral water	mi-ne-*raal*-vahs-ser	*Mineralwasser*
orange juice	o-*rō*-zhen-zahft	*Orangensaft*
water	*vahs*-ser	*Wasser*
coffee	*kahf*-feh	*Kaffee*
latte	*milkh*-kahf-feh	*Milchkaffee*
tea	teh	*Tee*
Vienna coffee (black, topped with whipped cream)	*kahf*-feh mit *zaa*-ne	*Kaffee mit Sahne*
with/without ...	mit/*aw*-ne ...	*mit/ohne* ...
cream	*zaa*-ne	*Sahne*
milk	milkh	*Milch*
sugar	*tsuk*-ker	*Zucker*

Alcoholic Drinks

apple brandy	*ahp*-fel-shnahps	*Apfelschnaps*
apple cider	*ahp*-fel-vain	*Apfelwein*
champagne	zekt/ shahm-*pahn*-yer	*Sektl Champagner*
spirit made from grain	shnahps	*Schnaps*
draught beer	beer fom *fahs*	*Bier vom Fass*
bitter	*ahlt*-beer	*Altbier*
dark beer	*bok*-beer	*Bockbier*
wheat-based beer	*vai*-tsen-beer	*Weizenbier*
strong beer	*shtahrk*-beer	*Starkbier*
... wine	... vain	... *wein*
dry	*trok*-ken	*trocken*
mulled	glüü	*Glüh*
red	rawt	*Rot*
sparkling	showm	*Schaum*
sweet	züüs	*süß*
white	vais	*Weiß*

GERMAN

GERMAN

AT THE MARKET

Basics

bread	brawt	Brot
butter	*but*-ter	Butter
cereal	tse-re-*aa*-li-en	Zerealien
cheese	*kair*-ze	Käse
chocolate	sho-ko-*laa*-de	Schokolade
croissant	kro-ah-*sō*	Croissant
eggs	*ai*-er	Eier
flour	mayl	Mehl
margarine	mahr-gah-*ree*-ne	Margarine
marmalade	o-rō-zhen-mahr-me-*laa*-de	Orangenmarmelade
milk	milkh	Milch
olive oil	o-*lee*-ven-erl/erl	Olivenöl/Öl
pasta	*pahs*-tah/*noo*-deln	Pasta/Nudeln
rice	rais	Reis
sugar	*tsuk*-kehr	Zucker (m)
yogurt	*yaw*-gurt	Joghurt
(mineral) water	(mi-ne-*raal*) vahs-ser	(Mineral)wasser

Meat & Poultry

beef	*rint*-flaish	Rindfleisch
chicken	*hüün*-khen	Hühnchen
ham	*shing-ken*	Schinken
meat	flaish	Fleisch
pork	*shvai*-neh-flaish	Schweinefleisch
sausage	vurst	Wurst
turkey	*troot*-haan	Truthahn
veal	*kahlp*-flaish	Kalbfleisch

Vegetables

beans	*baw*-ne	Bohnen
beetroot	*raw*-te *beh*-te	Rote Beete
cabbage	kawl	Kohl
carrot	kah-*rot*-te	Karotte
cauliflower	*bloo*-men-kawl	Blumenkohl

AT THE MARKET

celery	zel-le-ree	Sellerie
cucumber	gur-ke	Gurke
lettuce	kopf-zah-laat	Kopfsalat
mushroom	pilts	Pilz
onion	tsvee-bel	Zwiebel
peas	erp-se	Erbse
potatoes	kahr-to-feln	Kartoffeln
pumpkin	kür-bis	Kürbis
spinach	shpi-naat	Spinat
tomato	to-maa-te	Tomate
vegetables	ge-müü-ze	Gemüse

Seafood

fish	fish	Fisch
lobster	hum-mer	Hummer
mussels	mu-sheln	Muschel
oysters	ows-tern	Austern
shrimp	gahr-neh-le	Garnele

Pulses

broad beans	sow-baw-ne	Saubohne
chickpeas	keekh-ehr-erb-se	Kichererbse
lentils	leen-se	Linse

Fruit

apple	ahp-fel	Apfel
apricot	ah-pri-kaw-ze	Aprikose
banana	bah-naa-ne	Banane
date	daht-tel	Dattel
fruit	frükh-te/awpst	Früchte/Obst
grapes	vain-trow-be	Weintraube
lemon	tsi-traw-ne	Zitrone
orange	ahp-fel-zee-ne	Apfelsine
peach	pfir-zikh	Pfirsich
pear	bir-ne	Birne
plum	pflow-me	Pflaume
strawberry	ert-bair-re	Erdbeere

GERMAN

SHOPPING

Do you accept credit cards?
neh-men zee kre-*deet*-kahr-ten? *Nehmen Sie Kreditkarten?*

bakery	bek-ke-*rai*	*Bäckerei*
bookshop	*bookh*-hahn-dlung	*Buchhandlung*
chemist	ah-po-*teh*-ke	*Apotheke*
delicatessen	de-li-kah-*tes*-s en-ge-sheft	*Delikatessen-geschäft*
grocer	*leh*-bens-mit-tel-laa-den	*Lebensmittelladen*
hairdresser	fri-*zerr*	*Friseur*
laundry	ve-she-*rai*	*Wäscherei*
market	mah*rkt*	*Markt*
newsagent	*tsai*-tungks-hen-dler	*Zeitungshändler*
supermarket	*zoo*-per-mahrkt	*Supermarkt*

Essential Groceries

I'd like to buy ...	ikh *merkh*-te ...	*Ich möchte ...*
batteries	baht-te-*ree*-en	*Batterien*
bread	brawt	*Brot*
butter	*but*-ter	*Butter*
cheese	*kair*-ze	*Käse*
chocolate	sho-ko-*laa*-de	*Schokolade*
coffee	*kahf*-feh	*Kaffee*
ham	*shing*-ken	*Schinken*
matches	*shtraikh*-herl-tser	*Streichhölzer*
milk	milkh	*Milch*
mineral water	mi-ne-*raal*-vahs-ser	*Mineralwasser*
flour	mehl	*Mehl*
shampoo	shahm-*poo*	*Shampoo*
soap	*zai*-fe	*Seife*
sugar	*tsuk*-ker	*Zucker*
tea	teh	*Tee*
toilet paper	to-ah-*let*-ten-pah-peer	*Toilettenpapier*
toothpaste	*tsaan*-pahs-tah	*Zahnpasta*
washing powder	*ahsh*-pul-ver	*Waschpulver*
yogurt	*yaw*-gurt	*Joghurt*

Souvenirs

beer stein/mug	*beer*-krook	*Bierkrug*
cuckoo clock	kuk-*kuks*-oor	*Kuckucksuhr*
earrings	*awr*-ring-e	*Ohrringe*
embroidery	shtik-ke-*rai*	*Stickerei*
handicraft	*kunst*-hahnt-verk	*Kunsthandwerk*
necklace	*hahls*-ket-te	*Halskette*
porcelain	por-tsel-*laan*	*Porzellan*
ring	ring	*Ring*

GERMAN

Clothing

belt	*gür*-tel	*Gürtel*
bra	*büs*-ten-hahl-ter	*Büstenhalter*
button	knopf	*Knopf*
clothing	*klai*-dung	*Kleidung*
coat	*mahn*-tel	*Mantel*
dress	klait	*Kleid*
jacket	*yahk*-ke	*Jacke*
jumper (sweater)	*pul*-law-ver	*Pullover*
raincoat	*reh*-gen-mahn-tel	*Regenmantel*
panties	*shlüp*-fer; slip	*Schlüpfer*
scarf	*hahls*-tookh	*Halstuch*
shirt	hemt	*Hemd*
shoes	*shoo*-e	*Schuhe*
skirt	rok	*Rock*
trousers	*haw*-ze	*Hose*
T-shirt	*tee*-shert	*T-Shirt*

GERMAN

Materials

brass	*mes*-sing	*Messing*
cotton	*bowm*-vol-le	*Baumwolle*
gold	golt	*Gold*
leather	*leh*-der	*Leder*
linen	*lai*-nen	*Leinen*
silk	*zai*-de	*Seide*
silver	*zil*-ber	*Silber*
velvet	zahmt	*Samt*
wool	vol-le	*Wolle*

Colours

black	shvahrts	*schwarz*
blue	blow	*blau*
brown	brown	*braun*
green	grüün	*grün*
grey	grow	*grau*
orange	o-*rōzh*	*orange*
pink	*raw*-zah	*rosa*
purple	*lee*-lah	*lila*
red	rawt	*rot*
white	vais	*weiß*
yellow	gelp	*gelb*

Toiletries

comb	kahm	*Kamm*
condoms	kon-*daw*-me	*Kondome*
deodorant	de-o-do-*rahnt*	*Deodorant*
moisturiser	*foykh*-tikh-kaits-krehm	*Feuchtigkeitscreme*
razor	rah-*zee*-rer	*Rasierer*
razor blades	rah-*zeer*-kling-en	*Rasierklingen*
sanitary napkins	*daa*-men-bin-den	*Damenbinden*
shampoo	shahm-*poo*	*Shampoo*
shaving cream	rah-*zeer*-krehm	*Rasiercreme*
sunscreen	*zon*-nen-shuts-krehm	*Sonnenschutzcreme*
tampons	tahm-*pons*	*Tampons*
tissues	pah-*peer*-tüü-kher	*Papiertücher*
toothbrush	*tsaan*-bürs-te	*Zahnbürste*

Stationery & Publications

envelope	*breef*-um-shlaak	*Briefumschlag*
map	*kahr*-te	*Karte*
paper	pah-*peer*	*Papier*
pen	*koo*-gel-shrai-ber	*Kugelschreiber*
postcard	*pawst*-kahr-te	*Postkarte*
writing paper	*breef*-pah-peer	*Briefpapier*
English-language ...	... owf *eng*-lish	... *auf Englisch*
newspaper	*tsai*-tung	*Zeitung*
novels	ro-*maa*-ne	*Romane*

Photography

I'd like to have this film developed.
  bit-te ent-*vik*-keln   *Bitte entwickeln*
  zee dee-zen *film*   *Sie diesen Film.*
When will the photos be ready?
  vahn zint dee faw-tos   *Wann sind die Fotos*
  fer-tikh?   *fertig?*
I'd like a film for this camera.
  ikh merkh-te ai-nen *film*   *Ich möchte einen Film*
  füür dee-ze *kah*-me-rah   *für diese Kamera.*

B&W	*shvahrts*-vais	*schwarzweiß*
battery	baht-te-*ree*	*Batterie*
camera	*kah*-me-rah	*Kamera*
colour film	*fahrp*-film	*Farbfilm*
colour slide film	fahrp-*di*-ah-film	*Farbdiafilm*
film	film	*Film*
flash	blits	*Blitz*
lens	op-yek-*teef*	*Objektiv*
print	*ahp*-tsook	*Abzug*
slide	*di*-ah	*Dia*

GERMAN

Smoking

A packet of cigarettes, please.

ai-ne shahkh-tel	*Eine Schachtel*	
tsi-gah-*ret*-ten, bit-te	*Zigaretten bitte.*	

Do you have a light?

haa-ben zee *foy*-er?	*Haben Sie Feuer?*

cigarette papers	tsi-gah-*ret*-ten-pah-peer	*Zigarettenpapier*
cigarettes	tsi-gah-*ret*-ten	*Zigaretten*
filtered	mit *fil*-ter	*mit Filter*
lighter	*foy*-er-tsoyk	*Feuerzeug*
matches	*shtraikh*-herl-tser	*Streichhölzer*
menthol	men-*tawl*	*Menthol*
pipe	*pfai*-fe	*Pfeife*
tobacco (pipe)	tah-*bahk*	*Tabak*

Sizes & Comparisons

also	owkh	*auch*
big	graws	*groß*
enough	ge-*nookh*	*genug*
heavy	shvair	*schwer*
light	laikht	*leicht*
a little bit	ain *bis*-khen	*ein bisschen*
many	*fee*-le	*viele*
more	mair	*mehr*
less (not so much/ many)	nikht zaw feel/*fee*-le	*nicht so viel/viele*
small	klain	*klein*
too much/many	tsu feel/fee-le	*zu viel/viele*

HEALTH

Parts of the Body

ankle	*kner*-khel	*Knöchel*	head	kopf	*Kopf*
arm	ahrm	*Arm*	knee	knee	*Knie*
back	*rük*-ken	*Rücken*	leg	bain	*Bein*
chest	brust	*Brust*	nose	*naa*-ze	*Nase*
ear	awr	*Ohr*	skin	howt	*Haut*
eye	*ow*-ge	*Auge*	stomach	*maa*-gen	*Magen*
finger	*fing*-er	*Finger*	teeth	*tsair*-ne	*Zähne*
foot	foos	*Fuß*	throat	hahls	*Hals*
hand	hahnt	*Hand*			

GERMAN

Ailments

I'm sick.	meer ist *shlekht*	*Mir ist schlecht.*
My ... hurt/s.	meer toot ... veh	*Mir tut ... weh.*

I have (a/an) ...	ikh *haa*-be ...	*Ich habe ...*
allergy	ai-ne ahl-ler-*gee*	*eine Allergie*
constipation	fer-*shtop*-fung	*Verstopfung*
cough	*hoo*-sten	*Husten*
diarrhoea	*durkh*-fahl	*Durchfall*
fever	*fee*-ber	*Fieber*
infection	ai-ne in-fek-*tsyawn*	*eine Infektion*
influenza	dee *grip*-pe	*die Grippe*
nausea	*üü*-bel-kait	*Übelkeit*
pain	*shmer*-tsen	*Schmerzen*
sore throat	*hahls*-shmer-tsen	*Halsschmerzen*
sprain	ai-ne *mus*-kel-tser-rung	*eine Muskelzerrung*
venereal disease	ai-ne ge-*shlekhts*-krahngk-hait	*eine Geschlechtskrankheit*
worms	*vür*-mer	*Würmer*

GERMAN

Useful Words & Phrases

Where's a/the ...?	vaw ist ...?	*Wo ist ...?*
chemist	dee ah-po-*teh*-ke	*die Apotheke*
dentist	der *tsaan*-ahrtst	*der Zahnarzt*
doctor	ain ahrtst	*ein Arzt*
hospital	dahs *krahng*-ken-hows	*das Krankenhaus*
I'm allergic	ikh bin ahl-*ler*-gish	*Ich bin allergisch*
to ...	geh-gen ...	*gegen ...*
antibiotics	ahn-ti-bi-*aw*-ti-kah	*Antibiotika*
penicillin	pe-ni-tsi-*leen*	*Penizillin*

At the Chemist

Which chemist is open at night?

vel-khe ah-po-*teh*-ke	*Welche Apotheke*
haht *nahkht*-deenst	*hat Nachtdienst*
ge-*erf*-net?	*geöffnet?*

I need medication for ...

ikh *brow*-khe et-vahs	*Ich brauche etwas*
geh-gen ...	*gegen ...*

antiseptic	ahn-ti-*zep*-ti-kum	*Antiseptikum*
bandage	fer-*bahnts*-mah-te-ri-aal	*Verbandsmaterial*
cough mixture	*hoo*-sten-zahft	*Hustensaft*
laxative	*ahp*-füür-mit-tel	*Abführmittel*
painkillers	*shmerts*-mit-tel	*Schmerzmittel*

At the Dentist

I have a toothache.

ikh haa-be *tsaan*-shmer-tsen	*Ich habe Zahnschmerzen.*

I've lost a filling.

ikh haa-be ai-ne *füil*-lung fer-*law*-ren	*Ich habe eine Füllung verloren.*

My gums hurt.

dahs *tsaan*-flaish toot meer veh	*Das Zahnfleisch tut mir weh.*

I don't want it extracted.
  ikh vil een nikht   *Ich will ihn nicht*
  tsee-en lahs-sen   *ziehen lassen.*
Can you fix it temporarily?
  kern-nen zee es pro-vi-   *Können Sie es provisorisch*
  zaw-rish be-hahn-deln?   *behandeln?*

abscess	*ahps*-tses	*Abszess*
anaesthetic	be-*toy*-bung	*Betäubung*
to extract	*tsee*-en	*ziehen*
infection	ent-*tsün*-dung	*Entzündung*
tooth	tsaan	*Zahn*
toothache	*tsaan*-shmer-tsen	*Zahnschmerzen*

GERMAN

TIME & DATES
Time

What time is it?	vee *spairt* ist es?	*Wie spät ist es?*

It's ...	es ist ...	*Es ist ...*
3 o'clock	*drai* oor	*drei Uhr*
3.15	feer-tel naakh *drai*	*Viertel nach drei*
3.30	hahlp *feer*	*halb vier*
3.45	feer-tel fawr *feer*	*Viertel vor vier*

Days

Monday	*mawn*-taak	*Montag*
Tuesday	*deens*-taak	*Dienstag*
Wednesday	*mit*-vokh	*Mittwoch*
Thursday	*don*-ners-taak	*Donnerstag*
Friday	*frai*-taak	*Freitag*
Saturday	*zahms*-taak/	*Samstag/*
	zon-*aa*-bent	*Sonnabend*
Sunday	*zon*-taak	*Sonntag*

GERMAN

Months

January	yahn-oo-*aar*	*Januar*
February	feh-broo-*aar*	*Februar*
March	mairts	*März*
April	ah-*pril*	*April*
May	mai	*Mai*
June	*yoo*-ni	*Juni*
July	*yoo*-li	*Juli*
August	ow-*gust*	*August*
September	zep-*tem*-ber	*September*
October	ok-*taw*-ber	*Oktober*
November	no-*vem*-ber	*November*
December	deh-*tsem*-ber	*Dezember*

Seasons

spring	*früü*-ling	*Frühling*
summer	*zom*-mer	*Sommer*
autumn	herpst	*Herbst*
winter	*vin*-ter	*Winter*

Present

now	yetst	*jetzt*
immediately	zo-*fort*/glaikh	*sofort/gleich*
today	*hoy*-te	*heute*
this morning	hoy-te *mor*-gen	*heute morgen*
this afternoon	hoy-te *naakh*-mit-taak	*heute nachmittag*
tonight	hoy-te *aa*-bent	*heute abend*
this week	dee-ze *vo*-khe	*diese Woche*
this month	dee-zen *maw*-naht	*diesen Monat*
this year	dee-zes *yaar*	*dieses Jahr*

Past

yesterday morning/ afternoon	*ges*-tern mor-*gen*/ *naakh*-mit-taak	*gestern Morgen/ Nachmittag*
last night	lets-te *nahkht*	*letzte Nacht*
day before yesterday	*foor*-ges-tern	*vorgestern*
last week	lets-te *vo*-khe	*letzte Woche*
last year	lets-tes *yaar*	*letztes Jahr*

Future

tomorrow ...	mor-gen ...	*morgen ...*
morning	*früü*	*früh*
afternoon	*naakh*-mit-taak	*nachmittag*
evening	*aa*-bent	*abend*
day after tomorrow	*üü*-ber-mor-gen	*übermorgen*
next week	nairkhs-te *vo*-khe	*nächste Woche*
next year	nairkhs-tes *yaar*	*nächstes Jahr*

During the Day

afternoon	*naakh*-mit-taak	*Nachmittag*
day	taak	*Tag*
early	früü	*früh*
midnight	*mit*-ter-nahkht	*Mitternacht*
morning	*mor*-gen	*Morgen*
night	nahkht	*Nacht*
noon	*mit*-taak	*Mittag*
sunrise	*zon*-nen-owf-gahng	*Sonnenaufgang*
sunset	*zon*-nen-un-ter-gahng	*Sonnenuntergang*

GERMAN

NUMBERS & AMOUNTS

0	nul	*null*
1	ains	*eins*
2	tsvai; (tsvaw)	*zwei; (zwo)*
3	drai	*drei*
4	feer	*vier*
5	fünf	*fünf*
6	zeks	*sechs*
7	zee-ben	*sieben*
8	ahkht	*acht*
9	noyn	*neun*
10	tsehn	*zehn*
11	elf	*elf*
12	tsverlf	*zwölf*

ZWEI – ZWO

Zwo is used instead of zwei when giving numbers over the phone. It's also used when giving someone your phone number.

GERMAN

13	*drai*-tsehn	dreizehn
14	*feer*-tsehn	vierzehn
15	*fünf*-tsehn	fünfzehn
16	*zekh*-tsehn	sechzehn
17	*zeep*-tsehn	siebzehn
18	*ahkht*-tsehn	achtzehn
19	*noyn*-tsehn	neunzehn
20	*tsvahn*-tsikh	zwanzig
21	*ain*-unt-tsvahn-tsikh	einundzwanzig
22	*tsvai*-unt-tsvahn-tsikh	zweiundzwanzig
30	*drai*-sikh	dreißig
40	*feer*-tsikh	vierzig
50	*fünf*-tsikh	fünfzig
60	*zekh*-tsikh	sechzig
70	*zeep*-tsikh	siebzig
80	*ahkht*-tsikh	achtzig
90	*noyn*-tsikh	neunzig
100	(ain-) *hun*-dert	(ein)hundert
1000	(ain-) *tow*-zent	(ein)tausend
one million	ai-ne mil-*yawn*	eine Million

ABBREVIATIONS

ADAC	AA (Automobile Association)	*Hbf.*	Main railway station
Ausw.	ID	*Hr./Fr.*	Mr/Mrs
Bhf.	Railway station	*KW*	Short Wave
BLZ	Bank code	*n. Chr./v. Chr.*	AD/BC
BRD	Federal Republic of Germany	*N/S*	Nth/Sth
		PLZ	Post code
DB	German Federal Railways	*Str.*	St/Rd/etc
DJH	Youth Hostel	*U(-Bahn)*	Underground (Railway)
DM	German Mark	*usw.*	etc
EG	EC	*vorm./nachm.*	am/pm
GB	UK	*z.B.*	eg

EMERGENCIES

Help!	*hil*-fe!	*Hilfe!*
Thief!	deep!	*Dieb!*
Fire!	*foy*-er!	*Feuer!*
Go away!	geh-en zee *vek*!	*Gehen Sie weg!*

Please call the police!
    roo-fen zee bit-te dee   *Rufen Sie bitte die*
    po-li-*tsai*!   *Polizei!*
Where's the nearest police station?
    vaw ist dahs nairkhs-te   *Wo ist das nächste*
    po-li-*tsai*-re-veer?   *Polizeirevier?*
Could you help me, please?
    kern-ten zee meer   *Könnten Sie mir*
    bit-te *hel*-fen?   *bitte helfen?*
Could I please use the telephone?
    kern-te ikh bit-te dahs   *Könnte ich bitte das*
    teh-le-*fawn* be-nut-tsen?   *Telefon benutzen?*
Call a doctor!
    haw-len zee ai-nen *ahrtst*!   *Holen Sie einen Arzt!*
Call an ambulance!
    roo-fen zee ai-nen   *Rufen Sie einen*
    krahng-ken-vaa-gen!   *Krankenwagen!*
I have medical insurance.
    ikh bin *krahng*-ken-   *Ich bin krankenversichert.*
    fer-*zi*-khert
I'm lost.
    ikh haa-be mikh fer-*irt*   *Ich habe mich verirrt.*

GERMAN

Dealing with the Police

I want to report a/an...	ikh merkh-te ai-nen ... *ahn*-tsai-gen	*Ich möchte einen ... anzeigen.*
accident	*un*-fahl	*Unfall*
attack	*üü*-ber-fahl	*Überfall*
loss	fer-*lust*	*Verlust*
theft	*deep*-shtaal	*Diebstahl*

GERMAN

I'm sorry. I apologise.
es toot meer *lait*. ent-*shul*-di-gen zee bit-te
Es tut mir leid. Entschuldigen Sie bitte.

Can I make a phone call?
kahn ikh maal teh-le-fo-*nee*-ren?
Kann ich mal telefonieren?

I want to see a lawyer.
ikh merkh-te ai-nen *ahn*-vahlt shpre-khen
Ich möchte einen Anwalt sprechen.

I want to contact my ...	ikh *merkh*-te mikh mit ... in fer-*bin*-dung zet-tsen	*Ich möchte mich mit ... in Verbindung setzen.*
consulate	mai-nem kon-zu-*laat*	*meinem Konsulat*
embassy	mai-ner *bawt*-shahft	*meiner Botschaft*

GREEK

QUICK REFERENCE

Hello.	yi-a sas	Γειά σας.
Goodbye.	che-re-te/an-di-o	Χαίρετε./Αντίο.
Please.	pa-ra-ka-lo	Παρακαλώ.
Thank you.	ef-cha-ri-sto	Ευχαριστώ.
You're welcome.	pa-ra-ka-lo	Παρακαλώ.
Excuse me.	sigh-no-mi	Συγγνώμη.
Yes./No.	ne/o-chi	Ναι./Όχι.
How are you?	ti ka-ne-te?	Τι κάνετε;
Well thanks.	ka-la ef-cha-ri-sto	Καλά ευχαριστώ.
How do I get to ...?	pos pa-ne sto ...?	Πώς πάνε στο ...;
Straight ahead.	o-lo ef-thi-a	Όλο ευθεία.
Turn left/right.	strip-ste a-ris-te-ra/ dhek-si-a.	Στρίψτε αριστερά/ δεξιά.
What time is it?	ti o-ra i-ne?	Τι ώρα είναι;
How much is it?	po-so ka-ni?	Πόσο κάνει;

I'd like (a) ...	tha i-thel-a (e-na) ...	Θα ήθελα (ένα) ...
ticket.	i-si-ti-ri-o	εισιτήριο.
one-way	ap-lo	απλό
return	e-na	ένα

I (don't) understand.
  (dhen) ka-ta-la-ve-no   (Δεν) καταλαβαίνω.
Do you speak English?
  mi-la-te ang-li-ka?   Μιλάτε Αγγλικά;
Do you have any rooms?
  e-che-te e-lef-the-ra   Έχετε ελεύθερα
  dho-ma-ti-a?   δωμάτια;
Where are the toilets?
  pu i-ne i tu-a-le-tes?   Πού είναι οι τουαλέτες;

1	e-nas	ένας	6	ek-si	έξι
2	dhi-o	δύο	7	ef-ta/ep-ta	εφτά/επτά
3	tris	τρεις	8	och-to/ok-to	οχτώ/οκτώ
4	te-se-ris	τέσσερις	9	e-ni-a/e-ne-a	εννιά/εννέα
5	pen-de	πέντε	10	dhe-ka	δέκα

GREEK

Some of the most influential texts in Western European history have been written in Greek – the works of Homer, the first ever history by Herodotus, and the philosophical works of Plato and Aristotle.

With the rise in power of the Athenian state in the 5th century BC, *Attic* became the predominant Greek dialect used in literary works and all forms of intellectual expression. This form of Greek spread with Alexander the Great's empire stretching from Macedon to the shores of the Indus river. By the end of the first millennium BC, the conquered people of western Asia, Egypt and southern Italy used Greek to conduct all their commercial, administrative and military affairs.

Attic was the foundation of *Koine*, 'the common language' – a very simplified form of the language. Stripped of much of its grammatical complexity, *Koine* had assimilated elements of dialects spoken by the conquered peoples of the empire.

Centuries later, after the liberation of Greece in 1832, the dilemma of which language to adopt as the official language split scholars into two camps. It was clear that *Attic* in its pure, classical form was no longer viable, but many supported a language, close to *Attic*, that was 'cleansed' of all foreign elements. From this movement sprang *Katharevousa* (*katharos* means 'clean'). *Koine* or *laiki* (meaning 'popular') had equally strong support as the language most people used and understood, and one that could be implemented into the education system to raise literacy levels.

By the early 20th century, the *Koine*, now known as *Dhimotiki*, 'popular', became the accepted form of Greek.

GENDER

Some nouns have both masculine and feminine forms. Where nouns have two genders, these are separated with a slash, with the masculine form first.

Dhimotiki suffered a temporary blow during the years of the military dictatorship (1967–1974) when the purist *Katharevousa* was 'declared' as the official language, and many works written in demotic Greek were banned. However, *Dhimotiki* was re-established as the official language in 1974. The language underwent another wave of simplification in 1981, when all the accents, aspiration marks and archaic noun endings were abolished (at least in theory). More recently, and despite efforts from scholars, it has been impossible to stop the invasion of American-English and French words from being accepted into the language.

This strong linguistic dichotomy between purist *Katharevousa* and *Dhimotiki* has plagued education and the development of the language to the present day. Doctors, lawyers, professors and even some journalists use *Katharevousa* for all legal and official documents, and *Dhimotiki* for everything else. Some newspapers are even published entirely in *Katharevousa*. A 'smartened-up', austere *Dhimotiki* almost verging on *Katharevousa* is still the mark of a well-educated person. Another paradox is that the form of ancient Greek taught in schools today is written using the full aspiration and accent system – developed for the benefit of modern Greek – that it never had in classical times. Modern Greek no longer uses these systems.

Whether you're a speaker of English, French, German, or even a Slavonic language, you'll soon recognise similarities to Greek words in your own language (such as 'father', which resembles the Greek πατήρ, pronounced patir). After all, Greek is an Indo-European language, with grammar and syntax that are very similar to most European languages. Having mastered some Greek, you'll have the satisfaction of having learnt a small part of a 4000 year old piece of history.

Dhimotiki has been used throughout this chapter.

PRONUNCIATION

The Greek alphabet may look daunting and unfriendly at first sight. However, at closer inspection you'll recognise several letters from the Roman alphabet. The 24 letters of the alphabet are listed here in upper then lower case, along with the transliteration used throughout this chapter.

Vowels

alpha	A	α	a	as the 'a' in 'bat'
epsilon	E	ε	e	as the 'e' in 'bet'
ita	H	η	i	as the 'i' in 'kiss'
yiota	I	ι	i	as the 'i' in 'kiss'
omikron	O	o	o	as the 'o' in 'hot'
ipsilon	Y	υ	i	as the 'i' in 'kiss'
omegha	Ω	ω	o	as the 'o' in 'hot'

Consonants

vita	B	β	v	as the 'v' in 'velvet'
ghama	Γ	γ	y	before *e* and *i*, as the 'y' in 'yes';
			gh	before *a*, *o* and *u*, as the 'ch' in 'loch', but voiced
dhelta	Δ	δ	dh	as the 'th' in 'then'
zita	Z	ζ	z	as the 'z' in 'zoo'
thita	Θ	θ	th	as the 'th' in 'theatre'
kapa	K	κ	k	as the 'k' in 'king'
lamdha	Λ	λ	l	as the 'l' in 'like'
mi	M	μ	m	as the 'm' in 'meal'
ni	N	ν	n	as the 'n' in 'naughty'
ksi	Ξ	ξ	ks	as the 'ks' in 'yaks'
pi	Π	π	p	as the 'p' in 'pace'
ro	P	ρ	r	trilled
sighma	Σ	σ (ς at the end of a word)		
			z	as the 'z' in 'zoo' before the sounds v, gh and m;
			s	elsewhere, as the 's' in 'sin'
taf	T	τ	t	as the 't' in 'tame'
fi	Φ	φ	f	as the 'f' in 'fun'
chi	X	χ	ch	as the 'h' in 'huge' before *i* and *e*;
			ch	elsewhere, as the 'ch' in scottish 'loch'
psi	Ψ	ψ	ps	as the 'ps' in 'lapse'

GREEK

Combined Letters

Several combinations of sounds may be unfamiliar to English-speakers. Some of these take a bit of practice.

Vowels

αι	e	as the 'e' in 'bet'
ει	i	as the 'i' in 'kiss'
οι	i	as the 'i' in 'kiss'
ου	u	as the 'u' in put
υι	i	as the 'i' in 'kiss'
αυ	av	as the 'av' in 'average';
	af	as the 'af' in 'after'
ευ	ef	as the 'ev' in 'ever'
	ev	as the 'ef' in 'left'

> **NO QUESTION**
>
> Question marks in Greek are written as a semi-colon (;) at the end of a sentence.

Consonants

γκ/γγ	g	as the 'g' in 'gap' at the beginning of a word;
	ng	as the 'ng' in 'English' in the middle of a word
γχ	nch	there's no real equivalent in English; try saying 'ng' followed immediately by the 'ch' in Scottish 'loch'
μπ	b	at the beginning of a word, as the 'b' in 'bed';
	mb	in the middle of a word, as the 'mb' in 'amber'
ντ	d	as the 'd' in 'dog' at the beginning of a word;
	nd	as the 'nd' in 'indigo' in the middle of a word
τζ	dz	as the 'dds' in 'adds'
τσ	ts	as the 'ts' in 'hats'

If two vowels occur together and aren't listed above, they should be pronounced separately. This is indicated in the transliteration by a hyphen.

animal	zo-o	ζώο

Double consonants aren't pronounced twice:

other	*a*-los	άλλος

Elision

When a word that ends in a vowel is followed by another word that starts with the same or a similar vowel sound, one vowel can usually be omitted. The two words are pronounced as if they were one. This is called elision.

Thank you.   se ef-cha-ri-*sto*   Σε ευχαριστώ.

becomes

Thank you.   sef-cha-ri-*sto*   Σ' ευχαριστώ.

Accents

The accent (´) is written only on vowels in Greek. In the case of combined letters, it's only ever written on the second letter:

ού, οί, αί, αύ, εύ

Where the accent is placed on the first of two vowels, it means that those two vowels should be pronounced separately:

May   *ma*-i-os   Μάιος

Where this may be confused with a combined vowel sound (see page 214), a diaeresis (¨) is used, to indicate that the two vowels should be pronounced separately:

popular   *la*-i-kos   λαϊκός

PRONOUNS		
I	e-*gho*	εγώ
you (sg, inf)	e-*si*	εσύ
he	af-*tos*	αυτός
she	af-*ti*	αυτή
it	af-*to*	αυτό
we	e-*mis*	εμείς
you (pl; sg, pol)	e-*sis*	εσείς
they (m)	af-*ti*	αυτοί
they (f)	af-*tes*	αυτές
they (n)	af-*ta*	αυτά

GREEK

Stress

Where a word is stressed is quite important, as stressing the wrong syllable could change the meaning of a word quite drastically:

| half | mi-*sos* | μισός |
| hatred | *mi*-sos | μίσος |

All stressed syllables appear in italics in this chapter.

GREETINGS & CIVILITIES
You Should Know

Hello.	yi-*a* sas	Γειά σας.
Goodbye.	*che*-re-te/an-*di*-o	Χαίρετε./Αντίο.
Please.	pa-ra-ka-*lo*	Παρακαλώ.
Thank you.	ef-cha-ri-*sto*	Ευχαριστώ.
Yes./No.	ne/*o*-chi	Ναι./Όχι.
Excuse me.	sigh-*no*-mi	Συγγνώμη.
Good morning.	ka-li-*me*-ra	Καλημέρα.
Good afternoon.	ka-li-*spe*-ra	Καλησπέρα.
Good night.	ka-li-*nich*-ta	Καληνύχτα.
How are you?	ti *ka*-ne-te?	Τι κάνετε;
Well thanks.	ka-*la* ef-cha-ri-*sto*	Καλά ευχαριστώ.

GREEK

NICE ONE!

Greeks love the term 'Have a nice ...!', so there's a greeting for every occasion:

ka-li ev-tho-ma-dha!	Have a good week! (on Mondays)
ka-lo mi-na!	Have a good month! (on the 1st of every month)
ka-lo ka-lo-ke-ri!	Have a good summer!
ka-li dhi-as-ke-dha-si!	Have a nice time!
ka-li o-ra!	(lit: good hour) said when you've been expecting someone to return

Forms of Address

The vast majority of Greek male names end in -s. When speaking to the person, though, the final 's' is dropped.

Nick (speaking of the person)	*ni*-kos
Nick (speaking directly to that person)	*ni*-ko

With a few names, as well as the word for 'Mr', the final vowel changes to e:

Alexander (speaking of the person)	al-ek-*san*-dhros
Alexander (speaking directly to that person)	al-ek-*san*-dhre

Mr (speaking of a person)	*ki*-ri-os	Κύριος
Mr (when addressing someone directly)	*ki*-ri-e	Κύριε

Female names don't change in this way.

SMALL TALK
Meeting People

Excuse me! (to attract attention)	pa-ra-ka-*lo*!	Παρακαλώ!
What's your name?	pos sas *le*-ne?	Πώς σας λένε;
My name's ...	me *le*-ne ...	Με λένε ...
Pleased to meet you.	che-ro po-*li*	Χαίρω πολύ.
Where do you live; Where are you staying?		
	pu *me*-ne-te ?	Πού μένετε;
I'm/We're staying at ...		
	me-no/*me*-nu-me sto ...	Μένω/Μένουμε στο ...
Do you like it here?		
	sas a-*re*-si e-*dho*?	Σας αρέσει εδώ;
I like it here very much.		
	ma-*re*-si po-*li* e-*dho*	Μ' αρέσει πολύ εδώ.

GREEK

GREEK

I'm with (my/a) ...	*i*-me e-*dho* me ...	Σίμαι εδώ με ...
family	tin i-ko-*ye*-ni-a mu	την οικογένεια μου
friend (m)	ton *fi*-lo mu	τον φίλο μου
friend (f)	tin *fi*-li mu	την φίλη μου
partner	to zev-*gha*-ri mu	το ζευγάρι μου

Goodbye, nice to meet you.
an-*dio*, *cha*-ri-ka ya tin
ghno-ri-*mia*

Αντίο, χάρηκα για την
γνωριμία.

Nationalities

You'll find that many country names in Greek are similar to those in English. If your country isn't listed here, try saying it with Greek pronunciation and you might be understood.

What nationality are you?
ti eth-ni-*ko*-ti-ta *i*-ste ?   Τι εθνικότητα είστε;

I'm from ...	*i*-me ap-*o* ...	Είμαι από ...
Australia	tin af-stra-*li*-a	την Αυστραλία
Canada	ton ka-na-*dha*	τον Καναδά
Cyprus	tin *kip*-ro	την Κύπρο
England	tin ang-*lia*	την Αγγλία
Ireland	tin ir-lan-*dhi*-a	την Ιρλανδία
New Zealand	ti *ne*-a zi-lan-*dhi*-a	τη Νέα Ζηλανδία
Scotland	tin sko-*ti*-a	την Σκωτία
South Africa	ti *no*-ti-o af-ri-*ki*	τη Νότιο Αφρική
the USA	tis *i*-pa/tin a-me-ri-*ki*	τις ΗΠΑ/την Αμερική
Wales	ti o-al-*li*-a	τη Ουαλλία

Occupations

What work do you do?

ti dhu-*lia ka*-ne-te?   Τι δουλειά κάνετε;

I'm a/an ...	*i*-me ...	Είμαι ...
artist	ka-li-*tech*-nis	καλλιτέχνης
business person	e-pi-chi-ri-ma-*ti*-as	επιχειρηματίας
doctor	yia-*tros*	γιατρός
farmer	agh-*ro*-tis	αγρότης
journalist	dhi-mo-si-o-*ghra*-fos	δημοσιογράφος
lawyer	dhi-ki-*gho*-ros	δικηγόρος
nurse	no-so-*ko*-mos/	νοσοκόμος/
	no-so-*ko*-ma	νοσοκόμα
student	fi-ti-*tis*/fi-*ti*-tri-a	φοιτητής/φοιτήτρια
teacher	*dhas*-ka-los/	δάσκαλος/
	dhas-*ka*-la	δασκάλα
waiter	ser-vi-*to*-ros/	σερβιτόρος/
	ser-vi-*to*-ra	σερβιτόρα

DID YOU KNOW ... The days from Monday to Thursday in Greek are simply called second, third, fourth and fifth respectively. When Greece adopted the seven-day week, they considered the European names to be pagan. The word for 'Friday' (see page 253) means 'the day of preparation' and 'Sunday' means 'the day of the master'.

GREEK

Religion

What's your religion?

ti *thris*-kev-ma *i*-ste ?	Τι θρήσκευμα είστε;

I'm (m/f) not religious.

dhen *i*-me *thris*-kos/*thris*-ki	Δεν είμαι θρήσκος/θρήσκη.

I believe in God.

pis-*te*-vo sto the-*o*	Πιστεύω στο Θεό.

I'm an atheist.

i-me *a*-the-os/*a*-the-i	Είμαι άθεος/άθεη.

I'm agnostic.

i-me agh-nos-ti-kis-*tis*	Είμαι αγνωστικιστής.

I'm	*i*-me ...	Είμαι ...
Orthodox	or-*tho*-dho-xos/ or-*tho*-dho-xi	ορθόδοξος/ ορθόδοξη
Catholic	ka-tho-li-*kos*/ ka-tho-lik-*i*	καθολικός/ καθολική
Protestant	dhi-a-mar-ti-*ro*- me-nos/dhi-a- mar-ti-*ro*-me-ni	διαμαρτυρόμενος/ διαμαρτυρόμενη
Jewish	ev-*re*-os/ev-*re*-a	εβραίος/εβραία
Muslim	mo-a-me-tha-*nos*/ mo-a-me-tha-*ni*	μωαμεθανός/ μωαμεθανή

Family

Extended families in Greece tend to be very close. On feast days like Christmas, Easter Sunday and name days (see Festivals, page 236), families usually spend the day together.

Greeks are known for their hospitality. Don't be surprised if you're invited into somebody's home for no particular reason other than being a foreigner in Greece. This is the best way to get to meet local people.

Are you married(m/f)?

i-ste pan-dre-*me*-nos/ pan-dre-*me*-ni?	Είστε παντρεμένος/ παντρεμένη;

Do you have any children?
  e-che-te pe-dhi-*a*?   Έχετε παιδιά;
Do you have any siblings?
  e-che-te a-*dhel*-fia   Έχετε αδέλφια;
I'm (m/f) single.
  i-me e-*lef*-the-ros/e-*lef*-the-ri   Είμαι ελεύθερος/ελεύθερη.
I have a boyfriend/girlfriend.
  e-cho *fi*-lo/*fi*-li   Έχω φίλο/φίλη.
I'm married (m/f).
  i-me pan-dre-*me*-nos/   Είμαι παντρεμένος/
  pan-dre-*me*-ni   παντρεμένη.
I/We don't have any children.
  dhen *e*-cho/*e*-chu-me pe-dhi-*a*   Δεν έχω/έχουμε παιδιά.
I have a daughter/son.
  e-cho mi-*a* ko-ri/*e*-na yi-o   Έχω μια κόρη/ένα γιο.

aunt	i *thi*-a	η θεία
brother	o a-dhel-*fos*	ο αδελφός
cousin (m/f)	o *ksa*-dhel-fos/	ο ξάδελφος/
	i ksa-*dhel*-fi	η ξαδέλφη
daughter	i *ko*-ri	η κόρη
father	o pa-*te*-ras	ο πατέρας
granddaughter	i en-go-*ni*	η εγγονή
grandfather	o pa-*pus*	ο παππούς
grandmother	i yi-a-yi-*a*	η γιαγιά
grandson	o en-go-*nos*	ο εγγονός
husband	o *an*-dhras/*si*-zi-ghos	ο άνδρας/σύζυγος
mother	i mi-*te*-ra	η μητέρα
nephew	o a-ni-psi-*os*	ο ανηψιός
niece	i a-ni-psi-*a*	η ανηψιά
relatives	i sin-ge-*nis*	οι συγγενείς
sister	i a-dhel-*fi*	η αδελφή
son	o yi-os	ο γιος
uncle	o *thi*-os	ο θείος
wife	i yi-*ne*-ka/*si*-zi-ghos	η γυναίκα/σύζυγος

Feelings

I'm ...	*i*-me ...	Είμαι ...
afraid	fo-*va*-me	φοβάμαι
angry	thi-mo-*me*-nos/	θυμωμένος/
	thi-mo-*me*-ni	θυμωμένη
cold	kri-*o*-no	κρυώνω
happy	cha-*ru*-me-nos/	χαρούμενος/
	cha-*ru*-me-ni	χαρούμενη
hot	zes-*te*-no-me	ζεσταίνομαι
hungry	pi-*na*-o	πεινάω
sorry (regret)	li-*pa*-me	λυπάμαι
sad	li-pi-*me*-nos/li-pi-*me*-ni	λυπημένος/λυπημένη
thirsty	dhi-*psa*-o	διψάω.
tired	ku-raz-*me*-nos/	κουρασμένος/
	ku-raz-*me*-ni	κουρασμένη
well	ka-*la*	καλά

BREAKING THE LANGUAGE BARRIER

Do you speak English?
mi-*la*-te ang-li-*ka*?   Μιλάτε Αγγλικά;
Yes, I do (speak English).
ne, (mi-*la*-o ang-li-*ka*)   Ναι, (μιλάω Αγγλικά).
No, I don't (speak English).
o-chi, (dhen mi-*la*-o ang-li-*ka*)   Όχι, (δεν μιλάω Αγγλικά).
Does anyone speak English?
mi-*la*-i ka-*nis* ang-li-*ka*?   Μιλάει κανείς Αγγλικά;
Do you understand?
ka-ta-la-*ve*-ne-te?   Καταλαβαίνετε;
I (don't) understand.
(dhen) ka-ta-la-*ve*-no   (Δεν) καταλαβαίνω.
Could you speak more slowly?
bo-*ri*-te na mi-*la*-te
pi-o ar-*gha*?   Μπορείτε να μιλάτε πιο αργά;
Could you repeat that?
bo-*ri*-te na to
e-pa-na-*la*-ve-te?   Μπορείτε να το επαναλάβετε;

GREEK

BODY LANGUAGE

Greek people can sometimes be laconic with their replies. The single most confusing gesture is the tilting of the head backwards once, which means 'no'. This gesture is sometimes reduced to a mere raising of the eyebrows, and is often accompanied by a tongue-clicking sound. On the other hand, 'yes' is signified by a sideways tilt of the head. Shrugging your shoulders or raising your hands in the air (or both of these) means 'I don't know'.

An outward-facing palm with all five fingers splayed out (as if you're signifying the number five) is a very rude gesture, and it normally means that you've done something very offensive. Unsurprisingly, it's often used by angry taxi drivers to fellow drivers.

GETTING AROUND
Directions

How do I get to ...?	pos *pa*-ne sto ...?	Πώς πάνε στο ...;
Straight ahead.	*o*-lo ef-*thi*-a	Όλο ευθεία.
Turn left/right at the next ...	*strip*-ste a-ris-te-*ra*/ dhek-si-*a* ...	Στρίψτε αριστερά/ δεξιά ...
block	sto e-*po*-me-no tet-*ra*-gho-no	στο επόμενο τετράγωνο
corner	stin e-*po*-me-ni gho-*ni*-a	στην επόμενη γωνία
traffic lights	sta *fo*-ta	στα φώτα
behind	*pi*-so a-*po*	πίσω από
in front of	bros-*ta* a-*po*	μπροστά από
next to	*dhip*-la	δίπλα
opposite	a-*pe*-nan-di ap-*o*	απέναντι από
north	*vo*-ri-a	βόρεια
south	*no*-ti-a	νότια
east	a-na-to-li-*ka*	ανατολικά
west	dhi-ti-*ka*	δυτικά

GREEK

Buying Tickets

How much is a/(the cheapest)
ticket to (Thessaloniki)?

po-so *ka*-ni to/(fthi-*no*-te-ro)   Πόσο κάνει το/(φθηνότερο)
i-si-*ti*-ri-o ya tin   εισιτήριο για την
(the-sa-lo-*ni*-ki)?   (Θεσσαλονίκη);

I'd like (a) ...	tha *i*-thel-a (*e*-na) ...	Θα ήθελα (ένα) ...
one-way ticket	ap-*lo* i-si-*ti*-ri-o	απλό εισιτήριο
return ticket	*e*-na i-si-*ti*-ri-o	ένα εισιτήριο
	me-te-pis-tro-*fis*	επιστροφής μετ'
two ticket	*dhi*-o i-si-*ti*-ri-a	δύο εισιτήρια
first/second	*e*-na i-si-*ti*-ri-o	ένα εισιτήριο
class ticket	*pro*-tis/	πρώτης/
	dhef-te-ris *the*-sis	δεύτερης θέσης
student ticket	*e*-na fi-ti-ti-*ko*	ένα φοιτητικό
	i-si-*ti*-ri-o	εισιτήριο
child ticket	*e*-na pe-dhi-*ko*	ένα παιδικό
	i-si-*ti*-ri-o	εισιτήριο

One ticket, please.

e-na i-si-*ti*-ri-o, pa-ra-ka-*lo*   Ένα εισιτήριο, παρακαλώ.

A bunch of (10) tickets.

mi-*a* dhes-*mi*-dha (*dhe*-ka)   Μια δεσμίδα (δέκα)
i-si-ti-*ri*-on   εισιτηρίων.

Bus

In several Greek cities, Athens included, you have to buy your
bus tickets beforehand. They can be bought from booths
marked ΕΙΣΙΤΗΡΙΑ at main stops, or from the omnipresent
yellow kiosks, known as περίπτερο, pronounced pe-*rip*-te-ro
Punch them in the machine as you board.

Which bus goes to (Piraeus)?

pi-*o* le-o-fo-*ri*-o p*ai*   Ποιο λεωφορείο πάει
(ston pi-re-*a*)?   (στον Πειραιά);

Where can I buy a ticket
for the bus?
　　a-*po* pu bo-*ro* na a-gho-*ra*-so
　　i-si-*ti*-ri-o ya to le-o-fo-*ri*-o?
Από πού μπορώ να αγοράσω
εισιτήριο για το λεωφορείο;

Train

When's the next train for
(Thessaloniki)?
　　po-te *i*-ne to e-*po*-me-no
　　tre-no ya (tin the-sa-lo-*ni*-ki)?
Πότε είναι το επόμενο τραίνο
για (την Θεσσαλονίκη);

Which platform does the train
to (Patra) leave from?
　　a-*po* pi-a a-po-*vath*-ra *fev*-yi
　　to *tre*-no ya (tin *pat*-ra)?
Από ποια αποβάθρα φεύγει
το τραίνο για (την Πάτρα);

Is this the train to (Munich)?
　　af-*to i*-ne to *tre*-no ya
　　(to *mo*-na-cho)?
Αυτό είναι το τραίνο για
(το Μόναχο);

Do you accept Interail?
　　dhe-ches-te *kar*-ta interail?
Δέχεστε κάρτα Interail;

THEY MAY SAY ...	
to *tre*-no e-chi ka-this-te-ri-si	The train is delayed.

GREEK

Boat

Where does the boat to
(Chania) leave from?
　　a-*po* pu *fev*-yi to *pli*-o
　　ya (ta cha-ni-*a*)?
Από πού φεύγει το πλοίο
για (τα Χανιά);

When's the next boat for
(Naxos)?
　　po-te *i*-ne to e-*po*-me-no
　　pli-o ya (ti *na*-xo)?
Πότε είναι το επόμενο
πλοίο για (την Νάξο);

Does this ferry go to (Rhodes)?
　　af-*to* to fe-ri-*bot* pa-i
　　(sti *ro*-dho)?
Αυτό το φερυμπώτ πάει
(στην Ρόδο);

I'd like an inside/outside cabin.

    tha *i*-the-la mi-a e-so-te-ri-*ki*/ ek-so-te-ri-*ki* ka-*bi*-na

Θα ήθελα μια εσωτερική/ εξωτερική καμπίνα.

A cabin for one/two people, please.

    mi-a ka-*bi*-na ya *e*-na/*dhi*-o *a*-to-ma, pa-ra-ka-*lo*

Μια καμπίνα για ένα/δύο άτομα, παρακαλώ.

Where's (the) ...?	pu *i*-ne ... ?	Πού είναι ...;
deck	to ka-*ta*-stro-ma	το κατάστρωμα
cabin number ...	i ka-*bi*-na ...	η καμπίνα ...
car deck	to ga-*raz*	το γκαράζ
reception	i re-sep-si-*on*	η ρεσεψιόν
restaurant	to e-sti-a-*to*-ri-o	το εστιατόριο
purser's office	to lo-yi-*sti*-ri-o	το λογιστήριο

boat	to *pli*-o/va-*po*-ri/ ka-*ra*-vi	το πλοίο/βαπόρι/ καράβι
caique (large fishing boat)	to ka-*i*-ki	το καΐκι
ferryboat	to fe-ri-*bot*	το φερυμπώτ
sailing boat	to i-sti-o-plo-i-*ko*	το ιστιοπλοϊκό
small fishing boat	i psa-*ro*-var-ka/ *var*-ka	η ψαρόβαρκα/ βάρκα
yacht	to *ko*-te-ro/yi-*ot*	το κότερο/γιωτ

Taxi

At the airport, have a look at the taxi price lists posted in the baggage claim hall, and don't let a taxi driver charge you more.

Taxi drivers, especially in Athens, like taking a full load, so don't be surprised when you have to share your taxi with three other people. It also means that you can hail a taxi even if it already has passengers, as long as you are all going in the same direction. But don't expect to share the fare, as each passenger pays the full value displayed on the meter.

Taxi drivers charge more for carrying luggage, being called out, working at 'unsociable hours' – and they take a double tariff on holidays.

Where's the taxi rank?
   pu *i*-ne i *sta*-si ta-*xi*?   Πού είναι η στάση ταξί;
Are you free?
   is-te e-*lef*-the-ros?   Είστε ελεύθερος;
Can you take me to ...?
   bo-*ri*-te na me *pa*-te sto ...?   Μπορείτε να με πάτε στο ...;
How much is it to ...?
   po-so *i*-ne os to ...?   Πόσο είναι ως το ...;
How much do you charge
for the luggage?
   po-so chre-*o*-ne-te ya tis   Πόσο χρεώνετε για τις
   a-pos-ke-*ves*?   αποσκευές;
You've overcharged me!
   me chre-*o*-sa-te pa-ra-*pa*-no!   Με χρεώσατε παραπάνω!
Please, wait.
   pe-ri-*me*-ne-te, pa-ra-ka-*lo*   Περιμένετε, παρακαλώ.
Could you slow down, please?
   bo-*ri*-te na *pa*-te pi-o   Μπορείτε να πάτε πιο
   ar-*gha*, pa-ra-ka-*lo*?   αργά, παρακαλώ;

Car

Where can I rent a car/motorbike?
   pu bo-*ro* na ni-ki-*a*-so   Πού μπορώ να νοικιάσω
   af-to-*ki*-ni-to/mo-to-sik-*le*-ta?   αυτοκίνητο/μοτοσυκλέτα;

How much is it ...?   *po*-so *ka*-ni ...?   Πόσο κάνει ...;
   daily   tin i-*me*-ra   την ημέρα
   weekly   tin ev-dho-*ma*-dha   την εβδομάδα
   per kilometre   to chi-li-*o*-met-ro   το χιλιόμετρο

Is this the road to (Meteora)?
   af-*tos* o *dhro*-mos *pa*-i   Αυτός ο δρόμος πάει
   (sta me-*te*-o-ra)?   (στα Μετέωρα);
Can I park here?
   bo-*ro* na par-*ka*-ro e-*dho*?   Μπορώ να παρκάρω εδώ;
Where's the nearest garage?
   pu *i*-ne to kon-di-*no*-te-ro   Πού είναι το κοντινότερο
   ga-*raz*?   γκαράζ;

I need a mechanic.
   chri-a-zo-me mi-cha-ni-*ko*   Χρειάζομαι μηχανικό.
I've locked my keys in the car.
   kli-dho-sa ta kli-dhi-*a* mu   Κλείδωσα τα κλειδιά μου
   me-sa sto af-to-*ki*-ni-to   μέσα στο αυτοκίνητο.

indicator	o dhiktis	ο δείκτης
(main) road	o (kendrikos) dhromos	ο (κεντρικός) δρόμος
motorway	i ethniki odhos	η εθνική οδός
oil	to petreleo	το πετρέλαιο
petrol (gasoline)	i venzini	η βενζίνη
seatbelt	i zoni asfalias	η ζώνη ασφαλείας

SIGNS

ΑΝΔΡΩΝ	MEN'S
ΑΝΟΙΧΤΟ	OPEN
ΑΠΑΓΟΡΕΥΕΤΑΙ Η ...	NO ...
ΕΙΣΟΔΟΣ	ENTRY
ΦΩΤΟΓΡΑΦΗΣΗ	PHOTOGRAPHY
ΑΠΟΧΩΡΗΤΗΡΙΑ/ ΤΟΥΑΛΕΤΕΣ	TOILETS
ΓΥΝΑΙΚΩΝ	WOMEN'S
ΕΙΣΟΔΟΣ	ENTRANCE
ΕΞΟΔΟΣ	EXIT
ΙΛΙΩΤΙΚΟΣ ΧΩΡΟΣ	PRIVATE AREA
ΚΛΕΙΣΤΟ	CLOSED
ΜΗΝ ΑΓΓΙΖΕΤΕ	DO NOT TOUCH
Ο ΣΚΥΛΟΣ ΔΑΓΚΩΝΕΙ	BEWARE OF THE DOG! (lit: the dog bites)
ΤΟΥΑΛΕΤΕΣ	TOILETS

GREEK

ACCOMMODATION
At the Hotel

Do you have any rooms available?

e-che-te e-*lef*-the-ra dho-*ma*-ti-a?	Έχετε ελεύθερα δωμάτια;

I'd like a single/double room.

tha *i*-the-la *e*-na mo-*nok*-li-no/*dhik*-lino	Θα ήθελα ένα μονόκλινο/δίκλινο.

Where's the bathroom?

pu *i*-ne to *ba*-ni-o?	Πού είναι το μπάνιο;

How much is it ...? *po*-so *ka*-ni ...? Πόσο κάνει ...;

per night	tin vra-dhi-*a*	την βραδιά
for a week	ya mi-*a* ev-dho-*ma*-dha	για μια εβδομάδα

I want a room *the*-lo *e*-na Θέλω ένα
with a ... dho-*ma*-ti-o me ... δωμάτιο με ...

double bed	dhip-*lo* kre-*va*-ti	διπλό κρεβάτι
private bathroom	i-dhi-o-ti-*ko ba*-ni-o	ιδιωτικό μπάνιο
shower	dus	ντους
window	pa-*ra*-thi-ro	παράθυρο

(See also Camping, page 238.)

Requests & Complaints

Can I have another ...?	mu *dhi*-ne-te a-*ko*-mi ...?	Μού δίνετε ακόμη ...;
blanket	mi-*a* ku-*ver*-ta	μια κουβέρτα
pillow	*e*-na mak-si-*la*-ri	ένα μαξιλάρι
sheet	*e*-na sen-*do*-ni	ένα σεντόνι
towel	mi-*a* pet-se-ta	μια πετσέτα

Can you put the heating/
air-conditioning on?

bo-*ri*-te na-*nap*-se-te tin *ther*-man-si/ton kli-ma-tis-*mo*?	Μπορείτε ν' ανάψετε την θέρμανση/τον κλιματισμό;

Where can I leave my valuables?		Πού μπορώ ν' αφήσω
pu bo-*ro* na-*fi*-so po-*li*-ti-ma an-di-*ki*-me-na?		πολύτιμα αντικείμενα;
Where can I wash clothes?		Πού μπορώ να πλύνω ρούχα;
pu bo-*ro* na *pli*-no *ru*-cha?		

AROUND TOWN
At the Post Office

If you're sending parcels overseas, take them to the post office unsealed so they can be checked. You can usually change travellers cheques and send faxes at post offices, while stamps can be bought from most kiosks and souvenir shops.

I'd like to send a ...	*tha*-the-la na *sti*-lo ...	Θα 'θελα να στείλω ...
fax	*e*-na faks	ένα φαξ
letter	*e*-na *ghra*-ma	ένα γράμμα
parcel	*e*-na *dhe*-ma	ένα δέμα
postcard	mi-*a kar*-ta	μια κάρτα

I'd like some stamps for ...
tha-the-la me-ri-*ka*   Θα 'θελα μερικά
ghra-ma-*to*-si-ma ya ...   γραμματόσημα για ...
How much is it to send
this to ...?
po-so *ka*-ni ya na *sti*-lo   Πόσο κάνει για να στείλω
af-*to* stin ...?   αυτό στην ...;

air mail	a-e-ro-po-ri-*kos*	αεροπορικώς
express mail	ek-*spres*	εξπρές
post code	o ta-chi-dhro-mi-*kos* *ko*-dhi-kas	ο ταχυδρομικός κώδικας (Τ.Κ.)
registered mail	si-sti-*me*-no	συστημένο

GREEK

Telephone

With OTE (Οργανισμός Τηλεποικοινωνιών Ελλάδος), 'Greek Telecommunications Company', you can make both national and international phone calls from designated booths, marked ΤΗΛΕΦΩΝΙΚΕΣ ΘΥΡΙΔΕΣ. You don't need coins or phonecards for these, as you get charged after you've made the phone call.

Where's the OTE office?		
	pu *i*-ne o o-te?	Πού είναι ο ΟΤΕ;
I want to make a phone call to (Australia).		
	the-lo na *ka*-no *e*-na ti-le-*fo*-ni-ma (stin Af-stra-*li*-a)	Θέλω να κάνω ένα τηλεφώνημα (στην Αυστραλία).
How much does a five-minute call cost to ...?		
	po-so *ka*-ni *e*-na ti-le-*fo*-n-ma *pen*-de lep-*ton* stin ...?	Πόσο κάνει ένα τηλεφώνημα πέντε λεπτών στην ...;
I want to make a reverse-charge (collect) call.		
	the-lo na *ka*-no *e*-na ti-le-*fo*-ni-ma me *chre*-o-si tu ka-*lu*-me-nu	Θέλω να κάνω ένα τηλεφώνημα με χρέωση του καλούμενου.
What's the area code for ...?		
	pi-os *i*-ne o ti-le-fo-ni-*kos* *ko*-dhi-kas ya ...?	Ποιος είναι ο τηλεφωνικός κώδικας για ...;
It's engaged.		
	vu-*i*-zi	Βουΐζει.
How much is a fax per page?		
	po-so *ka*-ni i se-*li*-dha ya faks?	Πόσο κάνει η σελίδα για φαξ;

phone book	o ti-le-fo-ni-*kos* o-dhi-*ghos*	ο τηλεφωνικός οδηγός
phone box	o ti-le-fo-ni-*kos* *tha*-la-mos	ο τηλεφωνικός θάλαμος
phone card	i ti-le-*kar*-ta	η τηλεκάρτα

Internet

Where can I email from?

ap-*o* pu bo-*ro* na *sti*-lo e-mayl?	Από πού μπορώ να στείλω email;

Is there an Internet cafe near here?

i-*par*-chi *e*-na in-ter-n*et* cafe e-*dho* kon-*da*?	Υπάρχει ένα Internet cafe εδώ κοντά;

At the Bank

Can I change ...?	bo-*ro* na-*la*-kso ...?	Μπορώ ν' αλλάξω ...;
money	*chri*-ma-ta	χρήματα
travellers cheques	ta-ksi-dhi-o-ti-*kes* e-pi-ta-*yes*	ταξιδιωτικές επιταγές

Can I withdraw money with my credit card?

bo-*ro* na *ka*-no a-*na*-lip-si me tin pi-sto-ti-*ki* mu *kar*-ta?	Μπορώ να κάνω ανάληψη με την πιστωτική μου καρτα;

Can I use this card in the ATM?

bo-*ro* na chri-si-mo-pi-*i*-so af-*ti* tin *kar*-ta ston af-*to*-ma-to?	Μπορώ να χρησιμοποιήσω αυτή την κάρτα στον αυτόματο;

Can I have money transferred from my bank?

bo-*ro* na me-ta-*fe*-ro *chri*-ma-taa-*po* tin *tra*-pe-za mu?	Μπορώ να μεταφέρω χρήματα από την τράπεζα μου;

Has my money arrived?

e-chun *fta*-si ta *chri*-ma-ta mu	Έχουν φτάσει τα χρήματα μου;

banknotes	char-to-no-*mis*-ma-ta	χαρτονομίσματα
coins	*ker*-ma-ta	κέρματα
money	ta *chri*-ma-ta/lef-*ta*	τα χρήματα/λεφτά

GREEK

INTERESTS & ENTERTAINMENT
Sightseeing

Look out for the sign EOT (Ελληνικός Οργανισμός Τουρισμού), 'Greek Tourist Organization', which runs several tourist offices in airports, major cities and areas of interest.

Where's the EOT office?
  pu *i*-ne to ghra-*fi*-o e-*ot*?   Πού είναι το γραφείο ΕΟΤ;
Do you have a map of the
area/city?
  e-che-te *e*-na *char*-ti tis   Έχετε ένα χάρτη της
  pe-ri-o-*chis*/*po*-lis?   περιοχής/πόλης;
What time does it open/close?
  ti *o*-ra a-*ni*-yi/*kli*-ni?   Τι ώρα ανοίγει/κλείνει;
Is there an admission charge?
  pre-pi na pli-*ro*-so *i*-so-dho?   Πρέπει να πληρώσω είσοδο;
What's that building?
  ti *kti*-ri-o *i*-ne af-*to*?   Τι κτίριο είναι αυτό;
Can I take a photograph?
  bo-*ro* na *vgha*-lo   Μπορώ να βγάλω
  fo-to-ghra-*fi*-a?   φωτογραφία;

ancient	ar-*che*-os	αρχαίος
archaeological site	o ar-che-o-lo-yi-*kos* *cho*-ros	ο αρχαιολογικός χώρος
beach	i pa-ra-*li*-a	η παραλία
castle	to *ka*-stro	το κάστρο
city centre	to *ken*-dro tis *po*-lis	το κέντρο της πόλης
city walls	ta *ti*-chi	τα τείχη
fresco	i ti-cho-ghra-*fi*-a	η τοιχογραφία
main square	i ken-dri-*ki* pla-*ti*-a	η κεντρική πλατεία
market place	i a-gho-*ra*	η αγορά
mosaic	to psi-fi-dho-*to*	το ψηφιδωτό
museum	to mu-*si*-o	το μουσείο
mosque	to tza-*mi*	το τζαμί
old quarter	i pa-li-*a* *po*-li	η παλιά πόλη

Going Out

What can we do this evening?
ti bo-*ru*-me na *ka*-nu-me
a-*po*-pse?

Τι μπορούμε να κάνουμε
απόψε;

What's on tonight at the
theatre/cinema?
ti *pe*-ze-te a-*po*-pse sto
the-a-tro/si-ne-*ma*?

Τι παίζεται απόψε στο
θέατρο/σινεμά;

I'd like to go to a bouzouki restaurant.
tha-the-la na
pa-o sta bu-*zu*-ki-a

Θα'θελα να πάω
στα μπουζούκια.

I'd like to go to a/the ...	*tha*-the-la na *pa*-o ...	Θα'θελα να πάω ...
cinema	sto si-ne-*ma*	στο σινεμά
concert	se si-nav-*li*-a	σε συναυλία
nightclub	sti dis-ko-*tek*	στη ντισκοτέκ
restaurant	se es-ti-a-*to*-ri-o	σε εστιατόριο
theatre	sto *the*-a-tro	στο θέατρο

Do you want to go dancing?
the-lis na *pa*-me na
cho-*re*-psu-me?

Θέλεις να πάμε να
χορέψουμε;

Yes, I'd love to (come).
ne, (tha *er*-tho)ef-cha-*ri*-stos

Ναι, (θα έρθω) ευχαρίστως.

Are there any clubs here?
i-*par*-chun e-*dho* klab?

Υπάρχουν εδώ κλαμπ;

BOUZOUKI

The bouzouki, which looks something like a mandolin, features heavily in contemporary Greek music; you'll hear it everywhere around Greece.

What type of music do they play?
ti *i*-dhos mu-si-*kis pe*-zun?

Τι είδος μουσικής παίζουν;

When's the best night?
po-te *i*-ne i ka-*li*-te-ri vra-*dha*?

Πότε είναι η καλύτερη βραδιά;

GREEK

Sports & Interests

What do you do in your spare time?

ti *ka*-nis ton e-*lef*-the-ro su *chro*-no	Τι κάνεις τονελεύθερο σου χρόνο;

Do you like ...?	sas a-*re*-si ...?	Σας αρέσει ...;
I (don't) like ... (sg/pl)	(dhen) ma-*re*-si/ ma-*re*-sun ...	(Δεν) Μ' αρέσει/ αρέσουν ...
cooking	i ma-yi-ri-*ki*	η μαγειρική
films	i te-*ni*-es	οι ταινίες
listening to music	na-*ku*-o mu-si-*ki*	ν' ακούω μουσική
going to the cinema/theatre	na pi-*ye*-no sto si-ne-*mal the*-a-tro	να πηγαίνω στο σινεμά/θέατρο
reading	to dhi-*a*-vaz-ma	το διάβασμα
travelling	na tak-si-*de*-vo	να ταξιδεύω
walking (in the country)	na per-pa-*ta*-o (stin ek-so-*chi*)	να περπατάω (στην εξοχή)

Where can I play/go ...?	pu bo-*ro* na *pek*-so ...?	Πού μπορώ να παίξω ...;
sport	to spor/*ath*-li-ma	το σπορ/άθλημα
boxing	to boks	το μποξ
cycling	i po-dhi-la-*si*-a	η ποδηλασία
rowing	i ko-pi-la-*si*-a	η κωπηλασία
sailing	i i-sti-o-plo-*i*-a	η ιστιοπλοΐα
swimming	to ko-*lim*-bi	το κολύμπι
waterskiing	to tha-*la*-si-o ski	το θαλάσσιο σκι
weightlifting	i *ar*-si va-*ron*	η άρση βαρών

GREEK

I like watching sports.	
ma-*re*-si na pa-ra-ko-lu-*tho* spor	Μ' αρέσει να παρακολουθώ σπορ.
I follow ...	
pa-ra-ko-lu-*tho* ...	Παρακολουθώ ...
Which team do you support?	
ti o-*ma*-dha i-*se*?	Τι ομάδα είσαι;

Festivals

Every village in Greece has an annual feast to celebrate its patron saint. Most of the feasts tend to be during the months of June, July and August. They're usually noisy, colourful affairs with plenty of street markets, music and dancing.

to kar-na-*va*-li tis *pat*-ras (το καρναβάλι της Πάτρας)
    carnival of Patras, complete with parades and floats, held on the last Sunday before Lent, wich starts on Ash Wedsnesday

to fes-ti-*val* a-thi-*non* (το φεστιβάλ Αθηνών)
    Athens festival of music and dance, celebrated during the summer months

ta e-pi-*dha*-vri-a (τα Επιδαύρεια)
    festival of ancient plays, held during the months of summer

to pa-ni-*yi*-ri tis *ti*-nu (το πανηγύρι της Τήνου)
    a pilgrimage is made on 15 August on the island of Tinos, to what's believed to be the miracle-bearing icon of the Virgin in the island's main church

to fes-ti-*val* kra-si-*u* (το φεστιβάλ κρασιού)
    wine festival, held early in September in Dafni on the west side of Athens to celebrate the grape harvest

Birthdays & Saints' Days

Name days are dedicated to the saint after which a person has been named. Although birthdays are also celebrated, it's uncommon to send greeting cards for birthdays (or for any other occasion).

When's your name day?
    po-te y-ior-*ta*-zis?   Πότε γιορτάζεις;
When's your birthday?
    po-te *i*-ne ta ye-*ne*-thli-a su?   Πότε είναι τα γενέθλιά σου;
My name day's on (15 August).
    yi-or-*ta*-zo stis   Γιορτάζω στις
    (dhe-ka-*pen*-de av-*ghu*-stu)   (15 Αυγούστου).
Many happy returns!
    chro-ni-a po-*la*!   Χρόνια πολλά!

May you reach 100 years!
(for birthdays only)
  na ta e-ka-to-*sti*-sis!   Να τα εκατοστήσεις!

name day   i yi-or-*ti*   η γιορτή

Christmas & New Year

Christmas Eve
  i pa-ra-mon-*i* ton   η παραμονή των
  chri-stu-*ye*-non   Χριστουγέννων
Christmas Day
  i i-*me*-ra ton   η ημέρα των
  chri-stu-*ye*-non   Χριστουγέννων
New Year's Eve
  i pa-ra-mo-*ni* tis   η παραμονή της
  pro-toch-ro-ni-*as*   Πρωτοχρονιάς
New Year's Day
  i pro-toch-ro-ni-*a*   η Πρωτοχρονιά

Season's greetings!	*chro*-ni-a po-*la*!	Χρόνια Πολλά!
Happy New Year!	ka-*li* chro-ni-*a*!	Καλή Χρονιά!

IN THE COUNTRY
Weather

What will the weather be
like tomorrow?
  ti ke-*ro* tha *e*-chu-me *av*-ri-o?   Τι καιρό θα έχουμε αύριο;
We're having a heatwave.
  e-chu-me *kaf*-so-na   Έχουμε καύσωνα.

It's hot/cold.	*ka*-ni *ze*-sti/*kri*-o	Κάνει ζέστη/κρύο.
It's sunny.	e-chi li-a-*ka*-dha	Έχει λιακάδα.
It's raining.	*vre*-chi	Βρέχει.
It's snowing.	chi-o-*ni*-zi	Χιονίζει.
It's windy.	fi-*sa*-i	Φυσάει.

GREEK

Camping

Can we camp here?

	bo-*ru*-me na	Μπορούμε να
	ka-ta-ski-*no*-su-me e-*dho*?	κατασκηνώσουμε εδώ;

Is there a campsite nearby?

	i-*par*-chi kam-ping	Υπάρχει κάμπιγκ
	e-*dho* kon-*da*?	εδώ κοντά;

camping	i ka-tas-*ki*-no-si/	η κατασκήνωση/
	to *kam*-ping	το κάμπιγκ
campsite	o *cho*-ros	ο χώρος
	ka-tas-*ki*-no-sis	κατασκήνωσης
can opener	to a-nich-*ti*-ri	το ανοιχτήρι
fuel	ta *kaf*-si-ma	τα καύσιμα
hammock	i kre-ma-*sti ku*-ni-a	η κρεμαστή κούνια
hammer	to sfi-*ri*	το σφυρί
mattress	to *stro*-ma	το στρώμα
mosquito net	i ku-nu-pi-*e*-ra	η κουνουπιέρα
rope	to ski-*ni*	το σκοινί
sleeping bag	o ip-*no*-sa-kos	ο υπνόσακκος
tent	i ski-*ni*	η σκηνή
tent pegs	ta pa-*lu*-ki-a	τα παλούκια
torch (flashlight)	o fa-*kos*	ο φακός

GREEK

FOOD

Greek cuisine relies not so much on complicated recipes, but on getting the most from the flavours of fresh, local produce–fish straight from the sea, freshly made yogurt, locally grown vegetables and fruit, and an abundance of olive oil. All this – combined with pungent herbs, garlic and olive oil, or charcoal-grilled fish sprinkled with fresh oregano and lemon–pretty unbeatable.

breakfast	to pro-i-*no*	το πρωινό
lunch	to me-si-me-ri-a-*no*	το μεσημεριανό
dinner	to vra-dhi-*no*	το βραδινό

Vegetarian Meals

There are dozens of Greek dishes that are vegetable or pulse-based, and these are usually also suitable for vegans, as dairy products are rarely added. Food is always fried in olive or other vegetable oil, never in lard, and butter is rarely used.

I'm a vegetarian.
   i-me chor-to-*fa*-ghos   Είμαι χορτοφάγος.

I don't eat ...	dhen *tro-o* ...	Δεν τρώω ...
meat	*kre*-as	κρέας
seafood	ta tha-la-si-*na*	τα θαλασσινά

Staple Foods & Condiments

bread (dried)	to pak-si-*ma*-dhi	το παξιμάδι
coffee (instant)	o nes-ka-*fes*	ο νεσκαφές
eggplant	i me-lit-*za*-na	η μελιτζάνα
honey	to *me*-li	το μέλι
fish	to *psa*-ri	το ψάρι
fruit	*fru*-ta	φρούτα
meat	*kre*-as	κρέας
mustard	i mus-*tar*-dha	η μουστάρδα
olive oil	to e-le-*o*-la-dho	το ελαιόλαδο
olives	i e-li-*es*	οι ελιές
pepper	to pi-*pe*-ri	το πιπέρι
rice	to *ri*-zi	το ρύζι
salt	to a-*la*-ti	το αλάτι
sausages	ta lu-*ka*-ni-ka	τα λουκάνικα
vegetables	to la-cha-ni-*ko*	το λαχανικό
vinegar	to *ksi*-dhi	το ξύδι

MENU DECODER

Breakfast Menu

A Greek breakfast is usually a rather frugal affair – normally consisting of a cup of coffee and a piece of bread. In out of the way places, do as the Greeks do, and ask for some dried bread to dunk in your coffee. (See page 242 for ways to order coffee.)

bread	to psomi	το ψωμί
dried bread	to paksimadhi	το παξιμάδι
butter	to vutiro	το βούτυρο
coffee	e-na e-li-ni-ko	Ένα ελληνικό
orange juice	o chi-mos	ο χυμός
	por-to-ka-li	πορτοκάλι
toast	i fri-gha-ni-a	η φρυγανιά

Regional Specialities

Lunch is eaten rather late, at 2 pm but up to 4 pm. The afternoon siesta ends with a strong cup of coffee and perhaps some sweet cake. Don't expect to be served dinner before 9 pm, although most Greeks don't go out to eat before 10 or 11pm, especially on weekends.

Aegean Islands

fru-ta-li-a (φρουταλιά)
potato and spicy sausage 'omelette' (Andros)

sfu-ga-to (σφουγγάτο)
baked mince and zucchini omelette topped with breadcrumbs (Rhodes)

Crete

choch-li-i (χοχλιοί)
snails cooked with onions and tomato

kal-tsu-ni-a (καλτσούνια)
cheese pies made with soft *mizithra* cheese

pa-tu-dhi-a (πατούδια)
sesame and almond turnovers flavoured with orange-water

GREEK

Cyprus
a-*fe*-li-a (αφέλια)
  pork cooked in red wine and coriander
bo-*re*-ki-a (μπορέκια)
  small pies stuffed with cheese, mince or spinach
chu-mus (χούμους)
  chickpea and garlic dip

Northern Greece – Thessaly
a-tra-cho-*po*-dha-ra (βατραχοπόδαρα)
  fried frogs' legs (especially popular around Ioannina)
ri-gha-no-kef-*te*-dhes (ριγανοκεφτέδες)
  fish roe rissoles with oregano (Pilion)
spet-zo-*fai* (σπετζοφάι)
  spicy sausages cooked with eggplant (Pilion)

Ionian Islands
bur-*dhe*-to (μπουρδέτο)
  stewed fish with paprika (Corfu)
pa-stit-*sa*-dha (παστιτσάδα)
  veal cooked in wine and tomato with macaroni

North-Eastern Aegean
an-gi-*na*-res a-*la* po-*li*-ta (αγκινάρες αλά πολίτα)
  artichokes cooked with potato, carrot, dill and lemon
yi-us-le-*me*-dhes (γιουσλεμέδες)
  fried cheese pies (Mitilini)

Desserts
Filo pastry, a paper-thin sheet of flour pastry, features quite
heavily in Greek cuisine, especially in sweet-making.

bak-la-*vas* (μπακλαβάς)
  layers of nuts and filo pastry dripping with syrup
chal-*vas* po-*li*-ti-kos (χαλβάς πολίτικος)
  sweet made out of semolina, sugar, cinnamon, pine nuts,
  walnuts and raisins
gha-lak-to-*bu*-re-ko (γαλακτομπούρεκο)
  orange-flavoured custard in filo pastry

GREEK

ghli-*ka* ku-ta-li-*u* (γλυκά κουταλιού)
    fruit preserved in syrup made with pistachio, cherry,
    rosehip, bergamot (mint), bitter orange or baby eggplant
ka-ta-*i*-fi (καταΐφι)
    nuts wrapped in vermicelli-like pastry with syrup
man-do-*la*-to (μαντολάτο)
    nougat (especially popular in Zakinthos)
re-va-*ni* (ρεβανί)
    sponge-like cake with walnuts and syrup
tur-ta a-migh-*dha*-lu (τούρτα αμυγδάλου)
    almond gateau (cake)

GREEK COFFEE

Simply asking for:

a coffee, please!
e-nan ka-fe, pa-ra-ka-*lo*! έναν καφέ, παρακαλώ!

will most likely get you instant coffee in the winter and
an iced coffee in the summer. Here's how to get what
you want:

Greek coffee – a strong, thick brew served in a small cup	e-na e-li-ni-ko	Ένα ελληνικό
black, no sugar	e-na *ske*-to	Ένα σκέτο
medium strength with a little sugar	e-na *met*-ri-o	Ένα μέτριο
strong	e-na po-*la* va-*ri*	Ένα πολλά βαρύ
strong and sweet	e-na va-*ri* ghli-ko	Ένα βαρύ γλυκό
iced coffee	e-na fra-pe	Ένα φραπέ
with milk	me *gha*-la	με γάλα

GREEK

Non-Alcoholic Drinks

cherry juice (morello, sour)	i vi-si-*na*-dha	η βυσινάδα
... juice	o chi-*mos* ...	ο χυμός ...
apple	*mi*-lu	μήλου
orange	por-to-*ka*-li	πορτοκάλι
tea with ...	to *tsa*-i me ...	το τσάι με ...
lemon	le-*mo*-ni	λεμόνι
milk	*gha*-la	γάλα
herbal tea	to *tsa*-i tu vu-*nu*	το τσάι του βουνού
hot chocolate	i so-ko-*la*-ta	η σοκολάτα
	ro-fi-ma	ρόφημα
(mineral) water	to (me-ta-li-*ko*) ne-*ro*	το (μεταλλικό) νερό

Alcoholic Drinks

beer	i *bi*-ra	η μπύρα
bitter-orange liqueur	kum kuat	κουμ κουάτ
champagne	i sam-*pa*-ni-a	η σαμπάνια
Metaxa (five)	star me-tak-*sa*	Μεταξά (πέντε)
star brandy	(*pen*-de) as-*ter*-on	αστέρων
ouzo (aniseed drink)	to uzo	το ούζο
sweet red wine from Achaia	i mav-ro-*dhaf*-ni	η μαυροδάφνη
wine	to ... kra-*si*	το ... κρασί
dry	ksi-*ro*	ξηρό
red	*ko*-ki-no	κόκκινο
rosé	ro-*ze*	ροζέ
sweet	ghli-*ko*	γλυκό
white	*as*-pro	άσπρο

AT THE MARKET

GREEK

Basics

bread	to pso-*mi*	το ψωμί
bread (dried)	to pak-si-*ma*-dhi	το παξιμάδι
butter	to *vu*-ti-ro	το βούτυρο
cheese	to ti-*ri*	το τυρί
chocolate	i so-ko-*la*-ta	η σοκολάτα
flour	to a-*lev*-ri	το αλεύρι
milk	to *gha*-la	το γάλα
olive oil	to e-le-*o*-la-dho	το ελαιόλαδο
olives	i e-li-*es*	οι ελιές
rice	to *ri*-zi	το ρύζι
sugar	i *za*-cha-ri	η ζάχαρη
(mineral) water	to (me-ta-li-*ko*) ne-*ro*	το (μεταλλικό) νερό

Meat & Poultry

beef	to vo-dhi-*no*	το βοδινό
chicken	to ko-*to*-pu-lo	το κοτόπουλο
ham	to zam-*bon*	το ζαμπόν
lamb	ar-*ni*	αρνί
meat	*kre*-as	κρέας
pork	to chi-ri-*no*	το χοιρινό
salami	to sa-*la*-mi	το σαλάμι
sausages	ta lu-*ka*-ni-ka	τα λουκάνικα
turkey	i gha-lo-*pu*-la	η γαλοπούλα
veal	to mos-*cha*-ri	το μοσχάρι

Seafood

baby squid	to ka-la-ma-*ra*-ki	το καλαμαράκι
fish	to *psa*-ri	το ψάρι
lobster	o as-ta-*kos*	ο αστακός
mussels	ta *mi*-dhi-a	τα μύδια
prawns	i gha-*ri*-dhes	οι γαρίδες

Vegetables

artichoke	i an-gi-*na*-ra	η αγκινάρα
beetroot	to pat-*za*-ri	το πατζάρι
cabbage	to *la*-cha-no	το λάχανο
carrots	ta ka-*ro*-ta	τα καρότα

AT THE MARKET

capsicum	i pi-pe-ri-*a*	η πιπεριά
celery	i se-li-*no*-ri-za	η σελινόριζαη
cucumber	to an-*gu*-ri	το αγγούρι
eggplant	i me-lit-*za*-na	η μελιτζάνα
green beans	ta fa-so-*la*-ki-a	τα φασολάκια
lettuce	to ma-*ru*-li	το μαρούλι
mushrooms	ta ma-ni-*ta*-ri-a	τα μανιτάρια
onion	to kre-*mi*-dhi	το κρεμμύδι
parsley	o ma-in-da-*nos*	ὁ μαϊντανός
potatoes	i pa-*ta*-tes	οι πατάτες
spinach	to spa-*na*-ki	το σπανάκι
tomatoes	i do-*ma*-tes	οι ντομάτες
vegetable	to la-cha-ni-*ko*	το λαχανικό
zucchini	to ko-lo-ki-*tha*-ki	το κολοκυθάκι

Pulses

broad beans	ta ku-ki-*a*	τα κουκιά
chick peas	ta re-*vi*-thi-a	τα ρεβύθια
lentils	i fa-*kes*	οι φακές
split peas	i *fa*-va	η φάβα

Fruit

apples	ta *mi*-la	τα μήλα
apricots	ta ve-*ri*-ko-ka	τα βερίκοκα
bananas	i ba-*na*-nes	οι μπανάνες
figs	ta *si*-ka	τα σύκα
fruit	*fru*-ta	φρούτα
grapes	ta sta-*fi*-li-a	τα σταφύλια
lemon	to le-*mo*-ni	το λεμόνι
melon	to pe-*po*-ni	το πεπόνι
oranges	ta por-to-*ka*-li-a	τα πορτοκάλια
peaches	ta ro-*dha*-ki-na	τα ροδάκινα
pear	to ach-*la*-dhi	το αχλάδι
plums (red)	ta dha-*mas*-ki-na	τα δαμάσκηνα
plums (yellow)	i ne-*ram*-bu-les	οι νεράμπουλες
strawberries	i *fra*-u-les	οι φράουλες
watermelon	to kar-*pu*-zi	το καρπούζι

SHOPPING

Where's the	pu *i*-ne to	Πού είναι το
nearest ...?	kon-di-*no*-te-ro ...?	κοντινότερο ...;
barber	kur-*i*-o	κουρείο
bookshop	viv-li-o-po-*li*-o	βιβλιοπωλείο
clothing store	ka-*tas*-ti-ma *ru*-chon	κατάστημα ρούχων
department store	i-per-ka-*ta*-sti-ma	υπερκατάστημα
florist	an-tho-po-*li*-o	ανθοπωλείο
grocery	pan-do-po-*li*-o	παντοπωλείο
hairdresser	ko-mo-*ti*-ri-o	κομμωτήριο
laundrette	ka-tha-ri-*sti*-ri-o	καθαριστήριο
market	a-gho-*ra*	αγορά
shoe shop	i-po-dhi-ma-to-po-*li*-o	υποδηματοπωλείο
travel agency	tak-si-dhi-o-ti-*ko* ghra-*fi*-o	ταξιδιωτικό γραφείο

Do you accept credit cards?
dhe-che-ste pi-sto-ti-*ki* *kar*-ta?   Δέχεστε πιστωτική κάρτα;

Essential Groceries

batteries	i ba-ta-*ri*-es	οι μπαταρίες
bottled water	to em-fi-a-lo-*me*-no ne-*ro*	το εμφιαλωμένο νερό
bread	to pso-*mi*	το ψωμί
butter	to *vu*-ti-ro	το βούτυρο
chocolate	i so-ko-*la*-ta	η σοκολάτα
coffee	o ka-*fes*	ο καφές
cheese	to ka-*se*-ri/i *fe*-ta	το κασέρι/η φέτα
hard/soft		
gas cylinder	to igh-ra-*e*-ri-o	το υγραέριο
matches	ta *spir*-ta	τα σπίρτα
milk	to *gha*-la	το γάλα
sugar	i *za*-cha-ri	η ζάχαρη
tea	to *tsa*-i	το τσάι
toilet paper	to char-*ti* i-*yi*-as	το χαρτί υγείας
toothpaste	i o-dhon-*do*-pas-ta	η οδοντόπαστα
washing powder	to a-po-ri-pan-di-*ko*	το αποπαντικο

Souvenirs

It's made of ...	*i*-ne a-*po* ...	Είναι από ...
bronze	*brunt*-zo	μπρούντζο
copper	chal-*ko*	χαλκό
gold	chri-*so*	χρυσό
silver	a-*si*-mi	ασήμι

backgammon board	to *tav*-li	το τάβλι
bracelet	to vra-chi-*o*-li	το βραχιόλι
chain	i a-li-*si*-dha	η αλυσίδα
earrings	ta sku-la-*ri*-ki-a	τα σκουλαρίκια
evil eye	to *ma*-ti	το μάτι
(a blue eye worn to ward off evil spirits)		
necklace	to ko-li-*e*	το κολιέ
rug	to cha-*li*	το χαλί
statue	to *a*-ghal-ma	το άγαλμα
worry beads	to kom-bo-*lo*-i	το κομπολόι

Clothing

coat	to pal-*to*	το παλτό
dress	to *fo*-re-ma	το φόρεμα
hat	to ka-*pe*-lo	το καπέλο
jumper	to pu-*lo*-ver	το πουλόβερ
sandals	ta san-*dha*-li-a/ *pe*-dhi-la	τα σανδάλια/ πέδιλα
shirt	to pu-*ka*-mi-so	το πουκάμισο
shoes	ta pa-*pu*-tsi-a	τα παπούτσια
socks	i *kalt*-ses	οι κάλτσες
swimsuit	to ma-yi-*o*	το μαγιώ
T-shirt	to blu-*za*-ki	το μπλουζάκι
trousers	to pan-de-*lo*-ni	το παντελόνι
underwear	ta e-*so*-ru-cha	τα εσώρουχα

GREEK

Colours

black	*mav*-ros	μαύρος
blue	ble	μπλε
brown	ka-*fe*	καφέ
green	*pra*-si-nos	πράσινος
orange	por-to-ka-*li*	πορτοκαλί
pink	roz	ροζ
purple	mov	μωβ
white	lef-*kos*	λευκός

Toiletries

brush	i *vur*-tsa	η βούρτσα
comb	i *chte*-na	η χτένα
condoms	ta pro-fi-lak-ti-*ka*	τα προφυλακτικά
insect repellant	a-po-thi-ti-*ko* yi-a ta ku-*nu*-pi-a	απωθητικό για τα κουνούπια
razor blade	to ksi-ra-*fa*-ki	το ξυραφάκι
shampoo	to sam-pu-*an*	το σαμπουάν
shaving cream	o af-*ros* ksi-*ris*-ma-tos	ο αφρός ξυρίσματος
soap	to sa-*pu*-ni	το σαπούνι
scissors	to psa-*li*-dhi	το ψαλίδι
sunscreen	an-di-li-a-*ko*	αντηλιακό
tampons	ta tam-*pon*	τα ταμπόν
toothbrush	i o-dhon-*do*-vur-tsa	η οδοντόβουρτσα

Stationery & Publications

Where can I find books
in English?

pu bo-*ro* na vro viv-*li*-a stang-li-*ka*?	Πού μπορώ να βρω βιβλία στ' αγγλικά;

dictionary	to lek-si-*ko*	το λεξικό
English-language newspaper	i e-fi-me-*ri*-dha (stang-li-*ka*)	η εφημερίδα (στ' αγγλικά)
envelope	o *fa*-ke-los	ο φάκελλος
magazine	to pe-ri-o-dhi-*ko*	το περιοδικό

map	o *char*-tis	ο χάρτης
paper	to char-*ti*	το χαρτί
pen	to sti-*lo*	το στυλό
travel guide	o tak-si-dhi-o-ti-*kos*	ο ταξιδιωτικός
	o-dhi-*ghos*	οδηγός

Photography

How much does it cost to
have this film developed?

po-so *ka*-ni yi-a na mu
em-fa-*ni*-se-te af-*to* to film?

Πόσο κάνει για να μου
εμφανίσετε αυτό το φιλμ;

When will it be ready?

po-te tha *i*-ne *e*-ti-mo?

Πότε θα είναι έτοιμο;

I'd like film for this camera.

the-lo film yi-af-*ti* ti
mi-cha-*ni*

Θέλω φιλμ γι' αυτή
τη μηχανή.

Do you have (underwater)
disposable cameras?

e-che-te (i-pov-*ri*-chi-es)
mi-cha-*nes* mi-as *chri*-sis?

Έχετε (υποβρύχιες)
μηχανές μιας χρήσης;

camera	i (fo-to-ghra-fi-*ki*)	η (φωτογραφική)
	mi-cha-*ni*	μηχανή
film speed	i ta-*chi*-ti-ta	η ταχύτητα
flash	to flas	το φλας
slide film	to film yi-a	το φιλμ για
	dhi-a-*fan*-i-es	διαφάνειες

... film	to ... film	το ... φιλμ
B&W	as-*pro*-mav-ro	ασπρόμαυρο
colour	*en*-chro-mo	έγχρωμο

GREEK

Smoking

A packet of cigarettes, please.

e-na pa-*ke*-to tsi-*gha*-ra pa-ra-ka-*lo*

Ένα πακέτο τσιγάρα, παρακαλώ.

Can I smoke?

bo-*ro* na kap-*ni*-so?

Μπορώ να καπνίσω;

Do you have a light?

e-che-te fo-ti-*a*?

Έχετε φωτιά;

I don't smoke.	dhen kap-*ni*-zo	Δεν καπνίζω.
cigarettes	ta tsi-*gha*-ra	τα τσιγάρα
cigars	ta *pu*-ra	τα πούρα
lighter	o a-nap-*ti*-ras	ο αναπτήρας
matches	ta *spir*-ta	τα σπίρτα
tobacco	o kap-*nos*	ο καπνός

HEALTH
Parts of the Body

I can't	dhen bo-*ro* na	Δεν μπορώ να
move my ...	ku-*ni*-so ... mu	κουνήσω ... μου.
My ... hurts.	me po-*na*-i ... mu	Με πονάει ... μου.
ankle	o a-*stra*-gha-los	ο αστράγαλος
arm	to *che*-ri	το χέρι
back	i *pla*-ti	η πλάτη
chest	to *sti*-thos	το στήθος
ear	to af-*ti*	το αυτί
eye	to *ma*-ti	το μάτι
foot	to po-*dhi*	το πόδι
head	to ke-*fa*-li	το κεφάλι
jaw	to sa-*gho*-ni	το σαγόνι
leg	to po-dhi	το πόδι
muscle	o mis	ο μυς
ribs	ta pa-i-*dhi*-a	τα παΐδια
shoulder	o *o*-mos	ο ώμος
stomach	to sto-*ma*-chi	το στομάχι
throat	o le-*mos*/*fa*-rin-gas	ο λαιμός/φάρυγγας

Ailments

I'm sick.	*i*-me *a*-ros-tos	Είμαι άρρωστος.
I can't sleep.	*e*-cho a-ip-*nia*	Έχω αϋπνία.

I need a doctor.
   chri-*a*-zo-me *e*-na yi-a-*tro*   Χρειάζομαι ένα γιατρό.

I've been vomiting.
   e-ka-na e-me-*to*   Έκανα εμετό.

I've had diarrhoea for
(three) days.
   e-cho dhi-*a*-ri-a edh-*o* ke   Έχω διάρροια εδώ και
   (tris) *me*-res   (τρεις) μέρες.

I feel shivery/dizzy.
   e-cho *ri*-yi/za-*la*-dhes   Έχω ρίγη/ζαλάδες.

I need a new pair of glasses.
   chri-*a*-zo-me *e*-na   Χρειάζομαι ένα
   ke-*nur*-yi-o zev-*gha*-ri   καινούργιο ζευγάρι
   yi-a-li-*a*   γυαλιά.

I've been	me	Με
stung by a ...	*tsim*-bi-se ...	τσίμπησε ...
bee	*me*-li-sa	μέλισσα
jelly fish	*tsuch*-tra	τσούχτρα
wasp	*sfi*-ka	σφήκα

Useful Words

accident	to a-*ti*-chi-ma	το ατύχημα
blood group	i o-*ma*-dha *e*-ma-tos	η ομάδα αίματος
blood pressure	i *pi*-e-si	η πίεση
disease	i a-*ros*-ti-a	η αρρώστεια
injury/wound	to *trav*-ma	το τραύμα
virus	o i-*os*	ο ιός

At the Chemist

In Greece, all dispensing chemists (pharmacies) have a licence to take blood pressure, administer injections and carry out simple tests. For minor ailments, it might save you from having to go to a doctor. A lot of drugs that would need a prescription elsewhere can be given over the counter. Insulin is given free.

Where's the nearest
all-night chemist?
    pu *i*-ne to kon-di-*no*-te-ro   Πού είναι το κοντινότερο
    nich-te-ri-*no* far-ma-*ki*-o?   νυχτερινό φαρμακείο;
I need medication for ...
    chri-*a*-zo-me   Χρειάζομαι
    far-ma-ka ya ...   φάρμακα για ...
How many times a day?
    po-ses fo-*res* tin i-*me*-ra?   Πόσες φορές την ημέρα;

antibiotics	ta an-di-vi-o-ti-*ka*	τα αντιβιοτικά
bandage	i *gha*-za	η γάζα
contact lenses	i fa-*ki* e-pa-*fis*	οι φακοί επαφής
contraceptive	to pro-fi-lak-ti-*ko*	το προφυλακτικό
cough syrup	to *far*-ma-ko ya	το φάρμακο για
	ton *vi*-cha	τον βήχα
insect repellent	i a-li-*fi* ya ta	η αλειφή για τα
	ku-*nu*-pi-a	κουνούπια
laxative	to ka-*thar*-si-o	το καθάρσιο
painkillers	ta a-nal-ghi-ti-*ka*	τα αναλγητικά

At the Dentist

My gums hurt.
    me po-*na*-ne ta *u*-la mu   Με πονάνε τα ούλα μου.
This tooth is bothering me.
    me e-noch-*li* af-*to*   Με ενοχλεί αυτό
    to *dhon*-di   το δόντι.
I don't want it extracted.
    dhen *the*-lo na mu to   Δεν θέλω να μου το
    vgha-le-te   βγάλετε.

GREEK

TIME & DATES
Time

What time is it?	ti *o*-ra *i*-ne?	Τι ώρα είναι;

It's (one) o'clock.
  i-ne *(mi*-a) i *o*-ra — Είναι (μία) η ώρα.
It's quarter past four.
  i-ne *te*-se-ris ke *te*-tar-to — Είναι τέσσερις και τέταρτο.
It's half past four.
  i-ne *te*-se-ri-*si*-mi-si — Είναι τεσσερισήμιση.
It's quarter to four.
  i-ne *te*-se-ris pa-*ra te*-tar-to — Είναι τέσσερις παρά τέταρτο.

Days

Monday	dhef-*te*-ra	Δευτέρα
Tuesday	*tri*-ti	Τρίτη
Wednesday	te-*tar*-ti	Τετάρτη
Thursday	*pemp*-ti	Πέμπτη
Friday	pa-ras-ke-*vi*	Παρασκευή
Saturday	*sa*-va-to	Σάββατο
Sunday	ki-ri-a-*ki*	Κυριακή

Months

January	i-a-nu-*a*-ri-os	Ιανουάριος
February	fev-ru-*a*-ri-os	Φεβρουάριος
March	*mar*-ti-os	Μάρτιος
April	a-*pri*-li-os	Απρίλιος
May	*ma*-ios	Μάιος
June	i-*u*-ni-os	Ιούνιος
July	i-*u*-li-os	Ιούλιος
August	*av*-ghus-tos	Αύγουστος
September	sep-*tem*-vri-os	Σεπτέμβριος
October	ok-*tov*-ri-os	Οκτώβριος
November	no-*em*-vri-os	Νοέμβριος
December	dhe-*kem*-vri-os	Δεκέμβριος

GREEK

Present

now	*to*-ra	τώρα
immediately	a-*me*-sos	αμέσως
today	*si*-me-ra	σήμερα
this ...	*si*-me-ra to ...	σήμερα το ...
morning	pro-*i*	πρωί
afternoon	a-*po*-yev-ma	απόγευμα
tonight	a-*pop*-se	απόψε
this week	af-*ti* tin ev-dho-*ma*-dha	αυτή την εβδομάδα
this month	af-*to* ton *mi*-na	αυτό τον μήνα
this year	*fe*-tos	φέτος

Past

yesterday ...	chtes (chthes) ...	χτες (χθες) ...
morning	to pro-*i*	το πρωί
evening	to a-*po*-yev-ma	το απόγευμα
day before yesterday	proch-*tes* (proch-*thes*)	προχτές (προχθές)
last week	tin pro-i-*ghu*-me-ni ev-dho-*ma*-dha	την προηγούμενη εβδομάδα
last month	ton pro-i-*ghu*-me-no *mi*-na	τον προηγούμενο μήνα
last year	*per*-si	πέρσι

Future

soon	*sin*-do-ma	σύντομα
tomorrow ...	*av*-rio ...	αύριο ...
morning	to pro-*i*	το πρωί
night	to *vra*-dhi	το βράδι
day after tomorrow	me-*thav*-rio	μεθαύριο
next week	tin e-*po*-me-ni ev-dho-*ma*-dha	την επόμενη εβδομάδα
next month	ton e-*po*-me-no *mi*-na	τον επόμενο μήνα
next year	tu *chro*-nu	του χρόνου

GREEK

During the Day

day	i i-*me*-ra/*me*-ra	η ημέρα/μέρα
early	no-*ris*	νωρίς
evening	to *vra*-dhi	το βράδι
late afternoon; evening	to a-*po*-yev-ma	το απόγευμα
midday; early afternoon	to me-si-*me*-ri	το μεσημέρι
midnight	ta me-*sa*-nich-ta	τα μεσάνυχτα
morning	to pro-*i*	το πρωί
night	i *nich*-ta	η νύχτα

NUMBERS & AMOUNTS

Nouns in Greek are masculine, feminine or neuter in gender. The numbers one, three, four and 1000 and any number ending in one, three and four have masculine, feminine and neuter forms.

These numbers should agree in gender with the noun they quantify. While you're in Greece, you may hear many of these forms. However, if you don't know the gender of a particular noun, you'll still be understood if you just use the masculine form

0		mi-*dhen*	μηδέν
1	(m)	e-nas	ένας
	(f)	*mi*-a	μία
	(n)	e-na	ένα
2		*dhi*-o	δύο
3	(m)	tris	τρεις
	(f)	tris	τρεις
	(n)	*tri*-a	τρία
4	(m)	*te*-se-ris	τέσσερις
	(f)	*te*-se-ris	τέσσερις
	(n)	*te*-se-ra	τέσσερα
5		*pen*-de	πέντε
6		*ek*-si	έξι
7		ef-*ta*	εφτά
	(written form)	ep-*ta*	επτά
8		och-*to*	οχτώ
	(written form)	ok-*to*	οκτώ

GREEK

GREEK

9		e-ni-*a*	εννιά
	(written form)	e-*ne*-a	εννέα
10		*dhe*-ka	δέκα
11		*en*-de-ka	έντεκα
12		*dho*-dhe-ka	δώδεκα
13	(m)	dhe-kat-*ris*	δεκατρείς
	(f)	dhe-kat-*ris*	δεκατρείς
	(n)	dhe-kat-*ri*-a	δεκατρία
14	(m)	dhe-ka-*te*-se-ris	δεκατέσσερις
	(f)	dhe-ka-*te*-se-ris	δεκατέσσερις
	(n)	dhe-ka-*te*-se-ra	δεκατέσσερα
15		dhe-ka-*pen*-de	δεκαπέντε
16		dhe-ka-*ek*-si	δεκαέξι
17		dhe-ka-ef-*ta*	δεκαεφτά
18		dhe-ka-och-*to*	δεκαοχτώ
19		dhe-ka-e-*ne*-a	δεκαεννέα
20		*i*-ko-si	είκοσι
21	(m)	*i*-ko-si *e*-nas	είκοσι ένας
	(f)	*i*-ko-si *mi*-a	είκοσι μία
	(n)	*i*-ko-si *e*-na	είκοσι ένα
22		*i*-ko-si *dhi*-o	είκοσι δύο
30		tri-*an*-da	τριάντα
40		sa-*ran*-da	σαράντα
50		pe-*nin*-da	πενήντα
60		ek-*sin*-da	εξήντα
70		ev-dho-*min*-da	εβδομήντα
80		ogh-*dhon*-da	ογδόντα
90		e-ne-*nin*-da	ενενήντα
100		e-ka-*to*	εκατό
101		e-ka-*ton* e-na	εκατόν ένα
120		e-ka-*ton* *i*-ko-si	εκατόν είκοσι
1000	(m)	*chi*-li-i	χίλιοι
	(f)	*chi*-li-es	χίλιες
	(n)	*chi*-li-a	χίλια
2000		*dhi*-o chi-li-*a*-dhes	δύο χιλιάδες
3000		tris chi-li-*a*-dhes	τρεις χιλιάδες
one million		*e*-na e-ka-to-*mi*-ri-o	ένα εκατομμύριο

Useful Words & Phrases

double	dhip-*los*	διπλός
enough	ar-ke-*ta*	αρκετά
less	li-*gho*-te-ro	λιγότερο
a little bit	*li*-gho	λίγο
many/much/ a lot of (sg/pl)	po-*lis*/po-*li*	πολύς/πολλοί
more	pe-ri-*so*-te-ro	περισσότερο
once	*mi*-a fo-*ra*/*a*-paks	μια φορά/άπαξ
percent	tis e-ka-*to*	τοις εκατό
some	me-ri-*ki*	μερικοί

GREEK GODS

Aphrodite		goddess of love and beauty
afrodhiti	Αφροδίτη	
Apollo		god of reason and high moral
apolon	Απόλλων	principles
Ares		god of war
aris	Άρης	
Artemis		goddess of fertility and
artemis	Άρτεμις	childbirth
Athena		goddess of wisdom
athina	Αθηνά	and courage
Demeter		goddess of agriculture
dhimitra	Δήμητρα	
Hera		goddess of marriage and
ira	Ήρα	maternity
Hermes		messenger god and
ermis	Ερμής	protector of travellers
Hephaestus		god of metalwork
ifestos	Ήφαιστος	
Hestia		goddess of the sacred hearth
estia	Εστία	and protector of the home
Poseidon		god of the sea
posidhon	Ποσειδών	
Zeus		sovereign god
zefs/dhias	Ζευς/Δίας	

GREEK

ABBREVIATIONS

Some commonly used abbreviations that you might see around town are:

	In Full	
Αγ.	Άγιος/Αγία *a*-ghi-os/*a*-*ghi*-a	Saint
αρ.	αριθμός a-rith-*mos*	number
Δημ.	Δήμος *dhi*-mos	borough
δρχ.	δραχμές dhrach-*mes*	drachmas
ΕΛΤΑ	Ελληνικά Ταχυδρομεία e-li-ni-*ka* ta-chi-dhro-*mi*-a	Greek Post Office (found on post boxes)
Λεωφ.	Λεωφόρος le-o-*fo*-ros	avenue
Οδ.	Οδός o-*dhos*	street
Οσ.	Όσιος/Οσία o-si-os/o-*si*-a	saint
1ος, 2ος	πρώτος/δεύτερος *pro*-tos/*dhef*-te-ros	first/second

GREEK

EMERGENCIES

Go away!	*fi*-ye!	Φύγε!
Fire!	fo-ti-*a*!	Φωτιά!
Thief!	*klef*-tis!	Κλέφτης!

It's an emergency!
   i-ne *a*-me-si a-*nan*-gi!   Είναι άμεση ανάγκη!

There's been an accident.
   e-yi-ne a-*ti*-chi-ma   Έγινε ατύχημα.

Call a doctor.
   fo-*nak*-ste *e*-na yi-a-*tro*   Φωνάξτε ένα γιατρό.

Call the police.
   fo-*nak*-ste tin as-ti-no-*mi*-a   Φωνάξτε την αστυνομία.

Call an ambulance.
   fo-*nak*-ste *e*-na
   as-the-no-*fo*-ro   Φωνάξτε ένα
                ασθενοφόρο.

Where's the police station?
   pu *i*-ne to as-ti-no-mi-*ko*
   tmi-ma?   Πού είναι το αστυνομικό
                τμήμα;

Can you help me?
   bo-*ri*-te na me
   vo-i-*thi*-se-te?   Μπορείτε να με
                βοηθήσετε;

I've been raped.
   me *vi*-a-san   Με βίασαν.

I've been robbed.
   me *ek*-lep-san   Με έκλεψαν.

I'm ill.
   i-me *a*-ros-tos/*a*-ros-ti   Είμαι άρρωστος/άρρωστη.

I'm lost.
   e-cho cha-*thi*   Έχω χαθεί.

I have medical insurance.
   e-cho i-a-tri-*ki* as-*fa*-li-a   Έχω ιατρική ασφάλεια.

Where are the toilets?
   pu *i*-ne i tu-a-*le*-tes?   Πού είναι οι τουαλέτες;

GREEK

Dealing with the Police

I want to report an offence.

the-lo na ka-tan-*gi*-lo	Θέλω να καταγγείλω
e-na a-*dhi*-ki-ma	ένα αδίκημα.

I've lost my ...	*e*-cha-sa ...	Έχασα ...
My ... was stolen.	mu *ek*-lep-san ...	Μου έκλεψαν ...
credit card	tin pis-to-ti-*ki* *kar*-ta mu	την πιστωτική κάρτα μου
handbag	tin *tsan*-da mu	την τσάντα μου
luggage	tis a-pos-ke-*ves* mu	τις αποσκευές μου
money	ta *chri*-ma-*ta* mu	τα χρήματά μου
passport	to dhi-a-va-*ti*-ri-o mu	το διαβατήριό μου
travellers cheques	tis tak-si-dhi-o-ti-*kes* e-pi-ta-*yes* mu	τις ταξιδιωτικές επιταγές μου

I want to inform my embassy/consulate.

the-lo na i-dho-pi-*i*-so tin	Θέλω να ειδοποιήσω την
prez-*vi*-a/to prok-se-*ni*-o mu	πρεσβεία/το προξενείο μου.

Can I pay an on-the-spot fine?

bo-*ro* na pli-*ro*-so to	Μπορώ να πληρώσω το
pros-ti-mo ep-*i* to-pu?	πρόστιμο επι τοπου;

Do I have the right to make a phone call?

e-cho to dhi-*ke*-o-ma na	Έχω το δικαίωμα να
ka-no *e*-na ti-le-*fo*-ni-ma?	κάνω ένα τηλεφώνημα;

I apologise.

sas zi-*to* sigh-*no*-mi	Σας ζητώ συγγνώμη.

IRISH

QUICK REFERENCE

Hello.	dee-a gwit	*Dia duit.* (lit: God to you)
Goodbye.	slaan	*Slán.*
Welcome.	fawlcha	*Fáilte.*
What's new?	keyn shkey-al?	*Cén scéal?*
Please.	lyeh do hul	*Le do thoil.*
I'm ...	iss mish-a ...	*Is mise ...*
Yes.	taw/shah	*Tá./Sea.*
No.	nyeel; nyee hah	*Níl; Ní hea.*
Another pint.	pin-ta el-la	*Pionta eile.*
Cheers!	slawn-cha!	*Sláinte!*

Thank you (very much).
   go-ra (myee-la)   *Go raibh (míle)*
   mo o-got   *maith agat.*
You're welcome.
   taa faa-il-tyeh roht   *Tá fáilte romhat.*
Excuse me.
   gov mo lyeh-shkey-al   *Gabh mo leithscéal.*
What's your name?
   kod iss a-nim dit?   *Cad is ainm duit?*
I'd like to introduce you to ...
   sho ...   *Seo ...*
Pleased to meet you.
   taa aa-hass o-rom   *Tá áthas orm*
   boo-la lyat   *bualadh leat.*
How are you?
   ku-nass taa too?   *Conas tá tú?*
I'm fine.
   thawm goh moh   *Táim go maith.*
Bon appetit!
   slawn-cha uhn   *Sláinte an*
   vru-dawn chuwt!   *bradáin chugat!*

1	eyn	*aon*	6	shey	*sé*
2	doe	*dó*	7	shokt	*seacht*
3	three	*trí*	8	ukth	*ocht*
4	ka-hirr	*ceathair*	9	nay	*naoi*
5	koo-ig	*cúig*	10	jeh	*deich*

IRISH

IRISH

Irish is the national and first official language of Ireland, and the ancestral language of the 70-million-strong Irish diaspora, and of most Scots, throughout the world. It belongs, together with Breton, Cornish, Manx, Scottish Gaelic and Welsh, to the Celtic branch of the Indo-European language family, once spoken across Europe from Ireland to Anatolia (modern Turkey). Irish and Scottish Gaelic shared a common literary language from the 6th to the late 18th centuries. The Latin word Scotus meant simply an Irish speaker, whether from Ireland or Scotland.

The Irish language largely inspired the movement that brought about Ireland's national independence in the early 20th century. It's been an obligatory subject at all primary and secondary level schools since independence in 1922, and the number of Irish-medium schools has been rapidly growing in recent years. Since 1913, it's been a compulsory course for graduation at the National University of Ireland.

There are around one million Irish speakers in the Irish state, and about 140,000 Irish speakers in Northern Ireland. Irish is now the everyday language in the Gaeltacht, or traditional Irish-speaking areas, and is increasingly heard in urban areas, particularly in Dublin and Belfast. Irish literature is flourishing, and the language is part of the European Community LINGUA program, a project which promotes the teaching of European languages throughout the Member States. It's also one of the languages on the common EU passport.

PRONUNCIATION

Stress normally falls on the first syllable of a word. There are a number of Irish sounds not found in English – letters not pronounced as they are in English are described below.

Vowels

Vowels may be either long or short. Long vowels are marked by an acute accent – *dán*, 'a poem', is pronounced dawn.

	SHORT VOWELS			LONG VOWELS	
a	a	as the 'a' in 'sofa'; as the 'o' in 'hot'	*á*	aa aw	as the 'a' in 'father'; as the 'aw' in 'saw'
e	e	as the 'e' in 'hex'	*é*	ay	as the 'ey' in 'hey'
i	i	as the 'i' in 'sin'	*í*	ee	as the 'i' in 'marine'
o	o	as the 'o' in 'hot'	*ó*	oh	as the 'o' in 'rope'
u	u	as the 'u' in 'put'	*ú*	oo	as the 'u' in 'flute'

Both long and short vowels are divided into two categories – 'broad' and 'slender'. Long and short pronunciations of *a*, *o* and *u* are broad, while long and short *e* and *i* are slender. Vowels affect the pronunciation of a consonant which comes before or after, depending on which group they belong to (see Consonants, page 265).

Broad Vowels	Slender Vowels
a, á, o, ó, u, ú	*e, é, i, í*

Vowel Combinations

Irish also has the following vowel sounds, for which the spelling may differ.

ay	as the 'i' in 'spice'		
	a kind	says	*saghas*
ey	as in 'ey' in 'hey'		
	horn	eyrk	*adharc*

ISH

ow	as the 'ow' in 'cow'		
	river	ow-iny	*abhainn*
	world	down	*domhan*
ee-a	as the 'ee' in 'free' + the 'a' in 'father'		
	they	shee-ad	*siad*
oo-a	as the 'oo' in 'too' + the 'a' in 'father'		
	cold	foo-ar	*fuar*

Consonants

Some consonants have a broad pronunciation when preceded or followed by a broad vowel (*a, á, o, ó, u, ú*), and a slender pronunciation when followed or preceded by a slender vowel (*e, é, i, í*).

	SLENDER		BROAD	
bp	b	as the 'b' in 'box'		
c	k	as the 'c' in 'cat'; never as in 'celery'		
gc	g	as the 'g' in 'game'		
mb	m	as the 'm' in 'meal'		
nd	n	as the 'n' in 'naughty'		
ng	ng	as the 'ng' in 'sing'		
r	rr	trilled		
s	sh	as the 'sh' in 'shell'	s	as the 's' in 'sin'
t	ch	as the 'ch' in 'cheese'	t	as the 't' in 'tickle'
ts	t	as the 't' in 'tickle'		

When a consonant is followed by *h*, its sound changes.

bh(f)	v	as the 'v' in 'velvet'		
ch	h	as the 'h' in 'huge'	kh	as the 'ch' in Scottish 'loch'
dh	y	as the 'y' in 'yes'	g	as the 'g' in 'game'
fh		silent		
gh	y	as the 'y' in 'yes'	g	as the 'g' in 'game'
mh	v	as the 'v' in 'velvet'		
ph	f	as the 'f' in 'fun'		
sh	h	as the 'h' in 'hot'		
th	h	as the 'h' in 'hot'		

IRISH

GREETINGS & CIVILITIES
You Should Know

Hello.	dee-a gwit	*Dia duit.* (lit: God to you)
Welcome.	fawlcha	*Fáilte.*
Good night.	ee-ha vo	*Oíche mhaith.*
What's new?	keyn shkey-al?	*Cén scéal?*
Goodbye.	slaan	*Slán.*
See you later.	slaan go foh-il	*Slán go fóill.*
Take care.	toor a-ra	*Tabhair aire.*
Please.	lyeh do hul	*Le do thoil.*

Thank you (very much).	
go-ra (myee-la) mo o-got	*Go raibh (míle) maith agat.*
You're welcome.	
taa faa-il-tyeh roht	*Tá fáilte romhat.*
Excuse me.	
gov mo lyeh-shkey-al	*Gabh mo leithscéal.*
How are you?	
ku-nass taa too?	*Conas tá tú?*
I'm fine.	
thawm goh moh	*Táim go maith.*
Very well, thanks.	
go hon vo,	*Go han-mhaith,*
go-ra mo o-got	*go raibh maith agat.*

Yes.	taw/shah	*Tá./Sea.*
No.	nyeel; nyee hah	*Níl; Ní hea.*

Forms of Address

Sir/Mr	a gwi-na oo-a-sil	*A dhuine uasail*
Madam/Mrs	a van oo-as-al	*A bhean uasal*

IRISH

ON THE BUSES

Buses bound for the city centre have *An Lár* on their signboards.

SMALL TALK
Meeting People

I'm ...	iss mish-a ...	*Is mise ...*
I like ...	iss mo lyum ...	*Is maith liom ...*

I'd like to introduce you to ...
   sho ...   *Seo ...*

What's your name?
   kod iss a-nim dit?   *Cad is ainm duit?*

Pleased to meet you.
   taa aa-hass o-rom boo-la lyat   *Tá áthas orm bualadh leat.*

Where do you work?
   kaa wil too eg ob-ir?   *Cá bhfuil tú ag obair?*

Nationalities

Listed here are some countries where English-speaking travellers may come from. If your country isn't here, this could be a good starting point to talk with a local and find out how to pronounce the name of your country.

Where are you from?	kod oss dit?	*Cad as duit?*
Where do you live?	kaa wil koh-nee ort?	*Cá bhfuil cónaí ort?*

I'm from ...	oss ...	*As ...*
Australia	on os-traa-il	*an Astráil*
Canada	kya-na-da	*Ceanada*
England	soss-ana	*Sasana*
Ireland	ey-rin	*Éirinn*
New Zealand	on noo-a hay-lin	*an Nua-Shéalainn*
Scotland	ol-bwin	*Albain*
the US	me-ri-kaa	*Meiriceá*
Wales	an mra-tin vyug	*an mBreatain Bheag*

Family

Are you married?
   wil too pohs-ta?   *An bhfuil tú pósta?*

Do you have children?
   will paash-tyee ogot?   *An bhfuil páistí agat?*

IRISH

baby	lya-nuv	*leanbh*
brother	dri-harr	*deartháir*
child	paash-chuh	*páiste*
daughter	in-een	*iníonn*
father	a-hir	*athair*
grandfather	sha-na-hir	*seanathair*
grandmother	shan-vaa-hir	*seanmháthair*
husband	far key-luh	*fear céile*
mother	maa-hir	*máthair*
sister	dre-foor	*deirfiúr*
son	mak	*mac*
wife	ban kheyl-uh	*bean chéile*

Useful Phrases

Do you speak Irish?
    on wil gwayl-gye o-got?   *An bhfuil Gaeilge agat?*
Yes, a little.
    taa, byu-gaan   *Tá, beagán.*
How do you say that in Irish?
    ku-nass a dyair-faa   *Conas a déarfá*
    shin oss gwayl-gyeh?   *sin as Gaeilge?*
I don't understand you.
    nyee hi-gim hoo   *Ní thuigim thú.*
Say it again, please.
    ob-bir a-reesh ey,   *Abair arís é,*
    lyeh do hul   *le do thoil.*
I understand.
    ti-gim   *Tuigim.*
I disagree.
    nyee ayn-teem.   *Ní aontaím.*

IRISH

Agreed. You're right.
| ayn-teem. | Aontaím. |
| taa on kyart o-got | Tá an ceart agat. |

Where's the toilet, please?
| kaa wil on lyeh-aras, lyeh do hul? | Cá bhfuil an leithreas, le do thoil? |

What's this?	kod ey shawh?	Cad é seo?
What's that?	kod ey shin?	Cad é sin?
Why?	ka-ne faw?	Cén fáth?
Me too.	mish-a lyesh	Mise leis.
Neither do I.	naa mish-a	ná mise.
Amazing!	do-khred-tye!	Dochreidte!
How strange!	noch at ey!	nach ait é!
Impossible!	nyee fyey-dyir ey	Ní féidir é!
Nonsense!	raa-meysh	Ráiméis!
That's terrible!	guy hoo-ah-faa-ssoch!	Go huafásach!

SIGNS

ÁRAS AN UACHTARÁIN	PRESIDENTIAL RESIDENCE
CÉAD MÍLE FÁILTE	A HUNDRED THOUSAND WELCOMES
DÁIL ÉIREANN	LOWER HOUSE OF PARLIAMENT
DÚNTA	CLOSED
FIR	MEN
GARDAÍ	POLICE
MNÁ	WOMEN
NÁ CAITEAR TOBAC	NO SMOKING
OIFIG AN PHOIST	POST OFFICE
OIFIG EOLAIS	TOURIST INFORMATION
OSCAILTE	OPEN
PÁIRCEÁIL	PARKING

IRISH

PLACENAMES

Armagh	*Ard Mhacha*
Ballymena	*An Baile Meánach*
Bangor	*Beannchar*
Belfast	*Béal Feirste*
Cahir	*An Cathair*
Cork	*Corcaigh*
Derry	*Doire*
Drogheda	*Droichead Átha*
Dublin	*Baile Átha Cliath*
Galway	*Gaillimh*
Gortahork	*Gort an Choirce*
Kilkenny	*Cill Chainnigh*
Killarney	*Cill Airne*
Limerick	*Luimneach*
Lisburn	*Lios na gCearrbhach*
Republic of Ireland	*Éire*
Sligo	*Sligeach*
Waterford	*Port Láirge*

These words are often found in Irish placenames:

high	*Ard*
church	*Cill*
field	*Gort*
battle	*Cath*

AROUND TOWN

city	kaw-her	*cathair*
street	sroy-ed	*sráid*
town	bo-lyeh	*baile*
town square	lawr an vo-lyeh	*lár an bhaile*

IRISH

INTERESTS & ENTERTAINMENT
Going Out

Yes, I'd like to.
   bo vryaa lyum ey.   *Ba bhreá liom é.*
Great, good idea!
   har borr, on-smwee-nev   *Thar barr, an-smaoineamh.*
I'm sorry, I can't.
   broh-no-rom, nyee   *Brón orm, ní féidir liom.*
   fyey-dyir lyum

airneál	evening with story-telling by the fire
ceilí	session of traditional dancing and music
gealgháirí	relaxed party atmosphere
seisún	music session

YOUNG AT HEART

The Irish Youth Hostel Association is called *An Óige* (lit: the youth).

Sports & Interests

What interests do you have?
   ka-ne kah-iv aym-shi-ruh   *Cén caitheamh aimsire*
   taa a-gut?   *atá agat?*
What sports do you play?
   kad ee-ad nuh kli-hee sport   *Cad iad na cluichí spóirt a*
   uh im-reen too?   *imríonn tú?*

IRISH

I like ...	iss mo lyum ...	*Is maith liom ...*
art	a-leen	*ealaín*
basketball	kish-fel	*cispheil*
chess	fi-khul	*ficheall*
dancing	dou-suh	*damhsa*
food	bee-a	*bia*
football	pel	*peil*
Gaelic football	pel gey-lukh	*peil Ghaelach*
hiking	shoo-loid	*siúlóid*
hurling	u-naa-nee-ukht	*iománaíocht*
martial arts	a-lee-nuh mee-lu-tuh	*ealaíona mílaeata*
movies	skunaain	*scannáin*
music	kyowl	*ceol*
nightclubs	klu-bun-nuh ee-khuh	*clubanna oíche*
reading	lyey-how-i-rukht	*léitheoireacht*
shopping	shu-pa-doh-i-rukht	*siopadóireacht*
walking	shool	*siúl*
skiing	skee-aal	*sciáil*
swimming	snaav	*snámh*
tennis	lyadohg	*leadóg*
travelling	tash-tul	*taisteal*
photography	greeun-gra-fa-doh-i-rukht	*griangh-rafadóireacht*
visiting friends	koo-irt uh thoo-irt er khaar-juh	*cuairt a thabhaairt ar chairde*

FASTER PUSSYCAT!

Imeacht gan teacht ort.
  imucht gun chacht urt
  May you leave without returning.

Titim gan éirí ort.
  chichim gun ayree urt
  May you fall without rising.

Go n-ithe an cat thú is go n-ithe an diabhal an cat.
  gu ni-he uhn kat hoo iss gu ni-he an jowl uhn kat
  May the cat eat you, and may the cat be eaten by the devil.

IRISH

Festivals

Bloomsday
readings and dramatisation marking Leopold Bloom's Joycean journey around the city of Dublin

St Patrick's Day
March 17 is a national holiday, with parades held in Dublin and Armagh. The World Irish Dancing Championships also take place on this day.

Happy Christmas!	
no-lig ho-na!	*Nollaig shona!*
Happy Easter!	
kaashk ho-na!	*Cáisc shona!*
Bon voyage!	
guh nyai-ree on boh-har lyat!	*Go n-éirí an bóthar leat!*

FOOD

bread	a-raan	*arán*
dessert	myil-shohg	*milseog*
colcannon	kawl kya-nun	*cál ceannann*
(potato dish made with cabbage and leek)		
pie	pee-ohg	*pióg*
potato	praa-tee	*prátaí*
salmon & brown	bra-daan og-ass	*bradán agus arán*
bread	a-raan don	*donn*
soup	on-ra	*anraith*
stew	stow-uch	*stobhach*
vegetables	gloss-ree	*glasraí*

Bon appetit!	
slawn-cha uhn vru-dawn chuwt!	*Sláinte an bradáin chugat!*
	(lit: the health of the salmon to you!)

IRISH

Drinks

A 'drop' of ...	breen ...	*Braon ...*
apple juice	soo ool	*sú úll*
beer	byohr	*beoir*
mineral water	ish-keh myee-an-ree	*uisce mianraí*
orange juice	soo or-aash-the	*sú oráiste*
water	ish-keh	*uisce*
whisky	ish-keh ba-ha	*uisce beatha*
		(lit: water of life)
whisky (illicit)	po-tcheen	*poitín*
wine	fee-on	*fíon*

CHEERS!

Cheers!	slawn-cha!	*Sláinte!*
Good health to you!	slawn-cha hu-get!	*Sláinte chugat!*
Long life to you!	sal fa-da hu-get!	*Saol fada chugat!*
Guinness for strength!		
nee nyart gu gi-nis!		*Ní neart go Guinness!*
'wine lets out the truth'		
ski-lun feen fee-ri-nyeh		*Scileann fíon fírinne.*

SHOPPING

I'd like to buy (a) ...
    bah voh lum kya-nokh ...   *Ba mhaith liom ceannach ...*

How much/many?	key vaid	*Cé mhéid?*
ornament	owr-naaid	*ornáid*
photograph	gree-un-graf	*grianghraf*
picture	pik-choor	*pictiúr*
postcard	kaar-tuh pwisht	*árta poist*
shamrock	sham-rohg	*seamróg*
souvenir	kee-nu-khaan	*cuimhneachán*
T-shirt	tee ley-nuh	*t-léine*

TIME & DATES

Days

Monday	dey loon	*Dé Luain*
Tuesday	dey mawrt	*Dé Máirt*
Wednesday	dey kay-deen	*Dé Céadaoin*
Thursday	da-re-deen	*Déardaoin*
Friday	dey hee-na	*Dé Haoine*
Saturday	dey ssa-he-ren	*Dé Sathairn*
Sunday	dey dow-nick	*Dé Domhnaigh*

Months

January	ah-ner	*Eanair*
February	fyow-rah	*Feabhra*
March	mahr-tha	*Márta*
April	ah-brahn	*Aibreán*
May	byowl-the-na	*Bealtaine*
June	me-hev	*Meitheamh*
July	ool	*Iúil*
August	loo-na-sa	*Lúnasa*
September	man fohr	*Meán Fomhair*
October	dereh for	*Deireadh Fomhair*
November	sow-en	*Samhain*
December	nu-leg	*Nollaig*

Seasons

spring	ahn ta-rach	*an t-earrach*
summer	ahn ssow-ra	*an samhradh*
autumn	ahn fohr	*an fómhar*
winter	ahn gee-rah	*an geimhreadh*

Useful Words

hour	oor	*uair*
minute	no-ma-de	*noiméid*
week	shock-tin	*seachtain*
month	mee	*mí*
today	in-nyu	*inniu*
tomorrow	a-maw-rokk	*amárach*

IRISH

NUMBERS

1	eyn	*aon*	20	feekh	*fiche*	
2	doe	*dó*	21	feekh hayn	*fiche haon*	
3	three	*trí*	30	chree-o-kha	*tríocha*	
4	ka-hirr	*ceathair*	40	day-khayd	*daichead*	
5	koo-ig	*cúig*	50	ka-uga	*caoga*	
6	shey	*sé*	60	shay-ska	*seasca*	
7	shokt	*seacht*	70	shokt-oh	*seachtó*	
8	ukth	*ocht*	80	uk-thoh	*ochtó*	
9	nay	*naoi*	90	noh-kha	*nócha*	
10	jeh	*deich*	100	ka-de	*céad*	
11	ay-en dee-ug	*aon déag*	1000	mea-lah	*míle*	
12	doe yee-ugg	*dó dhéag*				

IRISH HERITAGE

ENGLISH	IRISH	
colleen	*cailín* (lit: a girl)	col-yeen
cairn	*carn* (lit: a pile of stones)	corr-an
clan	*clann* (lit: people with common ancestry)	klown
glen	*gleann* (lit: a valley)	gly-wan
slogan	*slua-ghairm* (lit: crowd call)	sloo-a gorr-im
tory	*tóraí* (lit: outlaw)	tohr-ee

ITALIAN

ITALIAN

QUICK REFERENCE

Hello.	bwon-*jor*-no/chao	Buongiorno./Ciao.
Goodbye.	ah-ree-ve-*der*-lah/chao	Arrivederla./Ciao.
Yes./No.	see/no	Sì./No.
Excuse me.	mee *sku*-zee	Mi scusi.
May I?	*pos*-so?	Posso?
Sorry.	mee dees-*pyah*-che	Mi dispiace.
Please.	per fah-*vo*-re	Per favore.
Thank you.	*grahts*-ye	Grazie
Cheers!	cheen cheen!	Cin cin!.
You're welcome.	*pre*-go	Prego.
Where's the ...	do-*ve* ...?	Dov'è ...?
What time is it?	che o-*rah* e?	Che ora è?

I'd like a ...	vor-*rey* ...	Vorrei ...
room	u-nah *kah*-me-rah	una camera
ticket to ...	un beel-*yet*-to per ...	un biglietto per ...

one-way	so-lah ahn-*dah*-tah	sola andata
return	ahn-*dah*-tah e ree-*tor*-no	andata e ritorno

I (don't) understand.		
(non) kah-*pee*-sko		(Non) capisco.
Do you speak English?		
pahr-lah ee-*gle*-ze?		Parla inglese?
Turn left/right ...		
jee-ree ah see-*nee*-strah/ de-strah ...		Giri a sinistra/ destra ...
Go straight ahead.		
see vah sem-pre *dreet*-to		Si va sempre diritto.
I'm looking for a public toilet.		
sto cher-*kan*-do ee gah-bee-*net*-tee		Sto cercando i gabinetti.
How much is it ...?		
kwahn-to ko-stah ...?		Quanto costa ...?

1	u-no	uno	6	sey	sei
2	du-e	due	7	set-te	sette
3	tre	tre	8	ot-to	otto
4	kwaht-tro	quattro	9	no-ve	nove
5	cheen-kwe	cinque	10	dee-e-chee	dieci

Italian is a Romance language – descended from Latin, the language of the Romans – and related to French, Spanish, Portuguese and Romanian. As English and Italian are both Indo-European languages and share common roots in Latin, you'll find many Italian words which are familiar.

While many and varied dialects are spoken in everyday conversation throughout Italy, standard Italian is the national language of schools, media and literature. A standard language began to be developed in the 13th and 14th centuries, predominantly through the works of Dante, Petrarch and Boccaccio, who wrote chiefly in the Florentine dialect, but also drawing on the dialect's Latin heritage as well as other dialects of Italy. Although there are still a great number of dialects spoken in Italy – some which are unintelligible to other Italian speakers – almost all Italians also speak, or at least understand, standard Italian.

There are around 60 million speakers of Italian in Italy, half a million in Switzerland where it's one of four official languages, and 1.5 million speakers in France and the former Yugoslavia.

Opera, film and literature, from the great Renaissance works to modern writers such as Umberto Eco and Alberto Moravia, have all contributed to portraying Italian as the vibrant, melodic and rich language that it is. It's not, however, a difficult language for English-speakers to learn, and Italians will welcome your attempts to communicate with them.

Although many Italians speak some English, it's more widely understood in the north – particularly in major centres such as Milan, Florence and Venice – than in the south. You'll find that staff at most hotels and restaurants speak some English, but you'll always receive a warm welcome if you attempt some Italian.

ITALIAN

PRONUNCIATION
Vowels
Vowels are generally more clipped than in English.

a	ah	as the 'a' in 'art', but shorter
e	e	as the 'e' in 'bed'
i	ee	as the 'i' in 'kiss', but slightly longer
o	o	as the 'o' in 'hot';
	o	sometimes as the 'o' in 'port'
u	u	as the 'u' in 'put'

Each vowel is pronounced, so, for example, the combination *ie* is pronounced as two sounds run together – 'i' as in 'kiss' and 'e' as in 'bed'.

GENDER

Some Italian nouns have both masculine and feminine forms. Often, masculine nouns end in *-o*, while feminine nouns end in *-a*. In this chapter, the masculine for appears first. The alternative feminine ending is separated by a slash. The phrase:

the child (m/f)   eel/lah   *il/la bambino/a*
bahm-*bee*-no/ah

indicates that the masculine form is *il bambino* and the feminine form is *la bambina*. In cases where the two forms are more complex, both forms of the word appear in full, separated by a slash.

student (m/f)   stu-*den*-te/   *studente/*
stu-den-*tes*-sah   *studentessa*

Consonants

The pronunciation of many consonants is the same as in English, but there are a few rules you should learn:

c	k	as the 'c' in 'cat' before *a*, *o*, *u* and *h*;
	ch	as the 'ch' in 'cheese' before *e* and *i*
g	g	before *a*, *o*, *u* and *h* as the 'g' in 'game';
	j	before *e* and *i* as the 'j' in 'joke'
sc	sk	before *a*, *o*, *u* and *h* as the 'sk' in 'skin'
	sh	before *e* and *i* as the 'sh' in 'shell'

CIAO GIOVANNI!

When *ci*, *gi* and *sci* are followed by *a*, *o* or *u*, the *i* isn't pronounced, unless it has an accent. Thus the name *Giovanni* is pronounced jo-*vahn*-nee and *ciao* is pronounced chao. Think of the *i* as being there simply to soften the sound.

h		always silent
r	r	trilled
z	dz	as the 'dz' sound in 'beds';
	ts	as the 'ts' in 'bits'
s	z	between two vowels, as the 's' in 'pose';
	s	elsewhere, as the 's' in 'sin'

BUONASERA

An exception to the above rule is the word *buonasera*, 'good evening'. The *s* in this word is pronounced as the 's' in 'sin'. This is because it's made up of two words that, over time, have come to be written as one word – *buona*, 'good', and *sera*, 'evening'.

ITALIAN

Combined Letters

Some letters, when combined, produce unexpected sounds:

gli	lyee	as the 'lli' in 'million'
gn	ny	as the 'ny' in 'canyon'

Double Consonants

These are pronounced as stronger, more intense sounds than single consonants. In contrast, the vowel that precedes a double consonant is shortened and clipped:

Pope	*papa*	*pah*-pah
baby food	*pappa*	*pahp*-pah
dog	*cane*	*cah*-ne
canes	*canne*	*can*-ne

Stress

Stress generally falls on the second-last syllable:

spaghetti	spa-*get*-ti	*spaghetti*

When a word has an accent, the stress should be pronounced on that syllable:

city	chit-*ta*	*città*

Intonation

Intonation is used much as it is in English. Questions are usually asked with rising intonation:

You're not from here.
    ley non *e* dee kwee   *Lei non è di qui.*
You're not from here?
    ley non *e* dee kwee?   *Lei non è di qui?*

While the first makes a statement, delivered in a flat tone, the second asks a question, delivered with rising intonation.

PRONOUNS					
SG			**PL**		
I	io	*io*	we	noi	*noi*
you (inf)	tu	*tu*	you (inf)	voi	*voi*
you (pol)	lei	*Lei*	you (pol)	lo-ro	*Loro*
he, it	lui	*lui*	they	lo-ro	*loro*
she, it	lei	*lei*			

ITALIAN

GREETINGS & CIVILITIES
You Should Know

Although *ciao* is a common greeting, it's best not to use it when addressing strangers unless they use it first. Use *buongiorno* and *arrivederla* (or *arrivederci*).

Good morning/ afternoon.	bwon-*jor*-no	*Buongiorno.*
Hello.	bwon-*jor*-no/chao	*Buongiorno./Ciao.*
Goodbye.	ah-ree-ve-*der*-lah/chao	*Arrivederla./Ciao.*
Good evening.	bwo-nah-*se*-rah	*Buonasera.*
Goodnight.	bwo-nah-*not*-te	*Buonanotte.*
See you later.	ah pyu *tahr*-dee	*A più tardi.*
How are you?	ko-me stah?	*Come sta?*
Well, thanks.	*be*-ne, *grahts*-ye	*Bene, grazie.*
Yes./No.	see/no	*Sì./No.*
Excuse me.	mee *sku*-zee	*Mi scusi.*
May I?	*pos*-so?	*Posso?*
Sorry. (Excuse/ forgive me.)	mee dees-*pyah*-che	*Mi dispiace.*
Please.	per fah-*vo*-re	*Per favore.*
Thank you (very much).	(tahn-te) *grahts*-ye	*(Tante) grazie.*
You're welcome.	pre-go	*Prego.*

ITALIAN

Forms of Address

Sir/Mr	see-*nyo*–re	*Signore (Sig.)*
Madam/Mrs/Ms	see-*nyo*-rah	*Signora (Sig.ra)*
companion	kom-*pahn*-yo/ah	*compagno/a*
friend	ah-*mee*-ko/ah	*amico/a*

SMALL TALK
Meeting People

What's your name?	ko-me see *kyah*-mah?	*Come si chiama?*
My name's ...	mee *kyah*-mo ...	*Mi chiamo ...*

I'd like to introduce you to ...
    vor-rey pre-sen-*tahr*-lah ah ...   *Vorrei presentarla a ...*
I'm pleased to meet you.
    pyah-*che*-re lye-to dee   *Piacere. Lieto di*
    ko-*no*-sher-lah   *conoscerla.*

I'm here ...	*so*-no kwee ...	*Sono qui ...*
on holiday	een vah-*kahn*-za	*in vacanza*
on business	per ahf-*fah*-ree	*per affari*
to study	per mo-*tee*-vee	*per motivi di*
	dee *stu*-dyo	*di studio*

I/We like Italy very much.
    mee/chee *pyah*-che   *Mi/Ci piace molto l'Italia.*
    mol-to lee-*tah*-lya

Nationalities

You'll find that many country names in Italian are similar to English. If your country isn't listed here, try saying it with Italian pronunciation and you'll most likely be understood. For example, 'Nigeria' is pronounced nee-jer-ee-ah

Where are you (sg/pl) from?
    dah do-ve vye-ne/ve-nee-te?   *Da dove viene/venite?*

I/We come from ...	ven-go/ve-nyah-mo ...	Vengo/Veniamo ...
Australia	dahl-lah-u-strah-lya	dall'Australia
Canada	dahl cah-nah-dah	dal Canadà
Ireland	dahl-leer-lahn-dah	dall'Irlanda
New Zealand	dahl-lah nwo-vah ze-lahn-dah	dalla Nuova Zelanda
Scotland	dahl-lah sko-zyah	dalla Scozia
South Africa	dah sud ah-free-kah	dal Sudafrica
the UK	dahl ren-yo u-nee-to	dal Regno Unito
the US	dahl-yee stah-tee u-nee-tee	dagli Stati Uniti
Wales	dahl gahl-les	dal Galles

ITALIAN

Occupations

What (work) do you do?
ke lah-vo-ro fah?   Che lavoro fa?

I'm (a/an) ...	so-no ...	Sono ...
artist	ahr-tee-stah	artista
business person	wo-mo/don-nah dahf-fah-ree	uomo/donna d'affari
doctor	me-dee-ko	medico
engineer	een-jen-ye-re	ingegnere
factory worker	o-pe-rah-yo/ah	operaio/a
homemaker	wo-mo/don-nah dee kah-zah	uomo/donna di casa
mechanic	mek-kah-nee-ko/ah	meccanico/a
musician	mu-zee-chee-stah	musicista
nurse	een-fer-mee-ye-re/ah	infermiere/a
office worker	eem-pee-ye-gah-to/ah	impiegato/a
retired	een pen-syo-ne	in pensione
secretary	se-gre-tah-ryo/ah	segretario/a
student	stu-den-te/ stu-den-tes-sah	studente/ studentessa
teacher	een-sen-yahn-te	insegnante
unemployed	dee-zok-ku-pah-to/ah	disoccupato/a
writer	skreet-tree-che/ skreet-to-re	scrittrice/ scrittore

ITALIAN

Religion

About 85 percent of Italians are Catholic, but only about 25 percent of these attend Mass regularly. Religious festivals always attract a large turnout, and many Italians are familiar with the saints and keep an interest in the activities of the Pope.

What's your religion?
    dee ke re-lee-*jo*-ne e ley?   *Di che religione è Lei?*

I'm ...	so-no ...	*Sono ...*
Anglican	ahn-glee-*kah*-no/ah	*anglicano/a*
Buddhist	bud-*dee*-stah	*buddista*
Catholic	kaht-*to*-lee-ko/ah	*cattolico/a*
Christian	kree-*styah*-no/ah	*cristiano/a*
Hindu	een-*du*	*indù*
Jewish	e-*bre*-o/ah	*ebreo/a*
Lutheran	lu-te-*rah*-no/ah	*luterano/a*
Muslim	mu-sul-*mah*-no/ah	*musulmano/a*
Orthodox	or-to-*dos*-so/ah	*ortodosso/a*
Protestant	pro-te-*stahn*-te	*protestante*

I'm not religious.
    non so-no re-lee-*jo*-zo/ah   *Non sono religioso/a.*
I believe in destiny/fate.
    so-no fah-tah-*lee*-stah   *Sono fatalista.*
I'm an atheist.
    so-no *ah*-te-o/ah   *Sono ateo/a.*
I'm agnostic.
    so-no an-yo-stee-ko/ah   *Sono agnostico/a.*

ITALIAN

Family

Do you have a girlfriend/boyfriend?
ahy u-nah rah-*gahts*-ah/   *Hai una ragazza/*
un rah-*gahts*-o?   *un ragazzo?*

How many children do you have?
kwahn-tee *fee*-lyee ahy?   *Quanti figli hai?*

I'm ...	so-no ...	*Sono ...*
divorced	dee-vor-*zyah*-to/ah	*divorziato/a*
separated	se-pah-*rah*-to/ah	*separato/a*
single	*che*-lee-be/*nu*-bee-le	*celibe/nubile*
widowed	*ve*-do-vo/ah	*vedovo/a*

I have a partner.
o un/u-nah kom-*pahn*-yo/ah   *Ho un/una compagno/a.*

I don't have any children.
non *o* feel-yee   *Non ho figli.*

I have a daughter/son.
o un feel-yo/u-nah feel-yah   *Ho un figlio/una figlia.*

baby	be-*be*	*bebé*
boy	eel bahm-*bee*-no	*il bambino*
brother	eel frah-*tel*-lo	*il fratello*
children	ee feel-yee	*i figli*
cousin (m/f)	eel/lah ku-*jee*-no/ah	*il/la cugino/a*
dad	eel pah-*pah*	*il papà*
daughter	lah feel-yah	*la figlia*
family	lah fah-*meel*-yah	*la famiglia*
father	eel pah-dre	*il padre*
girl	lah bahm-*bee*-nah	*la bambina*
grandfather	eel non-no	*il nonno*
grandmother	lah non-nah	*la nonna*
husband	eel mah-*ree*-to	*il marito*
mother	lah mah-dre	*la madre*
mum	lah mahm-mah	*la mamma*
sister	lah so-*rel*-lah	*la sorella*
son	eel feel-yo	*il figlio*
wife	lah mol-ye	*la moglie*

ITALIAN

Feelings

I (don't) like ...	(non) mee *pyah*-che ...	*(Non) mi piace ...*
I'm sorry. (condolence)	mee dee-*spyah*-che	*Mi dispiace.*
I'm well/fine.	sto *be*-ne	*Sto bene.*
I'm grateful.	lah reen-*grahts*-yo	*La ringrazio.*

I'm ...	o ...	*Ho ...*
Are you ...?	ah ...?	*Ha ...?*
cold	*fred*-do	*freddo*
hot	*kahl*-do	*caldo*
hungry	*fah*-me	*fame*
in a hurry	*fret*-tah	*fretta*
right	rah-*jo*-ne	*ragione*
sleepy	*son*-no	*sonno*
thirsty	*se*-te	*sete*
wrong	*tor*-to	*torto*

I'm ...	*so*-no ...	*Sono ...*
Are you ...?	e ...?	*È ...?*
angry	ahr-rahb-*byah*-to/ah	*arrabbiato/a*
happy	fe-*lee*-che	*felice*
sad	*tree*-ste	*triste*
tired	*stahn*-ko/ah	*stanco/a*
worried	pre-ok-ku-*pah*-to/ah	*preoccupato/a*

BREAKING THE LANGUAGE BARRIER

Do you speak English?
    pahr-lah ee-*gle*-ze?   *Parla inglese?*
Do you understand?
    kah-*pee*-she?   *Capisce?*
I (don't) understand.
    (non) kah-*pee*-sko   *(Non) capisco.*
I speak a little Italian.
    pahr-lo un *po* dee-tah-*lyah*-no   *Parlo un po' d'italiano.*

Could you speak more slowly please?
pwo par-*lah*-re pyoo
len-tah-*men*-te, per fah-*vo*-re?

*Può parlarepiù
lentamente, per favore?*

Could you repeat that, please?
pwo ree-*pe*-ter-lo, per fah-*vo*-re?

Può ripeterlo, per favore?

Could you write that down, please?
pwo *skree*-ver-lo, per fah-*vo*-re?

Può scriverlo, per favore?

How do you say ...?
ko-me see dee-che ...?

Come si dice ...?

ITALIAN

SIGNS

ACCETTAZIONE	CHECK-IN
ALT	STOP
BIGLIETTERIA	TICKET OFFICE
BINARIO	PLATFORM
DA QUESTA PARTE PER ...	THIS WAY TO ...
DARE LA PRECEDENZA	GIVE WAY
DEVIAZIONE	DETOUR
FERMATA ...	... STOP
DELL'AUTOBUS	BUS
DEL TRAM	TRAM
METRÒ	METRO/ UNDERGROUND
ORARIO	TIMETABLE
PARTENZE	DEPARTURES
POSTEGGIO TAXI	TAXI STAND
SENSO UNICO	ONE WAY
SOSTA VIETATA	NO PARKING
STAZIONE FERROVIARIA	TRAIN STATION
STOP	STOP
USCITA	EXIT

ITALIAN

PAPERWORK

certificato di nascita	birth certificate
data di nascita	date of birth
età	age
indirizzo	address
luogo di nascita	place of birth
motivi di viaggio	reason for travel
nazionalità	nationality
nome	name
patente (di guida)	drivers licence
(numero del) passaporto	passport (number)
professione	profession
registrazione	car registration
religione	religion
sesso	sex
stato civile	marital status
divorziata/o	divorced
nubile (f)/celibe (m)	single
sposata/o	married
visto consolare	visa

GETTING AROUND
Directions

Excuse me, can you help me please?
  sku-zee, mee pwo ah-yu-   *Scusi, mi può aiutare per*
  tah-re per fah-*vo*-re?   *favore?*
Can you show me (on the map)?
  pwo mo-*strahr*-mee   *Può mostrarmi (sulla carta)?*
  (sul-lah kahr-tah)?

Turn left ...	jee-ree ah see-*nee*-strah ...	*Giri a sinistra ...*
Turn right ...	jee-ree ah de-strah ...	*Giri a destra ...*
at the next corner	ahl pros-*see*-mo *ahn*-go-lo	*al prossimo angolo*
at the intersection	al-leen-*kro*-cho	*all'incrocio*
at the traffic lights	ahl se-*mah*-fo-ro	*al semaforo*

ITALIAN

Cross the road.
 see aht-trah-*ver*-sah lah   *Si attraversa la*
 strah-dah   *strada.*
Go straight ahead.
 see vah sem-pre *dreet*-to   *Si va sempre diritto.*

after	*do*-po	*dopo*
behind	*dye*-tro	*dietro*
between	frah/trah	*fra/tra*
far	lon-*tah*-no	*lontano*
in front of	dah-*vahn*-tee ah	*davanti a*
near	vee-*chee*-no	*vicino*
next to	ahk-*kahn*-to ah	*accanto a*
opposite	dee *fron*-te ah	*di fronte a*

avenue	vyah-le	*viale* (m)
square	*pyaht*-tsah	*piazza* (f)
street	*strah*-dah	*strada* (f)

north	nord	*nord*
south	sud	*sud*
east	est	*est*
west	o-vest	*ovest*

Buying Tickets

Excuse me, where's the ticket office?
 sku-zee, do-*ve* lah   *Scusi, dov'è la*
 beel-yet-te-*ree*-ah?   *biglietteria?*
I want to go to ...
 vor-rey ahn-*dah*-re ah ...   *Vorrei andare a ...*
How much is the fare to ...?
 kwahn-to ko-stah eel   *Quanto costa il*
 beel-*yet*-to per ...?   *biglietto per ...?*

I'd like (a) ...   vor-rey un   *Vorrei un*
ticket.   beel-*yet*-to dee ...   *biglietto di ...*
 one-way   so-lah ahn-*dah*-tah   *sola andata*
 return   ahn-*dah*-tah e ree-*tor*-no   *andata e ritorno.*
 (two) tickets   (du-e) beel-*yet*-tee   *(due) biglietti.*

ITALIAN

... fare	u-no skon-to per ...	*uno sconto per ...*
child's	bahm-*bee*-nee	*bambini*
pensioner's	pen-syo-*nah*-tee	*pensionati*
student's	stu-*den*-tee	*studenti.*

1st class	pree-mah klahs-se	*prima classe*
2nd class	se-*kon*-dah klahs-se	*seconda classe*

I'd like to ... my/ our reservation.	vor-rey ... lah mee-ah/no-strah pre-no-tahts-*yo*-ne	*Vorrei ... la mia/ nostra prenotazione.*
cancel	kahn-chel-*lah*-re	*cancellare*
change	kahm-*byah*-re	*cambiare*
confirm	kon-fer-*mah*-re	*confermare*

Bus & Coach

Where's the bus stop?
do-*ve* lah fer-*mah*-tah del-*lah*-u-to-bus?   *Dov'è la fermata dell'autobus?*
Which bus goes to ...?
kwah-le *ah*-u-to-bus vah ah ...?   *Quale autobus va a ...?*

Does this bus go to the ...?	kwe-sto *ah*-u-to-bus vah ah ...?	*Questo autobus va a ...?*
beach	lah spyahj-jah	*la spiaggia*
city centre	eel chen-tro	*il centro*
station	lah stahts-*yo*-ne	*la stazione*

What time's the ... bus?	ah ke o-rah pahs-sah ... *ah*-u-to-bus?	*A che ora passa ... autobus?*
first	eel pree-mo	*il primo*
last	*lul*-tee-mo	*l'ultimo*
next	eel *pros*-see-mo	*il prossimo*

Do you stop at ...?
see fer-mah ah ...?   *Si ferma a ...?*

Could you let me know when
we get to ...?
 mee pwo dee-re kwahn-do
 ahr-ree-*vyah*-mo ah ...?

*Mi può dire quando
arriviamo a ...?*

I want to get off!
 vor-rey *shen*-de-re!

Vorrei scendere!

ITALIAN

Metro

Which line takes me to ...?
 kwah-*le* lah *lee*-ne-ah per
 ahn-*dah*-re ah ...?

*Qual è la linea per
andare a ...?*

Where do I change for ...?
 do-ve de-vo
 kahm-*byah*-re per ...?

*Dove devo
cambiare per ...?*

What's the next station?
 kwah-*le* lah *pros*-see-mah
 staht*s-yo*-ne?

*Qual è la prossima
stazione?*

Train

Where's the nearest station?
 do-*ve* lah stahts-*yo*-ne pyu
 vee-*chee*-nah?

Dov'è la stazione più vicina?

Is this the right platform for ...?
 e kwe-sto eel
 bee-*nah*-ryo per ...?

È questo il binario per ...?

Is that seat taken?
 e ok-ku-*pah*-to
 kwe-sto po-sto?

*È occupato
quel posto?*

Do you mind if I open/close
the window?
 le dee-*spyah*-che se ah-pro/
 kyu-do eel fee-ne-*stree*-no?

*Le dispiace se apro/chiudo il
finestrino?*

ITALIAN

Taxi

Are you free?	e *lee*-be-ro?	*È libero?*

Please take me to the/this ...	mee por-tee ... per-pyah-*che*-re	*Mi porti ... per piacere.*
address	ah kwe-sto een-dee-*ree*-tso	*a questo indirizzo*
airport	ahl-lah-e-ro-*por*-to	*all'aeroporto*
city centre	een *chen*-tro	*in centro*
railway station	ahl-lah staht*s-yo*-ne	*alla stazione ferroviaria*

How much is it to go to ...?
kwahn-to ko-stah
ahn-*dah*-re ah ...?

Quanto costa andare a ...?

Does the price include luggage?
lah tah-*reef*-fah kom-*pren*-de
ahn-ke ee bah-*gahl*-yee?

La tariffa comprende anche i bagagli?

Can you take (five) people?
pwo por-*tah*-re (cheen-kwe)
per-*so*-ne?

Può portare (cinque) persone?

Please hurry.
pwo ahch-che-le-*rah*-re,
per fah-*vo*-re?

Può accelerare, per favore?

Please slow down.
pwo rahl-len-*tah*-re per
fah-*vo*-re?

Può rallentare, per favore?

Keep going!
ah-vahn-tee!

Avanti!

The next corner, please.
ahl *pros*-see-mo *ahn*-go-lo,
per fah-*vo*-re

Al prossimo angolo, per favore.

The next street to the left/right.
e lah *pros*-see-mah strah-dah
ah see-*nee*-strah/des-trah

È la prossima strada a sinistra/destra.

Here's fine, thanks.
kwee vah be-*nees*-see-mo, *Qui va benissimo,*
grahts-ye *grazie.*

Please wait here.
mee ah-*spet*-tee kwee, *Mi aspetti qui,*
per fah-*vo*-re *per favore.*

ITALIAN

Useful Phrases

What time does	ah ke o-rah pahr-te/	*A che ora*
the ... leave/arrive?	ahr-ree-vah ...?	*parte/arriva ...?*
airplane	lah-*e*-re-o	*l'aereo*
boat	lah nah-ve	*la nave*
bus	*lah*-u-to-bus	*l'autobus*
ferry	eel trah-*get*-to	*il traghetto*
train	eel tre-no	*il treno*

Car

Where can I rent a car?
do-ve pos-so no-lej-*jah*-re *Dove posso noleggiare*
u-nah *mahk*-kee-nah? *una macchina?*

How much is it ...?	kwahn-to ko-stah ...?	*Quanto costa ...?*
daily	ahl jor-no	*al giorno*
weekly	ahl-lah set-tee-*mah*-nah	*alla settimana*

Does that include insurance?
e kom-*pre*-sah *lahs*-see- *È compresa l'assicurazione?*
ku-rah*ts*-*yo*-ne?

Where's the next petrol station?
do-*ve* lah *pros*-see-mah *Dov'è la prossima*
stah*ts*-*yo*-ne dee ser-*veets*-yo? *stazione di servizio?*

Please fill the tank.
eel pee-ye-no, per fah-*vo*-re *Il pieno, per favore.*

I want ... litres of petrol (gas).
vor-rey ... lee-tree *Vorrei ... litri*
(dee ben-*zee*-nah) *(di benzina).*

ITALIAN

air	lah-ryah	l'aria
battery	lah baht-te-*ree*-ah	la batteria
brakes	ee *fre*-nee	i freni
clutch	lah freets-*yo*-ne	la frizione
diesel	eel gah-*so*-lee-o	il gasolio
drivers licence	lah pah-*ten*-te (dee *gwee*-dah)	la patente (di guida)
engine	eel mo-*to*-re	il motore
garage	eel gah-*rahj*	il garage
headlights	lyee ah-nahb-bahl-*yahn*-tee	gli anabbaglianti
high beam	lyee ahb-bahl-*yahn*-tee	gli abbaglianti
indicator	lah *spee*-ah	la spia
leaded	kon *pyom*-bo	con piombo
main road	lah *strah*-dah preen-chee-*pah*-le	la strada principale

motorway	*lah*-u-to-*strah*-dah	l'autostrada
oil	*lo*-lee-o	l'olio
puncture	lah fo-rah-*tu*-rah	la foratura
radiator	eel rah-dyah-*to*-re	il radiatore
road map	lah *kahr*-tah strah-*dah*-le	la carta stradale
seatbelt	lah cheen-*tu*-rah dee see-ku-*ret*-tsah	la cintura di sicurezza
speed limit	eel *lee*-mee-te dee ve-lo-chee-*tah*	il limite di velocità
super	eel *su*-per	il super
tail lights	ee fah-nah-*lee*-nee dee ko-dah	i fanalini di coda
tyre (sg/pl)	lah/le *gom*-mah/e	la/le gomma/e
unleaded	sen-zah *pyom*-bo	senza piombo
windscreen	eel *pah*-rah-*bret*-tsah	il parabrezza

ACCOMMODATION
At the Hotel

ITALIAN

I'd like ...	vor-rey ...	*Vorrei ...*
a bed	un let-to	*un letto*
a single room	u-nah *kah*-me-rah *seen*-go-lah	*una camera singola*
to share a room	dee-*vee*-de-re u-nah stahn-zah	*dividere una stanza*

I want a room with a ...	vor-rey u-nah *kah*-me-rah kon ...	*Vorrei una camera con ...*
bathroom	bahn-yo	*bagno*
double bed	u-nah dop-pyah mah-tree-mo-*nyah*-le	*una doppia matrimoniale*
twin beds	u-nah dop-pyah ah du-e let-tee	*una doppia a due letti*

I have a reservation.
  o u-nah pre-no-tahts-*yo*-ne   *Ho una prenotazione.*

Where's the bathroom?
  do-*ve* eel bahn-yo?   *Dov'è il bagno?*

Can I see it?
  pos-so ve-*der*-lah?   *Posso vederla?*

Do you have a safe?
  che u-nah kahs-*set*-tah
  dee see-ku-*ret*-tsah?   *C'è una cassetta disicurezza?*

The key for room ... please.
  lah kyah-ve per lah
  kah-me-rah ... per
  pyah-*che*-re   *La chiave per la camera ... per piacere.*

I've locked myself (m/f)
out of my room.
  mee so-no kyu-zo/ah
  fwo-ree dahl-lah mee-ah
  kah-me-rah   *Mi sono chiuso/a fuori dalla mia camera.*

Can you give me an extra blanket?
  pwo dahr-mee u-*nahl*-trah
  ko-*per*-tah?   *Può darmi un'altra coperta?*

ITALIAN

I'm/We're leaving now.
pahr-to/pahr-*tyah*-mo ah-*des*-so   *Parto/Partiamo adesso.*
Can I leave my backpack
at reception?
pos-so lah-*shah*-re eel mee-o   *Posso lasciare il mio*
zah-ee-no ahl-lah reception?   *zaino alla reception?*
Please call a taxi for me.
mee kyah-mah un tahk-see   *Mi chiama un taxi,*
per pyah-*che*-re?   *per piacere?*

(See also Camping, page 304.)

AROUND TOWN
At the Post Office

I'd like to send a/an ...   vor-rey mahn-   *Vorrei mandare ...*
dah-re ...

aerogram	un-*ah*-e-ro-*grahm*-mah	*un aerogramma*
letter	u-nah *let*-te-rah	*una lettera*
parcel	un pahk-*ket*-to	*un pacchetto*
postcard	u-nah kahr-to-*lee*-nah	*una cartolina*
telegram	un te-le-*grahm*-mah	*un telegramma*

I'd like some stamps, please.
vor-rey dey frahn-ko-*bol*-lee,   *Vorrei dei francobolli,*
per fah-*vo*-re   *perfavore.*
How much to send this to ...?
kwahn-*te* lahf-frahn-kah-   *Quant'è l'affrancatura*
tu-rah per ...?   *per ...?*

ITALIAN

Where's the poste restante section?
   do-*ve* eel fer-mo po-*stah*?   *Dov'è il fermo posta?*
Is there any mail for me?
   che po-*stah* per me?   *C'è posta per me?*

air mail	vee-ah ah-*e*-re-ah	*via aerea*
envelope	u-nah bu-stah	*una busta*
express	e-*spres*-so	*espresso*
insured mail	(lah po-stah) ahs-see-ku-*rah*-tah	*(la posta) assicurata*
mailbox	lah kahs-*set*-tah po-*stah*-le	*la cassetta postale*
postcode	eel *ko*-dee-che po-*stah*-le	*il codice postale*
poste restante	eel fer-mo po-stah	*il fermo posta*
registered mail	(lah po-stah) rahk-ko-mahn-*dah*-tah	*(la posta) raccomandata*
surface mail	lah po-stah or-dee-*nah*-ryah	*la posta ordinaria*

Telephone

I want to ring ...
   vor-rey te-le-fo-*nah*-re ah/een ...   *Vorrei telefonare a (+ city)/in (+ country) ...*
What's the area code for ...?
   kwah-*le* eel pre-*fees*-so per ...?   *Qual è il prefisso per ...?*
I'd like to make a reverse-charge (collect) phone call.
   vor-rey fah-re u-nah kyah-*mah*-tah ah *kah*-ree-ko del de-stee-nah-*tah*-ryo   *Vorrei fare una chiamata a carico del destinatario.*
The number is ...
   eel *nu*-me-ro *e* ...   *Il numero è ...*
It's engaged.
   lah *lee*-ne-ah *e* ok-ku-*pah*-tah   *La linea è occupata.*

ITALIAN

Hello!	pron-to!	*Pronto!*
It's ...	so-no ...	*Sono ...*
Is ... there?	che ...?	*C'è ...?*

I've been cut off.
  e kah-*du*-tah lah *lee*-ne-ah   *È caduta la linea.*

Internet

Where can I access email/the Internet?
  do-ve pos-so oo-*sah*-re
  lee-mah-eel/*leen*-ter-net?   *Dove posso usare*
                                         l'email/l'internet?
I'd like to check my email.
  vor-rey kon-trol-*lah*-re
  eel mee-o *ee*-ma-eel   *Vorrei controllare il mio*
                                email.

At the Bank

Can I use my credit card to
withdraw money?
  see pwo u-*sah*-re lah   *Si può usare la*
  kahr-tah dee *kre*-dee-to   *carta di credito*
  per fah-re pre-*lee-e*-vee?   *per fare prelievi?*
Can I change money here?
  see kahm-byah de-*nah*-ro kwee?   *Si cambia denaro qui?*

I want to exchange	vor-rey kahm-	*Vorrei*
some ...	*byah*-re ...	*cambiare ...*
money	del de-*nah*-ro	*del denaro*
travellers cheques	dey travellers	*dei travellers*
	che-kes	*cheques*

What's the exchange rate?
  kwahn-*te* eel kahm-byo?   *Quant'è il cambio?*
How many Euros/lire to the dollar?
  ah kwahn-tee e-u-ro/   *A quanti euro/*
  kwahn-te lee-re see   *quante lire si*
  kahm-byah eel *dol*-lah-ro?   *cambia il dollaro?*
Please write it down.
  pwo *skree*-ver-lo per fah-*vo*-re?   *Può scriverlo, per favore?*

ITALIAN

What's your commission?
kwah-*le* lah vo-strah
kom-mees-*syo*-ne?

Qual è la vostra commissione?

The automatic teller machine
swallowed my credit card.
eel *bahn*-ko-maht ah traht-
te-*nu*-to lah mee-ah kahr-
tah dee *kre*-dee-to

*Il Bancomat ha trattenuto la
mia carta di credito.*

INTERESTS & ENTERTAINMENT
Sightseeing
Do you have a local map?
ah u-nah pyahn-tah
del-lah cheet-*tah*?

*Ha una pianta
della città?*

What are the main attractions?
kwah-lee so-no le
mahj-*jo*-ree
aht-trah*ts*-yo-nee?

*Quali sono le
maggiori
attrazioni?*

What's that?
ko-*se*?

Cos'è?

Can I take photographs?
pos-so fah-re fo-to-grah-*fee*-e?

Posso fare fotografie?

What time does it open/close?
ah ke o-rah ah-pre/
kyu-de?

A che ora apre/chiude?

Is there an admission charge?
che un pret-tso deen-*gres*-so?

C'è un prezzo d'ingresso?

Going Out
What's there to do
in the evenings?
ko-sah see fah dee se-rah?

Cosa si fa di sera?

What's on tonight?
ke *che* een pro-*grahm*-mah
stah-*se*-rah?

*Che c'è in programma
stasera?*

ITALIAN

I feel like going to a/the ...	o vol-yah dee ahn-*dah*-re ...	*Ho voglia di andare ...*
bar	ahl bahr	*al bar*
cafe	ahl kahf-*fe*	*al caffè*
cinema	ahl *chee*-ne-mah	*al cinema*
concert/gig	ah un kon-*cher*-to	*a un concerto*
nightclub	een-un nait-klub	*in un nightclub*
opera	ahl-*lo*-pe-rah	*all'opera*
restaurant	een un ree-sto-*rahm*-te	*in un ristorante*
theatre	ahl te-*ah*-tro	*al teatro*

Do you (sg/pl) want to
go out tonight?
vwo-ee/vo-*le*-te u-*shee*-re
stah-*se*-rah?

*Vuoi/Volete uscire
stasera?*

Would you (sg/pl) like to
go for a drink/meal?
vwo-ee/vo-*le*-te ahn-*dah*-re
ah *pren*-de-re kwahl-*ko*-zah?

*Vuoi/Volete andare a
prendere qualcosa?*

| Yes, I'd love to. | *see* me pyah-che-*reb*-be | *Sì, mi piacerebbe.* |
| Sorry, I can't. | no *te*-mo dee no | *No, temo di no.* |

Sports & Interests

What do you do in your spare time?
ko-zah fahy nel tu-o tem-po
lee-be-ro?

*Cosa fai nel tuo tempo
libero?*

| What sport do you play? | kwah-le sport *prah*-tee-kee? | *Quale sport pratichi?* |

art	*lahr*-te	*l'arte*
basketball	lah pahl-lah-kah-*ne*-stro	*la pallacanestro*
cooking	ku-chee-*nah*-re	*cucinare*
fishing	lah pe-skah	*la pesca*
football	eel fut-bal	*il football*
going out	u-*shee*-re	*uscire*
going to the cinema	ahn-*dah*-re ahl *chee*-ne-mah	*andare al cinema*

ITALIAN

music	lah *mu*-zee-kah	*la musica*
photography	lah fo-to-grah-*fee*-ah	*la fotografia*
reading	lej-*je*-re	*leggere*
shopping	fah-re lo shop-ping	*fare lo shopping*
soccer	kahl-cho	*calcio*
sport	lo sport	*lo sport*
the theatre	eel te-*ah*-tro	*il teatro*
travelling	vyahj-*jah*-re	*viaggiare*
writing	*skree*-ve-re	*scrivere*

Festivals

Carnevale
during the period before Ash Wednesday, many towns stage carnivals and enjoy their last opportunity to indulge before Lent. The carnival held in Venice during the 10 days before Ash Wednesday is the most famous, but the more traditional and popular carnival celebrations are held at Viareggio on the north coast of Tuscany and at Ivrea, near Turin.

Corsa dei Ceri (Race of the Candles, 15 May)
this exciting and intensely traditional event is held at Gubbio, Umbria. Groups of men carrying huge wooden shrines race uphill to the town's basilica, dedicated to the patron saint Ubaldo.

Il Palio (2 July & 16 August)
the pride and joy of Siena, this famous traditional event is held twice a year in the town's beautiful Piazza del Campo. It involves a dangerous bareback horse race around the piazza, preceded by a parade of supporters in traditional costume.

Natale (Christmas)
during the weeks preceding Christmas, there are numerous processions, religious events and celebrations. Many churches set up elaborate cribs or nativity scenes known as *presepi*.

| Merry Christmas! | bwon nah-*tah*-le | *Buon Natale!* |
| Happy New Year! | bwo-*nahn*-no | *Buon Anno!* |

ITALIAN

IN THE COUNTRY
Weather

Will it be ... tomorrow?	do-*mah*-nee ... sah-*rah*?	*Domani ... sarà?*
The weather's ... today.	oj-jee e ...	*Oggi è ...*
cloudy	nu-vo-*lo*-zo	*nuvoloso*
cold	fred-do	*freddo*
drizzly	pyo-veej-jee-*no*-so	*piovigginoso*
foggy	neb-*byo*-zo	*nebbioso*
hot	kahl-do	*caldo*
sultry	ah-*fo*-zo	*afoso*
sunny	so-lej-*jah*-to	*soleggiato*

Camping

Where's the nearest campsite?	
do-*ve* eel kahm-*pej*-jo pyu vee-*chee*-no?	*Dov'è il campeggio più vicino?*
Am I allowed to camp here?	
see pwo pyahn-*tah*-re lah ten-dah kwee?	*Si può piantare la tenda qui?*
How much is it per night?	
kwahn-*te* per not-te?	*Quant'è per notte?*
Where can I get drinking water?	
do-ve tro-vo del-*lahk*-kwah po-*tah*-bee-le?	*Dove trovo dell'acqua potabile?*

ITALIAN

FOOD

Lunch is traditionally the main meal of the day, and shops and businesses close for three or four hours each afternoon to accommodate the meal and the siesta which usually follows.

breakfast	lah (pree-mah) ko-lah*ts*-yo-ne	*la (prima) colazione*
lunch	eel prahn-zo	*il pranzo*
dinner	lah che-nah	*la cena*

Vegetarian Meals

Vegetables are a staple of the Italian diet. *Contorni* are vegetable dishes prepared in various ways. *Antipasti* consist mainly of vegetables, and there are many vegetarian pasta sauces to choose from.

I'm (m/f) a vegetarian.
  so-no ve-je-tah-*ryah*-no/ah   *Sono vegetariano/a.*
Does this dish have meat?
  che kahr-ne een
  kwe-sto pyaht-to?   *C'è carne in questo piatto?*
Could you cook this
without meat?
  po-*tre*-ste pre-pah-*rah*-re
  kwe-sto pyaht-to sen-zah
  kahr-ne?   *Potreste preparare questo piatto senza carne?*

Staple Foods & Condiments

cured ham	pro-*shut*-to kru-do	*prosciutto crudo*
fish	eel pe-she	*il pesce*
fruit	lah frut-tah	*la frutta*
garlic	al-yo	*aglio*
meat	kahr-ne	*carne*
onion	lah chee-*pol*-lah	*la cipolla*
olive oil	eel o-lee-o	*il olio*
olives	le o-*lee*-ve	*le olive*
potato	lah pah-*tah*-tah	*la patata*
rice	ree-zo	*riso*
vegetables	ver-*du*-re	*verdure*

ITALIAN

Breakfast Menu

Breakfast usually consists of a quick cappuccino and a pastry, gulped down while standing at the bar.

cereal	ee fee-*ok*-kee	*i fiocchi*
pastry	eel kor-*net*-to	*il cornetto*
... eggs	le wo-vah ...	*le uova ...*
fried	freet-te	*fritte*
poached	een kah-*mee*-chah	*in camicia*
scrambled	strah-paht-*tsah*-te	*strapazzate*
soft-boiled	ahl-lah kok	*alla coque*

CAFFÈ

caffè llatte　　　kahf-fel-*laht*-te
coffee with milk – a breakfast drink.

caffè macchiato　　*kahf*-fe mahk-*kyah*-to
strong coffee with a little milk

cappuccino　　　kahp-pu-*chee*-no
named after the Capuchin monks who wore robes of chocolate and cream colours; considered a morning drink by Italians

corretto　　　kor-*ret*-to
coffee with a dash of liqueur; popular after-meal drink

doppio　　　*dop*-pyo
long and black; also known as *americano*

espresso　　　es-*pres*-so
very strong black coffee served in small cups and drunk at any time of the day

latte macchiato　　*laht*-te mahk-*kyah*-to
hot milk with a little coffee; enjoyed by children

ristretto　　　ree-*stret*-to
very concentrated, even stronger than the espresso; strictly for the initiated

MENU DECODER

ITALIAN

Starters

antipasto misto	assortment of cold appetisers
bruschetta	crisp, baked bread slices in oil, often with tomato on top (Florence, Tuscany)
cappelletti	a form of ravioli, with various stuffings, in broth
caponata (alla siciliana)	eggplant dish with capers, olives, onion and anchovies (Sicily)
ceci con origano	marinated chickpeas with oregano
condimento al pepe	pepper relish
cuscucu	fish soup (Sicily)
olive ascolane	stuffed, deep-fried olives
polenta	cornmeal, often sliced and deep-fried
prosciutto e melone	melon with cured ham
sottaceti	pickled vegetables
stracciatella	egg in broth
zuppa pavese	Pavian soup of bread, butter, chicken broth and eggs

Pasta Sauces

alfredo	butter, cream, Parmesan cheese and parsley
aglio e olio	garlic and olive oil
alla checca	cold summer sauce of ripe tomato, olives, basil, capers and oregano (Rome)
alla puttanesca	spicy tomato sauce with anchovies, capers, olives and basil
alla siciliana	eggplant, anchovies, olives, capers, tomato and garlic
al ragù	chunks of meat, tomato, onion and herbs
al tonno e funghi	tuna and mushrooms in a tomato and cream sauce
misto di mare	mixed seafood, often served in cream and wine

Main Meals

anelletti gratinati	crumbed fried cuttlefish rings (Sicily)
baccalà mantecato	puree of salt cod, served with polenta (Veneto)
bistecca alla fiorentina all'etto	huge grilled T-bone steak (Florence)

ITALIAN

bollito misto	various meats boiled and served with vegetables (Turin, Piedmont)
bomba di riso	rice with pigeon (Parma)
burrida/ciuppa	fish stew (Genoa, Liguria)
busella	tripe dish (Milan, Lombardy)
calzone	folded pizza (Naples)
capon magro	salad made with vegetables and fish (Genoa, Liguria)
cima	cold veal stuffed with pork, sweet breads, nuts, peas and egg (Genoa)
cotechino	sausage stuffed with raw, spiced pork (Emilia-Romagna)
involtini	stuffed veal rolls (Bologna, Emilia-Romagna)
risi e bisi	risotto with green peas (Venice, Veneto)
risotto in capro roman	risotto with mutton (Venice)
sartù	savoury rice dish (Naples)
supplì	deep-fried balls of rice filled with mozzarella cheese and tomato sauce
tacchino con sugo di melagrana	turkey with pomegranate sauce (Venice, Veneto)
tortino di abbacchio	flat omelette with vegetables (Florence, Tuscany)
zampone	pig's trotters stuffed with raw, spiced sausage (Modena)
zimmo sfogie in saòr	sole with herbs and garlic (Venice, Veneto)

Desserts

bignè alla cioccolata	puff pastry filled with cream and covered with chocolate
cannoli	tubes of sweet pastry filled with a rich cream
cassata	pudding made with sponge cake, cream, fruit and chocolate; also an ice-cream
granita di limone	lemon-water ice
macedonia	fruit salad
panettone	large, dry yeast cake
paste di mandorle	almond pastries
zabaglione	egg yolk whipped with sugar and Marsala
zuccotto	almond and hazelnut cake with brandy

ITALIAN

Non-Alcoholic Drinks

almond milk	lor-*zah*-tah	*l'orzata*
chinotto (some-thing like bitter cola)	eel kee-*not*-to	*il chinotto*
fruit juice	eel *suk*-ko dee *frut*-tah	*il succo di frutta*
milk	eel *laht*-te	*il latte*
orange juice	eel *suk*-ko dah-*rahn*-chah	*il succo d'arancia*
soft drink	lah *bee*-bee-tah	*la bibita*
(herbal) tea	eel te (*ahl*-le *er*-be)	*il tè (alle erbe)*
... water	*lahk*-kwah	*l'acqua ...*
mineral	mee-ne-*rah*-le	*minerale*
plain	nah-tu-*rah*-le	*naturale*

Alcoholic Drinks

I'll have a/an...	*pren*-do ...	*Prendo ...*
anise	u-nah sahm-*bu*-kah	*una sambuca*
aperitif	un*fah*-pe-ree-*tee*-vo	*un aperitivo*
beer	u-nah beer-rah	*una birra*
bitters	un-*ah*-mah-ro	*un amaro*
digestive liqueur	un dee-je-*stee*-vo	*un digestivo*
brandy	un ko-*nyahk*	*un cognac*
champagne	u-no shahm-*pahn*-ye	*uno champagne*
cocktail	un kok-tah-eel	*un cocktail*
cider	un see-dro	*un sidro*
grappa	u-nah grahp-pah	*una grappa*
martini	un mahr-*tee*-nee	*un martini*
rum	un rum	*un rum*
whisky	un wis-kee	*un whisky*
(glass of)	(un beek-*kye*-re dee)	*(un bicchiere di)*
wine	vee-no	*vino*
red	*ros*-so	*rosso*
white	bee-*ahn*-ko	*bianco*
rosé	ro-*zah*-to	*rosato*
Cheers!	cheen cheen!	*Cin cin!*

ITALIAN

AT THE MARKET

Basics

bread	eel *pah*-ne	il pane
butter	eel *bu*-ro	il burro
cereal	ee fee-*ok*-kee	i fiocchi
cheese	eel for-*mahj*-jo	il formaggio
chocolate	eel chok-ko-*lah*-to	il cioccolato
eggs	le *wo*-vah	le uova
flour	lah *fah*-ree-nah	la farina
margarine	lah mahr-gah-*ree*-nah	la margarina
milk	eel *laht*-te	il latte
olive oil	*lo*-lee-o	l'olio
olives	le o-*lee*-ve	le olive
pastry	eel eel kor-*net*-to	il cornetto
rice	eel *ree*-zo	il riso
sugar	lo *zuk*-ke-ro	lo zucchero
(mineral) water	*lahk*-kwah (mee-ne-rah-le)	l'acqua (minerale)
yogurt	*lyo*-gurt	l'yogurt

Meat & Poultry

beef	eel *mahnd*-zo	il manzo
chicken	eel *pol*-lo	il pollo
cured ham	eel pro-*shut*-to kru-do	il prosciutto crudo
lamb	lahn-*yel*-lo	l'agnello
meat	lah *kahr*-ne	la carne
pork	eel *may*-ah-le	il maiale
sausage	lah sahl-*see*-cha	la salsiccia
turkey	eel tu-*kee*-no	il tacchino
veal	eel vee-*tel*-lo	il vitello

Vegetables

beetroot	lah bahr-bah-*bye*-to-lah	la barbabietola
cabbage	eel *kah*-vo-lo	il cavolo
carrot	lah kah-*ro*-tah	la carota
capsicum	eel pe-pe-*ro*-ne	il peperone
cauliflower	eel kah-vol-*fyo*-re	il cavolfiore
celery	eel se-*dah*-no	il sedano
cucumber	eel che-tree-*yo*-lo	il cetriolo

AT THE MARKET

ITALIAN

eggplant	lah me-lahnd-*zah*-nah	*la melanzana*
lettuce	lah lah-*tu*-gah	*la lattuga*
mushrooms	ee *fun*-gee	*i funghi*
onion	lah chee-*pol*-lah	*la cipolla*
potato	lah pah-*tah*-tah	*la patata*
spinach	lyee spee-*nah*-chee	*gli spinaci*
string beans	ee fah-jo-*lee*-nee	*i fagiolini*
tomato	eel po-mo-*do*-ro	*il pomodoro*
vegetables	le ver-*du*-re	*le verdure*
zucchini	lyee zu-*kee*-nee	*gli zucchini*

Seafood

fish	eel *pe*-she	*il pesce*
mussels	le *kot*-se	*le cozze*
oysters	le os-*tree*-ke	*le ostriche*
shrimp	lyee *skahm*-pee	*gli scampi*

Pulses

borlotti beans	ee fah-*jo*-lee bor-*lot*-tee	*i fagioli borlotti*
broad beans	le *fah*-ve	*le fave*
chickpeas	ee *che*-chee	*i ceci*
lentils	le len-*teek*-ye	*le lenticchie*

Fruit

apple	lah *me*-lah	*la mela*
apricot	lahl-bee-*kok*-kah	*l'albicocca*
banana	lah bah-*nah*-nah	*la banana*
fig	eel *fee*-ko	*il fico*
fruit	lah *frut*-tah	*la frutta*
grapes	*lu*-vah	*l'uva*
lemon	eel lee-*mo*-ne	*il limone*
orange	lah-*rahn*-che	*l'arancia*
peach	lah *pes*-kah	*la pèsca*
pear	lah *pe*-rah	*la pera*
plum	lah su-*see*-nah	*la susina*
strawberry	lah *frah*-go-lah	*le fragole*

ITALIAN

SHOPPING

bakery	for-nah-ee-o	*fornaio*
bank	bahn-kah	*banca*
bookshop	lee-bre-ree-a	*libreria*
clothing store	ne-got-see-o dee ab-bee-lyee-ah-men-to	*negozio di abbigliamento*
chemist	fahr-mah-see-ah	*farmacia*
delicatessen	peet-see-ke-ree-ah	*pizzicheria*
department store	grahn-de mah-gaht-see-no	*grande magazzino*
grocer	ne-got-see-o dee ah-lee-men-tah-ri	*negozio di alimentari*
launderette	la-van-de-ree-ah	*lavanderia*
market	mer-kah-to	*mercato*
newsagency	e-dee-ko-lah	*edicola*
shoeshop	ne-got-see-o dee skahr-pe	*negozio di scarpe*
supermarket	su-per-mer-cah-to	*supermercato*
travel agency	ah-jen-tsee-ah dee vee-ahj-jee	*agenzia di viaggi*

Can I pay by credit card?
  pos-so pah-*gah*-re kon lah kahr-tah dee *kre*-dee-to?   *Posso pagare con la carta di credito?*

Can I have a receipt, please?
  pwo *dahr*-mee u-nah ree-che-*vu*-tah, per kor-te-*zee*-ah?   *Può darmi una ricevuta, per cortesia?*

ITALIAN

Essential Groceries

batteries	le pee-le	*le pile*
bread	eel pah-ne	*il pane*
cereal	ee che-re-*ah*-lee	*i cereali*
cheese	eel for-*mahj*-jo	*il formaggio*
chocolate	eel chok-ko-*lah*-to	*il cioccolato*
coffee	eel kahf-*fe*	*il caffè*
fruit juice	eel suk-ko	*il succo*
	dee frut-tah	*di frutta*
gas cylinder	lah *bom*-bo-lah	*la bombola*
	ah gahs	*a gas*
matches	ee fyahm-*mee*-fe-ree	*i fiammiferi*
milk	eel laht-te	*il latte*
soap	eel sah-*po*-ne	*il sapone*
sugar	lo *zuk*-ke-ro	*lo zucchero*
tissues	ee fat-tso-let-*tee*-nee	*i fazzolettini*
	dee kahr-tah	*di carta*
toilet paper	lah kahr-tah	*la carta igienica*
	ee-*je*-nee-kah	
toothpaste	eel den-tee-*free*-cho	*il dentifricio*
washing powder	eel de-ter-*see*-vo	*il detersivo*

Souvenirs

blown glass	eel ve-tro sof-*fyah*-to	*il vetro soffiato*
brooch	u-nah speel-lah	*una spilla*
ceramics	lah che-*rah*-mee-kah	*la ceramica*
earrings	lyee o-rek-*kee*-nee	*gli orecchini*
embroidery	eel ree-*kah*-mo	*il ricamo*
handicraft	eel lah-*vo*-ro	*il lavoro artigianale*
	ahr-tee-jah-*nah*-le	
jewellery	lah bee-jot-te-*ree*-ah	*la bigiotteria*
lace	eel mer-*let*-to	*il merletto*
leather bag	u-nah bor-sah	*una borsa di cuoio*
	dee kwo-yo	
miniature statue	u-nah stah-tu-*et*-tah	*una statuetta*
necklace	u-nah kol-*lah*-nah	*una collana*

ITALIAN

ornament	un so-prahm-*mo*-bee-le	*un soprammobile*
plate	un pyaht-to	*un piatto*
pottery	lyee oj-jet-*tee*-nee een che-*rah*-mee-kah	*gli oggetti in ceramica*
ring	un-ah-*nel*-lo	*un anello*
rug	un tap-*pe*-to	*un tappeto*
vase	un vah-zo	*un vaso*
woodcarving	len-yo	*legno*

Clothing

belt	u-nah cheen-*tu*-rah	*una cintura*
boots	lyee stee-*vah*-lee	*gli stivali*
clothing	lyee *ah*-bee-tee	*gli abiti*
coat	un kap-*pot*-to	*un cappotto*
dress	un ve-*stee*-to	*un vestito*
jacket	u-nah jahk-kah	*una giacca*
jeans	ee jeenz	*i jeans*
jumper (sweater)	un mahl-*yo*-ne	*un maglione*
hat	un kahp-*pel*-lo	*un cappello*
raincoat	un-eem-per-*myah*-bee-le	*un impermeabile*
sandals	ee *sahn*-dah-lee	*i sandali*
shirt	u-nah kah-*mee*-chah	*una camicia*
(sports) shoes	le skahr-pe (dah jeen-*nah*-stee-kah)	*le scarpe (da ginnastica)*
shorts	ee pahn-tah-*lo*-nee kor-tee	*i pantaloni corti*
skirt	u-nah gon-nah	*una gonna*
socks	ee kahl-*zee*-nee	*i calzini*
swimsuit	un ko-*stu*-me dah bahn-yo	*un costume da bagno*
T-shirt	u-nah mahl-*yet*-tah	*una maglietta;*
umbrella	un-om-*brel*-lo	*un ombrello*
trousers	ee pahn-tah-*lo*-nee	*i pantaloni*
underwear	lah byahn-ke-*ree*-ah *een*-tee-mah	*la biancheria intima*

ITALIAN

Materials

brass	ot-*to*-ne	ottone
bronze	bron-zo	bronzo
ceramic	che-*rah*-mee-kah	ceramica
cotton	ko-*to*-ne	cotone
glass	ve-tro	vetro
gold	o-ro	oro
leather	pel-le/kwo-yo	pelle/cuoio
marble	mahr-mo	marmo
metal	me-*tahl*-lo	metallo
paper	kahr-tah	carta
porcelain	por-chel-*lah*-nah	porcellana
copper	rah-me	rame
silk	se-tah	seta
silver	ahr-*jen*-to	argento
stone	pye-trah	pietra
wood	len-yo	legno
wool	lah-nah	ana

Colours

black	ne-ro/ah	nero/a
(dark) blue	blu	blu
(medium) blue	ad-*zur*-ro/ah	azzurro/a
(light) blue	che-*le*-ste	celeste
brown	mahr-*ro*-ne	marrone
dark	sku-ro/ah	scuro/a
green	ver-de	verde
grey	gree-jo/ah	grigio/a
light	kyah-ro/ah	chiaro/a
orange	ah-rahn-*cho*-ne	arancione
pink	ro-zah	rosa
purple	vyo-lah	viola
red	ros-so/ah	rosso/a
white	byan-ko/ah	bianco/a
yellow	jahl-lo/ah	giallo/a

ITALIAN

Toiletries

comb	un *pet*-tee-ne	*un pettine*
condoms	ee pre-ser-vah-*tee*-vee	*i preservativi*
deodorant	eel de-o-do-*rahn*-te	*il deodorante*
conditioner	eel *bahl*-sah-mo per ee kah-*pel*-lee	*il balsamo per i capelli*
moisturiser	lah kre-mah ee-drah-*tahn*-te	*la crema idratante*
razor blades	le lah-*met*-te dah bahr-bah	*le lamette da barba*
sanitary napkins	lyee ahs-sor-*ben*-tee ee-*je*-nee-chee	*gli assorbenti igienici*
shampoo	lo shahm-po	*lo shampoo*
shaving cream	lah kre-mah dah bahr-bah	*la crema da barba*
sunscreen	lah kre-mah so-*lah*-re	*la crema solare*
tampons	ee tahm-*po*-nee	*i tamponi*
tissues	ee fatːtso-let-*tee*-nee dee kahr-tah	*i fazzolettini di carta*
toothbrush	lo spaht-tso-*lee*-no dah den-tee	*lo spazzolino da denti*

Stationery & Publications

The two major dailies are Rome's *La Repubblica* and Milan's *Corriere della Sera*. There are also a number of English-language newspapers available.

Where's the English-language section?
do-*ve* lah se-*zyo*-ne dee   *Dov'è la sezione di*
leen-gwah een-*gle*-ze?   *lingua inglese?*

dictionary	un dee-tsyo-*nah*-ryo	*un dizionario*
envelope	u-nah bu-stah	*una busta*
paper	lah kahr-tah	*la carta*
pen	u-nah pen-nah	*una penna*
postcards	le kahr-to-*lee*-ne	*le cartoline*

ITALIAN

English-language ...	un ... een-*gle*-ze	un ... in inglese
newspaper	jor-*nah*-le	giornale
novel	ro-*mahn*-zo	romanzo
... map	u-nah kahr-*tee*-nah ...	una cartina ...
city	del-lah cheet-*tah*	della città
regional	del-lah re-*jo*-ne	della regione
road	strah-*dah*-le	stradale

Photography

How much is it to process this film?
kwahn-to ko-stah svee-lup-*pah*-re   *Quanto costa sviluppare*
kwe-stah pel-*lee*-ko-lah?   *questa pellicola?*
When will it be ready?
kwahn-do sah-*rahn*-no   *Quando saranno*
pron-te le fo-to?   *pronte le foto?*
I'd like a film for this camera.
vor-rey u-nah pel-*lee*-ko-lah   *Vorrei una pellicola*
per kwe-stah *mahk*-kee-nah   *per questa macchina*
fo-to-*grah*-fee-kah   *fotografica.*
Do you have one-hour processing?
ah-*ve*-te un ser-*veets*-yo dee   *Avete un servizio di*
svee-*lup*-po ee-stahn-*tah*-neo?   *sviluppo istantaneo?*

battery	u-nah pee-lah	una pila
B&W	byahn-ko e ne-ro	bianco e nero
camera	u-nah mahk-*kee*-nah	una macchina
	fo-to-*grah*-fee-kah	fotografica
colour	eel ko-*lo*-re	il colore
film	u-nah pel-*lee*-ko-lah	una pellicola
film speed	lah sen-see-bee-lee-*tah*	la sensibilità
flash	eel flahsh	il flash
lens	lo-byet-*tee*-vo	l'obiettivo
light meter	le-spo-*zee*-me-tro	l'esposimetro
slides	le dyah-po-zee-*tee*-ve	le diapositive
videotape	un vee-deo-*nah*-stro	un videonastro

ITALIAN

Sizes & Comparisons

also	ahn-ke	*anche*
big	grahn-de	*grande*
enough	ahb-bah-*stahn*-zah	*abbastanza*
few	po-ko/ah	*poco/a*
heavy	pe-*zahn*-te	*pesante*
less	(dee) me-no	*(di) meno*
light	lej-*je*-ro/ah	*leggero/a*
a little (bit)	un po	*un po'*
a lot	mol-to/ah	*molto/a*
many	tahn-te/ee	*tante/i*
more	(dee) pyu	*una macchina (di) più*
small	*peek*-ko-lo/ah	*piccolo/a*
some	ahl-*ku*-ne/ee	*alcune/i*
too much/many	trop-po/ah/e/ee	*troppo/a/e/i*

Smoking

carton	u-nah *skah*-to-lah	*una scatola*
cigarette machine	un dee-stree-bu-*to*-re dee see-gah-*ret*-te	*un distributore di sigarette*
cigarette papers	le kahr-*tee*-ne (per see-gah-*ret*-te)	*le cartine (per sigarette)*
cigarettes	le see-gah-*ret*-te	*le sigarette*
cigar	un *see*-gah-ro	*un sigaro*
filtered/unfiltered	kon/sen-zah feel-tro	*con/senza filtro*
lighter	un ahch-chen-*dee*-no	*un accendino*
matches	ee fyahm-*mee*-fe-ree	*i fiammiferi*
menthol	ahl-lah men-tah	*alla menta*
pipe	u-nah pee-pah	*una pipa*
tobacconist	lah tah-bahk-ke-*ree*-ah	*la tabaccheria*
tobacco (pipe)	eel tah-*bahk*-ko (dah pee-pah)	*il tabacco (da pipa)*

A packet of cigarettes, please.
un pahk-*ket*-to dee *Un pacchetto di*
see-gah-*ret*-te per fah-*vo*-re *ßigarette, per avore.*

Do you have a light?
mee fahy ahch-*chen*-de-re? *Mi fai accendere?*
Do you have an ashtray?
ahy un por-tah-*ce*-ne-re? *Hai un portacenere?*

HEALTH
Parts of the Body
It hurts here.
mee fah mah-le kwee *Mi fa male qui.*

ankle	lah kah-*veel*-yah	*la caviglia*
arm	eel brah-cho	*il braccio*
	(le brah-chah)	(pl: *le braccia*)
back	lah skye-nah	*la schiena*
breast	lah mahm-*mel*-lah	*la mammella*
buttocks	le nah-*tee*-ke	*le natiche*
chest	eel to-*rah*-che	*il torace*
ear	lo-*rek*-kyo	*l'orecchio*
elbow	eel *go*-mee-to	*il gomito*
eyes	lyee ok-kee	*gli occhi*
finger	eel dee-to (le dee-tah)	*il dito* (pl: *le dita*)
foot	eel pye-de	*il piede*
hand	lah mah-no	*la mano*
head	lah te-stah	*la testa*
hip	lahn-kah	*l'anca*
knee	eel jee-*no*-kyo	*il ginocchio*
leg	lah gahm-bah	*la gamba*
mouth	lah bok-kah	*la bocca*
neck	eel kol-lo	*il collo*
nose	eel nah-zo	*il naso*
shoulder	lah spahl-lah	*la spalla*
stomach	lo *sto*-mah-ko	*lo stomaco*
throat	lah go-lah	*la gola*

ITALIAN

Ailments

I'm ill.   sto mah-le   *Sto male.*
I've been vomiting.
   kon-*tee*-nu-o ah vo-mee-*tah*-re   *Continuo a vomitare.*

I feel ...   o ...   *Ho ...*
   dizzy   eel kah-po-*jee*-ro   *il capogiro*
   nauseous   lah nah-u-ze-ah   *la nausea*

I have (a/an) ...   o ...   *Ho ...*
   bite   un mor-so   *un morso*
   burn   u-nah skot-tah-*tu*-rah   *una scottatura*
   cold   eel rahf-fred-*do*-re   *il raffreddore*
   constipation   lah stee-tee-*ket*-tsa   *la stitichezza*
   cough   lah tos-se   *la tosse*
   diarrhoea   lah dyahr-*re*-ah   *la diarrea*
   fever   lah feb-bre   *la febbre*
   hayfever   lah feb-bre dah   *la febbre da*
                      fye-no   *fieno*
   headache   eel mahl dee te-stah   *il mal di testa*
   indigestion   leen-dee-jest-*yo*-ne   *l'indigestione*
   infection   un-een-fets-*yo*-ne   *un'infezione*
   inflammation   u-neen-fyahm-   *un'infiam-*
                      mahts-*yo*-ne   *mazione*
   itch   un pru-*ree*-to   *un prurito*
   migraine   un-e-mee-*krah*-nyah   *un'emicrania*
   rash   u-no sfo-go   *uno sfogo*
   rheumatism   ee re-u-mah-*tee*-zmee   *i reumatismi*
   sore throat   eel mal dee go-lah   *il mal di gola*
   stomachache   eel mahl dee   *il mal di*
                      sto-mah-ko   *stomaco*
   sunburn   u-nah skot-tah-*tu*-rah   *una scottatura*
   travel sickness   eel mal *dah*-u-to   *il mal d'auto*
   venereal disease   u-nah mah-laht-*tee*-ah   *una malattia*
                      ve-*ne*-reah   *venerea*
   worms   ee ver-mee   *i vermi*

Useful phrases

Where's the nearest ...?	do-*ve* ... pyu vee-*chee*-no/ah?	*Dov'è ... più vicino/a?*
chemist	eel/lah fahr-mah-*chee*-stah	*il/la farmacista*
dentist	eel/lah den-*tee*-stah	*il/la dentista*
doctor	eel/lah *me*-dee-ko	*il/la medico*
hospital	lo-spe-*dah*-le	*l'ospedale*

I need a doctor (who speaks English).
o bee-*zon*-yo dee un *me*-dee-ko (ke pahr-lee een-*gle*-ze)

Ho bisogno di un medico (che parli inglese).

Can I have a receipt for my health insurance?
po-*treb*-be dahr-mee u-nah ree-che-*vu*-tah per lahs-see-ku-rah*ts*-*yo*-ne?

Potrebbe darmi una ricevuta per l'assicurazione?

At the Chemist

Where's the nearest (all-night) chemist?
do-*ve* lah pyu vee-*chee*-nah fahr-mah-*chee*-ah (dee tur-no)?

Dov'è la piu vicina farmacia (di turno)?

I need something for ...
o bee-*zon*-yo de kwahl-*ko*-zah per ...

Ho bisogno di qualcosa per ...

How many times a day?
kwahn-te vol-te ahl jor-no?

Quante volte al giorno?

ITALIAN

Could I please have ...	po-*treb*-be dahr-mee ... per fah-*vo*-re?	*Potrebbe darmi ... per favore?*
antibiotics	del-yee ahn-tee-*byo*-tee-chee	*degli antibiotici*
aspirins	del-le ah-spee-*ree*-ne	*delle aspirine*
contraceptives	dey kon-trah-chet-*tee*-vee	*dei contraccettivi*
cough syrup	u-no shee-*rop*-po	*uno sciroppo*
cough lozenges	del-le pah-*steel*-ye kon-tro lah tos-se	*delle pastiglie contro la tosse*
laxatives	dey lahs-sah-*tee*-vee	*dei lassativi*
painkillers	un ah-nahl-*je*-zee-ko	*un analgesico*
sleeping pills	dey son-*nee*-fe-ree	*dei sonniferi*

At the Dentist

I have a toothache.
o mahl dee den-tee — *Ho mal di denti.*

I've lost a filling.
o per-so u-not-tu-rah*ts*-yo-ne — *Ho perso un'otturazione.*

My gums hurt.
mee fahn-no mah-le le jen-*jee*-ve — *Mi fanno male le gengive.*

I don't want it extracted.
non vol-yo ke mee ven-gah tol-to — *Non voglio che mi venga tolto.*

Please give me an anaesthetic.
mee dyah un-ah-ne-*ste*-tee-ko per fah-*vo*-re — *Mi dia un anestetico, per favore.*

TIME & DATES
Time

The 24-hour clock is commonly used in Italy – 1pm is 13.00,
2pm is 14.00.

ITALIAN

What time is it?	che o-rah e?	*Che ora è?*
It's one o'clock.	e lu-na	*È l'una.*
It's (two o'clock).	so-no le (du-e)	*Sono le (due).*
It's five past six.	so-no le sei e cheen-ke	*Sono le sei e cinque.*
It's a quarter to four.	so-no le kwaht-tro me-no un kwar-to	*Sono le quattro meno un quarto.*

Days

Monday	lu-ne-*dee*	*lunedì*
Tuesday	mahr-te-*dee*	*martedì*
Wednesday	mer-ko-le-*dee*	*mercoledì*
Thursday	jo-ve-*dee*	*giovedì*
Friday	ve-ner-*dee*	*venerdì*
Saturday	*sah*-bah-to	*sabato*
Sunday	do-*me*-nee-kah	*domenica*

Months

January	jen-*nah*-yo	*gennaio*
February	feb-*brah*-yo	*febbraio*
March	mahr-tso	*marzo*
April	ah-*pree*-le	*aprile*
May	mahj-jo	*maggio*
June	jun-yo	*giugno*
July	lul-yo	*luglio*
August	ah-*go*-sto	*agosto*
September	set-*tem*-bre	*settembre*
October	ot-*to*-bre	*ottobre*
November	no-*vem*-bre	*novembre*
December	dee-*chem*-bre	*dicembre*

ITALIAN

Seasons

spring	lah pree-mah-*ve*-rah	*la primavera*
summer	le-*stah*-te	*l'estate*
autumn	lah-u-*tun*-no	*l'autunno*
winter	leen-*ver*-no	*l'inverno*

Present

right now	een kwe-sto mo-*men*-to	*in questo momento*
now	ah-*des*-so	*adesso*
today	oj-jee	*oggi*
this morning	stah-maht-*tee*-nah	*stamattina*
this afternoon	oj-jee po-me-*reej*-jo	*oggi pomeriggio*
tonight	stah-*se*-rah	*stasera*
this week	kwe-stah set-tee-*mah*-nah	*questa settimana*
this month	kwe-sto me-ze	*questo mese*
this year	kwe-*stahn*-no	*quest'anno*

Past

yesterday ...	ye-ree ...	*ieri ...*
morning	maht-*tee*-nah	*mattina*
afternoon	po-me-*reej*-jo	*pomeriggio*
day before yesterday	lahl-tro ye-ree	*l'altro ieri*
last night	ye-ree se-rah	*ieri sera*
last week	lah set-tee-*mah*-nah skor-sah	*la settimana scorsa*
last month	eel me-ze skor-so	*il mese scorso*
last year	lahn-no skor-so	*l'anno scorso*

Future

tomorrow ...	do-*mah*-nee ...	*domani ...*
morning	maht-*tee*-nah	*mattina*
afternoon	po-me-*reej*-jo	*pomeriggio*
evening	se-rah	*sera*
night	not-te	*notte*

day after tomorrow	do-po-do-*mah*-nee	*dopodomani*
next week	lah set-tee-*mah*-nah *pros*-see-mah	*la settimana prossima*
next month	eel me-ze *pros*-see-mo	*il mese prossimo*
next year	lahn-no *pros*-see-mo	*l'anno prossimo*

ITALIAN

During the Day

afternoon	eel po-me-*reej*-jo	*il pomeriggio*
day	eel *jor*-no	*il giorno*
dinner time	*lo*-rah dee *che*-nah	*l'ora di cena*
evening	lah *se*-rah	*la sera*
lunchtime	*lo*-rah dee *prah*n-zo	*l'ora di pranzo*
midday	eel med-dzo-*jor*-no	*il mezzogiorno*
midnight	lah med-dzah-*not*-te	*la mezzanotte*
morning	lah maht-*tee*-nah	*la mattina*
night	lah *not*-te	*la notte*
sunrise	*lahl*-bah	*l'alba*
sunset	eel trah-*mon*-to	*il tramonto*

NUMBERS

0	ze-ro	*zero*
1	*u*-no	*uno*
2	*du*-e	*due*
3	tre	*tre*
4	*kwaht*-tro	*quattro*
5	*cheen*-kwe	*cinque*
6	sey	*sei*
7	*set*-te	*sette*
8	*ot*-to	*otto*
9	*no*-ve	*nove*
10	dee-*e*-chee	*dieci*
11	*un*-dee-chee	*undici*
12	*do*-dee-chee	*dodici*
13	*tre*-dee-chee	*tredici*
14	kwaht-*tor*-dee-chee	*quattordici*
15	*kween*-dee-chee	*quindici*

ITALIAN

16	*se*-dee-chee	*sedici*
17	dee-chah-*set*-te	*diciassette*
18	dee-*chot*-to	*diciotto*
19	dee-chahn-*no*-ve	*diciannove*
20	ven-tee	*venti*
21	ven-*tu*-no	*ventuno*
22	ven-tee-*du*-e	*ventidue*
30	*tren*-tah	*trenta*
40	kwah-*rahn*-tah	*quaranta*
50	cheen-*kwah*-tah	*cinquanta*
60	ses-*sahn*-tah	*sessanta*
70	set-*tahn*-tah	*settanta*
80	ot-*tahn*-tah	*ottanta*
90	no-*vahn*-tah	*novanta*
100	*chen*-to	*cento*
101	chen-to *u*-no	*cento uno*
1000	*meel*-le	*mille*
2000	du-e-*mee*-lah	*duemila*
10, 000	dee-e-chee-*mee*-lah	*diecimila*
one million	un mee-*lyo*-ne	*un milione*

ABBREVIATIONS

AA	*assistenza automobilistica*	Automobile Association
ac	*anno corrente*	this year
AC	*Avanti Cristo*	BC (Before Christ)
CC	*Carabinieri*	military police
DC	*Dopo Cristo*	AD (Anno Domini)
FS	*Ferrovie dello Stato*	National Railway
ONU	*Nazioni Unite*	United Nations
S	*santo*	saint
SS	*Santi/Santissimi*	holy
UE	*Unione Europea*	European Union

EMERGENCIES

Help!	ah-*yu*-to!	*Aiuto!*
Call the police!	kyah-mee lah po-lee-*tsee*-ah!	*Chiami la polizia!*
Look out!	aht-ten-*tsyo*-ne!	*Attenzione!*
Fire!	ahl fwo-ko!	*Al fuoco!*
Go away!	vah *vee*-ah!	*Va' via!*
Thief!	ahl lah-dro!	*Al ladro!*

ITALIAN

Where's the police station?
do-*ve* lah kwe-*stu*-rah? — *Dov'è la questura?*

It's an emergency!
e un e-mer-*jen*-za! — *È un'emergenza!*

Could you help me please?
mee pwo ah-yu-*tah*-re? — *Mi può aiutare?*

Could I please use the telephone?
pos-so fah-re u-nah te-le-fo-*nah*-tah? — *Posso fare una telefonata?*

There's been an accident!
che stah-to u-neen-chee-*den*-te! — *C'è stato un incidente!*

Call a doctor!
kyah-mee un *me*-dee-ko! — *Chiami un medico!*

Call an ambulance!
kyah-mee u-nahm-bu-*lahn*-za! — *Chiami un'ambulanza!*

I have medical insurance.
o lahs-see-ku-rahts-*yo*-ne *me*-dee-kah — *Ho l'assicurazione medica.*

I've (m/f) been robbed!
mee ahn-no de-ru-*bah*-to/ah! — *Mi hanno derubato/a!*

I've (m/f) been raped.
so-no stah-to/ah vyo-len-*tah*-to/ah! — *Sono stato/a violentato/a.*

I'm (m/f) lost.
mee so-no per-so/ah — *Mi sono perso/a.*

I'm looking for a public toilet.
sto-ser-*kan*-do ee gah-bee-*net*-tee — *Sto cercando i gabinetti.*

ITALIAN

Dealing with Police

I want to report an offence.

vol-yo *spor*-je-re u-nah
de-*nun*-chah

*Voglio sporgere una
denuncia.*

I've lost my...	o per-so ...	*Ho perso ...*
backpack	eel mee-o *zah*-ee-no	*il mio zaino*
handbag	lah mee-ah bor-*set*-tah	*la mia borsetta*
luggage	ee mee-ey bah-*gahl*-yee	*i miei bagagli*
money	ee mee-ey sol-dee	*i miei soldi*
papers	ee mee-ey do-ku-*men*-tee	*i miei documenti*
passport	eel mee-o pahs-sah-*por*-to	*il mio passaporto*
travellers cheques	ee mee-ey travelers che-kes	*i miei travellers cheques*
wallet	eel mee-o por-tah-*fol*-yee	*il mio portafogli*

I'm sorry. I apologise.

mee sku-zee mee dee-*spyah*-che

Mi scusi. Mi dispiace.

Can I speak with someone in English?

pos-so pahr-*lah*-re kon
kwahl-*ku*-no een een-*gle*-ze?

*Posso parlare con
qualcuno in inglese?*

I want to contact my
embassy/consulate.

vor-rey kon-taht-*tah*-re lah
mee-ah ahm-bah-*shah*-tah/
eel mee-o kon-so-*lah*-to

*Vorrei contattare la
mia ambasciata/
il mio consolato.*

MALTESE

MALTESE

QUICK REFERENCE

Good day.	bon-ju	Bonġu.
Good night.	il-lejl it-tahy-yeb	Il-lejl it-tajjeb.
How are you?	kif in-ti?	Kif inti?
I'm (m) fine, thanks.	tahy-yeb grahz-zi	Tajjeb, grazzi.
I'm (f) fine, thanks.	tahy-bah grahz-zi	Tajba, grazzi.
Goodbye.	sah-hah	Saħħa.
Yes./No.	i-vah/le	Iva./Le.
Please.	yekk yoj-bok	Jekk jogħġbok.
Thank you.	grahz-zi	Grazzi.
You're welcome.	mniesh	Mniex.
Excuse me.	sku-zah-ni	Skużani.
What's your name?	shyis-mek?	X'jismek?
My name's ...	yi-sim-ni ...	Jisimni ...

I'd like to introduce you to ...
    nish-tie' nin-tro-doo-chik lil ...   Nixtieq nintroduċik lil ...
I'm pleased to meet you.
    ahn-di pyah-chir   Għandi pjaċir.
How do I get to ...?
    kif im-moor il ...?   Kif immur il-...?
Turn left/right.
    door fu' ish-shel-lug/   Dur fuq ix-xellug/
    il-le-min   il-lemin.
Go straight ahead.
    mur dritt   Mur dritt.
Where's the toilet, please?
    feyn oo-mah toy-lits   Fejn huma t-toilets,
    yek yoj-bok?   jekk jogħġbok?

1	wie-hed	wieħed	6	sit-tah	sitta
2	tneyn	tnejn	7	se-bah	sebgħa
3	tlie-tah	tlieta	8	tmie-nyah	tmienja
4	er-bah	erbgħa	9	di-sah	disgħa
5	hahm-sah	ħamsa	10	ah-shrah	għaxra

MALTESE

Maltese is the language of a small, ancient Mediterranean culture. Located in the Mediterranean Sea, just south of Sicily, the Maltese archipelago consists of three islands – Malta, Gozo and Comino, of which Malta is the largest, with a total population of around 350,000. From early times, the Maltese have settled in many parts of the Mediterranean, especially in North Africa. Today there are as many Maltese living abroad as there are in Malta, mainly in Australia, North America and the UK.

Archaeological finds account for a human presence in Malta since 5000 BC. Malta's famous prehistoric temples are a rich heritage of flourishing ancient civilisations which ebbed and flowed in the Mediterranean region between 3200 and 800 BC. In 800 BC, the Phoenicians, who were moving westward into most parts of the Mediterranean from the Levant and the headlands of the Nile, settled in Malta. The Phoenicians were succeeded by various cultures, including the Normans, who arrived from Sicily in the latter part of the 11th century. The British, who ruled from 1800 to 1964, were the last of Malta's colonisers.

This long history of colonisation had its effect on the language now spoken in modern Malta. Some linguists attribute the origins of the language to the Phoenician occupation of Malta, and consider Maltese to be a Semitic offshoot of Phoenician. This school of thought maintains that 220 years of Arab domination served only to consolidate the Semitic structure of the language.

Others consider the Arab period, and not the Phoenician, to be the more significant linguistic force in the origins of Maltese. Either way, the Semitic base of Maltese grammar has persisted to this day, despite the prominence of the Romance languages ushered in with the Europeanisation of Malta, giving the language words from Sicilian, Italian, Spanish and French, as well as English. The Maltese alphabet is a successful transliteration of Semitic sounds but, uniquely, written in Roman characters.

Italian was Malta's official language during the period of the Knights of St John (1530-1798). During the British period, English and Italian became the official languages. It wasn't until 1934 that Italian was withdrawn and substituted by the native Maltese language. Together with English, Maltese finally became officially accepted and used in the public administration of the islands. For the first time, Maltese also became the official language of the law courts.

Today, Maltese people are generally trilingual, speaking fluent English and Italian as well at their native Maltese. Although you won't have any trouble getting by in English during your stay in Malta, this chapter will introduce you to the language you'll hear spoken around you.

PRONUNCIATION
Vowels

Vowels in Maltese can be long or short, depending on their position in a word. There are a few general rules to remember:

Vowels are short when:
- at the end of a word
- followed by more than one consonant

Vowels are long when:
- stressed (see page 334)
- followed by one consonant

Short Vowels

a	a	as the 'u' in 'shut'
e	e	as the 'e' in 'elf'
i	i	as the 'i' in 'sin'
o	o	as the 'o' in 'hot'
u	u	as the 'u' in 'put'

MALTESE

Long Vowels

a	ah	as the 'a' in 'far'
e	e	as the 'ei' in 'heir'
i	i	as the 'ee' in 'see'
o	o	as the 'o' in 'for'
u	oo	as the 'u' in 'flu'

PRONUNCIATION HINTS

The letter *ħ* sounds like the 'h' in 'horse', only stronger, while *h* is silent except at the end of a word.

The overdot on *ġ* makes this sound softer, and it's pronounced as the 'g' in 'gentle', not in 'game'.

Vowel Combinations

ie	ie	as the 'ie' in 'tier'

Consonants

All double consonants have a stressed, slightly extended sound compared to their single counterparts. Consonants not described here are pronounced approximately as they are in English.

ċ	ch	as the 'ch' in 'cheese'
ġ	j	as the 'g' in 'gentle' – the overdot makes the 'g' a soft 'g'
għ		silent. Lengthens the preceding and/or the following vowel.
h	h	at the end of a word, as the 'h' in 'horse', but stronger; in the middle of a word, silent, but lengthens the preceding and/or the following vowel; elsewhere, silent
ħ	h	as the 'h' in 'horse', but stronger
j	y	as the 'y' in 'yes'
q	'	glottal stop; as the sound between the words in 'uh-oh', or as the 'tt' in Cockney 'bottle'
x	sh	as the 'sh' in 'shiver'
z	ts	as the 'ts' in 'bits'
ż	z	as the 'zz' in 'buzz'

MALTESE

Stress

Stress generally falls on the second-last syllable of a word. However, words containing *ie* or *għ* are always stressed on the syllable where these letter combinations occur.

| to do | *għamel* | *ah*-mel |
| they were | *kienu* | *kie*-nu |

When a word has both these letter combinations, stress always falls on *ie*.

| female bird | *għammiela* | am-*mie*-la |

Many Maltese words that have been borrowed from a Romance language take stress on the final syllable. This is indicated by an accent on the final vowel.

| pope | *Papa* | *pa*-pa |
| father | *papá* | pa-*pa* |

GREETINGS & CIVILITIES
You Should Know

Good day.	*bon*-ju	*Bonġu.*
Good night.	il-lejl it-*tahy*-yeb	*Il-lejl it-tajjeb.*
How are you?	kif *in*-ti?	*Kif inti?*
I'm (m) fine, thanks.	*tahy*-yeb *grahz*-zi	*Tajjeb, grazzi.*
I'm (f) fine, thanks.	*tahy*-bah *grahz*-zi	*Tajba, grazzi.*
Take care.	hoo hsieb	*ħu ħsieb.*
Goodbye.	*sah*-hah	*Saħħa.*
Yes./No.	*i*-vah/le	*Iva./Le.*
Please.	yekk *yoj*-bok	*Jekk jogħġbok.*
Thank you (very much).	*grahz*-zi (*hahf*-nah)	*Grazzi (ħafna).*
You're welcome.	mniesh	*Mniex.*
Excuse me.	sku-*tsah*-ni	*Skużani.*

Forms of Address

Mr Smith	sur smith	*Sur Smith*
Mrs Smith	sin-*yu*-rah smith	*Sinjura Smith*
Miss Smith	sin-yo-*ri*-nah smith	*Sinjorina Smith*
friend	hah-*bib*	*ħabib*
mate	shbin	*xbin*

PRONOUNS					
SG			**PL**		
I	yien	*jien*	we	ah-nah	*aħna*
you	int(i)	*int(i)*	you	in-tom	*intom*
he	u(wah)	*hu(wa)*	they	u-mah	*huma*
she	i(yah)	*hi(ja)*			

MALTESE

SMALL TALK
Meeting People

What's your name?	*shyis*-mek?	*X'jismek?*
My name's ...	yi-*sim*-ni ...	*Jisimni ...*
I like ...	*in*-hob ...	*Inhobb ...*

I'd like to introduce you to ...
   nish-*tie'* nin-tro-doo-*chik* lil ...   *Nixtieq nintroduċik lil ...*
I'm pleased to meet you.
   ahn-di *pyah*-chir.   *Għandi pjaċir.*
How do you say ... in Maltese?
   kif teyd ... *bil* mahl-*ti*?   *Kif tgħid ... bil-Malti?*

Nationalities

Where do you live?	feyn to-'od?	*Fejn toqgħod?*
Where are you from?	minn feyn *in*-ti?	*Minn fejn inti?*

I'm from ...	*yie*-nah mil ...	*Jiena mill- ...*
Australia	lahw-*strahl*-yah	*l-Awstralja*
Canada	il-*kah*-nah-dah	*il-Kanada*
the UK	lin-gil-*ter*-rah	*l-Ingilterra*
the US	lah-*mer*-kah	*l-Amerka*

MALTESE

GETTING AROUND
Directions

How do I get to ...?
  kif im-*moor* il ...?   *Kif immur il-...?*

Where's a/the ...?
  feyn i ...?   *Fejn hi ...?*

Where's the toilet, please?
  feyn *oo*-mah *toy*-lits   *Fejn huma t-toilets,*
  yek *yoj*-bok?   *jekk jogħġbok?*

Turn left/right.
  door fu' ish-shel-*lug*/   *Dur fuq ix-xellug/*
  il-le-*min*   *il-lemin.*

Go straight ahead.   mur dritt   *Mur dritt.*
Keep on going.   *ib*-'ah *sey*-yer   *Ibqa' sejjer.*

far/near   il-*bod*/vi-*chin*   *'il boghod/viċin*

Useful Words & Phrases

When does the boat leave/arrive?
  me-tah *yit*-lah'   *Meta jitlaq il-vapur?*
  il-vah-*pur*?

When does the bus leave/arrive?
  me-tah *tit*-lah'   *Meta titlaq il-karozza?*
  il-kah-*roz*-zah?

Which bus do I catch to go to ...
  shkah-*roz*-zah *nah*'-bahd ahl ...   *X'karozza naqbad għal ...*

I'd like to hire a ...   nish-*tie*' *nik*-ri ...   *Nixtieq nikri ...*
  bicycle   *ro*-tah   rota
  car   kah-*roz*-zah   karozza
  motorbike   mu-*tur*   mutur

I'd like a one-way/return ticket.
  nish-*tie*' bil-*yet* *wun*-way/   *Nixtieq biljett one-way/*
  re-*tern*   *return.*

ACCOMMODATION

Do you have a room available?
ahn-dek kam-ra yek
yoj-bok?

*Ghandek kamra jekk
joghġbok?*

Is breakfast included?
il-brek-fast in-kluz?

Il-breakfast inkluż?

Do you have a room for ...?	*ahn*-dek *kahm*-rah ahl ...?	*Ghandek kamra għal ...?*
one/two people	*wie*-hed/tnayn	*wieħed/tnejn*
one/two nights	leyl/zewj til-*yie*-li	*lejl/żewġt iljieli*

AROUND TOWN
At the Post Office

I'd like to send a letter/parcel.
nish-*tie'* ni-baht
it-trah/pak

*Nixtieq nibgħat
ittra/pakk.*

I'd like some stamps.
nish-*tie'* shi bol-li

Nixtieq xi bolli.

How much is it to send this to ...?
kemm ti-*ji*-ni biesh
ni-baht din l...?

*Kemm tiġini biex
nibgħat din 'l...?*

envelope	*en*-ve-lop	*envelop*
paper	*kahr*-tah	*karta*
pen	*pin*-na	*pinna*
postcards	*kahr*-to-*li*-ni	*kartolini*
stamps	*bol*-li	*bolli*

MALTESE

MALTESE

Telephone

Hello!	hel-lo!	*Hello!*
Who's calling?	min *in*-ti?	*Min inti?*

I want to call (Australia).
    ir-*rid* in-*chem*-pel
    (*lahw*-strahl-yah)   *Irrid inċempel*
    (l-Awstralja).

The number is ...
    in-*num*-roo oo ...   *In-numru hu ...*

I want to make a reverse-charge
(collect) phone call.
    nish-*tie'* in-*chem*-pel   *Nixtieq inċempel*
    bir-revers-charg   *bir-reverse charge.*

Can I speak to...?
    nis-tah *nkel*-lem lil...?   *Nista' nkellem lil...?*

At the Bank

I'd like to	nish-*tie'*	*Nixtieq*
exchange some ...	in-*sahr*-rahf shi ...	*insarraf xi ...*
money	flus	*flus*
travellers cheques	tra-ve-lers cheks	*travellers cheques*

What's the exchange rate?
    shi-*ni rrah*-tah tahl-*kam*-byu?   *X'inhi r-rata tal-kambju?*

Please write it down.
    ik-*ti*-bah yek *yoj*-bok   *Iktibha jekk jogħġbok.*

What's your commission?
    kem *tieh*-du ko-mi-shon?   *Kemm tieħdu commission?*

INTERESTS & ENTERTAINMENT
Sightseeing

What are the main attractions?

shi-*noo*-mah laht-traz-zyo-
ni-*yiet* ew-le-*nin*?

*X'inhuma l-attrazzjonijiet
ewlenin?*

I'd like to go to a/the ...

nish-*tie'* im-*moor* sahl ...

Nixtieq immur sal ...

ancient	ahn-*tik*	*antik*
archaeological	ahr-ke-o-*lo*-ji-ku	*arkeoloġiku*
building	*bi*-ni	*bini*
harbour	port	*port*
main square	*pyahz*-zah	*pjazza*
	prin-ci-*pah*-li	*prinċipali*
monument	mo-nu-*ment*	*monument*
old city	belt 'ah-*di*-mah	*belt qadima*
temple	*tem*-pyu	*tempju*

MALTESE

Going Out

What's there to do
in the evenings?

shtis-tah *tah*-mel
fil-ash-i-*yiet*?

*X' tista' tagħmel
fil-għaxijiet?*

Would you like to go
for a drink/meal?

trid no-*hor*-ju ahl
drink/*ik*-lah?

*Trid noħorġu għall-
drink/ikla?*

Yes, I'd love to.

i-vah bil-'ahlb *kol*-lah

Iva bil-qalb kollha.

Sorry I can't. How about
tomorrow?

sku-*hah*-ni mah nis-*tahsh*
for-si *ah*-dah?

*Skużani ma nistax.
Forsi għada?*

I'd like to go to a/the …	nish-*tie'* im-*moor* f ...	*Nixtieq immur* f...
bar	bahr	*bar*
beach	*bahy*-yah	*bajja*
nightclub	*nait*-klub	*nightclub*
men's musical/ political club	kah-*ħin*	*każin*
traditional restaurant	*res*-to-rahnt trah-diz-zyo-*nah*-li *mahl*-ti	*restorant tradizzjonali Malti*

MALTESE

PLACES TO BE

Bugibba	bu-*jib*-bah	Bugibba (active summer nightlife)
Għajn Tuffieħa	ahyn tuf-*fee*-hah	Golden Sands beach (Malta)
Għawdex	*ahw*-dex	Gozo (second island in the archipelago – thriving traditional lifestyle)
Ir-Ramla l-Hamra	ir-*rahm*-lah l-*hahm*-rah	Ramla l-Hamra beach (Gozo)
l-Għadira	lah-*di*-rah	Ghadira beach (Malta)
Paceville	*pah*-ce-vil	Paceville (year-round nightlife)
l-Imdina	lim-*di*-na	Mdina (mediaeval walled city)
Valletta; Il-Belt	vahl-*let*-ta; il-belt	Valletta (the Baroque, walled capital city)
Wied il-Għajn	weed il-*ahyn*	Marsascala (known for summer nightlife)

Sports & Interests

What do you do in your spare time?
   shtah-mel fil-hin *li*-be-ru?   *X'taghmel fil-hin liberu?*
What sports do you play?
   shtah-mel *bhah*-lah sports?   *X'taghmel bhala sports?*
Which side do you support?
   mah min iz-*zom*?   *Ma' min iżżomm?*

How's the ...	kif i-*ni*	*Kif inhi*
going?	*sey*-rah ...?	*sejra ...?*
game	*lo*-bah	*il-loghba*
match	*lo*-bah	*l-loghba*
race	it-tel-*lie*-'ah	*it-tellieqa*

My/our team ...!		
won	*ir*-bah-hna!	*Irbahna!*
lost	*tlif*-nah!	*Tlifna!*

How am I playing?	kif 'ed *ni*-lahb?	*Kif qed nilghab?*
I won/lost!	ir-*bahht*/tlift!	*Irbaht/Tlift!*
I beat you! (teasing)	ir-*bahh*-tlek!	*Irbahtlek!*
Do you play ...?	*ti*-lahb il ...?	*Tilghab il ...?*

art	*ahr*-ti	*arti*
basketball	bas-ket-bal	*basketball*
chess	ich-*chess*	*iċ-ċess*
dancing	is-*sfin*	*iż-żfin*
food	*li*-kel	*l-ikel*
football	*fut*-bol	*futbol*
hiking	mish-*yiet*	*mixjiet*
	fil-kahm-*pahn*-yah	*fil-kampanja*
movies	films	*films*
music	*mu*-hi-kah	*mużika*
nightclubs	*nait*-klubs	*nightclubs*
photography	fo-to-grah-*fi*-yah	*fotografija*
reading	il-*'ah*-ri	*il-qari*

MALTESE

MALTESE

shopping	ish-*shi*-ri	*ix-xiri*
skiing	lis-kiy-*yar*	*l-iskijjar*
swimming	lahwm	*l-għawm*
tennis	it-*te*-nis	*it-tennis*
travelling	liv-yaj-*jar*	*l-ivjaġġar*
visiting friends	sahnd il-*hbieb*	*s'għand il-ħbieb*
walking	il-*mi*-shi	*il-mixi*

Festivals

Il-Vitorja   il vi-*tor*-yah
  Our Lady of Victories (8 September)

L-Imnarja   lim-*nahr*-yah
  the feast of St Peter and St Paul (29 June)

San Pawl   sahn pahwl
  the feast of St Paul (10 February)

Santa Marija   *sahn*-tah mah-*ri*-yah
  the feast of St Mary (15 August)

What feasts are being celebrated today?
  shfes-ti em il-*lum*?   *X'festi hemm illum?*
How much is the entrance fee?
  kem u d-dhul?   *Kemm hu d-dhul?*

IN THE COUNTRY
Weather

What's the weather like today?
  kif i-*nu* t-temp il-lum?   *Kif inhu t-temp illum?*

It's ...	u ...	*hu ...*
cloudy	im-*sahh*-hahb	*imsaħħab*
cold	il-bahrd	*il-bard*
fine	il-*bnahz*-zi	*bnazzi*
hot	is-*shah*-nah	*is-shana*
hot and humid	rih *is*-fel	*rih isfel*
windy	ir-rih	*ir-rih*

FOOD

Like the intriguing blend of Semitic and Romance in the Maltese language, Middle Eastern and Italian influences are prominent in Maltese cuisine. However, the Maltese have preserved a strongly indigenous quality in their cooking techniques. Some traditional foods are intimately related to the country's folklore. Other dishes that, at first sight, resemble those of other countries, are found to be typically Maltese in preparation, cooking methods and in taste.

Some Maltese produce has been world-famous for centuries. Maltese oranges, *laring*, have a strong flavour. Most popular are the so-called blood oranges, *laring tad-demm*, whose flesh is a blood-red colour. Maltese honey, *ghasel*, is famous for its healing properties. Another Maltese goody of international repute is *hobż*, a loaf with a very crisp, aerated crumb.

I'm a vegetarian.	yien ve-je-tahr-*yahn*	*Jien veġetarjan.*
Waiter!	il-kont, yek *yoj*-bok!	*Il-kont, jekk joghġbok!*

Typical Foods & Dishes

fenek

rabbit is reputedly Malta's national dish. Maltese rabbit – reared in backyard hutches – is cooked with flair and imagination.

fenek bit-tewm u l-inbid	rabbit cooked in garlic & wine
fenek moqli	fried rabbit
stuffat tal-fenek	stewed rabbit

MALTESE

MALTESE

lampuki
fish is very popular in Malta, and perhaps most popular of all is the *lampuki*, a migratory species in season from mid-August until November. Although found throughout the Mediterranean, *lampuki* are mostly caught in the waters surrounding the Maltese islands.

lampuki biz-zalza pikkanti	lampuki in piquant sauce
torta tal-lampuki	lampuki pie

pastizzi
a Maltese speciality made with a pastry similar to puff pastry, and filled with either ricotta or peas. Best eaten hot and fresh.

pastizz ta' l-irkotta	pastizz made with ricotta
pastizz tal-piżelli	pastizz made with peas

ġbejniet (tal-bżar)
Maltese (peppered) cheese

ħobż biż-żejt
bread with oil, tomato and capers

insalata
salad

Drinks

coffee	kah-*fe*	*kafè*
(mineral) water	*il*-mah (mi-ne-*rah*-li)	*ilma (minerali)*
... tea	te ...	*te ...*
black	*is*-wed	*iswed*
white	*ahb*-yahd	*abjad*
with/without	biz/blah *zok*-kor	*biz-/bla zokkor*
red/white wine	in-*bid ah*-mahr/ *ahb*-yahd	*inbid ahmar/ abjad*
(cold) beer	bir-*rah* (*kies*-hah)	*birra (kiesha)*
bottle	flish-*kun*	*flixkun*
glass	*tahz*-zah	*tazza*

SHOPPING

Where's the nearest ...?	feyn u *leq*-reb ...?	*Fejn hu l-eqreb ...?*
bookshop	hah-*nut* tahl-*kot*-bah	*ħanut tal-kotba*
camera shop	hah-*nut* tahl-*kah*-me-rahs	*ħanut tal-kameras*
chemist	spi-ze-*ri*-yah	*spiżerija*
greengrocer	tahl-hah-*shish*	*tal-ħaxix*
market	is-suq	*is-suq*
newsagency	ah-jen-*zi*-yah tah lahh-bah-ri-*yiet*	*aġenzija ta' l-aħbarijiet*
travel agency	ah-jen-*zi*-yah tah liv-vyahj-*jahr*	*aġenzija ta' l-ivvjaġġar*

| I'm just looking. | qed *nah*-rah bis | *Qed nara biss.* |
| I'd like to buy ... | nish-*tie*' nish-tri ... | *nixtieq nixtri ...* |

Do you have anything cheaper?	*ahn*-dek shi *hah*-jah *ir*-hahs?	*Għandek xi ħaġa irħas?*
I'll take it.	se nish-trih/nish-tri-ah	*Se nixtrih/a.*
Do you accept credit cards?	*tieh*-du kre-dit kards?	*Tieħdu credit cards?*
Can I have a receipt?	*tis*-tah tah-*ti*-ni ir-che-*vu*-tah?	*Tista' tagħtini irċevuta?*

Essential Groceries

Do you sell ...?	*tbie*-ow ...?	*tbiegħu ...?*
bread	hobz	*ħobż*
sanitary napkins	srie-vet tahl *kahr*-ti	*srievet tal-karti*
shampoo	shahm-*poo*	*xampu*
soap	sah-*pu*-nah	*sapuna*
toothbrush	shku-*pil*-ya tahs-snien	*xkupilja tas-snien*

Souvenirs

filigree	fil-u-*grah*-nu	*filugranu*
glassware	hjiej tah *mahl*-tah	*ħġieġ ta' Malta*
lace	biz-*zil*-lah tah *mahl*-tah	*bizzilla ta' Malta*
traditional boat	il *luz*-zu/*dahy*-sah	*il-luzzu/dgħajsa*

TIME & DATES

Days

Monday	it-tneyn	*it-tnejn*
Tuesday	it-*tlie*-tah	*it-tlieta*
Wednesday	*ler*-bah	*l-erbgħa*
Thursday	il-hah-*mis*	*il-ħamis*
Friday	il-*ji*-mah	*il-ġimgħa*
Saturday	is-*sibt*	*is-sibt*
Sunday	il-*hahdd*	*il-ħadd*

Months

January	yahn-*nahr*	*Jannar*
February	frahr	*Frar*
March	*mahr*-zu	*Marzu*
April	ahp-*ril*	*April*
May	*mey*-yu	*Mejju*
June	*jun*-yu	*Ġunju*
July	*lul*-yu	*Lulju*
August	ahw-*wis*-su	*Awwissu*
September	set-*tem*-bru	*Settembru*
October	ot-*tu*-bru	*Ottubru*
November	no-*vem*-bru	*Novembru*
December	di-*chem*-bru	*Diċembru*

Seasons

spring	ir-reb-*bie*-ah	*ir-Rebbiegħa*
summer	is-sahyf	*is-Sajf*
autumn	il-hah-*ri*-fah	*il-ħarifa*
winter	ish-*shit*-wah	*ix-Xitwa*

MALTESE

Useful Words

afternoon	*wah*-rah nofs in-*nahr*	wara nofs in-nhar
morning	fi-*lo*-du	fil-għodu
today	il-*lum*	illum
tomorrow	*ah*-dah	għada
yesterday	il-*bie*-rahh	il-bierah

NUMBERS

1	*wie*-hed	wieħed
2	tneyn	tnejn
3	*tlie*-tah	tlieta
4	er-bah	erbgħa
5	*hahm*-sah	ħamsa
6	*sit*-tah	sitta
7	se-bah	sebgħa
8	*tmie*-nyah	tmienja
9	*di*-sah	disgħa
10	*ah*-shrah	għaxra
100	*mi*-yah	mija
1000	elf	elf
one million	mil-*yun*	miljun

MALTESE

SIGNS

Signs in Malta are usually in English or in both Maltese and English.

DHUL	ENTRANCE
HRUG	EXIT
MIFTUH	OPEN
MAGHLUQ	CLOSED
NISA	WOMEN
PULIZIJA	POLICE
RGIEL	MEN
TIDHOLX	NO ENTRY

MALTESE

EMERGENCIES

Help!	ahy-*yut*!	*Ajjut!*
Police!	pu-li-*zi*-ya!	*Pulizija!*
Call a doctor!	*i*-baht aht tah-*bib*!	*Ibghat ghat-tabib!*
I'm lost.	int-*lift*	*Intlift.*

PORTUGUESE

PORTUGUESE

QUICK REFERENCE

Hello.	oh-lah!	*Olá!*
Goodbye.	uh-de-wsh!	*Adeus!*
Yes/No.	sing/nõw	*Sim/Não.*
Please.	Se fahsh fuh-vor	*Se faz favor.*
Thank you. (m/f)	ob-ree-gah-doo/uh	*Obrigado/a.*
You're welcome.	de nah-duh	*De nada.*
Excuse me.	dsh-koolp	*Desculpe.*
I'm sorry.	peh-soo d-shkool-puh	*Peço desculpa.*
What time is it?	ke ohruhsh sõw	*Que horas são?*
left	ah shkerduh	*à esquerda*
right	ah deeraytuh	*à direita*
straight ahead	vah ãy frengt	*vá em frente*

I'd like a ...	kreeuh ...	*Queria ...*
room	oong kwartoo	*um quarto*
ticket	oong beelyet	*um bilhete*

one-way	de eeduh	*de ida*
return	de eeduh	*de ida*
	ee vohltuh	*e volta*

Do you speak English?
fah-luh ing-glesh?   *Fala inglês?*

I (don't) understand.
(nõw) per-seboo   *(Não) percebo.*

How do you get to ...?
ko-moo eh ke se vai   *Como é que se vai*
puh-ruh ...?   *para ...?*

How much is this/that?
kwangtoo eh ke kooshtuh   *Quanto é que custa*
eeshtoo/uhkeeloo?   *isto/aquilo?*

Where's the toilet?
ongd eh oomuh   *Onde é uma casa*
kahzuh de buhnyoo?   *de banho?*

0	zehroo	*zero*	6	saysh	*seis*
1	oong/oomuh	*um/uma*	7	seht	*sete*
2	doysh/dwuhsh	*dois/duas*	8	oytoo	*oito*
3	tresh	*três*	9	nohv	*nove*
4	kwatroo	*quatro*	10	dehsh	*dez*
5	singkoo	*cinco*			

PORTUGUESE

Portuguese is a Romance language, which means it evolved from the Latin that was spoken by Roman settlers. Yet, Portuguese as we know it today, has also adopted a number of features from other languages it has come in contact with throughout the ages.

The vocabulary and structure of Portuguese will seem familiar to travellers who've studied Spanish, Italian or French, and in its written form, the language seems fairly decipherable. The pronunciation, however, is much more complex, and often makes first contact with the language a frustrating experience for those expecting to be aided by their knowledge of Spanish or Italian. There's a tendency to reduce vowel sounds, which makes the language sound like a series of consonants in which 'zh' and 'sh' mysteriously seem to predominate. There are also a number of nasalised vowels and diphthongs. These two features in particular can make pronouncing and understanding the spoken word a challenge for the foreign visitor.

GENDER

Some nouns in Portuguese have have both masculine and feminine forms, usually indicated by the ending of the word. Masculine nouns usually end in -o, while feminine nouns often end in -a. In this chapter, the masculine form of a word appears first. The alternative feminine ending is separated with a slash.

| lawyer (m/f) | uhd-voo-gah-doo/uh | advogado/a |

This indicates that the masculine form is *advogado*, while the feminine form is *advogada*.

In cases where masculine and feminine forms follow a different pattern, both forms appear in full, separated by a slash.

| farmer (m/f) | uh-gree-kool-tor/ | agricultor/ |
| | uh-gree-kool-to-ruh | agricultora |

PORTUGUESE

PRONUNCIATION

Many letters have alternate pronunciations, depending on their position in a word or a phrase. Because Portuguese has many muted vowels and 'sh' and 'zh' sounds, one startled tourist was said to have remarked that it sounded like 'a drunken Frenchman trying to speak Spanish'. However, most often visitors say the language sounds Slavic.

In spite of its complexity, the pronunciation of Portuguese is quite regular and most sounds aren't difficult for English speakers to produce, although the nasal sounds require a bit of practice.

Three of the accent marks can be keys to better pronunciation. The acute accent (′) and the grave accent (`) signify that a vowel is pronounced with the mouth opened a little more. The circumflex (^) signals a closed vowel, made with the mouth a bit more closed.

Vowels

To the visitor, Portuguese can sound like a long succession of consonants with no vowels except a nasalised sound at the end of certain words. You can be sure, though, that there *are* vowels, and that most of them have more than one pronunciation.

a (stressed, open)	ah	as the 'a' in 'father'
a (stressed, closed; unstressed)	uh	as the 'u' in 'cut'
e (stressed, open)	eh	as the 'e' in 'bed'
e (stressed, closed)	e	as the 'e' in 'berry'
e (unstressed)		barely perceptible in speech, and not represented in the transliterations
i	ee	as the 'ee' in 'see'
o (stressed, open)	oh	as the 'o' in 'hot'
o (stressed, closed)	o	as the 'o' in 'port'
o (unstressed)	oo	as the 'oo' in 'too'
u	oo	as the 'oo' in 'too'

Vowel Combinations

Sometimes two vowel sounds are combined in the same syllable.

ai	ai	as the 'y' in 'fly'
au	ow	as the 'ow' in 'now'
ei	ay	as the 'ay' in 'day'
eu	e-w	as the 'e' in 'bet' + the 'oo' in 'too'
oi	oy	as the 'oy' in 'boy', but shorter
ua	wa	as the 'w' in 'wind' + the 'a' in 'far'
ue	we	as the 'whe' in 'when'
ui	wi	as the word 'we'
uo	wo	as the 'wo' in 'wobble'

Nasal Vowels

When a vowel is followed by n or m, or is marked with a tilde (~), the vowel is nasalised. Imagining an 'ng' at the end of the syllable, as in the word 'sing', can help you make this nasal sound. Remember, though, that the 'g' isn't actually pronounced.

ã/an	ang	as the 'an' in 'fan' + 'ng'
em/en	eng	as the 'e' in 'Ben' + 'ng'
im/in	ing	as the 'i' in 'marine' + 'ng'
õ/om/on	ong	as the 'o' in 'bone' + 'ng'
um/un	oong	as the 'oo' in 'moon' + 'ng'

Nasal Vowel Combinations

Almost all transliterations of vowel combinations include a 'w' or 'y', depending on the sound.

ão	õw	as the 'oun' in 'ounce'
am	õw	as ão, but unstressed
ãe/em/en	ãy	at the end of a word, as the 'i' in 'wine' + 'ng'
õe	õy	as the 'oy' in 'boy' + 'ng'

THROUGH THE NOSE

A common word, muito, 'much/very', is pronounced as a nasal vowel combination, even though the letter combination 'ui' isn't normally nasalised.

PORTUGUESE

Consonants

Consonants not described here are pronounced as they are in English.

c	k	as the 'c' in 'cat' before *a*, *o* or *u*;
		as the 'c' in 'celery' before *e* or *i*
ç	s	as the 'c' in 'celery'. This letter is known as 'c-cedilha'.
ch	sh	as the 'sh' in 'ship'
g	g	as the 'g' in 'game' before *a*, *o* or *u*;
	zh	as the 's' in 'pleasure' before *e* or *i*
h		always silent
j	zh	as the 's' in 'pleasure'
lh	ly	as the 'lli' in 'million'
nh	ny	as the 'ny' in 'canyon'
q(u)	k	as the 'k' in 'king' before *e* or *i*;
	kw	as the 'qu' in 'queen' before *a* or *o*
r	rr	at the beginning of a word or when written as *rr*, this is a very guttural, raspy sound;
	r	elsewhere, as the 'tt' in 'butter' when pronounced quickly
s	s	as the 's' in 'sin' at the beginning of a word or when written as *ss*;
	sh	as the 'sh' in 'ship' at the end of a phrase or before *p*, *t*, *c(k)* or *f*;
	z	between vowels, as the 'z' in 'zebra'
	zh	as the 's' in 'pleasure' before *b*, *d*, *g*, *m*, *n*, *r* or *x*;
	sh	elsewhere, as the 'sh' in 'ship'
x	ks	in some words, such as *próxima*, as the 'x' in 'taxi';
	s	in a few words, as the 's' in 'sin'
z	z	as the 'z' in 'zebra' between two vowels;
	zh	elsewhere, as the 's' in 'pleasure'

Stress

Stress falls on a syllable which contains a vowel marked with an acute accent (´) or a circumflex (^). The grave accent (`) shows a contraction of two *a*'s – it doesn't show stress.

| | Saturday | *sah*-buh-doo | *sábado* |

but ...

| | that one | *ah*-kel | *àquele* |

If a word contains both an acute accent ( ) and a tilde ( ), stress falls on the vowel with the accent. Otherwise, the vowel with the tilde is stressed.

| | attic | *soh*-tõw | *sótão* |

Words with no accent that end in *m*, *s*, *a*, *e* or *o* are stressed on the second-last syllable.

| | phone call | te-le-foo-*ne*-muh | *telefonema* |

When a word ends in two vowels which have no accent marks, stress falls on the syllable containing the second-last vowel.

| | cold | *free*-oo | *frio* |

When a word ends in three vowels which have no accent marks, the first two vowels combine to form one sound, and stress falls on that syllable.

| | beach | *prai*-uh | *praia* |
| | idea | ee-*day*-uh | *ideia* |

Words ending in *i*, *im*, *l*, *r*, *z*, *u* or *um* are always stressed on the last syllable.

| | to sleep | door-*meer* | *dormir* |

PORTUGUESE

PRONOUNS

SG			PL		
I	e-w	*eu*	we	nohs	*nós*
you (inf)	too	*tu*	they	eh-les	*eles*
you (pol)	voo-seh	*você*	(m & f)		
he/it	eh-le	*ele*	they (f)	eh-luhs	*elas*
she/it	eh-luh	*ela*			

GREETINGS & CIVILITIES
You Should Know

Hello./Hi.	oh-lah!	*Olá!*
Goodbye.	uh-dewsh!/tshow!	*Adeus!/Ciao!*
Yes./No.	sing/nõw	*Sim./Não.*
Please.	(se) fahsh fuh-vor	*(Se) faz favor.*
Thank you.	o-bree-gah-doo/uh	*Obrigado/a.*
You're welcome.	de nah-duh	*De nada.*
Excuse me.	d-shkoolp	*Desculpe.*
May I?	poh-soo?	*Posso?*
I'm sorry.	peh-soo d-shkool-puh	*Peço desculpa.*
OK.	shtah bãy	*Está bem.*

Forms of Address

In a first encounter, the Portuguese shake hands and address each other using the polite form of the pronoun 'you' (see page 355).

- A courteous and formal way of addressing someone is to use the expression *o senhor* or *a senhora*, without a name or surname after it.

- A person's academic title is used as the equivalent of Mr, Mrs, Ms or Miss. The title:

  Dr (m/f)   *Doutor/Doutora*

  can be used to address anyone who has a university degree. Alternatively, you can add the person's professional title, such as:

  Mr/Mrs Engineer   *Senhor/Senhora Engenheiro/a*

  For women, the expression *Dona* can be used if you don't know the person's title or if they don't have one.

- Children are addressed using the informal pronoun *tu*, 'you', and this is how they address one another. *Tu* is also commonly used among close friends or students.

SMALL TALK
Meeting People

| How are you? | ko-moo shtah? | *Como está?* |
| Fine, thanks. | bāy o-bree-gah-doo/uh | *Bem, obrigado/a.* |

I'm here ...	shto uh-kee ...	*Estou aqui ...*
on holiday	de feh-ree-uhs	*de férias*
on business	āy n-goh-siwsh	*em negócios*
to study	puh-ruh shtoo-dahr	*para estudar*

What's your name?
  ko-moo se shuh-muh? *Como se chama?*
My name's ...
  shuh-moom ... *Chamo-me ...*
I'd like to introduce you to ...
  kree-uh uh-pr-zeng-tahr-ly ... *Queria apresentar-lhe ...*
I'm pleased to meet you.
  mwing-too gosh-too *Muito gosto.*

Do you live here?
  veev uh-kee? *Vive aqui?*
What's this called?
  ko-moo se shuh-muh eesh-too? *Como se chama isto?*
Beautiful, isn't it!
  shpeh-tuh-koo-lahr nōw eh? *Espectacular, não é?*
We love it here.
  uh-doo-ruh-moosh eesh-too! *Adoramos isto!*
Are you waiting too?
  tang-bāy shtah ah shpeh-ruh? *Também está à espera?*
That's strange!
  ke shtruhn-yoo/shkzee-too! *Que estranho/esquisito!*
That's funny! (amusing)
  ke eng-gruh-sah-doo! *Que engraçado!*
Can I take a photo of you?
  pohsoo teerahrly
  oomuh footoogruhfeeuh? *Posso tirar-lhe
  uma fotografia?*

Nationalities

You'll find that many names of countries and cities in Portuguese are similar to those in English. Remember, though, that even if a word looks like the English equivalent, it will have a Portuguese pronunciation.

Where are you from?	de ongd eh?	*De onde é?*
I'm from ...	so ...	*Sou ...*
Australia	duh owsh-trah-lee-uh	*da Austrália*
Canada	doo kuh-nuh-dah	*do Canadá*
England	duh ing-gluh-tehr-ruh	*da Inglaterra*
Europe	duh ew-roh-puh	*da Europa*
India	duh ing-dee-uh	*da Índia*
Ireland	duh eer-lang-duh	*da Irlanda*
New Zealand	duh noh-vuh zlang-dyuh	*da Nova Zelândia*
Scotland	duh shkoh-syuh	*da Escócia*
Spain	de shpuh-nyuh	*de Espanha*
the US	dooz shtah-dooz oo-nee-doosh	*dos Estados Unidos*
Wales	doo puh-eezh de gah-lesh	*do País de Gales*

DID YOU KNOW ...	The 25 April 1974 revolution is also know as the 'carnation revolution' because on that day a woman handed out carnations to soldiers.

Occupations

What work do you do?	oo ke fahsh?	*O que faz?*
I'm a/an ...	so ...	*Sou ...*
actor	ah-tor/ah-treesh	*actor/actriz*
architect	uhr-kee-teh-too/uh	*arquitecto/a*
artist	uhr-teesh-tuh	*artista*

doctor	meh-dee-koo/uh	*médico/a*
electrician	ee-leh-tree-seesh-tuh	*electricista*
engineer	eng-zh-nyay-roo/uh	*engenheiro/a*
journalist	zhoor-nuh-leesh-tuh	*jornalista*
lawyer	uhd-voo-gah-doo/uh	*advogado/a*
mechanic	m-kuh-nee-koo/uh	*mecânico/a*
nurse	eng-fer-may-roo/uh	*enfermeiro/a*
office worker	eng-pr-gah-doo/uh	*empregado/a*
	de shkree-toh-riw	*de escritório*
secretary	skre-tah-riw/skre-tah-ryuh	*secretário/a*
student	shtoo-dangt	*estudante*
teacher	proof-sor/uh	*professor/a*
translator	truh-doo-tor/uh	*tradutor/a*
waiter	eng-pr-gah-doo/uh	*empregado/a*
	de me-zuh	*de mesa*
writer	shkree-tor/shkree-tor-uh	*escritor/ escritora*

Family

Are you married?
  eh kuhzahdoo/uh? *É casado/a?*
Do you have any children?
  tãy feelyoosh? *Tem filhos?*
Do you live with your family?
  veev kong uh swuh fuhmeelyuh? *Vive com a sua família?*
I'm involved with someone.
  shto kongproomteedoo/uh *Estou comprometido/a.*
I live with my partner (m/f).
  veevoo kong (oo me-w *Vivo com (o meu*
  kongpuhnyayroo/uh *companheiro/a*
  meenyuh kongpuhnyayruh) *minha companheira).*
I don't have any children.
  nõw tuhnyoo feelyoosh *Não tenho filhos.*
I/we have a boy and a girl.
  tuhnyoo/temooz *Tenho/temos*
  oong kuhzuhleenyoo *um casalinho.*

PORTUGUESE

I'm ...	so ...	*Sou ...*
single	soltayroo/uh	*solteiro/a*
married	kuhzahdoo/uh	*casado/a*
a widower/widow	veeoovoo/uh	*viuvo/a*
divorced	deevoorseeahdoo/uh	*divorciado/a*

aunt	teeuh	*tia*
baby	behbeh	*bebé*
brother	eermōw	*irmão*
children	feelyoosh/kreeangsuhsh	*filhos/crianças*
cousin	preemoo/preemuh	*primo/prima*
daughter	feelyuh	*filha*
family	fuhmeelyuh	*família*
father	pai	*pai*
grandfather	oo uhvo	*o avô*
grandmother	uh uhvoh	*a avó*
husband	muhreedoo	*marido*
mother	mãy	*mãe*
niece	soobreenyuh	*sobrinha*
nephew	soobreenyoo	*sobrinho*
sister	eermang	*irmã*
son	feelyoo	*filho*
uncle	teeoo	*tio*
wife	moolyehr	*mulher*

Feelings

I'm ...	tuhn-yoo ...	*Tenho ...*
Are you ...?	tãy ...?	*Tem ...?*
afraid	me-doo	*medo*
cold	free-oo	*frio*
hot	kuh-lor	*calor*
hungry	fohm	*fome*
in a hurry	preh-suh	*pressa*
right	rruh-zōw	*razão*
sorry (regret)	pe-nuh	*pena*
thirsty	sed	*sede*

PORTUGUESE

I'm ...	shto kong ...	*Estou com ...*
keen to ...	vong-tahd de ...	*vontade de ...*
sleepy	so-noo	*sono*

I'm ...	shto ...?	*Estou ...*
Are you ...?	shtah ...?	*Está ...?*
angry	zang-gah-do/a	*zangado/a*
annoyed	shuh-tee-ah-doo/uh	*chateado/a*
happy	fleesh	*feliz*
sad	treesht	*triste*
tired	kang-sah-doo/uh	*cansado/a*
upset	shuh-tee-ahd-oo/uh	*chateado/a*
well	bãy	*bem*
worried	pree-o-koo-pah-doo/uh	*preocupado/a*

I feel great.
  shto oh-tee-moo/uh   *Estou óptimo/a.*
I'm sorry. (condolence)
  sing-too mwing-too;   *Sinto muito;*
  oozh me-wsh seng-ti-meng-toosh   *Os meus sentimentos.*
I'm grateful.
  mwing-too uhg-ruhd-see-doo/uh   *Muito agradecido/a.*

PORTUGUESE

Useful Phrases

Sure.	klah-roo	*Claro.*
It's OK.	too-doo bãy	*Tudo bem.*

Just a minute.
  eh soh oong moo-meng-too   *É só um momento.*
It's (not) important.
  (nõw) eh ing-poor-tangt   *(Não) é importante.*
Don't worry about it.
  nõw fahzh mahl   *Não faz mal.*

It's (not) possible.
(nõw) eh poo-see-vehl   *(Não) é possível.*

That's enough!	she-guh!	*Chega!*
Look!	oh-ly!/rr-pahr!	*Olhe!/Repare!*
Listen (to this)!	oy-suh (eesh-too)!	*Oiça (isto)!*
I'm ready.	shto prong-too/uh	*Estou pronto/a.*
Are you ready?	shtah prong-too/uh?	*Está pronto/a?*
Wait!	shpeh-ruh!	*Espera!*
Good luck!	bo-uh sohrt!	*Boa sorte!*

BREAKING THE LANGUAGE BARRIER

Do you speak English?
  fah-luh ing-glesh?   *Fala inglês?*

Yes, I do.	fah-loo	*Falo.*
No, I don't.	nõw (nõw fahl-oo)	*Não (não falo).*

Does anyone speak English?
  ah ahl-gãy ke fahl   *Há alguém que fale*
  ing-glesh?   *inglês?*

I (don't) understand.
  (nõw) per-se-boo   *(Não) percebo.*

Could you speak more slowly?
  poo-dee-uh fuh-lahr   *Podia falar*
  maizh dvuh-gahr?   *mais devagar?*

Could you repeat that?
  pohd rr-p-teer ee-soo?   *Pode repetir isso?*

Please write it down.
  shkre-vuh, se fash fuh-vor   *Escreva, se faz favor.*

How do you say ...?
  ko-moo eh ke se deesh ...?   *Como é que se diz ...?*

BODY LANGUAGE

When greeting each other, people in professional situations will usually shake hands. Young people, women, and friends of the opposite sex often kiss each other first on the left cheek, then on the right, while men may greet with a hug.

The Portuguese are fairly expressive physically. During a conversation, people will often move close to one another and touch.

PAPERWORK

carta de condução	drivers licence
data de emissão	date of issue
data de nascimento	date of birth
estado civil	marital status
casado/a	married
divorciado/a	divorced
solteiro/a	single
viúvo/a	widowed
idade	age
identificação	identification
imigração	immigration
lugar del nascimento	place of birth
morada	address
motivo da viagem	reason for travel
férias	holiday
negócios	business
visita a familiares/a parentes	visiting relatives
nacionalidade	nationality
nome	name
número do passaporte	passport number
profissão	profession
religião	religion
sexo	sex
valido até ...	expiry date
visto	visa

PORTUGUESE

GETTING AROUND
Directions

How do you get to ...?
  ko-moo eh ke se vai   *Como é que se vai*
  puh-ruh ...?   *para ...?*
Straight ahead.
  vah ãy frengt   *Vá em frente.*
In the next block.
  noo proh-see-moo   *No próximo quarteirão.*
  kwuhr-tay-rõw

Turn (at the) ...	veer ...	*Vire ...*
left	ah shker-duh	*à esquerda*
right	ah dee-ray-tuh	*à direita*
intersection	noo kroo-zuh-meng-too	*no cruzamento*
traffic lights	noo smah-foor-oo	*no semáforo*
next corner	nuh proh-see-muh	*na próxima*
	shkee-nuh	*esquina*

behind	uh-trahzh de	*atrás de*
in front of	dee-angt de;	*diante de;*
	ãy frengt de	*em frente de*
far	longzh	*longe*
near	pehr-too	*perto*
opposite	doo ot-roo lah-doo;	*do outro lado;*
	ãy frengt doo/duh	*em frente do/da*

here	uh-kee	*aqui*
there	uh-lee	*ali*

north	uh nohrt	*a norte*
south	uh sool	*a sul*
east	uh ehsht	*a este*
west	uh oh-ehsht	*a oeste*

Buying Tickets

Excuse me, where's the ticket office?	
desh-koolp, ongd eh	*Desculpe, onde é*
uh beely-tay-ruh?	*a bilheteira?*
I'd like to book a seat to ...	
kree-uh r-zer-vahr oong	*Queria reservar um*
loo-gahr puh-ruh ...	*lugar para ...*

I'd like (a) ...	kree-uh ...	*Queria ...*
one-way ticket	oong bee-lyet	*um bilhete*
	de ee-duh	*de ida*
return ticket	oong bee-lyet de	*um bilhete de*
	ee-duh ee vohl-tuh	*ida e volta*
two tickets	doysh bee-lyetsh	*dois bilhetes*
a/an ... fare	oong bee-lyet kong	*um bilhete*
	desh-kong-too	*com desconto*
	puh-ruh ...	*para ...*
senior	ter-say-ruh ee-dahd	*terceira idade*
student	shtoo-dangtsh	*estudantes*
youth	zhoh-vãysh	*jovens*
... ticket	bee-lyet ...	*bilhete ...*
daily	dee-ah-riw	*diário*
weekly	smuh-nahl	*semanal*
10-trip	de dehsh	*de dez*
	viahzhãysh	*viagens*
1st/2nd class	ãy pree-may-ruh/	*em primeira/*
	sgoong-duh klahs	*segunda classe*

Bus

City buses are called *autocarros*, while intercity buses are *camionetes*, which may or may not provide an express service.

Where do I get the bus for ...?	
ongd eh ke poh-soo uh-puh-nyahr	*Onde é que posso apanhar*
oo ow-toh-kahr-roo puh-ruh ...?	*o autocarro para ...?*

Which bus goes to ...?
   kwal eh oo ow-toh-kahr-roo/uh   *Qual é o autocarro/a*
   kuh-miw-neht ke vai puh-ruh ...?   *camionete que vai para ...?*
Does this bus go to ...?
   esht ow-toh-kahr-roo/ehs-tuh   *Este autocarro/esta*
   kuh-miw-neht vai puh-ruh ...?   *camionete vai para ...?*
How often do buses come?
   de kwang-too ãy kwang-too   *De quanto em quanto*
   teng-poo vãy ooz   *tempo vêm os*
   ow-toh-kahr-roosh?   *autocarros?*
Could you let me know when
we get to ...?
   poo-dree-uh uh-vee-zahrm   *Poderia avisar-me*
   kwang-doo shgahr-moosh uh ...?   *quando chegarmos a ...?*

What time's the ... bus?	uh ke oh-ruhsh sai oo ... ow-toh-kahr-roo?	*A que horas sai o ... autocarro?*
first	pree-may-roo	*primeiro*
last	ool-teem-oo	*último*
next	proh-see-moo	*próximo*

Train

Aside from the commuter trains that serve the Cascais and Sintra
lines, Portugal has a complete network of regional and intercity
trains. The intercity trains, called *inter-cidades*, are the fastest and
most direct way of getting to some of Portugal's major cities.
Lisbon and Oporto both have underground subway systems.

What station is this?
   ke shtuh-sõw eh eh-shtuh   *Que estação é esta?*
Does this train stop at ...?
   esht kong-bo-yoo pah-ruh ãy ...?   *Este comboio para em ...?*
Is this seat taken?
   esht loo-gahr shtah o-koo-pah-doo?   *Este lugar está ocupado?*
Which line goes to ...?
   kwal eh uh lee-nyuh puh-ruh ...?   *Qual é a linha para ...?*

Do I have to change lines
to get to ...?
  tuh-nyoo de moo-dahr de   *Tenho de mudar de*
  lee-nyuh puh-ruh shgahr uh ...?   *linha para chegar a ...?*
What's the next station?
  kwal eh uh proh-see-muh   *Qual é a próxima*
  shtuh-sōw?   *estação?*
How long will it be delayed?
  kwal eh oo uh-trah-zoo?   *Qual é o atraso?*

THEY MAY SAY ...

oo kong-bo-yoo shtah ...	The train is ...
uh-truh-zah-doo	delayed
foy kang-slah-doo	cancelled

Taxi

Is this taxi free?	shtah leevr?	*Está livre?*
Please take	lehvm puh-ruh ...,	*Leve-me para ...,*
me to (the) ...	fahsh fuh-vor	*faz favor.*
airport	oo uh-eh-roh-por-too	*o aeroporto*
this address	ehsh-tuh moo-rah-duh	*esta morada*
... station	uh shtuh-sōw de ...	*a estação de ...*
bus	ow-toh-kahr-roosh	*autocarros*
coach	kah-miw-neh-tsh	*camionetes*
train	kong-boy-oosh	*comboios*

How much does it cost to go to ...?
  kwang-to eh ke   *Quanto é que*
  koo-shtuh eer uh ...?   *custa ir a ...?*
Do we pay extra for luggage?
  pah-guhs maish pe-luh   *Paga-se mais pela*
  buh-gah-zhāy?   *bagagem?*
Can you take (five) passengers?
  pohd lvahr (sing-koo)   *Pode levar (cinco)*
  pso-uhsh?   *pessoas?*

PORTUGUESE

The next street to the left/right.
  nuh proh-see-muh roo-uh veer
  ah shker-duh/ah dee-ray-tuh

*Na próxima rua vire
à esquerda/direita.*

Please slow down.
  poor fuh-vor, vah
  maizh-dvuh-gahr!

*Por favor, vá mais
devagar!*

Please wait here.
  shpehr, se fash fuh-vor

Espere, se faz favor.

Stop here!
  pahr uh-kee!

Pare aqui!

Stop at the corner.
  pahr nuh shkee-nuh

Pare na esquina.

Continue!
  kong-tee-noo-e!

Continue!

Boat

Where does the ferry leave from?
  de ongd eh ke sai/
  pahrt oo bahr-koo?

*De onde é que sai/
parte o barco?*

Where does the ferry dock?
  oo bahr-koo she-guh/pah-ruh
  ãy ke shtuh-sõw?

*O barco chega/pára
em que estação?*

What time does the ferry leave/arrive?
  uh ke oh-ruhsh pahrt/
  she-guh oo bahr-koo?

*A que horas parte/
chega o barco?*

How much is it if I bring my car?
  kwang-too koosh-tuh oo bee-lyet
  doo-muh pso-uh kong kahr-roo?

*Quanto custa o bilhete
duma pessoa com carro?*

Useful Phrases

I'm looking for ...
  shto ah proh-koo-ruh duh ...

Estou à procura da ...

Where does this ... go?
  puh-ruh ongd vai esht ...?

Para onde vai este ...?

PORTUGUESE

Where's the ...?	ongd eh uh ...?	*Onde é a ...?*
bus stop	puh-rah-zhãy doo	*paragem do*
	ow-toh-kah-rroo	*autocarro*
road to	shtrah-duh puh-ruh ...	*estrada para ...*
... station	shtuh-sõw ...	*estação ...*
train	de kong-boy-oosh	*de comboios*
underground	doo meh-troo	*do metro*
taxi stand	prah-suh de	*praça de*
	tahk-seesh	*táxis*

What time does the	uh ke ohruhsh	*A que horas*
... leave/arrive?	sheguh/pahrt oo ...?	*chega/parte o ...?*
boat	bahrkoo	*barco*
bus	owtohkahrroo	*autocarro*
plane	uhveeõw	*avião*
train	kongboyoo	*comboio*
underground	mehtroo	*metro*

Car

Where can I rent a car?
    ongd poh-soo uh-loo-gahr   *Onde posso alugar*
    oong kahr-roo?   *um carro?*
How much is it daily/weekly?
    kwang-too koosh-tuh poor   *Quanto custa por*
    dee-uh/smuh-nuh?   *dia/semana?*

Does that	noo pre-soo shtah ...?	*No preço está ...?*
include ...?	ing-kloo-ee-doo	*incluído*
insurance	oo sgoo-roo	*o seguro*
mileage	ing-kloo-ee-duh	*incluída*
	uh-kee-loom-trah-zhãy	*aquilometragem?*

Does this road lead to ...?
    eh-shtuh shtrah-duh   *Esta estrada*
    vai uh-teh ...?   *vai até ...?*
We need a mechanic.
    pre-see-zuh-moosh   *Precisamos dum*
    doong mkuh-nee-koo   *mecânico.*

PORTUGUESE

I've lost my car keys.

per-dee uhsh shahvsh	*Perdi as chaves*
doo kahr-roo	*do carro.*

I've run out of petrol.

fee-kay sãy guh-zoo-lee-nuh	*Fiquei sem gasolina.*

Where's the nearest petrol station?

ongd fee-kuh uh proh-see-muh	*Onde fica a próxima*
bong-buh de guh-zoo-lee-nuh?	*bomba de gasolina?*

I have a flat tyre.

tuhn-yoo oong pne-w	*Tenho um pneu*
foo-rah-doo	*furado.*

air	ahr	*ar*
battery	buh-tree-uh	*bateria*
brakes	truh-võysh	*travões*
clutch	eng-bri-ah-zhãy	*embriagem*
drivers licence	kahr-tuh de kong-doo-sõw	*carta de condução*
engine	moo-tor	*motor*
garage	oh-fee-see-nuh	*oficina*
highway	ow-tohsh-trah-duh	*auto-estrada*
indicator	peesh-kuhsh	*piscas*
lights	fuh-roysh	*faróis*
leaded	guh-zoo-lee-nuh kong	*gasolina com*
	shoong-boo	*chumbo*
regular	guh-zoo-lee-nuh	*gasolina*
	sãy shoong-boo	*sem chumbo*
oil	oh- liw	*óleo*
motorway	ow-tohsh-trah-duh	*auto-estrada*
radiator	rruhd-yuh-dor	*radiador*
(main) road	shtrah-duh (pring-see-pahl)	*estrada (principal)*
roadmap	mah-puh de shtrah-duhsh	*mapa de estradas*
seatbelt	sing-too de	*cinto de*
	sgoo-rang-suh	*segurança*
speed limit	lee-meet de	*limite de*
	vloo-see-dahd	*velocidade*
tyres	pnew-sh	*pneus*
windscreen	pah-ruh-bree-zuhsh	*parabrisas*

SIGNS

CEDA A VEZ	GIVE WAY
DESVIO	DETOUR
NÃO ULTRAPASSAR	DO NOT OVERTAKE
OBRAS	ROAD WORK
PEÕES	PEDESTRIAN CROSSING
PROIBIDO ESTACIONAR	NO PARKING
REDUZA A VELOCIDADE	REDUCE SPEED
SAÍDA	EXIT
SENTIDO PROIBIDO	NO ENTRY
SENTIDO ÚNICO	ONE WAY
PARQUE DE ESTACIONAMENTO (P)	CAR PARK

ACCOMMODATION
At the Hotel

I have a reservation
in the name of ...
   feezh oo-muh rrsehr-vuh   *Fiz uma reserva*
   ãy nom de ...   *em nome de ...*
Do you have any
rooms available?
   tãy ahl-goong kwar-too   *Tem algum quarto*
   deesh-poo-nee-vehl?   *disponível?*

Do you have a ...?	tãy ahl-goong kwar-too ...?	*Tem algum quarto ...?*
single room	ing-dee-veed-wal	*individual*
room with two beds	doop-loo	*duplo*
room with a double bed	kong kuh-muh de kuh-sahl	*com cama de casal*

PORTUGUESE

I'd like to share a room.
  kree-uh pur-tee-lyahr   *Queria partilhar*
  oong kwar-too   *um quarto.*

We want a	kree-uh-moozh oong	*Queríamos um*
room with a ...	kwar-too kong ...	*quarto com ...*
bathroom	kah-zuh de buh-nyoo	*casa de banho*
shower	doosh	*duche*
window	zhuh-neh-luh	*janela*

Can I see it?
  poh-soo ve-loo?   *Posso vê-lo?*
Is there hot water all day?
  ah ahg-wuh kengt   *Há água quente*
  to-doo oo dee-uh?   *todo o dia?*
It's fine. I'll take it.
  mwing-too bãy   *Muito bem.*
  fee-koo kong el   *Fico com ele.*

(See also Camping, page 383.)

PORTUGUESE

SIGNS

HOTEL (H)	HOTEL
PARQUE DE CAMPISMO	CAMPING SITE
PENSÃO (P)	PENSION
POUSADA DA JUVENTUDE	YOUTH HOSTEL
RESIDENCIAL (R)	GUESTHOUSE

Requests & Complaints

Do you have a safe?
  tãy oong kohfr?   *Tem um cofre?*
Can we use the telephone?
  poh-soo oo-zahr oo tlfohn? *Posso usar o telefone?*
I locked myself out.
  fshay uh pohr-tuh ee   *Fechei a porta*
  shkeh-see-m duhsh   *e esqueci-me das*
  shahvzh dengt-roo   *chaves dentro.*

The key to room (seven), please.
uh shahv doo kwar-too
(seht), se fahsh fuh-vor

*A chave do quarto
(sete), se faz favor.*

Could I have the bill please?
kree-uh uh kong-tuh
poor fuh-vor

*Queria a conta
por favor.*

I need another ...	pre-see-zah-vuh de ...	*Precisava de ...*
blanket	ot-roo koo-ber-tor	*outro cobertor*
pillow	ot-ruh ahl-moo-fah-duh	*outra almofada*
towel	ot-ruh twa-lyuh	*outra toalha*

PORTUGUESE

AROUND TOWN
At the Post Office

I want to buy ...	kree-uh kong-prahr ...	*Queria comprar ...*
an envelope	oong eng-vlohp	*um envelope*
postcards	poosh-taish	*postais*
stamps	se-loosh	*selos*

I want to send a ...	kree-uh eng-vee-ahr ...	*Queria enviar ...*
fax	oong fahks	*um fax*
letter	oo-muh kahr-tuh	*uma carta*
parcel	oo-muh eng-koo-meng-duh	*uma encomenda*
telegram	oong t-leg-ruh-muh	*um telegrama*

How much does it cost to
send this to ...?

	kwang-too eh ke koosh-tuh eng-vee-ahr eesh-too puh-ruh ...?	*Quanto é que custa enviar isto para ...?*

Please send it
by ... mail.

	poor fuh-vor, eng-vee-e eesh-too ...	*Por favor, envie isto ...*
air	vee-uh uh-eh-ree-uh	*via aérea*
express	ehks-prehs mayl	*express mail*
fast	koor-ray-oo uh-zool	*correio azul*
registered	koor-ray-oo rrzheesh-tah-doo	*correio registado*
regular	koor-ray-oo nohr-mahl	*correio normal*
surface	vee-uh trrehsh-tre/ muh-ree-tee-muh	*via terrestre/ marítima*
mailbox	oo mahr-koo doo kor-ray-oo	*o marco do correio*
padded envelope	oo eng-vlohp ahl-moo-fuh-dah-doo	*o envelope almofadado*
pen	uh kuh-ne-tuh/ shfeh-roh-grah-fee-kuh	*a caneta/ esferográfica*
postcode	oo koh-dee-goo poosh-tahl	*o código postal*
receiver	desh-tee-nuh-tah-riw	*destinatário*
sender	rrem-tengt	*remetente*

Telephone

Could I please use the telephone?

poh-soo oo-zahr oo tle-fohn se fahsh fuh-vor?	*Posso usar o telefone, se faz favor?*

Please connect me to
directory assistance.

leeg-m ahz ing-foor-muh-sõyshs, poor fuh-vor	*Ligue-me às informações, por favor.*

How much does a (three)
minute call cost?

    kwang-to eh ke koosh-tuh   *Quanto é que custa*
    oo-muh shuh-mah-duh de   *uma chamada de*
    (trezh) meenootoosh?   *(três) minutos?*

I want to make	kree-uh fuh-zer oo-muh	*Queria fazer uma*
a(n) ... call.	shuh-mah-duh ...	*chamada ...*
international	ing-ter-nuh-siw-nahl	*internacional*
local	loo-kahl	*local*
long distance	nuh-siw-nahl	*nacional*
(within Portugal)		
regional	ing-teh-roor-buh-nuh	*interurbana*

The number is ...   oo noom-roo eh ...   *O número é ...*
I want to make a reverse-charge
(collect) call.

    kree-uh fuh-zer oo-muh   *Queria fazer uma*
    shuh-mah-duh uh puh-gahr   *chamada a pagar*
    no desh-tee-noo   *no destino.*

What's the area code for ...?

    kwal eh oo ing-dee-kuh-tee-voo   *Qual é o indicativo*
    puh-ruh ...?   *para ...?*

Hello, is ... there?	shtah sing? shtah ...?	*Está sim? Está ...?*
Hello. (answering call)	shtah sing	*Está sim.*
May I speak to ...?	pohsoo fuhlahr kong ...?	*Posso falar com ...?*
It's	eh ...	*É ...*

phone book	uh lish-tuh tle-foh-nee-kuh	*a lista telefónica*
phone box	uh kah-been tle-foh-nee-kuh	*a cabine telefónica*
phonecard	oo kuhr-tõw de tle-fohn	*o cartão de telefone*
telephone	oo tle-fohn	*o telefone*
telephone number	oo noo-mroo de tle-fohn	*o número de telefone*

PORTUGUESE

Internet

Where can I get Internet access?
 ongd eh ke pohsoo
 fuhzer oomuh leeguhsõw
 ah ingtehrneht?

*Onde é que posso
fazer uma ligação
à Internet?*

I want to access the Internet.
 prseezoo de uhseder
 ah ingtehrneht

*Preciso de aceder
à Internet.*

I'd like to check my email.
 prseezoo de ver
 oo me-w eemayl

*Preciso de ver
o meu email.*

At the Bank

Banks typically open at 8.30 am and close at 3 pm, and don't
close for lunch.

I want to exchange (a) ...	kree-uh troo-kahr ...	*Queria trocar ...*
cash	dee-nyay-roo	*dinheiro*
cheque	oong shehk	*um cheque*
travellers cheque	oong treh-vuh-luhrs shehk	*um travellers' cheque*

Can I use my credit card to
withdraw money?
 poh-soo lvang-tahr dee-nyay-roo
 kong oo me-w kuhr-tõw
 de kreh-dee-too?

*Posso levantar dinheiro
com o meu cartão
de crédito?*

What's the exchange rate?
 kwal eh uh tah-shuh de kang-biw?

Qual é a taxa de câmbio?

Please write it down.
   poor fuh-vor, shkre-vuh-oo   *Por favor, escreva-o.*

The ATM swallowed my card.
   oo mool-tee-bang-koo ko-me-w   *O multibanco comeu*
   oo me-w kuhr-tõw   *o meu cartão.*

automatic teller machine	oo moolteebangkoo	*o multibanco*
bank notes	uhzh noh-tuhsh (de bang-koo)	*as notas (de banco)*
coins	uzh mweh-duhsh	*as moedas*
credit card	oo kuhr-tõw de kreh-dee-too	*o cartão de crédito*
identification	uh ee-deng-tee-fee-kuh-sõw	*a identificação*
signature	uh uh-seen-uh-too-ruh	*a assinatura*

SIGNS

ABERTO	OPEN
CASA DE BANHO	TOILETS
CENTRO	CITY CENTRE
CORREIO (CTT)	POST OFFICE
ENCERRADO	CLOSED
ENTRADA	ENTRANCE
ENTRADA PROIBIDA	NO ENTRY
FECHADO	CLOSED
FRIO	COLD
FUMAR	SMOKING
HOMENS	MEN'S TOILETS
INFORMAÇÃO	INFORMATION
PONTO DE ENCONTRO	MEETING POINT
PROIBIDO ...	... PROHIBITED
QUENTE	HOT
SAÍDA (DE EMERGÊNCIA)	(EMERGENCY) EXIT
SENHORAS	WOMEN'S TOILETS
TURISMO (i)	TOURIST INFORMATION

PORTUGUESE

INTERESTS & ENTERTAINMENT
Sightseeing

Where's the tourist information office?

ongd eh oo posh-too
de too-reezh-moo?

*Onde é o posto
de turismo?*

Can we take photographs?

poo-de-moosh tee-rahr
foo-too-gruh-fee-uhsh?

*Podemos tirar
fotografias?*

Is there an entrance fee?

eh nse-sah-riw puh-gahr
uh eng-trah-duh?

*É necessário pagar
a entrada?*

I'd like to see the ...	goosh-tah-vuh de ver ...	*Gostava de ver ...*
city/town centre	oo sengtroo duh seedahd/veeluh	*o centro da cidade/vila*
castle	oo kuhsh-teh-loo	*o castelo*
church	uh ee-grezh-uh	*a igreja*
cathedral	uh kuht-drahl	*a catedral*
convent	oo kong-veng-too	*o convento*
market	oo merkahdoo	*o mercado*
monastery	oo moosh-tay-roo	*o mosteiro*
museum	oo moo-se-w	*o museu*
park	oo zhuhr-ding	*o jardim*
statue	uh shtaht-wuh	*a estátua*
university	uh oo-nee-ver-see-dahd	*a universidade*

Going Out

Fado is Portugal's most well-known and best-loved musical genre. Though *Fado* is sung throughout the country, Lisbon and Coimbra *fado* are the most famous. Lisbon *fado* is sung by a single vocalist, who's usually accompanied by at least two instrumentalists, one playing the Portuguese guitar and the other playing the classical six-stringed guitar. Though the *fado corrido*, or fast *fado*, is captivating with its flair and liveliness, it's the standard slow *fado*, with its plaintive, sorrowful tale of tragedy and unrequited love, that holds the audience in thrall.

PORTUGUESE

What's there to do in the evening?

ke uhk-tee-vee-dahdzh
ah ah noyt?

*Que actividades
há à noite?*

I'd like to go to a/the ...	tuh-nyoo vong-tahd deer ...	*Tenho vontade de ir ...*
bar	uh oong bahr	*a um bar*
cafe	uh oong kuh-feh	*a um café*
cinema	ow see-ne-muh	*ao cinema*
club	uh oo-muh deesh-koo-teh-kuh	*a uma discoteca*
concert	uh oong kong-ser-too	*a um concerto*
opera	ah oh-pruh	*à opera*
restaurant	uh oong rresh-tow-rangt	*a um restaurante*
theatre	ow tee-ah-troo	*ao teatro*

Are you doing anything ...?	tãysh pluh-noosh puh-ruh ...?	*Tens planos para ...?*
tonight	ehsh-tuh noyt	*esta noite*
this weekend	esht fing de smuh-nuh	*este fim de semana*

Do you want to dance?

kehrsh dang-sahr?

Queres dançar?

Sure!

klah-roo (ke sing)!

Claro (que sim)!

I can't. I have other plans.

nõw poh-soo, zhah tuh-nyoo
oong eng-kont-roo
muhr-kah-doo

*Não posso, já tenho
um encontro
marcado.*

PORTUGUESE

concert	kong-ser-too	*concerto*
fado house	kah-zuh de fah-doo	*casa de fado*
fado singer	fuh-deesh-tuh	*fadista*
fado night	noyt de fah-doosh	*noite de fados*
folk group	rrang-shoo	*prancho*
music	moo-zee-kuh	*música*
seats	loo-gahr seng-tah-doo	*lugar sentado*
show	shpeh-tah-koo-loo	*espectáculo*
singer	kang-tor/kang-to-ruh	*rcantor/cantora*
stage	pahl-koo	*palco*
ticket	bee-lyet/eng-trah-duh	*bilhete/entrada*
ticket office	beely-tay-ruh	*bilheteira*

Sports & Interests

What do you do in your spare time?

oo ke eh ke fazh noosh se-wsh teng-poosh leevrsh?	*O que é que faz nos seus tempos livres?*

Do you like ...?	gohsh-tuh de ...?	*Gosta de ...?*
Do you play ...?	zhoh-guh ...?	*Joga ...?*
Would you like to play ...?	kehr zhoo-gahr ...?	*Quer jogar ...?*
art	ahrt	*arte*
basketball	bahs-keht-bohl	*basquetebol*
cooking	koo-zee-nyahr	*cozinhar*
cycling	seek-leezh-moo	*ciclismo*
dancing	dang-sahr	*dançar*
drawing	dze-nyahr	*desenhar*
film	see-ne-muh	*cinema*
football (soccer)	foot-bohl	*futebol*
gardening	zhuhr-dee-nah-zãy	*jardinagem*
going out	suh-eer	*sair*
going to the beach	eer ah prai-uh	*ir à praia*
martial arts	ahrtsh muhr-syaish	*artes marciais*
music	moo-zee-kuh	*música*
painting	ping-tahr	*pintar*

photography	fuh-zer	*fazer*
	foo-too-gruh-fee-uh	*fotografia*
reading books	ler	*ler*
skiing	skee	*ski*
surfing	suhrf	*surf*
swimming	nuh-tuh-sōw	*natação*
tennis	teh-neesh	*ténis*
the theatre	tyah-troo	*teatro*
travelling	vee-uh-zhahr	*viajar*
writing	shkre-ver	*escrever*

Festivals

Camões Day
on 10 June, the Portuguese commemorate *Camões*, the 16th century writer who's considered to be Portugal's greatest poet and one of the greatest epic writers of all time

Carnaval
celebrated in February. While the island of Madeira boasts large, showy parades, throughout the rest of Portugal, *Carnaval* is mainly celebrated by children, who set off firecrackers and play pranks.

Dias de Santos e Padroeiros
each Portuguese city and village has a patron saint, and each celebrates the saint's particular day with a holiday. Streets are decorated, and there's usually a religious procession.

At night an *arraial*, 'block party', is set up, and grilled sardines, bread and wine are provided free or for a nominal charge. You can eat while listening to music and dance to the sounds of traditional songs called *modinhas*. St Anthony is the patron saint of Lisbon, and the Portuguese capital celebrates its municipal holiday on 13 June.

Liberty Day
Portugal's most important national holiday is celebrated on 25 April. On this day in 1974, the 'Carnation Revolution' established a democratic regime.

PORTUGUESE

Happy Holidays! (Christmas & Easter)	bo-uhsh fehsh-tuhsh	*Boas festas!*
Merry Christmas!	fleezh nuh-tahl!	*Feliz Natal!*
Happy Easter!	pahsh-kwuh fleesh!	*Páscoa feliz!*
Happy New Year!	fleesh uh-noo no-voo!	*Feliz Ano Novo!*
Happy Mardi Gras!	bong kuhr-nuh-vahl!	*Bom Carnaval!*
Happy Birthday!	mwing-toosh puh-ruh-bāysh!	*Muitos parabéns!*

IN THE COUNTRY
Weather

What's the weather like?
  ko-moo shtah oo teng-poo?   *Como está o tempo?*

Today it's ...	ozh shtah ...	*Hoje está ...*
cloudy	kong noo-vāysh	*com nuvens*
cold	free-oo	*frio*
foggy	nvoo-ay-roo	*nevoeiro*
hot	kuh-lor	*calor*
warm	kengt	*quente*
windy	veng-too	*vento*
downpour	uh trong-buh dahg-wuh	*a tromba d'água*
dry season	eh-poo-kuh se-kuh	*época seca*
rainy season	eh-poo-kuh duhsh shoo-vuhsh	*época das chuvas*
snow	uh nehv	*a neve*
sun	oo sohl	*o sol*

PORTUGUESE

Camping

Where's the nearest campsite?
ongd fee-kuh oo
uh-kang-puh-meng-too
maish proh-see-moo?

Onde fica o
acampamento
mais próximo?

Can we camp here?
poo-de-mooz
uh-kang-pahr uh-kee?

Podemos
acampar aqui?

How much is it per...?	kwang-too koosh-tuh poor ...?	*Quanto custa por ...?*
person	psouh	*pessoa*
tent	teng-duh	*tenda*
vehicle	vuh-ee-koo-loo	*veículo*

backpack	uh moo-shee-luh	*a mochila*
camping	(fuh-zer) kang-peezh-moo	*(fazer) campismo*
campsite	oo uh-kang-puh-meng-too	*o acampamento*
can opener	oo ah-brlah-tuhsh	*o abre-latas*
gas stove	oo foo-gõw uh gahzh	*o fogão a gás*
hammer	oo muhr-teh-loo	*o martelo*
mattress	oo kol-shõw	*o colchão*
pad	uh shtay-ruh	*a esteira*
pocket knife	uh nuh-vah-lyuh	*a navalha*
rope	uh kohr-duh	*a corda*
sleeping bag	oo sah-koo kuh-muh	*o saco-cama*
tent	uh teng-duh	*a tenda*
tent peg	uh shtah-kuh	*a estaca*
thermos	oo ter-moo	*o termo*
torch (flashlight)	uh lang-tehr-nuh	*a lanterna*
wood	uh luh-nyuh	*a lenha*

PORTUGUESE

CROSSING THAT BRIDGE

A day that falls between an official holiday and the week-end is declared a holiday for public service workers. These days are called *ponte*, which literally means 'bridge'.

FOOD

Lunch often consists of soup, a main dish, dessert and coffee, and there's a similar menu for dinner. It's also very common to have a mid-morning and mid-afternoon snack of a *salgadinho*, 'savoury', or a cake.

Vegetarian Meals

Do you have any vegetarian dishes?
tãy ahl-goong prah-too vzhe-tuh-ree-uh-noo? — *Tem algum prato vegetariano?*

Does this dish have any meat in it?
esht prah-too tãy kahrn? — *Este prato tem carne?*

Can I get this without meat?
pohdm ser-veer eesh-too sãy kahrn? — *Pode-me servir isto sem carne?*

Does it contain eggs?
leh-vuh oh-voos? — *Leva ovos?*

I don't eat ...	nõw ko-moo ...	*Não como ...*
chicken	frang-goo	*frango*
dairy products	luhk-tee-see-niwsh	*lacticínios*
fish	paysh	*peixe*
meat	kahrn	*carne*

Staple Foods & Condiments

fish	paysh	*peixe*
fruit	froo-tuh	*fruta*
garlic	ah-lyoo	*alho*
ginger	zheng-zheebr	*gengibre*
hot pepper	pee-ree pee-ree/	*piri piri/*
	muh-luh-ge-tuh	*malagueta*
mayonnaise	mai-oh-nez	*maionese*
meat	kahrn	*maionese*
mint	ort-lang	*hortelã*

PORTUGUESE

mustard	moosh-tahr-duh	*mostarda*
olives	uh-zay-to-nuhsh	*azeitonas*
olive oil	uh-zayt	*azeite*
pasta	mah-suh	*massa*
parsley	sahl-suh	*salsa*
pepper	pee-meng-tuh	*pimenta*
potato	buh-tah-tuh	*batata*
rice	uhr-roz	*arroz*
salt	sahl	*sal*
vinegar	vee-nahgr	*vinagre*
vegetable oil	oh-liw	*óleo*
	uh-lee-meng-tahr	*alimentar*
vegetables	ohr-tuh-lee-suhsh	*hortaliças*

PORTUGUESE

Breakfast Menu

The typical Portuguese breakfast consists of bread with ham or cheese and a cup of coffee (see page 391 for ways to order coffee).

bread	pōw	*pão*
butter	mang-tay-guh	*manteiga*
cheese	kay-zhoo	*queijo*
ham	fee-angbr	*fiambre*
juice	oong soo-moo	*sumo*
toast	toor-rah-duh	*torrada*

PORTUGUESE

MENU DECODER

Starters

amêijoas à Bulhão Pato
  small clams in wine and garlic sauce with coriander
camarões com piripiri
  shrimp sauteed in garlic, seasoned with hot pepper
chouriço assado
  grilled sausage
cogumelos recheados
  stuffed mushrooms
crepe de galinha/legumes
  chicken/vegetable filled crepe, fried to a crisp
croquete
  meat croquette
folhado de vitela/salsicha/galinha/carne/legumes
  puff-pastry filled with veal/sausage/chicken/ground meat/
  vegetables

gambas fritas com alho
  prawns sauteed with garlic
melão com presunto
  prosciutto and melon
pastel de bacalhau
  deep fried, oval-shaped patties of seasoned potato,
  onion and salt cod
queijo fresco
  fresh, fine-curd cheese
rissol de camarão/carne/peixe
  fried pasty with shrimp/meat/fish filling
salgados
  savoury pastries

In Portugal, a soup that's called *creme de ...*, 'cream of ...', contains neither cream nor milk. It simply has a creamy texture because it's been pureed.

caldo verde
  potato-based soup with shredded Galician cabbage and garlicky sausage
creme de camarão
  spicy shrimp soup
sopa de espinafres
  spinach soup
sopa de feijão verdes
  green bean soup

Main Meals

Portuguese menus don't usually list what's served with meat or fish because there are standard combinations:

- fried meat or fish; grilled meat
  rice and/or chips, lettuce and tomato
- grilled or boiled fish
  boiled potatoes and vegetables
- oven-roasted meat and fish
  roasted potatoes

arroz de cabidela
  chicken and rice casserole prepared with fresh chicken blood
arroz de marisco
  casserole of seafood and rice in a tomato sauce
arroz de pato
  oven-baked casserole of duck with rice and sausages
açorda de marisco
  bread-based dish studded with seafood and flavoured with garlic and coriander
amêijoas na cataplana
  small clams prepared with tomato, green pepper and onions
caldeirada
  stew of assorted seafood in a tomato and wine sauce

PORTUGUESE

PORTUGUESE

peixe assado no forno
  oven baked fish
bacalhau à Gomes de Sá
  oven-baked casserole of flaked salt cod with potato and onion
bacalhau com natas
  casserole of creamed salt cod and potato
bacalhau á lagareiro/com batatas á murro
  grilled salt cod served with potatoes baked in their skin with
  garlic-scented olive oil
bife à casa (or *bife à* plus the name of the restaurant)
  thin, pan-fried steak served with chips, rice and a bit of
  salad
cabrito assado
  kid roasted with wine, garlic and bay laurel. Lamb
  (*borrego*) is also prepared this way.
coelho à caçador
  rabbit stewed with red wine and tomato

cozido à portuguesa
  a hearty meal made with chunks of assorted meat,
  sausages and vegetables
feijoada
  hearty bean stew with sausages or other meat; each
  region has its own variety
frango no churrasco
  grilled chicken seasoned with garlic, bay leaves, paprika
  and olive oil, and sometimes hot pepper
carne de porco à alentejana
  cubes of marinated pork and clams simmered with
  onions, garlic and tomato
rojões
  a typical northern dish made with chunks of pork,
  marinated and browned, then stewed in wine; often
  garnished with fried pork liver

Desserts

In general, desserts tend to be very sweet and rich. Lemon and cinnamon are preferred flavourings. Many desserts are *doces de colher* – soft and creamy concoctions eaten with a spoon rather than a fork.

Regional specialities include almond and fig desserts from the Algarve, such as excellent *maçapão*, 'marzipan', which come in an assortment of shapes and have tiny centres of *fios de ovos*, 'sweetened egg yolk'. There's also sweet soft eggs, from Aveiro, and *pastéis de Tentugal*, a flaky filled pastry.

bolo de amêndoa
    cake made of ground almonds, usually with two layers and
    a filling of *doce de ovos* (see *ovos moles*)
bolo de bolacha
    cake made with biscuit and layered with sweetened
    buttercream frosting
doce da avó/casa
    chilled desserts, typically made with cream or condensed
    milk, sweetened egg, crumbled biscuit and chopped nuts
gelado
    ice cream
leite creme
    custard cream with caramelised sugar (similar to creme
    brulee)
ovos moles
    sweetened egg yolks thickened to a soft, creamy
    texture. A similar concoction, *doce de ovos*, is also used
    as an ingredient in other sweets and cakes.
pão de ló (de Alfeizarão)
    a rich yellow sponge cake, eaten plain or used as a
    base for other desserts
pudim molotov
    poached meringue with caramel sauce
tarte de amêndoa
    sweet almond filling in a pastry shell

PORTUGUESE

Pastries

arrepiadas
clusters of sliced almonds, held together with meringue

bolo de mel
honey and spice cake, studded with candied fruit

palmier
flat, palm-shaped puff-pastry. Variations include *simples* (plain), *recheado* (two *palmiers* sandwiched with sweet filling), and *coberto* (with icing)

pastel de nata
small rich custard cream tart in flaky pastry shell. You can ask to have it sprinkled with cinnamon.

sonhos
fried sweet dough, sprinkled with sugar and cinnamon

torta
cake roll with filling

PORTUGUESE

WHAT'S BACALHAU?

Bacalhau, a Portuguese staple, is usually translated into English as 'codfish'. This can lead the unsuspecting tourist to believe they're ordering fresh fish. But in Portugal, *bacalhau* is always dried salt cod unless stated otherwise.

Non-Alcoholic Drinks

(orange) juice	oong soo-moo (de luh-rang-zhuh)	*um sumo (de laranja)*
lemonade	lee-moo-nah-duh	*limonada*
milk	layt	*leite*
(herbal) tea	oong shah (dehr-vush)	*um chá (de ervas)*
(mineral) water	ah-gwa (meen-rahl)	*água (mineral)*

Portuguese coffee is among the best in the world. It's strong and full-bodied, without being bitter. It's typically drunk as espresso, either with milk in the morning or black during the day.

Many cafes have coffee and hot milk prepared in advance for the popular morning drinks *meia de leite* and *galão*. If you want your coffee with milk freshly made, ask for it *de máquina*.

espresso coffee
  kuh-feh (ping-gah-doo);   *café (pingado);*
  oo-muh bee-kuh;   *uma bica;*
  oong sing-buh-lee-noo   *um cimbalino* (in the north)
espresso coffee with a dash of milk
  kuh-feh ping-gah-doo   *café pingado*
short shot of espresso coffee
  ee-tuh-lee-uh-nuh   *italiana*
full shot of espresso coffee
  kuh-feh sha-yoo   *café cheio*
coffee with milk, espresso size
  guh-ro-too   *garoto*
cafe au lait
  may-uh de layt   *meia de leite*
  (de mah-kee-nuh)   *(de máquina)*
coffee with milk in a glass
  oong guh-lōw   *um galão*

with/without ...	kong/sāy ...	*com/sem ...*
milk	layt	*leite*
sugar	uh-soo-kahr	*açúcar*

PORTUGUESE

AT THE MARKET

Basics

bread	pōw	*pão*
butter	mang-tay-guh	*manteiga*
cheese	kay-zhoo	*queijo*
chocolate	shoo-koo-laht	*chocolate*
eggs	oh-voosh	*ovos*
flour	fuh-ree-nyuh	*farinha*
honey	mehl	*mel*
margarine	muhr-guh-ree-nuh	*margarina*
milk	layt	*leite*
olive oil	uh-zayt	*azeite*
olives	uh-zay-to-nuhsh	*azeitonas*
pasta	mah-suh	*massa*
rice	uh-rroz	*arroz*
sugar	uh-soo-kahr	*açúcar*
(mineral) water	ah-gwa (meen-rahl)	*água (mineral)*
yogurt	ee-oh-goort	*yogurte/iogurte*

Meat & Poultry

beef	kahrn de vah-kuh	*carne de vaca*
chicken	frang-goo	*frango*
ham	fee-angbr	*fiambre*
lamb	boo-rre-goo	*borrego*
meat	kahrn	*carne*
pork	kahrn de por-koo	*carne de porco*
chourizo	sho-ree-soo	*chouriço*
turkey	proo	*perú*
veal	vee-teh-luh	*vitela*

Vegetables

beans (green)	fay-zhōw (verd)	*feijão (verde)*
cabbage	kov	*couve*
capsicum	pee-meng-too	*pimento*
(red/green)	(ver-mel-hoo/verd)	*(vermelho/verde)*
carrots	sno-ruh	*cenoura*
cauliflower	kov flor	*couve-flor*
cucumber	pe-pee-noo	*pepino*
eggplant	bring-zheh-luh	*beringela*

AT THE MARKET

lettuce	ahl-fahs	*alface*
mushrooms	koo-goo-meh-loosh	*cogumelos*
onion	sbo-luh	*cebola*
peas	eer-veel-yuhs	*ervilhas*
potato	buh-tah-tuh	*batata*
spinach	shpee-nah-fresh	*espinafres*
tomato	too-maht	*tomate*
vegetable	ohr-tuh-lee-suh/lgoom	*hortaliça/legume*

Seafood

dried salt cod	buh-kuhl-yow	*bacalhau*
fish	paysh	*peixe*
mussels	msheel-yōysh	*mexilhões*
prawns	gang-buhsh	*gambas*
oysters	osh-truhsh	*ostras*

Pulses

... beans	fay-zhōw ...	*feijão ...*
red	eng-kuhr-nah-doo	*encarnado*
white	brang-koo	*branco*
chickpeas	grōw (de bee-koo)	*grão (de bico)*
fava beans	fah-vuhsh	*favas*

Fruit

apple	muh-sang	*maçã*
avocado	uh-buh-kaht	*abacate*
banana	buh-nuh-nuh	*banana*
cantaloupe	mlo-uh	*meloa*
fig	fee-goo	*figo*
fruit	froo-tuh	*fruta*
grape	oo-vuh	*uva*
kiwi	kee-vee	*kiwi*
lemon	lee-mōw	*limão*
mango	mang-guh	*manga*
orange	luh-rang-zhuh	*laranja*
peach	pes-goo	*pêssego*
pear	pe-ruh	*pêra*
strawberry	moorang-goo	*morango*
watermelon	mlang-see-uh	*melancia*

Alcoholic Drinks

Vinho verde (lit: green wine) is a light, effervescent white wine with a low alcohol content that should be served well chilled. There's also a *vinho verde tinto* (lit: red green wine).

The best known of all Portuguese wines are Port and Madeira wines. These are fortified wines usually served as an after-dinner drink or as an aperitif, chilled or on ice. Moscatel and Carcavelos wines are other popular dessert wines.

The wine list, please.
   uh kahr-tuh de veen-yoosh,
   poor fuh-vor
A carta de vinhos, por favor.

The house wine, please.
   oo veen-yoo duh kah-zuh,
   poor fuh-vor
O vinho da casa, por favor.

A glass of Port/Madeira wine, please.
   oong kah-lees de vee-nyoo doo
   por-too/duh muh-day-ruh,
   poor fuh-vor
Um cálice de vinho do Porto/da Madeira, por favor.

I'd like a (half) bottle of ... wine.	kree-uh oo-muh (may-uh) guhr-rah-fuh de ...	*Queria uma(meia) garrafa de ...*
champagne	shang-puhny	*champanhe*
dry	se-koo	*seco*
green	vee-nyoo verd	*vinho verde*
house	vee-nyo duh kah-zuh	*vinho da casa*
red	vee-nyoo ting-too	*vinho tinto*
sweet	dos	*doce*
white	vee-nyoo brang-koo	*vinho branco*

gin & tonic	oong dzheen toh-neek	*um gin tonic*
shot	oo-muh oo-nyuh	*uma unha*
slammer	oong boong boong	*um bum-bum*
vodka & orange	oong vohd-kuh luh-rang-zhuh	*um vodka laranja*
whisky	oong wis-kee	*um whisky*

PORTUGUESE

SHOPPING

Can I pay by credit card?
poh-soo puh-gahr kong   *Posso pagar com*
kuhr-tõw de kreh-dee-too?   *cartão de crédito?*

bookshop	uh lee-vruh-ree-uh	*a livraria*
camera shop	uh loh-zhuh de foo-to-gruh-fee-uhsh	*a loja de fotografias*
chemist	uh fuhr-mahs-yuh	*a farmácia*
clothes store	uh loh-zhuh de rro-puh	*a loja de roupa*
crafts shop	uh loh-zhuh de uhrt-zuh-nah-too	*a loja de artesanato*
general store	oo mee-nee mer-kah-doo	*o mini-mercado*
grocery store	uh mer-syuh-ree-uh	*a mercearia*
laundry	uh luh-vang-duh-ree-uh	*a lavandaria*
market	oo mer-kah-doo; uh prah-suh	*o mercado; a praça*
souvenir shop	uh loh-zhuh de rr-koor-duh-sõysh	*a loja de recordações*
supermarket	oo soo-pehr- mer-kah-doo	*o supermercado*

PORTUGUESE

Essential Groceries

batteries	pee-lyuhsh	*pilhas*
bread	põw	*pão*
butter	mang-tay-guh	*manteiga*
cheese	kay-zhoo	*queijo*
chocolate	shoo-koo-laht	*chocolate*
eggs	oh-voosh	*ovos*
flour	fuh-ree-nyuh	*farinha*
gas cylinder	oong kuhr-too-shoo de gahsh	*um cartucho de gás*
ham	fee-angbr	*fiambre*
honey	mehl	*mel*

PORTUGUESE

margarine	muhr-guh-ree-nuh	*margarina*
milk	layt	*leite*
pepper	pee-meng-tuh	*pimenta*
salt	sahl	*sal*
soap	suh-boo-net	*sabonete*
sugar	uh-soo-kahr	*açúcar*
toilet paper	puh-pehl	*papel*
	eezh-yeh-nee-koo	*higiénico*
toothpaste	pahsh-tuh de dengtsh	*pasta de dentes*
washing powder	dte-rgengt puh-ruh	*detergente para*
	uh rro-puh	*a roupa*
yogurt	ee-oh-goort	*yogurte/iogurte*

Souvenirs

ceramics	sruh-mee-kuh	*cerâmica*
ceramic tiles	uh-zoo-luhzh-oosh	*azulejos*
clay pottery	o-luh-ree-uh/	*olaria/*
	uhr-tee-goosh	*artigos*
	ãy bahr-roo	*em barro*
copperware	truh-bah-lyooz ãy	*trabalhos em*
	kohbr	*cobre*
embroidery	boor-dah-doosh	*bordados*
gold/silver filigree	fee-lee-gruh-nuh ãy	*filigrana em*
	o-roo/ãy prah-tuh	*ouro/em prata*
leather footwear	kahl-sah-doo ãy pehl	*calçado em pele*
pewter ware	uhr-tee-goozh ãy	*artigos em*
	shtuhn-yoo	*estanho*
rugs	tuh-petsh	*tapetes*
... wine	vee-nyoo ...	*vinho ...*
Madeira	duh muh-day-ruh	*da Madeira*
Port	doo por-to	*do Porto*

Clothing

bathrobe	oong rro-pōw	*um roupão*
belt	oong sing-too	*um cinto*
blouse	oo-muh bloo-zuh	*uma blusa*
bra	oong soo-tee-ang	*um soutien*
dress	oong vsh-tee-doo	*um vestido*
hat	oong shuh-peh-oo	*um chapéu*
jacket	oong kuh-zah-koo	*um casaco*
raincoat	oo-muh gah-bahr-dee-nuh	*uma gabardina*
sandals	oo-mush sang-dah-lyuhsh	*umas sandálias*
shorts	oongsh kahl-sōysh	*uns calções*
skirt	oo-muh sai-uh	*uma saia*
socks	oo-mush ma-yuhsh/ pee-oo-guhsh	*umas meias/ peúgas*
trousers	oo-mush kahl-suhsh	*umas calças*
T-shirt	oo-muh tee-shuhrt	*uma Tshirt*
underwear	rro-puh ingt-ryor	*roupa interior*

Materials

brass	luh-tōw	*latão*
copper	kohbr	*cobre*
ceramic	sruh-mee-kuh	*cerâmica*
clay	bahr-roo	*barro*
cork	koor-tee-suh	*cortiça*
cotton	ahl-goo-dōw	*algodão*
gold	o-roo	*ouro*
linen	lee-nyoo	*linho*
marble	mahr-moor	*mármore*
mother-of-pearl	mahdr-peh-roo-luh	*madrepérola*
pewter	shtuh-nyoo	*estanho*
silk	se-duh	*seda*
silver	prah-tuh	*prata*
tile	uh-zoo-luh-zhoo	*azulejo*

PORTUGUESE

PORTUGUESE

Colours

black	pre-too	*preto*
blue	uh-zool	*azul*
brown	kuhsh-tuhn-yoo	*castanho*
dark ...	... shkoo-roo	*... escuro*
green	verd	*verde*
grey	sing-zeng-too	*cinzento*
light ...	... klah-roo	*... claro*
orange	kor de luh-rang-zhuh	*cor-de-laranja*
pink	kor de rroh-zuh	*cor-de-rosa*
purple	viw-le-tuh/rro-shoo	*violeta/roxo*
red	ver-me-lyoo	*vermelho*
white	brang-koo	*branco*
yellow	uh-muh-reh-loo	*amarelo*

Toiletries

condoms	przer-vuh-tee-voosh	*preservativos*
deodorant	dzoh-doo-ree-zangt	*desodorizante*
hairbrush	shko-vuh (puh-ruh oo kuh-be-loo)	*escova (para o cabelo)*
moisturiser	krehm ee-druh-tangt	*creme hidratante*
razor	mah-kee-nuh de buhr-byahr	*máquina de barbear*
sanitary napkins	peng-sooz eezh-yeh-nee-koosh	*pensos higiénicos*
shampoo	shang-po	*champô*
shaving cream	krehm de fuh-zer uh bahr-buh	*creme de fazer a barba*
sunscreen	proo-teh-tor doo sohl	*protector do sol*
tampons	tang-põysh	*tampões*
toothbrush	shko-vuh de dengtsh	*escova de dentes*

Stationery & Publications

Is there an English-language ... here?	ah ahl-goo-muh ... de leev-rooz ãy ing-glesh?	Há alguma ... de livros em inglês?
bookshop	leev-ruh-ree-uh	livraria
section	sehk-sõw	secção

Do you sell ...?	vengd ...?	Vende ...?
city maps	plang-tuhzh duh see-dahd	plantas da cidade
dictionaries	dee-siw-nahr-ywsh	dicionários
envelopes	eng-vlohpsh	envelopes
magazines	rr-veesh-tuhsh	revistas
(English-language) newspapers	zhoor-naiz (ãy ing-glesh)	jornais (em inglês)
notebooks	bloh-koozh de noh-tush	blocos de notas
pens	shfeh-roh-grah-fee-kuhsh	esferográficas
postcards	poosh-taish	postais
stamps	se-loosh	selos
writing paper	puh-pehl de kahr-tuh	papel de carta

... maps	mah-puhsh ...	mapas ...
regional	rr-zhiw-naish	regionais
road	duhzh shtrah-duhsh	das estradas

Photography

How much is it to process this film?

| kwang-too koosh-tuh rr-vlahr esht rro-loo? | Quanto custa revelar este rolo? |

When will it be ready?

| kwang-doo eh ke shtah prong-too? | Quando é que está pronto? |

I'd like a roll of film for this camera.

| kree-uh oong rro-loo puh-ruh ehsh-tuh mah-kee-nuh | Queria um rolo para esta máquina. |

PORTUGUESE

I'd like to have some
passport photos taken.

> kree-uh ke me fee-zehs   *Queria que me fizesse*
> oo-muhsh foo-too-gruh-fee-uhsh   *umas fotografias*
> tee-poo pahs   *tipo passe.*

B&W film	oo feelm uh pre-too ee brang-koo	*o filme a preto e branco*
camera	uh mahkeenuh footoograhfeekuh	*a máquina fotográfica*
(colour) film	oo rroloo (uh korsh)	*o rolo (a cores)*
flash bulb	oo flahsh	*o flash*
lens	uh ohbjehkteevuh	*a objectiva*
light metre	oo foo-tohm-troo	*o fotómetro*
slides	oosh sla-idsh/dee-uh-poo-zee-tee-voosh	*os slides/ diapositivos*
videotape	uh kah-seht de vee-diw	*a cassette de vídeo*

Smoking

A packet of cigarettes, please.

> oong mah-soo de tuh-bah-koo/   *Um maço de tabaco/*
> see-gahr-roosh,se fahsh fuh-vor   *cigarros, se faz favor.*

Do you have a light?	tãy loom?	*Tem lume?*
Can I smoke?	poh-soo foo-mahr?	*Posso fumar?*

ashtray	oo singzayroo	*o cinzeiro*
cigarettes	seegahrroosh	*cigarros*
cigarette papers	oomuzh moortahlyuhsh	*umas mortalhas* (lit: shrouds)
filtered	kong feel-troo	*com filtro*
lighter	oo eeshkayroo	*o isqueiro*
matches	oosh fohshfooroosh	*os fósforos*
pipe	oo kuh-shing-boo	*o cachimbo*
(non)smoking section	zo-nuh de (nõw) foo-muh-dorsh	*zona de (não) fumadores*
tobacco	oo tuh-bah-koo	*o tabaco*

Sizes & Comparisons

big	grangd	*grande*
enough	soo-fee-syengt	*suficiente*
few	po-koosh	*poucos*
heavy	pzah-doo	*pesado*
less	me-noosh	*menos*
light	lehv	*leve*
little (amount)	po-koo	*pouco*
a lot	mwing-too	*muito*
many	mwing-toosh	*muitos*
more	ma-ish	*mais*
small	pke-noo	*pequeno*
too much/many	dmuh-zee-ah-doo	*demasiado*

HEALTH
Parts of the Body

My ... hurts.	doym ...	*Doi-me ...*
abdomen	oo uhb-dohmehn	*o abdómen*
ankle	oo toor-noo-ze-loo	*o tornozelo*
arm	oo brah-soo	*o braço*
back	uhsh kohsh-tuhsh	*as costas*
bone	oo o-soo	*o osso*
breast	uh muh-muh	*a mama*
buttocks	uhzh nahd-guhsh	*as nádegas*
chest	oo pay-too/toh-rahks	*o peito/tórax*
ear (exterior)	uh oo-ruh-lyuh	*a orelha*
ear (interior)	oo o-vee-doo	*o ouvido*
elbow	oo koo-too-ve-loo	*o cotovelo*
eye	oo o-lyoo	*o olho*
eyes	ooz oh-lyoosh	*os olhos*

PORTUGUESE

finger	oo de-doo (duh mōw)	o dedo (da mão)
foot	oo peh	o pé
hand	uh mōw	a mão
head	uh kuh-be-suh	a cabeça
hip	uh ang-kuh	a anca
joints	uhz uhr-tee-koo-luh-sōysh	as articulações
knee	oo zhwuh-lyoo	o joelho
leg	uh pehr-nuh	a perna
mouth	uh bo-kuh	a boca
neck	oo pshko-soo	o pescoço
nose	oo nuh-reezh	o nariz
shoulder	oo ong-broo	o ombro
stomach	oo shto-muh-goo	o estômago
thigh	uh ko-shuh	a coxa
throat	uh guhr-gang-tuh	a garganta
toes	oozh de-doozh doo peh	os dedos do pé

PORTUGUESE

Ailments

I can't sleep.
   nōw kong-see-goo door-meer   *Não consigo dormir.*

I've been vomiting.
   tuh-nyoo shtah-doo uh   *Tenho estado a*
   voo-mee-tahr   *vomitar.*

I feel ...	shto ...	Estou ...
dizzy	kong tong-toor-uhsh	com tonturas
feverish	kong fehbr	com febre
nauseous	kong nowz-yuhsh	com naúseas
weak	frah-koo/uh	fraco/a

I'm on medication for (a/an) ...	shto uh tom-ahr mdee-kuh-meng-toosh puh-ruh ...	*Estou a tomar medicamentos para ...*
asthma	ahzh-muh	*asma*
bite (insect)	oo-muh pee-kah-duh (ding-seh-too)	*uma picada (de insecto)*
bronchitis	brong-keet	*bronquite*
burn	oo-muh kay-muh-doo-ruh	*uma queimadura*
chills	kuh-luh-free-oosh	*calafrios*
constipation	oo-muh kong-shtee-puh-sõw pree-zõw de veng-tr	*uma constipação prisão de ventre*
cough	oo-muh tohs	*uma tosse*
diarrhoea	dee-uhr-ray-uh	*diarreia*
fever	feh-br	*febre*
(bad) headache	oo-muh dor de kuh-be-suh (mwing-too fohrt)	*uma dor de cabeça (muito forte)*
heartburn	uhz-ee-uh	*azia*
indigestion	ing-dee-zhesh-tõw	*indigestão*
infection	oo-muh in-feh-sõw	*uma infecção*
inflammation	oo-muh ing-fluh-muh-sõw	*uma inflamação*
the flu	oo-muh greep	*uma gripe*
itch	koo-mee-shõw	*comichão*
lice	pyo-lyoosh	*piolhos*
lump	oong kuh-ro-soo	*um caroço*
migraine	oo-muh eng-shuh-keh-kuh	*uma enxaqueca*
motion/sea sickness	eng-zho-oo de kahr-roo/doo mahr	*enjoo de carro/do mar*
pain	dorsh	*dores*
rash	oo-muh ee-roop-sõw duh pehl	*uma erupção da pele*

PORTUGUESE

sexually transmitted disease	oo-muh doo-eng-suh vneh-ryuh	*uma doença venérea*
sore throat	dorzh de guhr-gang-tuh	*dores de garganta*
stomachache	dorzh de buhr-ree-guh	*dores de barriga*
sunburn	kay-muh-doo-ruh doo sohl	*queimadura do sol*
urinary tract infection	oo-muh ing-feh-sõw nuhsh vee-uhz oo-ree-nah-ryuhsh	*uma infecção nas vias urinárias*

Useful Words & Phrases

I'm sick.	shto doo-engt	*Estou doente.*

I need a doctor who speaks English.

	pr-see-zoo doong meh-dee-koo ke fahl ing-glesh	*Preciso de um médico que fale inglês.*
Where's the nearest ...?	ongd fee-kuh oo ... maish proh-see-moo?	*Onde fica o ... mais próximo?*
dentist	deng-teesh-tuh	*dentista*
doctor	meh-dee-koo	*médico*
hospital	osh-pee-tahl	*hospital*

At the Chemist

Where's the nearest after-hours chemist?

	ongd fee-kuh uh fuhr-mah-syuh de ser-vee-soo maish proh-see-muh?	*Onde fica a farmácia de serviço mais próxima?*

I need something for ...

	pr-see-zoo dahl-goo-muh koy-zuh puh-ruh ...	*Preciso de alguma coisa para ...*

How many times a day should
I take this medicine?

    kwang-tuhsh ve-zesh   *Quantas vezes*
    poor dee-uh de-voo   *por dia devo*
    too-mahr esht rrmeh-diw?   *tomar este remédio?*

Could you give
me (a/an/some)...,
please?

    dah-vuhm ..., se   *Dava-me ..., se*
    fash fuh-vor?   *faz favor?*

analgesic	oong uh-nahl-zheh-zee-koo	*um analgésico*
antibiotic	oong ang-teebee-oh-tee-koo	*um antibiótico*
aspirin	oo-muh kai-shuh duhsh-pee-ree-nuhsh	*uma caixa de aspirinas*
Band-Aids	peng-soosh rrah-pee-doosh	*pensos rápidos*
cold remedy	oong rrmeh-diw puh-ruh uh kongsh-tee-puh-sōw	*um remédio para a constipação*
contraceptive	oong ang-tee-kong-seh-tee-voo	*um anticonceptivo*
tranquillisers	oongsh kahlm-angtsh	*uns calmantes*

At the Dentist

My ... hurts.   doym ...   *Dói-me ...*
    gum   zheng-zhee-vuhsh   *a gengiva*
    tooth   oong dengt   *um dente*

I don't want the tooth extracted.
    nōw keh-roo ke   *Não quero que*
    muhr-rangk oo dengt   *me arranque o dente.*

Can you give me an anaesthetic?
    pohd uhn-esht-zyah-rm?   *Pode anestesiar-me?*

Stop! You're hurting me!
    pahr! shtah uh fuh-zer doo-er!   *Pare! Está a fazer doer!*

PORTUGUESE

TIME & DATES
Time

To make it clear whether a time like 6 o'clock, *às seis horas*, is in the morning or in the afternoon, add the expression *da manhã*, 'in the morning' or *da tarde*, 'in the afternoon'. For very early hours you can say *da madrugada*, 'in the early morning'.

Another way to avoid confusion is to use a 24-hour clock, which is common in Portugal.

What time is it?	ke oh-ruhsh sōw?	*Que horas são?*
It's one o'clock.	eh oo-muh oh-ruh	*É uma hora.*
It's noon.	eh may-oo dee-uh	*É meio-dia.*
It's midnight.	eh may-uh noyt	*É meia-noite.*
It's ten o'clock.	sōw dehz oh-ruhsh	*São dez horas.*
It's ... past one (in the morning/afternoon).	eh oo-muh ee ... (duh muhn-yang/tahrd)	*É uma e ... (da manhã/tarde).*
half	may-uh	*meia*
quarter	oong kwar-too	*um quarto*

Days

Monday	uh sgoong-duh fay-ruh	*a segunda-feira*
Tuesday	uh ter-suh fay-ruh	*a terça-feira*
Wednesday	uh kwar-tuh fay-ruh	*a quarta-feira*
Thursday	uh king-tuh fay-ruh	*a quinta-feira*
Friday	uh saysh-tuh fay-ruh	*a sexta-feira*
Saturday	oo sah-buh-doo	*o sábado*
Sunday	oo doo-ming-goo	*o domingo*
weekend	oo fing de smuh-nuh	*o fim de semana*

Months

January	zhuh-nay-roo	*Janeiro*
February	fev-ray-roo	*Fevereiro*
March	mahr-soo	*Março*
April	uh-bril	*Abril*
May	mai-oo	*Maio*
June	zhoon-yoo	*Junho*
July	zhoo-lyoo	*Julho*
August	uh-gosh-too	*Agosto*
September	steng-broo	*Setembro*
October	otoo-broo	*Outubro*
November	noo-veng-broo	*Novembro*
December	dzeng-broo	*Dezembro*

Present

now	uh-goh-ruh	*agora*
this morning	ehsh-tuh muh-nyang	*esta manhã*
today	ozh	*hoje*
tonight	ehsh-tuh noyt	*esta noite*
this week	ehsh-tuh smuh-nuh	*esta semana*
this month	esht mesh	*este mês*
this year	esht uh-noo	*este ano*

Past

yesterday	ong-tãy	*ontem*
last night	ong-tãy ah noyt	*ontem à noite*
yesterday ...	ong-tãy de ...,	*ontem de ...*
morning	muhn-yang	*manhã*
afternoon	ah tahrd	*à tarde*
day before yesterday	ang-tee-ong-tãy	*anteontem*
last week	uh smuh-nuh puh-sah-duh	*a semana passada*
last month	oo mesh puh-sah-doo	*o mês passado*
last year	oo uh-noo puh-sah-doo	*o ano passado*

PORTUGUESE

Future

tomorrow ...	ah-muhn-yang ...	*amanhã ...*
morning	de muhn-yang	*de manhã*
afternoon	ah tahrd	*à tarde*
evening	ow fing duh tahrd	*ao fim da tarde*
day after tomorrow	dpoysh de	*depois de*
	ah-muhn-yang	*amanhã*
next ...	... ke vãy	*... que vem*
week	uh smuh-nuh	*a semana*
month	o mesh	*o mês*
year	o uh-noo	*o ano*

During the Day

afternoon	uh tahrd	*a tarde*
dawn	uh muhd-roo-gah-duh	*a madrugada*
day	oo dee-uh	*o dia*
early	se-doo	*cedo*
early evening	ow fing duh tard	*ao fim da tarde*
late	tahrd	*tarde*
midnight	may-uh noyt	*meia-noite*
morning	muhn-yang	*manhã*
night	noyt	*noite*
noon	may-oo dee-uh	*meio-dia*
sunrise	uh-muhny-ser	*amanhecer*
sunset	por doo sohl	*pôr do sol*

PORTUGUESE

NUMBERS & AMOUNTS

0	zeh-roo	*zero*
1 (m/f)	oong/oo-muh	*um/uma*
2 (m/f)	doysh/dwuhsh	*dois/duas*
3	tresh	*três*
4	kwat-roo	*quatro*
5	sing-koo	*cinco*
6	saysh	*seis*
7	seht	*sete*
8	oy-too	*oito*
9	nohv	*nove*
10	dehsh	*dez*
11	ongz	*onze*
12	doz	*doze*
13	trez	*treze*
14	kuh-torz	*catorze*
15	kingz	*quinze*
16	dzuh-saysh	*dezasseis*
17	dzuh-seht	*dezassete*
18	dzoi-too	*dezoito*
19	dzuh-nohv	*dezanove*
20	vingt	*vinte*
21 (m/f)	vingt ee oong/oomuh	*vinte e um/uma*
22 (m/f)	vingt ee doysh/dwuhsh	*vinte e dois/duas*
30	tring-tuh	*trinta*
40	kwuh-reng-tuh	*quarenta*
50	sing-kweng-tuh	*cinquenta*
60	ses-eng-tuh	*sessenta*
70	steng-tuh	*setenta*
80	oy-teng-tuh	*oitenta*
90	noo-veng-tuh	*noventa*
100	sãy	*cem*
1000	meel	*mil*
one million	oong meel-yõw	*um milhão*

Useful Words

all	to-doo	*todo*
double	oo dob-roo	*o dobro*
a dozen	oo-muh dooz-yuh	*uma dúzia*
half	m-tahd	*metade*
a half dozen	may-uh dooz-yuh	*meia dúzia*
a little	oong po-koo	*um pouco*
once	oo-muh vesh	*uma vez*
a pair	oong pahr	*um par*
percent	poor seng-too	*por cento*
twice	doo-uhsh vezsh	*duas vezes*

PORTUGUESE

ABBREVIATIONS

AMI	ah-mee	International Medical Assistance
CDS	se de es	Social Democratic Central Party (right)
CDU	se de oo	Unified Democratic Coalition (left)
ONU	oh-noo	United Nations
PPD	pe pe de	Popular Democratic Party
PSD	pe es de	Social Democratic Party
UE	oo eh	European Union

EMERGENCIES

Help!	soo-kor-roo!	*Socorro!*
Stop!	pahr!	*Pare!*
Go away!	vahs eng-boh-ruh!	*Vá-se embora!*
Thief!	luh-drõw!	*Ladrão!*
Fire!	fo-goo!	*Fogo!*
Watch out!	kwi-dah-doo!	*Cuidado!*

Call a doctor!
   shuh-mãy oong meh-dee-koo!   *Chamem um médico!*

Call an ambulance!
   shuh-mãy oo-muh
   ang-boo-langs-yuh!   *Chamem uma ambulância!*

Call the police!
   shuhm uh poo-lee-syuh!   *Chame a polícia!*

Where's the police station?
   ongd eh uh sh-kwad-ruh
   duh poo-lees-yuh?   *Onde é a esquadra da polícia?*

Could you help me please?
   pohd uh-zhoo-dahr-me,
   fahsh fuh-vor?   *Pode ajudar-me, faz favor?*

I've been raped.
   fwi viw-lah-duh   *Fui violada.*

I've/We've been robbed.
   fwi/fo-mooz
   uh-sahl-tah-doosh/uhsh   *Fui/Fomos assaltados/as.*

Where's a public toilet?
   ongd eh oo-muh kah-zuh
   de buhn-yoo poo-blee-kuh?   *Onde é uma casa de banho pública?*

Dealing with the Police

Larger cities have their own police departments, known as the *PSP (Polícia de Segurança Pública)*. Everywhere else, policing is carried out by the *GNR (Guarda Nacional Republicana)*.

We want to report an offence.
   kree-uh-muhs d-noong-see-ahr   *Queríamos denunciar*
   oong kreem   *um crime.*

PORTUGUESE

My ... was/ were stolen.	rro-bah-rõwm ...	*Roubaram-me ...*
backpack	uh moo-shee-luh	*a mochila*
bags	uhzh mah-luhsh	*as malas*
camera	uh mah-kee-nuh foo-too-grah-fee-kuh	*a máquina fotográfica*
car	oo kahr-roo	*o carro*
handbag	a kuhr-tay-ruh	*a carteira*
money	oo deen-yay-roo	*o dinheiro*
travellers cheques	oosh trah-ve-lersh sheh-kesh	*os travellers cheques*
passport	oo pah-suh-pohrt	*o passaporte*
wallet	uh kuhr-tay-ruh	*a carteira*

Can I call someone?
   poh-soo shuh-mahr ahl-gãy?   *Posso chamar alguém?*
Can I have a lawyer who speaks English?
   poh-soo ter oong uhd-voo-gah-doo   *Posso ter um advogado*
   ke fahl ing-glesh?   *que fale inglês?*
Is there a fine we can pay to clear this?
   ah ahl-goo-muh mool-tuh ke   *Há alguma multa que*
   poo-suh-moosh puh-gahr puh-ruh   *possamos pagar para*
   rr-sol-ver uh seet-wuh-sõw?   *resolver a situação?*
I want to contact my embassy/consulate.
   kree-uh kong-tuhk-tahr kong   *Queria contactar com*
   uh mee-nyuh eng-bai-shah-duh/   *a minha embaixada/*
   oo me-w kong-soo-lah-doo   *o meu consulado.*

SCOTTISH
GAELIC

QUICK REFERENCE

Please.	ma-sheh ur tol eh	Mas e ur toil e.
Thank you.	ta-puh laiv	Tapadh leibh.
You're welcome.	shey ur beh-huh	'Se ur beatha.
Excuse me.	ga muh lyesh-kyal	Gabh mo lethsgeul.
I'm sorry.	ha mee doo-leech	Tha mi duilich.
Good morning.	matiny vah	Madainn mhath.
Good afternoon/ evening.	feskur mah	Feasgar math.
Good night.	ai-khuh vah	Oidhche mhath.
It's a lovely day.	ha lah-uh bree-a-uh own	Tha latha brèagha ann.
It's cold today.	a eh foo-ar un joo	Tha e fuar an-diugh.
Goodbye.	mar shin laiv	Mar sin leibh.
How are you?	kemur uh ha oo/shiv?	Ciamar a tha thu/sibh?
Well.	ha guh mah	Tha gu math.

What's your name?		
jen ta-nam a hu-ryuf?		Dé an t-ainm a tha oirbh?
Do you speak Gaelic?		
uh vel gaa-lik a-kut/a-kif?		Am bheil Gàidhlig agad/agaibh?
Cheers!		
slaan-chuh voer!		Slàinte mhór!

I'd like a(n) ...	bu tul lum ...		bu toil leam ...
ale	lyoonn		lionn
lager	lyoonn		lionn
pint	peenj		pinnt
whisky	ush-kyuh beh-huh		uisge-beatha

1	a h-aon	uh hoon	6	a sia	uh shea
2	a dhà	uh ghaa	7	a seachd	uh shakhk
3	a trì	uh tree	8	a hochd	uh hokhk
4	a ceithir	uh ke-hiry	9	a naoi	uh nai
5	a cóig	uh coe-ik	10	a deich	uh jekh

SCOTTISH GAELIC

SCOTTISH GAELIC

Scottish Gaelic (*Gàidhlig*, pronounced gah-lik) is spoken by about 66,000 people, mainly in the traditional Gaelic-speaking areas of the Highlands and Islands in the west and north-west of Scotland. All speakers are bilingual in Gaelic and English. Migration during the last two centuries, mainly due to socio-economic factors, has meant that increasing numbers now live in or near large urban areas such as Glasgow and Edinburgh.

Scottish Gaelic belongs to the Goedelic branch of Celtic. Irish (*Gaeilge)* spoken in Ireland, and Manx (*Gaelg)*, a language formerly spoken on the Isle of Man that's recently been revived, are closely related to Scottish Gaelic.

Gaelic wasn't the first language spoken in Scotland – Scotland was home to a set of tribes called Picts who spoke a language or set of languages usually referred to as *Pictish*. It's generally believed that Gaelic was brought to Scotland by Irish settlers some time before the 5th century AD. The Romans called these settlers 'Scotti' (lit: Irishmen), which later gave rise to the country's name. By the 11th and 12th centuries, Gaelic was spoken in most parts of modern Scotland and placenames give ample evidence of this (see page 425).

Due to geographical factors and contact with different cultures – such as the Picts, the Britons, the Vikings and the Anglo-Saxons – Scottish Gaelic gradually began to diverge from the mother language Irish.

The decline of Scottish Gaelic began with the Anglicisation of the Scottish dynasty, and the establishment of English-speaking burghs from roughly the 12th century in the Lowlands of Scotland (eastern and central Scotland). The Scottish court spoke English and Norman-French, and the northern dialect of English replaced Gaelic as the official language. Trading with these burghs led to the eventual spread of English and the gradual demise of Gaelic in outlying Lowland areas.

The Lordship of the Isles, founded in the mid-12th century, and partly based on the earlier Norse kingdom of the Western and Southern Isles, became an important focus and centre of Gaelic culture and learning. This continued until the late 15th century, when the Lordship was destroyed by the central authorities of Scotland. All of these factors together served to reduce the formerly high status of Gaelic in Scottish society.

Meanwhile, Gaelic flourished as a vernacular in the Highlands and Islands right up to the 18th century, the time of the Jacobite rebellions and wars. Following the Battle of Culloden in 1746, the Gaels were punished for their involvement in these wars by a variety of measures including the banning of traditional costumes and music.

One of the most drastic measures taken against the Gaels were what are normally called the Highland Clearances (*na Fuadaichean*) of the 19th century. After realising that sheep were more profitable than tenants, some landlords drove the Gaels from their ancestral lands and homes, with many of them ending up in far-away lands such as Canada.

Needless to say, the Clearances delivered a severe blow to the Gaelic language in Scotland. However, the 1872 Education Act (Scotland), which imposed a national system of education, largely destroyed the Gaelic school system set up in the 19th century. Under the new regime, the use of Gaelic was actively discouraged in schools.

Efforts to revive and restore Gaelic began in the later 19th century, and significant progress has been made, especially in education and the media.

Teaching in the Gaelic language has expanded considerably in the past two decades both in traditional areas and in cities, with more than 2000 children taught through the medium of Gaelic, and some subjects taught at secondary level. Gaelic is also taught in Scotland's four main universities. The Gaelic College on the Isle of Skye, Sabhal Mór Ostaig, conducts a wide variety of tertiary-level courses in Gaelic.

Gaelic television and radio are broadcast regularly. There is a Gaelic newspaper and Gaelic articles appear regularly in some national and regional weekly newspapers. The Government has recently signed the European Charter for Minority Languages, which should ensure a small measure of security for the language in the future.

All of these developments have served to raise the profile of Gaelic, and more importantly to increase the confidence of speakers in their language and culture. The tide has turned.

PRONUNCIATION

The stress in Scottish Gaelic almost always falls on the first syllable of a word. Even the word *poileas* (borrowed from English 'police') is stressed on the first syllable. Although Scottish Gaelic spelling may seem complicated, it's in fact more regular than that of English, and pronunciation becomes easier once you're familiar with the spelling system. Although Gaelic uses only 18 letters in its alphabet, it has more individual sounds than English, with some sounds being made by combining letters.

Vowels

Vowels may have either short or long pronunciations. Accents are used to indicate long vowels. Grave accents (*è*) are the norm nowadays, although some writers also use acute accents (*é, ó*) with the vowels *e* and *o* to indicate vowels of a different sound quality.

foot	*cas*	(short *a*)	cas
difficulty	*càs*	(long *à*)	cahs

SCOTTISH GAELIC

Both long and short vowels fall into two groups, called 'broad' and 'slender'. Most vowels also have both 'broad' and 'slender' pronunciations, and affect the pronunciation of a consonant they appear next to depending on which group they belong to (see pages 419-20).

a, o, u	broad vowels
i, e	slender vowels

	SHORT	LONG	
a	a		as the 'a' in 'bat'
		ah	as the 'a' in 'father'
	u		as the 'u' in 'put'
	uh		as the 'u' in 'cut'
e	e		as the 'e' in 'bet'
		eh	as the 'a' in 'scare'
	uh		as the 'u' in 'cut'
i	i	i	as the 'i' in 'marine'
o	o		as the 'o' in 'hot'
		oe	as the 'u' in 'burn'
u	oo		as the 'oo' in 'food'
	u		as the 'u' in 'put'
	uh		as the 'u' in 'cut'

Vowel Combinations

Vowels are combined in various ways to represent different vowel sounds, some of which don't occur in English. The help of a native speaker is invaluable for these. These sounds are represented in this chapter as:

ai	as the 'i' in 'dive'		
	night	ai-khuh	*oidhche*
	thank you	ta-puh laiv	*tapadh leibh*

ay	as the 'ay' in 'play'		
	James	shaym-uhs	*Seumas*
ea	as the 'ea' in 'near'		
	meal	beagh	*biadh*
	wine	fean	*fion*
ee-a	as the 'ee' in 'free' plus the 'a' in father, but shorter		
	mouth	bee-ahl	*beul*
	Christmas	chree-al	*Chridheil*
oh	as the 'oa' in 'boat'		
	slow	soh-kiry	*socair*
ow	as the 'ow' in 'vow'		
	alive	byow	*beò*
	family	chow-lukh	*teaghlach*

PRONOUNS

SG			PL		
I	mee	*mi*	we	shiny	*sinn*
you	oo/doo	*thu/tu*	you (pol)	shiv	*sibh*
he/it	eh	*e*	they	at	*iad*
she/it	ee	*i*			

Consonants

The consonants *l*, *n* and *r* may be doubled to *ll*, *nn* and *rr*. Double consonants are generally stronger than single ones.

Broad & Slender Consonants

All consonants except *h* have two pronunciations, one 'broad', the other 'slender'. Broad consonants are pronounced approximately as in English. Slender consonants have an inbuilt 'y' sound which can be approximated by placing a 'y' sound after the sound.

beò	byow	alive
ceò	kyow	smoke/mist

When a consonant comes next to, or is surrounded by broad vowels (*a, o, u*), the consonant is said to be 'broad'. When next to or surrounded by a slender vowel (*e, i*), a consonant is said to be 'slender'. In other words, broad goes with broad, and slender with slender. When a consonant is preceded by a broad vowel it's followed by a broad vowel and when it's preceded by a slender vowel it must be followed by a slender vowel.

balach   'a boy'   *caileag*   'a girl'

In the latter example the *i* and *e* aren't pronounced – they merely indicate that the *l* is to be pronounced as a slender *l*.

Consonants not listed here are pronounced as in English.

	BROAD	SLENDER	
b	b		at the start of a word, as the 'b' in 'bet';
	p		elsewhere as the 'p' in 'pet'
		by	as the 'beau' in 'beauty'
c	k		as the 'k' in 'king'
		ky	as the 'cu' in 'cute'
d	d		as the 'd' in 'dog'
		j	as the 'j' in 'joke'
l	l		as the 'l' in 'like'
		ly	as the 'lli' in 'stallion'
n	n		as the 'n' in 'naughty'
		ny	as the 'ny' in 'canyon'
ng	ng		as the 'ng' in 'fling'
r	r		as the 'r' in 'rat'
		ry	an 'r' sound followed by a 'y' sound; has no equivalent in English, but can sound like the 'th' in 'then'
rr	rr		trilled

	BROAD	SLENDER	
s	s		as the 's' in 'sin'
		sh	as the 'sh' in 'shoe'
t	t		as the 't' in 'tickle'
		ch	as the 'ch' in 'cheese'
y	y		as the 'y' in 'yacht'

The Letter 'h'

The letter *h* can occur before a vowel or be added to the letters *b*, *c*, *d*, *f*, *g*, *m*, *p*, *s* and *t* to provide a new set of softened sounds. This process is called lenition.

	BROAD	SLENDER	
bh	v		as the 'v' in 'velvet'
ch	kh		as the 'ch' in Scottish 'loch'
		kh	as the 'ch' in German 'ich'
			(never pronounced as the 'ch' in 'cheese')
dh	gh		as the 'ch' in Scottish 'loch' but with voicing
		y	as the 'y' in 'yes'
fh			silent
gh	gh		as the 'ch' in Scottish 'loch' but with voicing
		y	as the 'y' in 'yes'
mh	v		as the 'v' in 'velvet'
ph	f		as the 'f' in 'fun'
sh	h		as the 'h' in 'horse'
th	h		as the 'h' in 'horse'

SCOTTISH GAELIC

GREETINGS & CIVILITIES
You Should Know

Please.	ma-sheh ur tol eh	*Mas e ur toil e.*
Thank you.	ta-puh laiv	*Tapadh leibh.*
(Many) thanks.	(moe-ran) tah-eeng	*(Móran) taing.*
You're welcome.	shey ur beh-huh	*'Se ur beatha.*
Excuse me.	ga muh lyesh-kyal	*Gabh mo lethsgeul.*
Pardon me.	(je) baal laiv	*(Dé) b'àill leibh.*
I'm sorry.	ha mee doo-leech	*Tha mi duilich.*
I don't mind.	ha mee ko-muh	*Tha mi coma.*
Come on.	tro-ut	*Trobhad.*
Let's go.	hu-kiny	*Thugainn.*

Greetings & Goodbyes

Scottish Gaelic has no word that directly corresponds to 'hello'. Instead, people greet each other by asking how the other person is and making comments on the weather, although expressions based on English idioms are becoming more common.

Good morning.	matiny vah	*Madainn mhath.*
Good afternoon/ evening.	feskur mah	*Feasgar math.*
Good night.	ai-khuh vah	*Oidhche mhath.*
How are you?	kemur uh ha oo/shiv?	*Ciamar a tha thu/sibh?*
Well.	ha guh mah	*Tha gu math.*
Not bad.	chany el donuh	*Chan eil dona.*
It's a lovely day.	ha lah-uh bree-a-uh own	*Tha latha brèagha ann.*
It's cold today.	a eh foo-ar un joo	*Tha e fuar an-diugh.*
It's ...	ha ... own	*Tha ... ann.*
misty	kyo	*ceò*
raining	un tush-kyeh	*an t-uisge*
snowing	snyakh	*sneachd*
Goodbye.	mar shin laiv	*Mar sin leibh.*

HEY SHEUMAIS!

When addressing someone in Gaelic, *a* is placed before the name, which corresponds to English 'hey!'. The letter *h* is also added after the first letter of the name.

| (Hey) Mary. | uh va-ryee | *A Mhàiri.* |
| (Hey) Morag. | uh voe-rak | *A Mhórag.* |

If the person is male, an *i* is also added before the final sound of the man's name.

| (Hey) James. | uh hay-mish | *A Sheumais.* |
| (Hey) Donald. | uh ghoe-ily | *A Dhomhnaill.* |

SMALL TALK
Meeting People

What's your name?
  jen ta-nam a hu-ryuf?   *Dé an t-ainm a tha oirbh?*
Do you speak Gaelic?
  uh vel gaa-lik a-kut/a-kif?   *Am bheil Gàidhlig agad/agaibh?*

| Yes, a little. | ha be-kan | *Tha beagan.* |
| Not much. | chany el moe-ran | *Chan eil móran.* |

I'm learning.
  ha mee kyoo-sukh-ugh   *Tha mi ag ionnsachadh.*
What's this in Gaelic?
  e ha sho owns uh ghaa-lik?   *Dé tha seo anns a' Ghàidhlig?*
I don't understand.
  khany el mee tuky-shiny   *Chan eil mi a' tuigsinn.*
Could you say that again?
  un ka-nuh shiv shin   *An canadh sibh sin*
  uh ryee-ishch?   *a-rithist?*
Could you speak
more slowly please?
  um bru-ee-nuh shiv ery ur   *Am bruidhneadh sibh ar*
  soh-kiry ma-sheh ur tol eh?   *ur socair mas e ur toil e?*

SIGNS

CEUD MÌLE FÀILTE	A HUNDRED THOUSAND WELCOMES
FÀILTE GU ...	WELCOME TO ...
FIR	MEN
FÓN	TELEPHONE
IONAD FÁILTEACHAIDH	RECEPTION
IONAD-FIOSRACHAIDH	TOURIST INFORMATION CENTRE
MNATHAN	WOMEN
POILEAS	POLICE
SRÀID (A' PHRIONNSA)	(PRINCES) STREET
TAIGH-BEAG	TOILET
TAIGH-TASGAIDH	MUSEUM

Family

Do you have a partner?
    uh vel keluh a-kut/a-kif?   *Am bheil céile agad/agaibh?*
Do you have any children?
    uh vel klown a-kif?   *Am bheil clann agaibh?*

brother	brah-hiry	*bràthair*
family	chow-lukh	*teaghlach*
father	ahiry	*athair*
grandfather	shen-ary	*seanair*
grandmother	she-ne-vuhry	*seanmhair*
mother	mah-hiry	*màthair*
sister	pyoo-uhr	*piuthar*

INTERESTS & ENTERTAINMENT
Finding Your Way

I want to go to the ...	ha mee gea-ree uh ghol duh ...	*Tha mi ag iarraidh a dhol do ...*
church	un ek-lish	*an eaglais*
ferry	un ta-shuk	*an t-aiseag*
toilet	an taigh-bek	*an taigh-beag*
tourist information centre	in-ut fees-rukh-ee lukhk tu-rish	*ionad fiosrachaidh luchd turais*
town centre	mee-an uh va-luh	*meadhan a' bhaile*

PLACENAMES

Edinburgh	*Dùn Éideann* (lit: the fort of Éideann)	dun e-junn
Fort William	*An Gearrasdan* (lit: the Garrison)	un gye-ra-stan
Glasgow	*Glaschu*	gla-sa-khoo
Harri	*na Hearadh*	nuh he-rugh
the Highlands	*a' Ghàidhealtachd* (lit: the place of the Gaels)	uh ghe-yul-takhk
Inverness	*Inbhir Nis* (lit: the outlet of Ness)	i-nyor nyish
the Isle of Skye	*An t-Eilean Sgitheanach*	un che-lan skee-a-nukh
Lewis	*Leódhas* (lit: the small bay)	lyoe-us
Oban	*An t-Òban*	un to-ban
Portree	*Port Rìgh* (lit: the harbour of the king)	porsht ru-i
Scotland	*Alba*	a-la-puh
Uist	*Uibhist*	u-isch

SCOTTISH GAELIC

Going Out

What are you doing this evening?
   je ha shiv uh jee-a-nuv   *Dé tha sibh a' dèanamh*
   fes-gur?   *feasgar?*

Would you like to   um buh tul laiv   *Am bu toil*
go for a …?   uh ghol …?   *leibh a dhol …?*
   drink   uh gha-al dra-muh   *a ghabhail drama*
   meal   guh beagh   *dhol gu biadh*

That'd be great.
   vee-ugh shin sku-nyal   *Bhiodh sin sgoinneil.*
I'm sorry, I can't.
   ha mee du-likh khan   *Tha mi duilich, chan*
   u-rriny gho   *urrainn dhomh.*

Sports & Interests

What do you like doing in
your spare time?
   jes tul laiv uh vih uh   *Dé as toil leibh a bhith a'*
   dee-anuv?   *dèanamh?*
Do you like (sport)?
   un tul laiv (sporsh)   *An toil leibh (spòrs)?*
What kind of music do you like?
   jen shor-shuh kyoo-il is   *Dé an seòrsa ciùil as toil leibh?*
   tul laiv?

I like …   stul lum …   *Is toil leam …*
I don't like …   kha tul lum …   *Cha toil leam …*

Festivals

a' Bhliadhna Ùr	uh vluh noor	New Year
A' Chàisg	uh chaashk	Easter
am Mòd	um mot	annual Gaelic arts festival, usually held in early October, with a wide range of competitive music and theatre events
an Nollaig	un no-laky	Christmas
Latha Bealltainn	lah-huh byowl-tiny	May Day
Latha Fhéill Brighde	lah-huh ely bree-juh	first day of spring
Latha Lùnastail	lah-huh loo-nu-stal	Lammas Day
Latha na Bliadhna Ùire	lah-huh nuh bluh noo-ryuh	New Year's Day
Oidhche Challainn	aikh-uh cha-liny	Hogmanay (New Year's Eve). People normally visit friends and relatives after the New Year has been rung in, exchanging drinks. This is commonly referred to as 'first-footing'.
Oidhche Shamhna	ai-khuh how-nuh	Hallowe'en

PARTY HARD DUDE

Happy Birthday!
 koe lah-uh breh
 so-nuh ghuht!   *Co-latha breith sona dhut!*

Happy Christmas!
 no-lik chree-al!   *Nollaig Chridheil!*

Happy New Year!
 blu-nuh vah oor!   *Bliadhna Mhath Ùr!*

Congratulations!
 myal ur ne-yachk!   *Meal ur naidheachd!*

FOOD

breakfast	bra-kishch	*bracaist*
dinner	jee-nary	*dìnnear*
beans	po-nary	*pònair*
black pudding	ma-rak ghoo	*marag dhubh*
bread	a-ran	*aran*
butter	eem	*ìm*
carrot	ku-rran	*curran*
cheese	kaa-shuh	*càise*
chicken	kyark	*cearc*
crab	kroo-pak	*crùbag*
dessert	meel-shan	*mìlsean*
eggs	u-yun	*uighean*
fish	eask	*iasg*
meat	fyol	*feòil*
oatcake	a-ran kory-kyuh	*aran-coirce*
peas	pe-siry	*peasair*
porridge	lyi-chuh/bro-khan	*lite/brochan*
potato	bun taa-tuh	*buntàta*
salmon	bra-tan	*bradan*
sandwich	ke-piry-uh	*ceipire*
soup	brot	*brot*
toast	a-ran ery uh lo-skugh	*aran air a losgadh*
vegetables	glas-rikh	*glasraich*

Non-Alcoholic Drinks

a cup of ...	ku-puh ...	*cupa ...*
coffee	ko-fee	*ofaidh*
tea	tee	*tì*
with milk	leh ba-nyuh	*le bainne*
without milk	gun va-nuh	*gun bhainne*
with sugar	leh shoo-kary	*le siùcar*
without sugar	gun shoo-kary	*gun siùcar*
orange juice	soo o-rinsh	*sùgh orains*
water	ush-gyuh	*uisge*

Alcoholic Drinks

It's my round.
shey un tu-rus
a-kum-suh hown

'Se an turas agamsa
a tha ann.

I'll get this one.
yoe mee-shuh um
fer/un che sho

Gheobh mise am
fear/an té seo.

What will you have?
je ghah-us doo?

Dé ghabhas tu?

The same again.
un oon rut uh ree-ishch

An aon rud a-rithist.

Cheers!
slaan-chuh voer!

Slàinte mhór!

I'd like a ... of	bu tul lum ...	Bu toil leam ...
glass	glu-nyuh	gloine
pint	peenj	pinnt
half-pint	leh feenj	leth phinnt
ale	lyoonn	lionn
lager	lyoonn	lionn
red/white wine	fean ja-rak/gyal	fìon dearg/geal
whisky	ush-kyuh beh-huh	uisge-beatha

INSULTS

Shut your mouth!	doon duh veal!	Dùn do bheul!
Get lost!	hala!	Fhalbh!
Misfortune on you.	du-nai orsht	Dunaidh ort.
Bad luck to you.	go-nugh orsht	Gonadh ort.
Bad cess (luck) to you.	gu-muh holk ghuht	Gum bu h-olc dhut.
You fool!	a-ma-tan!	A amadain!
You idiot!	uh ghlaichk!	A ghloidhc!

SOUVENIRS

heather	fruhkh	*fraoch*
kilt	feylugh	*féileadh*
Loch Ness Monster	uluh vehshch lokh nyish	*uile-bhéist Loch Nis*
pipes	peebuhn	*pìoban*
ornament	bal mashuh	*ball-maise*
photograph	jalav kamarah	*dealbh camara*
picture	jalav	*dealbh*
postcard	karshch fushch	*cairt phuist*
tartan	tarshtan	*tartan*
T-shirt	lyeynuh	*léine*
thistle	kluharan	*cluaran*

TIME & DATES
Days

There are two words used for 'Sunday' – the first tends to be used by Catholics and Episcopalians, the second by Presbyterians.

Monday	ji loo-any	*Di-Luain*
Tuesday	ji maarshch	*Di-Màirt*
Wednesday	ji kee-a-tany	*Di-Ciadaoin*
Thursday	jur doony	*Diar-daoin*
Friday	ji hoo-nyuh	*Di-hAoine*
Saturday	ji sa-hur-nuh	*Di-Sathairne*
Sunday	ji doe-nikh; lah-uh nuh saa-pach	*Di-Domhnaich; Latha na Sàbaid*

Months

January	um fool-chakh	*am Faoilteach*
February	un gya-rran	*an Gearran*
March	um maarsht	*am Màrt*
April	un gip-lun	*an Giblean*
May	un ke-chan	*an Céitean*
June	un tok-vee-as	*an t-Ògmhìos*
July	un chu-khary	*an t-Iuchar*
August	un loo-nu-stal	*an Lùnastal*
September	un tul-tiny	*an t-Sultain*
October	un da-vary	*an Damhair*
November	un tow-iny	*an t-Samhain*
December	un doo-lakhk	*an Dubhlachd*

Seasons

spring	un tcha-rruch	*an t-Earrach*
summer	un sow-rugh	*an Samhradh*
autumn	um fu-ur	*am Foghar*
winter	un gyow-rugh	*an Geamhradh*

NUMBERS

0	nyo-nee	*neoini*
1	uh hoon	*a h-aon*
2	uh ghaa	*a dhà*
3	uh tree	*a trì*
4	uh ke-hiry	*a ceithir*
5	uh coe-ik	*a cóig*
6	uh shea	*a sia*
7	uh shakhk	*a seachd*
8	uh hokhk	*a hochd*
9	uh nai	*a naoi*
10	uh jekh	*a deich*

To form the numbers 11 to 19, *deug* is added to numbers from one to ten – *deug* being an old form of deich '10' (cf. English *-teen* and *ten*).

SCOTTISH GAELIC

11	uh hoon jeak	*a h-aon deug*
12	uh ghaa yeak	*a dhà dheug*
13	uh tree jeak	*a trì deug*
14	uh ke-hiry jeak	*a ceithir deug*
15	uh koe-ik jeak	*a còig deug*
16	uh shea jeak	*a sia deug*
17	uh shakhk jeak	*a seachd deug*
18	uh hokhk jeak	*a h-ochd deug*
19	a nai jeak	*a naoi deug*

The Celts used to count in twenties, and this ancient way of counting is still used in Gaelic and Welsh. The decimal system shown here has recently been devised for use in schools, and is taught alongside the older *vigesimal* system.

	VIGESIMAL	DECIMAL
20	*fichead*	*fichead*
30	*deich ar fhichead*	*trithead*
40	*dà fhichead*	*ceathrad*
50	*dà fhichead is a deich*	*caogad/lethcheud*
60	*trì fichead*	*seasgad*
70	*trì fichead is a deich*	*seachdad*
80	*ceithir fichead*	*ochdad*
90	*ceithir fichead is a deich*	*naochad*
100	*ceud*	*ceud*

SPANISH

SPANISH

QUICK REFERENCE

Hello.	*oh*-luh!	¡Hola!
Goodbye.	uh-dee-*os*	¡Adiós!
Yes./No.	see/no	Sí./No.
Excuse me.	per-*don*	Perdón.
Please.	por fuh-*vor*	Por favor.
Thank you.	*gra*-si-as	Gracias.
May I?	*pwe*-doh?	¿Puedo?
Sorry.	loh see-*en*-toh	Lo siento.
You're welcome.	day *na*-duh	De nada.
Do you speak English?	*ab*-la in-*glays*?	¿Habla inglés?
I (don't) understand.	(noh) en-tee-*en*-doh	(No) Entiendo
What time is it?	kay or-ruh es?	¿Qué hora es?
How much is it?	*kwan*-toh *kwes*-tuh?	¿Cuánto cuesta?
How do I get to ...?	*koh*-moh say vuh a ...?	¿Cómo se va a...?

I'd like a room.
kee-see-*eh*-ruh *oo*-nuh   *Quisiera una*
uh-bee-tuh-see-*ohn*   *habitación.*

Where are the toilets?
dohn-day ke-dan lohs   ¿Dónde quedan los
sehr-vih-see-ohs?   servicios?

Go straight ahead.
see-guh; vai-yuh toh-doh   Siga; Vaya todo
de-reh-choh/rek-toh   derecho/recto.

Turn ...	*doh*-blay a la ...	Doble a la ...
left	iz-kee-*ehr*-duh	izquierda
right	de-*reh*-chuh	derecha

I'd like a ...	kee-see-*eh*-ruh	Quisiera un billete ...
ticket.	oon bihl-*yet*-ay ...	
one-way	sen-*seel*-yoh	sencillo
return	day *ee*-duh	de ida
	ee *vwel*-tuh	y vuelta

0	*say*-roh	cero	6	says	seis
1	*oon*-oh/uh	uno/a	7	see-*et*-ay	siete
2	dohs	dos	8	*oh*-choh	ocho
3	trays	tres	9	noo-*eh*-vay	nueve
4	*kwat*-roh	cuatro	10	dee-*eth*	diez
5	*sin*-koh	cinco			

Spanish, or 'Castilian', as it's often and more precisely called, is the most widely spoken of the Romance languages – the group of languages derived from Latin which includes French, Italian, Portuguese and Romanian. Spanish is one of four official languages in Spain – alongside Basque, Catalan and Galician. Castilian itself has many dialects, which mainly involve differences in pronunciation.

Spanish is the neo-Latin language derived from the Vulgar Latin that Roman soldiers and merchants brought to the Iberian Peninsula during the period of the Roman conquest (from the 3rd to the 1st century BC). By 19 BC, Latin had become the language of the Peninsula, almost completely obliterating the languages of the Celtic and Iberian indigenous tribes. Only Basque has survived in its original form.

Castilian-speakers today are intensely proud of their language, and generally expect visitors to know at least a little. English is less widely spoken in Spain than in many other European countries, especially outside the major cities.

GENDER

Nouns in Spanish are either masculine or feminine in gender. Some nouns have both masculine and feminine forms. Often, but not always, masculine nouns end in -o while feminine nouns end in -a. Where the difference between feminine and masculine forms is simply an -o or -a ending, these choices are separated with a slash, with the masculine form first:

| nurse (m/f) | en-fer-*mer*-oh/uh | enfermero/a |

When the masculine and feminine forms of a word vary from this pattern, each word is given in full:

| teacher (m/f) | proh-fe-*sor*/
proh-fe-*sor*-uh | profesor/
profesora |

PRONUNCIATION

Spanish pronunciation isn't difficult, as there's a fairly consistent relationship between pronunciation and spelling.

Vowels

Vowels are pronounced clearly, even when they're not stressed or at the end of a word. Some letters have several pronunciations.

a	uh	as the 'u' in 'nut';
	a	as the 'a' in 'father', but shorter
e	e	as the 'e' in 'bet';
	eh	as the 'a' in 'dare';
	ay	as the 'ay' in 'day', but shorter
i	ih	as the 'i' in 'kiss';
	ee	as the 'i' in 'marine'
o	oh	as the 'o' in 'hot';
	o	as the 'o' in 'port'
u	oo	as the 'oo' in 'zoo'

Vowel Combinations

au	ow	as the 'ow' in 'cow'
ay	ai	as the 'y' in 'sky'
ei	ay	as the 'ay' in 'day'
oy	oy	as the 'oy' in 'toy'
ua	wa	as the 'wa' in 'Swahili'
ue	we	as the 'we' in 'wet';
	way	as the word 'way';
	oo-eh	as the 'oo' in 'zoo' + the 'a' in 'dare';
	oo-ay	as the 'oo' in 'zoo' + the 'ay' in 'day'
		(Remember that 'u' is silent after 'q' and when it's between 'g' and 'e/i')

What?	kay?	*Que?*
guerilla band	gehr-*rihl*-yuh	*guerrilla*
guide	*gee*-uh	*guía*

SPANISH

Consonants

The Spanish alphabet contains three consonants which aren't found
in the English alphabet – *ch*, *ll* and *ñ*.

b	b	as the 'b' in 'big' at the start of a word or after *m*, *n* or *ñ*;
	v	elsewhere, somewhere between the 'b' in 'big' and the 'v' in 'velvet'
c	th	as the 'th' in 'thin' before *e* or *i*;
	k	elsewhere, as the 'c' in 'cat'
ch	ch	as the 'ch' in 'cheese'
d	d	as the 'd' in 'dog' at the start of a word; elsewhere, as the 'th' in 'then'
g	h	before *e* and *i*, as the 'h' in 'hot';
	g	elsewhere, as the 'g' in 'game'
h		silent
j	kh	as the 'ch' in Scottish 'loch'
ll	ly	between the 'ly' sound in 'million' and the 'y' in 'yes'
ñ	ny	as the 'ny' in 'canyon'
q	k	as the 'k' in 'king'; always followed by a silent 'u'
r	r	trilled
s	s	as the 's' in 'sin'
v	b	as the 'b' in 'big' at the start of a word or after *m*, *n* or *ñ*;
	v	elsewhere, somewhere between the 'b' in 'big' and the 'v' in 'velvet'
x	ks	between vowels, as the 'x' in 'taxi';
	s	before a consonant, as the 's' in 'sin'
z	th	as the 'th' in 'thin'

SPANISH

PRONOUNS		
SG		
I	yoh	yo
you (inf)	too	tú
you (pol)	oo-*sted*	usted
he/it	el	él
she/it	*el*-yuh	ella
PL		
we (m/f)	noh-*sot*-rohs/as	nosotros/as
you (inf, m/f)	voh-*soh*-trohs/as	vosotros/as
you (pol)	oo-*ste*-des	ustedes

GREETINGS & CIVILITIES
You Should Know

Hello.	*oh*-luh!	¡Hola!
Good morning.	*bwe*-nohs *dee*-as	Buenos días.
Good afternoon. (until about 8pm)	*bwe*-nas *tar*-des	Buenas tardes.
Good evening/night.	*bwe*-nas *noh*-ches	Buenas noches.
How are you?	kay tal?	¿Qué tal?
Well, thanks.	bee-*en*, *gra*-sih-as	Bien, gracias.
Goodbye.	uh-*dee*-os	¡Adiós!
See you later.	*as*-tuh loo-*ay*-goh	Hasta luego.
Yes./No.	see/no	Sí./No.
Excuse me.	per-*don*	Perdón.
Please.	por fuh-*vor*	Por favor.
Thank you.	*gra*-sih-as	Gracias.
Many thanks.	*moo*-chas *gra*-sih-as	Muchas gracias.
May I? Do you mind?	*pwe*-doh?	¿Puedo?
Sorry. (excuse/ forgive me)	loh see-*en*-toh	Lo siento.
That's fine. You're welcome.	day *na*-duh	De nada.

SPANISH

Forms of Address

It's become less common for women to be addressed as *Señorita*. All women are usually addressed as *Señora*, regardless of age or marital status.

Miss	sen-yo-*ree*-tuh	*Señorita*
Mr	sen-*yo*	*Señor*
Mrs	sen-*yo*-ruh	*Señora*
companion	kohm-pan-*yeh*-roh/uh	*compañero/a*
friend	a-*mee*-goh/uh	*amigo/a*

SMALL TALK
Meeting People

What's your name?
    koh-moh say *yuh*-muh oo-*sted*? ¿Cómo se llama usted?

My name's ...
    may *yuh*-moh ...   *Me llamo ...*

I'm (m/f) a friend of (Maria).
    soy a-*mee*-goh/uh day   *Soy amigo/a de (María).*
    (Ma-*ree*-uh)

I'd like to introduce you to ...
    kee-see-*ehr*-uh   *Quisiera*
    pre-sen-*tar*-lay uh ...   *presentarle a ...*

Pleased to meet you.
    moo-choh *goos*-toh   *Mucho gusto.*

I like (Spain) very much.
    may en-*kan*-tuh (es-*pan*-yuh)   *Me encanta (España).*

It was good talking to you.
    may uh en-kan-*tuh*-doh   *Me ha encantado*
    char-*luhr* kohn-*see*-goh   *charlar consigo.*

I had a great day/evening.
    may loh eh puh-*suh*-doh en   *Me lo he pasado*
    gran-day   *en grande.*

See you soon.
    as-tuh *prohn*-toh   *Hasta pronto.*

SPANISH

Nationalities

Spain is very much a regional country – it's said that Spaniards are loyal firstly to their home town, then to their region and only finally to Spain. A great conversation-starter in Spain is to ask someone where they come from.

You'll find that many country names in Spanish are similar to English. Remember though that even if a word looks like the English equivalent, it will have Spanish pronunciation. For instance, 'Japan' is pronounced hah-*pon*

Where are you from?		
day *dohn*-day es?		¿De dónde es?

I'm from ...	soy day ...	Soy de ...
Australia	a-oo-*stra*-lee-uh	Australia
England	ihn-gluh-*tehr*-ruh	Inglaterra
Germany	uh-leh-*man*-yuh	Alemania
The Netherlands	lohs pay-*ih*-ses buh-kohs	los Países Bajos
Ireland	ihr-*lan*-da	Irlanda
New Zealand	noo-*eh*-vuh zee-*lan*-dee-uh	Nueva Zelanda
Scotland	es-*kohs*-see-uh	Escocia
the US	lohs es-*tuh*-dohs oo-*nee*-dohs	los Estados Unidos
Wales	pay-*ihs* day *ga*-les	País de Gales

Occupations

What do you do?		
uh kay lay de-*dee*-ka?		¿A qué le dedica?

I'm (a/an ...)	soy ...	Soy ...
artist	uhr-*tee*-stuh	artista
business person	koh-mer-see-*an*-tay	comerciante
doctor	*meh*-dee-koh/uh	médico/a
engineer	ihn-he-nee-*ehr*-oh/uh	ingeniero/a
homemaker	*uh*-muh day *ka*-suh	amo/a de casa

SPANISH

lawyer	uh-boh-*ga*-doh/uh	*abogado/a*
mechanic	meh-*ka*-nee-koh/uh	*mecánico/a*
musician	*moo*-see-koh/uh	*músico/a*
nurse	en-fer-*mer*-oh/uh	*enfermero/a*
office worker	oh-fee-see-*nihs*-tuh	*oficinista*
secretary	sek-reh-*ta*-ree-oh/uh	*secretario/a*
self-employed	truh-bak-uh-*dohr*/	*trabajador/*
	truh-bak-uh-*doh*-ruh	*trabajadora*
	ow-*toh*-noh-moh/uh	*autónomo/a*
student	es-too-dee-*an*-tay	*estudiante*
teacher	proh-fe-*sor*/	*profesor/*
	proh-fe-*so*-ruh	*profesora*
waiter	kuh-muh-*rehr*-oh/uh	*camarero/a*
writer	es-kree-*tohr*/	*escritor/*
	es-kree-*toh*-ruhr	*escritora*

I'm ...	es-*toy* ...	*Estoy ...*
retired	hoo-bee-*luh*-doh/duh	*jubilado/a*
unemployed	en el *puh*-roh	*en el paro*

Religion

What's your religion?
kwal es soo reh-lee-hee-*ohn*? ¿*Cuál es su religión?*

I'm ...	soy ...	*Soy ...*
Buddhist	boo-*dihs*-tuh	*budista*
Catholic	ka-*toh*-leek-oh/uh	*católico/a*
Christian	krihs-tee-*oon*-oh/uh	*cristiano/a*
Hindu	hihn-*doo*	*hindú*
Jewish	hoo-dee-oh/uh	*judío/a*
Muslim	moo-sul-*man*/	*musulmán/*
	moo-sul-*man*-uh	*musulmana*

I'm not religious.	noh soy reh-lee-hee-*oh*-soh/suh	*No soy religioso/a.*
I'm agnostic.	soy ag-*nohs*-tih-koh/uh	*Soy agnóstico/a.*
I'm an atheist.	soy at-*ay*-oh/uh	*Soy ateo/a.*

SPANISH

Family

Are you married?
es-*ta* kuh-*suh*-doh/uh? ¿*Está casado/a?*

Do you have a boyfriend/girlfriend?
tee-*en*-ay noh-vee-oh/uh? ¿*Tiene novio/a?*

How many children do you have?
kwan-tohs ee-kohs tee-*en*-ay? ¿*Cuántos hijos tiene?*

How many brothers/
sisters do you have?
kwan-tohs/as er-*man*-os/as ¿*Cuántos/as hermanos/as*
tee-*en*-ay? *tiene?*

I'm ...	es-*toy* ...	Estoy ...
divorced	dee-vor-see-*uh*-doh/uh	*divorciado/a*
married	kuh-*suh*-doh/uh	*casado/a*
separated	sep-uh-*ruh*-doh/uh	*separado/a*

I'm ...	soy ...	Soy ...
single	sohl-*teh*-roh/uh	*soltero/a*
widowed	vee-*oo*-doh/uh	*viudo/a*

I have a partner.
ten-goh puh-*rek*-uh *Tengo pareja.*

I don't have any children.
noh *ten*-goh ee-kohs *No tengo hijos.*

I have (one) son/daughter.
ten-goh (oon/*oo*-nuh) *Tengo (un/una) hijo/a.*
ee-koh/uh

baby	el bay-*bay*	*el bebé*
boy	el *chee*-coh	*el chico*
brother	el er-*man*-oh	*el hermano*
children	lohs ee-kohs	*los hijos*
dad	el puh-*puh*	*el papá*
daughter	la ee-kuh	*la hija*
family	la fuh-*mee*-lee-uh	*la familia*
father	el *pad*-ray	*el padre*

girl	la *chee*-cuh	la chica
grandfather	el ab-*way*-loh	el abuelo
grandmother	la ab-*way*-luh	la abuela
husband	el es-*poh*-soh/muh-*ree*-doh	el esposo/marido
mother	la *mad*-ray/muh-*muh*	la madre/mamá
mum	la *muh*-muh	la mamá
sister	la er-*ma*-nuh	la hermana
son	el ee-khoh	el hijo
wife	la es-*poh*-suh/moo-*khehr*	la esposa/mujer

SPANISH

Feelings

I'm ...	*ten*-goh ...	Tengo ...
Are you ...?	tee-en-ay ...?	¿Tiene ...?
afraid	mee-e-doh	miedo
cold	*free*-oh	frío
hot	kuh-*lohr*	calor
hungry	am-bray	hambre
in a hurry	*pree*-suh	prisa
keen to ...	*guh*-nas day ...	ganas de ...
right	ra-*thohn*	razón
sleepy	*swen*-yoh	sueño
thirsty	sed	sed

I'm ...	es-*toy* ...	Estoy ...
Are you ...?	es-*ta* ...?	¿Está ...?
angry	en-oh-*khuh*-doh/uh	enojado/a
happy	fay-*lees*	feliz
sad	*trihs*-tay	triste
tired	kan-*suh*-doh/uh	cansado/a
well	bee-*en*	bien
worried	pray-ohk-yoo-*puh*-doh/uh	preocupado/a

I'm sorry. (condolence)
 loh see-*en*-toh *moo*-choh — *Lo siento mucho.*

I'm grateful.
 lay ag-ruh-*dez*-koh *moo*-choh — *Le agradezco mucho.*

SPANISH

BREAKING THE LANGUAGE BARRIER

Do you speak English?
ab-la ihn-*glays*?   *¿Habla inglés?*

Does anyone speak English?
ai al-gee-*en* kay *ab*-lay ihn-*glays*   *¿Hay alguien que hable inglés?*

I'm learning.
es-*toy* ap-ren-dee-*en*-doh   *Estoy aprendiendo.*

I (don't) understand.
(noh) en-tee-*en*-doh   *(No) Entiendo.*

Do you understand?
may en-tee-*en*-day?   *¿Me entiende?*

Could you speak more slowly please?
mas des-*puh*-see-oh   *Más despacio,*
por fuh-*vor*   *por favor.*

Could you repeat that?
pwe-day reh-pe-*tihr*?   *¿Puede repetir?*

Could you write that down please?
pwe-day es-kree-*beer*-loh   *¿Puede escribirlo,*
por fuh-*vor*?   *por favor?*

How do you say ...?
koh-moh say dee-*say* ...?   *¿Cómo se dice ...?*

What's this called in Spanish?
koh-moh say dee-*say es*-to   *¿Cómo se dice esto en*
en kas-tel-*yuh*-noh?   *castellano?*

GETTING AROUND
Directions

How do I get to ...?
koh-moh say vuh a ...?   *Cómo se va a ...?*

Can you show me (on the map)?
loh *pwe*-day mohs-*truhr*   *¿Lo puede mostrar*
(en el *muh*-puh)?   *(en el mapa)?*

Turn ...	*doh*-blay a la ...	*Doble a la ...*
left	ihz-kee-*ehr*-duh	*izquierda*
right	de-*reh*-chuh	*derecha*

SIGNS

ABIERTO	OPEN
ASEOS	TOILETS
CALIENTE	HOT
CERRADO	CLOSED
ENTRADA (GRATIS)	(FREE) ADMISSION
FRÍO	COLD
INFORMACIÓN	INFORMATION
NO TOCAR	DO NOT TOUCH
NO (USAR EL) FLASH	DO NOT USE FLASH
PROHIBIDO ...	... PROHIBITED
EL PASO	ENTRY
FUMAR	SMOKING
TOMAR FOTOS	PHOTOGRAPHY
RESERVADO	RESERVED
SALIDA (DE EMERGENCIA)	(EMERGENCY) EXIT
SERVICIOS	TOILETS

SPANISH

Cross the road at the ...	*kroo*-say la *cal*-yay ...	*Cruce la calle ...*
next corner	en la *prohx*-ee-ma es-*kee*-nuh	*en la próxima esquina*
roundabout	en la roht-*ohn*-duh	*en la rotonda*
traffic lights	en el se-*ma*-for-oh	*en el semáforo*

Go straight ahead.
see-guh; *vai*-yuh *toh*-doh
de-*reh*-choh/ *rek*-toh

Siga; Vaya todo derecho/recto.

after	des-*pwes* day	*después de*
behind	deh-*tras* day	*detrás de*
between	en-*tray*	*entre*
far	*leh*-khohs	*lejos*
in front of	en-*fren*-tay day	*enfrente de*

SPANISH

near	*sihr*-kuh	*cerca*
next to	al *luh*-doh day	*al lado de*
opposite	*fren*-tay a	*frente a*
avenue	uh-ve-*nee*-duh	*avenida*
square	*pla*-thuh	*plaza*
street	*cal*-yay/puh-*say*-oh	*calle/paseo*
north	*nor*-tay	*norte*
south	soor	*sur*
east	*ehs*-teh	*este*
west	oh-*ehs*-teh	*oeste*

Buying Tickets

Excuse me, where's the ticket office?
    per-*dohn, dohn*-day es-*tuh*   *¿Perdón, dónde está*
    la tuh-*keel*-yuh?   *la taquilla?*
Do you have a timetable?
    tee-*en*-ay oon or-*ruh*-ree-oh?   *¿Tiene un horario?*
I want to go to ...
    kee-*ehr*-oh eer a ...   *Quiero ir a ...*
How much is the fare to ...
    kwan-toh *vuh*-lay el   *¿Cuánto vale el*
    bihl-*yet*-ay a ...?   *billete a ...?*

... sale window	*ben*-tuh ...	*venta ...*
immediate	ihn-meh-dee-*a*-tuh	*inmediata*
advance	uhn-tih-sih-*pa*-duh	*anticipada*

I'd like ...	kee-see-*eh*-ruh ...	*Quisiera ...*
a one-way ticket	oon bihl-*yet*-ay	*un billete*
	sen-*seel*-yoh	*sencillo*
a return ticket	oon bihl-*yet*-ay	*un billete*
	day *ee*-duh ee	*de ida y*
	vwel-tuh	*vuelta*
two tickets	dohs bihl-*yet*-ays	*dos billetes*

A(n) ... fare	oo-nuh tuh-ree-fuh ...	una tarifa ...
adult	day a-dul-toh	de adulto
child's	ihn-fan-teel	infantil
senior	day pen-see-ohn-ihs-tuh	de pensionista
student	day es-too-dee-an-tay	de estudiante
1st class	pree-mehr-uh cla-say	primera clase
2nd class	se-goon-duh clas-say	segunda clase

SPANISH

Bus

Where's the bus stop?
dohn-day es-tuh la puh-ruh-duh day ow-toh-boo-ses? — ¿Dónde está la parada de autobúses?

Which bus goes to ...?
kay ow-toh-bus va a ...? — ¿Qué autobús va a ...?

Do you stop at ...?
tee-en-ay puh-ruh-duh en ...? — ¿Tiene parada en ...?

Could you let me know when we get to ...?
pwe-day uh-vee-suhr-may kwan-doh yeh-ge-mohs a ...? — ¿Puede avisarme cuando lleguemos a ...?

I want to get off!
kee-ehr-oh buh-khar-may! — ¡Quiero bajarme!

What time's the ... bus/coach?	a kay or-uh es el ... ow-toh-bus/ ow-toh-car?	¿A qué hora es el ...autobús/ autocar?
first	pree-mehr	primer
last	ul-tee-moh	último
next	prohx-ee-moh	próximo

Does this bus go to the ...?	es-tay ow-toh-bus va a ...?	¿Este autobús va a ...?
beach	la pla-yuh	la playa
city centre	el sen-troh de la see-oo-dad	el centro de la ciudad
station	la es-tuh-see-ohn	la estación

SPANISH

Metro

Which line takes me to ...?
kay *lih*-nee-uh *koh*-khoh
puh-ruh ...?
¿Qué línea cojo para ...?

What's the next station?
kwal es la *prohx*-ee-ma
es-tuh-see-*ohn*?
¿Cuál es la próxima estación?

Where do I change for ...?
dohn-day uh-*goh* el
trans-*bor*-doh *puh*-ruh ...?
*¿Dónde hago el
transbordo para ...?*

change (coins)	*kam*-bee-oh	*cambio*
destination	des-*tee*-noh	*destino*
line	*lih*-nee-uh	*línea*
ticket machine	*ven*-tuh ow-toh-*ma*-tee-kuh day bihl-*ye*-tays	*venta automática de billetes*

Train

RENFE is the name of the Spanish national railway. The fastest services are *Talgo, Expreso* and *Rápido.*

Where's the nearest train station?
don-day es-*ta* la
es-tah-see-*on* dee tren
mas sihr-*kah*-nah?
*¿Dónde está la
estación de tren
más cercana?*

Is this the right platform for ...?
el tren *pah*-rah ... *sa*-lay
day *es*-tay an-*den*?
*¿El tren para ... sale
de este andén?*

Is that seat taken?
es-*tah* ok-you-*pah*-dah
es-tay a-see-*en*-toh?
*¿Está ocupado
este asiento?*

THEY MAY SAY ...

el tren *sah*-lay del an-*den noo*-meh-roh ...
The train leaves from platform ...

los pah-sa-*khe*-ros *deh*-ben
kam-bee-*ahr* de tren/an-*den*
Passengers must change trains/platforms.

Taxi

Are you free?	es-*tuh lee*-bray?	*Está libre?*
Please take me to the/this ...	por fuh-*vor*, yeh-vuh-may ...	*Por favor, lléveme ...*
address	a es-tuh dee-rek-see-*ohn*	*a este dirrección*
airport	al ay-roh-*pwer*-toh	*al aeropuerto*
city centre	al *sen*-troh day la see-oo-*dad*	*al centro de las ciudad*
railway station	a la es-tuh-see-*ohn* day tren	*a la estación de tren*

How much is it to go to ...?
  kwan-toh *kwes*-tuh eer a ...?   *¿Cuánto cuesta ir a ...?*

Does that include luggage?
  el *preh*-see-oh ihn-*kloo*-yay
  el eh-kee-*pa*-khay?   *¿El precio incluye el equipaje?*

Can you take (five) people?
  pwe-day yeh-*vuhr* a
  (*sihn*-koh) per-*soh*-nas?   *¿Puede llevar a (cinco) personas?*

Please hurry.
  por *fuh*-vor, *day*-say *pree*-suh   *Por favor, dese prisa.*

The next corner, please.
  la *prohx*-ee-muh
  es-*kee*-nuh, por *fuh*-vor   *La próxima esquina, por favor.*

SPANISH

Keep going!
   see-guh!   ¡*Siga!*

The next street to the left/right.
   la *prohx*-ee-ma *cal*-yay a la   *La próxima calle a la*
   ihz-kee-*ehr*-duh/de-*reh*-cha   *izquierda/derecha.*

Here's fine, thanks.
   uh-*kee* es-*tuh* bee-*en* gra-*sih*-as   *Aquí está bien, gracias.*

Stop here!
   puh-ray uh-*kee*!   ¡*Para aquí!*

Please wait here.
   por fuh-*vor*, es-*peh*-ray uh-*kee*   *Por favor, espere aquí.*

Car

How much is it daily/weekly?
   kwan-toh *kwes*-tuh por   ¿*Cuánto cuesta por*
   dee-uh/seh-*ma*-nuh?   *día/semana?*

Does that include insurance/mileage?
   ihn-*kloo*-yay el seh-*goo*-roh/   ¿*Incluye el seguro/*
   kih-loh-me-*tra*-khay?   *kilometraje?*

Where's the next petrol station?
   ai al-*goo*-nuh ga-soh-   ¿*Hay alguna gasolinera*
   lee-*neh*-ruh por uh-*kee*?   *por aquí?*

Please fill the tank.
   por *fuh*-vor, *yeh*-neh-may   *Por favor, lléneme*
   el deh-*poh*-sih-toh   *el depósito.*

I need a mechanic.
   ne-seh-*see*-toh oon   *Necesito un*
   meh-*kan*-ee-koh   *mecánico.*

I've lost my car keys.
eh per-*dee*-doh las *yuh*-vays *He perdido las llaves*
day mee *koh*-chay *de mi coche.*

I've run out of petrol.
may eh kay-*duh*-doh sihn *Me he quedado sin*
ga-soh-*lee*-nuh *gasolina.*

I have a flat tyre.
ten-goh uhn pihn-*chuh*-thoh *Tengo un pinchazo.*

brakes	*fray*-nohs	*frenos*
drivers licence	*kar*-nay	*carnet*
engine	moh-*tor*	*motor*
indicator	ihn-ter-mih-*ten*-tay	*intermitente*
main road	kuhr-ret-*teh*-ruh	*carretera*
(road) map	*muh*-puh (day	*mapa (de*
	kuhr-ret-*teh*-ras)	*carreteras)*
tollway	ow-toh-*pees*-tuh	*autopista*
oil	a-*say*-tay	*aceite*
petrol (gasoline)	gas-oh-*lee*-nuh	*gasolina*
leaded/unleaded	kohn/sihn *ploh*-moh	*con/sin plomo*
radiator	ruh-dee-uh-*dor*	*radiador*
speed limit	*lih*-mee-tay day	*límite de velocidad*
	veh-*lohs*-see-dad	
toll free motorway	ow-toh-*vee*-uh	*autovía*
tyres	nay-oo-*ma*-tee-kohs	*neumáticos*
windscreen	puh-ruh-*bree*-sas	*parabrisas*

SIGNS

CEDA EL PASO	GIVE WAY
DESVÍO	DETOUR
DIRECCIÓN PROHIBIDA	NO ENTRY
NO ADELANTAR	DO NOT OVERTAKE
PARE	STOP
PROHIBIDO ESTACIONARY	NO PARKING

SPANISH

SPANISH

ACCOMMODATION
At the Hotel

I have a reservation.

eh *eh*-choh *oo*-nuh re-*sehr*-vuh   *He hecho una reserva.*

I'd like to share a dorm.

kee-see-*eh*-ruh kohm-par-*teer*   *Quisiera compartir un*
oon dor-mee-*tor*-ee-oh   *dormitorio.*

I'd like a ... room.	kee-see-*eh*-ruh *oo*-nuh uh-bee-tuh-see-*ohn* ...	*Quisiera una habitación* ...
single	ihn-dee-vihd-yoo-*al*	*individual*
double	*doh*-blay	*doble*

I want a room with a ...	kee-*eh*-roh *oo*-nuh uh-bee-tuh-see-*ohn* kohn ...	*Quiero una habitación con* ...
bathroom	*ban*-yoh	*baño*
double bed	*kuh*-muh mat-ree-moh-nee-*al*	*cama de matrimonio*
twin beds	dohs *kuh*-mas	*dos camas*

Can I see it?	*pwe*-doh *ver*-luh?	*¿Puedo verla?*
It's fine, I'll take it.	*vuh*-lay, la al-*kee*-loh	*Vale, la alquilo.*

I'd like to pay the bill.

kee-*ehr*-oh puh-*gar* la   *Quiero pagar la*
kwen-tuh   *cuenta.*

Requests & Complaints

Do you have a safe?

tee-*en*-ay *oo*-nuh   *¿Tiene una*
kuh-khuh *fwer*-tay?   *caja fuerte?*

I've locked myself out of my room.

ser-*ray* la *pwer*-tuh ee say   *Cerré la puerta y se*
may ohl-vee-*duhr*-ohn las   *me olvidaron las*
yuh-vays *den*-troh   *llaves dentro.*

Can I have an extra blanket?
pwe-day *dar*-may *oh*-truh   ¿Puede darme otra
man-tuh?   manta?

Can I leave my backpack at
reception until tonight?
pwe-doh deh-*khar* mee   ¿Puedo dejar mi
moh-*chee*-luh en la   mochila en la
reh-sep-see-*ohn* as-tuh   recepción hasta
es-tuh *noh*-chay?   esta noche?

Please call a taxi for me.
pwe-day yuh-*muhr* a oon   ¿Puede llamar a un taxi,
tak-see, por fuh-*vor*?   por favor?

(See also Camping, page 461.)

AROUND TOWN
At the Post Office

I'd like to send   kee-see-*ehr*-uh   Quisiera enviar ...
a ...   en-vee-*uhr* ...
    letter   *oo*-nuh *kar*-tuh   una carta
    postcard   *oo*-nuh pohs-*tal*   una postal
    parcel   oon puh-*ke*-tay   un paquete
    telegram   oon teh-lay-*gra*-muh   un telegrama

I'd like some stamps.
kee-see-*ehr*-uh *oo*-nohs   Quisiera unos sellos.
sel-yohs

How much is the postage?
kwan-toh *vuh*-lay el   ¿Cuánto vale el franqueo?
fran-*kay*-oh?

Where's the poste restante section?
dohn-day es-*tuh* la *lihs*-tuh   ¿Dónde está la lista de correos?
day koh-*ray*-ohs?

Is there any mail for me?
ai al-*goo*-nuh *kar*-tuh   ¿Hay alguna carta para mí?
puh-ruh mee?

SPANISH

air mail	por *vee*-uh *ay*-ree-uh	*por vía aérea*
envelope	un *soh*-bray	*un sobre*
mail box	el boo-*sohn*	*el buzón*
parcel	oon puh-*ke*-tay	*un paquete*
postcode	el *koh*-dee-goh pohs-*tal*	*el código postal*
surface mail	por *vee*-uh tehr-*rest*-ray	*por vía terrestre*
... mail	el koh-*ray*-oh ...	*el correo ...*
express	oohr-*hen*-tay	*urgente*
registered	ser-tee-fih-*kuh*-doh	*certificado*

Telephone

Local and international calls can be made from any public telephone, or from a *locutorio*, where you pay afterwards. All calls are charged by the minute.

I'd like to make a call.
    kee-*eh*-roh uh-*ser oo*-nuh   *Quiero hacer una*
    yuh-*muh*-duh   *llamada.*
I want to ring (Australia).
    kee-*eh*-roh yuh-*muhr* a   *Quiero llamar a*
    (ows-*tra*-lee-uh)   *(Australia).*
The number is ...
    el *noo*-mer-oh es ...   *El número es ...*
What's the area code for ...?
    kwal es el preh-*fee*-khoh day ...?   *¿Cuál es el prefijo de ...?*
I want to make a reverse-charge
(collect) phone call.
    kee-*eh*-roh uh-*ser oo*-nuh   *Quiero hacer una*
    yuh-*muh*-duh a *kohb*-roh   *llamada a cobro*
    ray-ver-*tee*-doh   *revertido.*
It's engaged.
    es-*tuh* koh-moo-nee-*kan*-doh   *Está comunicando.*
I've been cut off.
    may an kor-*tuh*-doh   *Me han cortado.*

operator	la oh-per-uh-*door*;	*el operador;*
	el oh-per-uh-*doo*-ruh	*la operadora*
phone book	la *gee*-uh te-le-*foh*-nee-kuh	*la guía telefónica*
phone box	la kuh-*bee*-nuh	*la cabina telefónica*
	te-le-*foh*-nee-kuh	
phonecard	la tar-*he*-tuh day	*la tarjeta de*
	te-*le*-foh-noh	*teléfono*
telephone	el te-*le*-foh-noh	*el teléfono*
telephone	la sen-truh-*lee*-tuh	*la centralita*
office	te-le-*foh*-nee-kuh	*telefónica*

Hello! (making a call)	*oh*-luh!	*¡Hola!*
Hello! (answering a call)	*dee*-guh?	*¿Diga?*
It's	day ...	*De ...*
Can I speak to (Angel)?	es-*tuh* (an-*hel*)?	*¿Está (Angel)?*
Who's calling?	day *par*-tay de	*¿De parte de quién?*
	kee-*en*?	

Internet

Is there a local Internet cafe?
ai al-*goon* sehr-*vih*-see-oh
loh-*kuhl* day ihn-*tehr*-net?
¿Hay algún servicio local de Internet?

How can I get internet access?
koh-moh *pwe*-doh ak-se-*dehr* uh ihn-*tehr*-net?
¿Cómo puedo acceder a Internet?

I want to check my email.
ten-goh kay re-vih-*sar* mee koh-*ray*-oh e-lek-*troh*-nee-koh
Tengo que revisar mi correo electrónico.

I want to send an email.
ten-goh kay en-vee-*ar* oon ee-*mayl*
Tengo que enviar un email.

SPANISH

At the Bank

Can I use my credit card to
withdraw money?

pwe-doh oo-sar mee
tar-het-uh day kreh-dee-toh
puh-ruh suh-kar dih-ne-roh?

¿Puedo usar mi tarjeta de
crédito para sacar dinero?

Can I exchange money here?

say kam-bee-uh dih-ne-roh
uh-kee?

¿Se cambia dinero aquí?

I want to exchange some ...

kee-ehr-oh kam-bee-uhr ...

Quiero cambiar ...

What's the exchange rate?

kwal es el tee-poh day
kam-bee-oh?

¿Cuál es el tipo de cambio?

What's your commission?

kwal es soo
koh-mih-see-ohn?

¿Cuál es su comisión?

Please write it down.

pwe-day es-kree-beer-loh,
por fuh-vor?

¿Puede escribirlo, por favor?

The automatic teller machine
has swallowed my credit card.

el kuh-khehr-oh ow-toh-
mat-ee-koh say uh
truh-guh-doh mee
tar-het-uh day creh-dee-toh

El cajero automático se ha
tragado mi tarjeta de crédito.

INTERESTS & ENTERTAINMENT
Sightseeing

Do you have a ...?	tee-e-nay ...?	¿Tiene ...?
guidebook	oo-nuh gee-uh	una guía
local map	oon muh-puh day	un mapa de
	la see-oo-dad	la ciudad?

What are the main attractions?

kwa-les sohn las uh-trak-
see-ow-nes prihn-see-pa-les?

¿Cuáles son las atracciones
principales?

What's that?
    kay es *e*-soh?   *¿Qué es eso?*
Can I take photographs?
    pwe-doh toh-*muhr foh*-tohs?   *¿Puedo tomar fotos?*
What time does it open/close?
    a kay *or*-ruh *ab*-ren/   *¿A qué hora abren/cierran?*
    see-*ehr*-ran?
Is there an admission charge?
    ai kay puh-*gar*?   *¿Hay que pagar?*

Going Out

Socialising is a national pastime in Spain, especially at night when
Spaniards of all ages hit the streets in search of friends, food, music
and a good time. On weekends, the evening doesn't get started
until after 11 pm and can go on all night.

What's there to do in the evenings?
    kay say *pwe*-day uh-*ser*   *¿Qué se puede hacer*
    por las *noh*-ches?   *por las noches?*
What's on tonight?
    kay ai *es*-tuh *noh*-chay?   *¿Qué hay esta noche?*
Where can I find out what's on?
    dohn-day *pwe*-doh uh-*veh*-   *¿Dónde puedo averiguar*
    ree-*gwar* kay ai *es*-tuh   *qué hay esta noche?*
    noh-chay?

I feel like going to a/the ...	*ten*-goh *guh*-nas day eer ...	*Tengo ganas de ir ...*
cinema	al *sih*-nay	*al cine*
concert	a oon kohn-see-*ehr*-toh	*a un concierto*
theatre	al tay-*at*-roh	*al teatro*

SPANISH

Would you like to go out somewhere?	kee-*ehr*-es sal-*eer* kohn-mee-goh?	*¿Quieres salir conmigo?*
Would you like to go for a ...?	kee-*ehr*-es kay va-ya-*mohs* a ...?	*¿Quieres que vayamos a ...?*
drink	toh-*muhr* al-goh	*tomar algo*
meal	se-*nuhr*	*cenar*

Yes, I'd love to.	may en-kan-tuh-*ree*-uh	*Me encantaría.*
Where can we dance some (salsa)?	*dohn*-day say *pwe*-day bai-*luhr* (*sal*-suh)?	*¿Dónde se puede bailar (salsa)?*
This place is great!	es-tay loo-*gar* may en-*kan*-tuh!	*¡Este lugar me encanta!*
See you later/tomorrow.	*as*-tuh loo-*ay*-goh/ man-*yuh*-nuh	*Hasta luego/mañana.*

Sports & Interests

What do you do in your spare time?	kay lay *gus*-tuh uh-*ser* en soo tee-*em*-poh *lee*-bray?	*¿Qué le gusta hacer en su tiempo libre?*
What sport do you play?	kay day-*por*-tay prak-*tee*-kas?	*¿Qué deporte practicas?*

SPANISH

I like/play/practise ...	prak-*tee*-koh ...	*Practico ...*
art	el *ar*-tay	*el arte*
basketball	el buh-lohn-*ses*-toh	*el baloncesto*
chess	el a-khed-*reth*	*el ajedrez*
dancing	bai-*lar*	*bailar*
films	el *sih*-nay	*el cine*
food	la koh-*mee*-duh	*la comida*
football	el *foot*-bohl	*el fútbol*
hiking	el ex-koor-see-oh-*nees*-moh	*el excursionismo*
martial arts	las *ar*-tays mar-see-*al*-es	*las artes marciales*
music	la *moo*-see-kuh	*la música*
nightclubs	lohs *kloo*-bes nohk-*toor*-nohs	*los clubes nocturnos*
reading	lay-*eer*	*leer*
shopping	eer day *kohm*-pras	*ir de compras*
skiing	es-kee-*ar*	*esquiar*
swimming	na-*dar*	*nadar*
travelling	vee-uh-*khar*	*viajar*
walking	puh-say-*ar*-say	*pasearse*

Festivals

El Año Nuevo y Las uvas

a much-loved Spanish tradition is eating twelve grapes at midnight on New Year's Eve. They must be eaten in rapid succession, one for each consecutive strike of the clock. It's not as easy as it sounds!

Happy New Year!	fay-leece an-yoh noo-eh-voh!	*¡Feliz año nuevo!*

Cabalgata de reyes

on the evening of 5 January, in villages, towns and cities throughout Spain, you can see a Christmas procession featuring the Three Wise Men and other Christmas characters

SPANISH

Cotillón

> on New Year's Eve you can go from party to party, collecting a *cotillón* at each one, which is a kind of party bag containing sweets, party whistles and other goodies

La Navidad

> Christmas in Spain begins on 24 December, but gifts aren't usually exchanged until Epiphany on 6 January

Happy Christmas!   fay-leece nuh-vee-dad!   ¡Feliz navidad!

Poner el belén

> (lit: to place the nativity scene) this tradition involves placing figures of the Three Kings at a distance from a set of nativity figures on 24 December and moving them a little closer each day. This ritual culminates on 6 January, *el día de los reyos magos*, 'the day of the Three Wise Men'.

IN THE COUNTRY
Weather

What's the weather like?

> kay tee-*em*-poh *a*-say   *¿Qué tiempo hace?*

The weather's fine/bad today.

> *a*-say bwen/mal   *Hace buen/mal*
> tee-*em*-poh oy   *tiempo hoy.*

Its ...

cloudy	es-*tuh* noo-*bluh*-doh	*Está nublado.*
cold	*a*-say *free*-oh	*Hace frío.*
foggy	ai nee-*eb*-luh	*Hay niebla.*
frosty	es-*tuh* eh-*lan*-doh	*Está helando.*
hot	a-*say* kuh-*lohr*	*Hace calor.*
raining	yoo-*e*-vay	*Llueve.*
snowing	nee-*e*-vuh	*Nieva.*
sunny	*a*-say sohl	*Hace sol.*
windy	*a*-say vee-*en*-toh	*Hace viento.*

SPANISH

Camping

Where's the nearest campsite?
dohn-day es-*tuh* el *kam*-ping
mas sihr-*kuh*-noh?
¿Dónde está el camping
más cercano?

Do you have any sites available?
tee-*e*-nay par-*se*-las *lee*-brays?
¿Tiene parcelas libres?

Can I camp here?
say *pwe*-day uh-kam-*par* uh-*kee*?
¿Se puede acampar aquí?

How much is it per ...?	*kwan*-toh *vuh*-lay por ...?	¿Cuánto vale por ...?
person	per-*soh*-nuh	persona
tent	tee-*en*-duh	tienda
vehicle	vay-*ihk*-yu-loh	vehículo
firewood	la *len*-yuh	la leña
gas cartridge	el kar-*too*-choh day gas	el cartucho de gas
hammer	el mar-*teel*-yoh	el martillo
mat	la es-teh-*reel*-yuh	la esterilla
mattress	el kohl-*chohn*	el colchón
rope	la *kwer*-duh	la cuerda
sleeping bag	el *suh*-koh day dor-*meer*	el saco de dormir
stove	la es-*too*-fa	la estufa
tent	la tee-*en*-duh (day kam-*pan*-yuh)	la tienda (de campaña)
tent pegs	las pee-*ke*-tas	las piquetas
torch (flashlight)	la lihn-*ter*-nuh	la linterna
water bottle	la kan-tihm-plor-uh	la cantimplora

SPANISH

FOOD

Breakfast in Spain usually consists of a light snack. Lunch is the principal meal, often including soup, bread, a main course, fruit or dessert and coffee, taken between 2 and 4 pm. A light evening meal is eaten at about 10 pm.

Vegetarian Meals

Finding vegetarian food is a real headache in Spain once you've tired of tortillas. Vegetables are normally listed (and served) separately in Spanish menus, so you can always order them as separate courses. Look under *Legumbres* or *Entremeses* on the menu. Visitors familiar with the Mexican tortilla (a kind of thin maize pancake) should be aware that the Spanish tortilla is quite different. It is, in fact, an omelette.

I'm a vegetarian(m/f).
  soy ve-ge-ta-ree-*an*-oh/uh   *Soy vegetariano/a.*
Do you have any vegetarian dishes?
  tee-e-nen al-*goon* pla-toh
  ve-get-a-ree-*a*-noh?   *¿Tienen algún plato*
                                vegetariano?
Does this dish have meat?
  yeh-vuh *kar*-nay *es*-tay *pla*-toh?   *¿Lleva carne este plato?*
Can I get this without the meat?
  may *pwe*-day preh-pay-*ruhr*
  es-tay *pla*-toh sihn *kar*-nay?   *¿Me puede preparar*
                                este plato sin carne?
Does it contain eggs/dairy products?
  yeh-vuh *hway*-vohs/
  proh-*duk*-tohs lak-*tay*-ohs?   *¿Lleva huevos/*
                                productos lácteos?

Staple Foods & Condiments

beans	hoo-*dee*-as	*judías*
(white/green)	(*blan*-kas/ *ver*-days)	*(blancas/verdes)*
cheese	*ke*-soh	*queso*
fish	pes-*kuh*-doh	*pescado*
fruit	*froo*-tuh	*fruta*
cured ham	ha-*mohn* se-*ruh*-noh	*jamón serrano*

SPANISH

garlic	uh-khoh	ajo
meat	kar-nay	carne
mustard	mohs-ta-thuh	mostaza
omelette	tor-tihl-yuh	tortilla
pastry	puhs-tel	pastel
pepper	pih-mee-en-tuh	pimienta
pork sausage	sal-chee-chuh	salchicha
potato	pa-ta-tuh	patata
rice	uh-rroth	arroz
salt	sal	sal
vegetables	or-tuh-lee-thas	hortalizas
vinegar	vih-nag-reh	vinagre

Non-Alcoholic Drinks

almond drink	or-chuh-ta	horchata
fruit juice	soo-moh	zumo
soft drink	re-fres-koh	refresco
(mineral) water	ag-wuh (mih-ne-ral)	agua (mineral)
tap water	ag-wuh del gree-foh	agua del grifo

coffee with ...	ka-fay ...	café ...
liqueur	ka-rakh-ihl-yoh	carajillo
milk	kohn le-chay	con leche
a little milk	kor-tuh-doh	cortado

... coffee	ka-fay ...	café ...
black	soh-loh	solo
decaffeinated	des-kaf-ay-ih-nuh-doh	descafeinado
iced	e-luh-doh	helado

| long black | doh-blay | doble |
| tea | teh | té |

SPANISH

Alcoholic Drinks

Bar-hopping is a favourite pastime in Spain. Most residential streets have at least one local bar, and town centres have a whole range of bars. *Mesones* and *tabernas* are old-style inns with plenty of atmosphere. *Cervecerías*, *champañerías* and *sidrerías* specialise in beer, champagnes and cider respectively. Drinking and eating always go together in Spain, so join the locals in selecting a different morsel from the tapas bar each time you order.

In most bars, don't expect to pay until you're ready to leave.

Do you want to go for a drink?
    kee-*ehr*-es eer a toh-*muhr* al-goh?   *¿Quieres ir a tomar algo?*

anise	oon uh-*nees*	*un anís*
beer	*oo*-nuh ser-*veh*-suh	*una cerveza*
champagne	oon cham-*pan*	*un champán*
cider	*oo*-nuh *see*-druh	*una sidra*
cocktail	oon kohm-bih-*nuh*-doh	*un combinado*
brandy	oon *kohn*-yak	*un coñac*
rum	oon rohn	*un ron*
sangría	*oo*-nuh san-*gree*-uh	*una sangría*
sherry	oon he-*reth*	*un jerez*
whisky	oon *gwihs*-kee	*un güisqui*
glass of red/	oon *vee*-noh	*un vino tinto/*
white wine	*tihn*-toh/ *blan*-koh	*blanco*

CHEERS, BIG EARS!

Cheers!;
To your (inf/pol) health!
    sa-*lood*!   ¡*Salud*!
    uh too/soo sa-*lood*!   ¡*A tu/su salud*!
Best of luck!
    toh-duh la *swer*-tay!   ¡*Toda la suerte*!
Here's to you (sg/pl)!
    por tee/voh-*soht*-rohs!   ¡*Por ti/vosotros*!
Here's to us!
    por noh-*soht*-rohs!   ¡*Por nosotros*!

MENU DECODER

SPANISH

Breakfast Menu

Breakfast in Spain usually consists of a large bowl of coffee with bread, biscuits or cakes. Those used to more healthy or substantial fare can, however, find the following snacks in bars and cafes throughout the day:

bocadillo	sandwich
bollos	bread roll
churros con chocolate	fried pastry strips for dunking in hot chocolate
croissants	croissants, often with sweet or savoury fillings
magdalena	fairy cake, often dunked in coffee
pastas	small cakes, available in a variety of flavours

Tapas

Almost every bar in Spain offers a selection of *tapas*, or snacks. *Tapas* are usually cheap, and you may even be offered bite-sized portions free with your drink. The best way to discover these delicious snacks is to experiment by pointing at any interesting dish and asking for:

a little of this   oon *pihn*-cho day *es*-toh   un pincho de esto

aceitunas rellenas	stuffed olives
berberechos	cockles
boquerones en vinagre	anchovies in vinaigrette
boquerones fritos	fried anchovies
calamares a la romana	squid rings fried in butter
callos	tripe
champiñones al ajillo	garlic mushrooms
ensaladilla rusa	vegetable salad with mayonnaise
gambas a la plancha	grilled prawns
mejillones al vapor	steamed mussels
patatas alioli	potatoes in garlic sauce
patatas bravas	potatoes in tomato sauce
pescaíto frito	tiny fried fish
pulpo a la gallega	octopus in sauce
tortilla de patata	potato omelette

SPANISH

Starters

caldo gallego	white bean and potato soup with turnip, greens and chorizo sausage
crema de cangrejos de segovia	freshwater crab-and-fish soup
ensalada	salad
fideos	thin pasta noodles with sauce
garbanzos con carne	chickpea, pork, chorizo and vegetable soup
gazpacho	cold soup made with garlic, tomato and other vegetables
olla podrida	vegetable and meat stew served with fried slices of bread
sopa de ajo	garlic soup
sopa al cuarto de hora	(lit: fifteen-minute soup) clam, shrimp, ham and rice soup served with chopped hard-boiled egg
tortilla de patatas	egg-and-potato omelette

Main Meals

albóndigas	meatballs in an onion-and-chicken sauce
almejas a la marinera	clams in white wine with garlic, onion and parsley
bacalao al ajo arriero	salt cod cooked in olive oil with tomato, onion and garlic
besugo al horno	red snapper baked with sliced potato in olive oil, onion and tomato
calamares en su tinta	squid fried with onion, garlic and parsley, with a sauce made from the squid's ink
cocido	stew made with chickpeas, pork and chorizo
cochifrito	lamb fricassee in lemon and garlic sauce
cordonices a la cazadora	quail stew with onion, leek, tomato, turnip and carrot
croquetas	fried croquettes, often filled with ham or chicken
changurro	crab meat with sherry and brandy
charcutería	cured pork meats
chorizo al horno	spicy baked sausages
churrasco	slabs of grilled meat or ribs in a tangy sauce (Galicia)

SPANISH

empanada	meat pie (Galicia)
filete empanado	pork, cheese and ham wrapped in breadcrumbs and fried
filete de ternera	veal steak
habas a la catalana	casserole of broad beans with chorizo sausage, parsley and mint
liebre a la cazadora	hare casserole with red wine and garlic
morcilla	blood sausage (black pudding)
paella	saffron rice with seafoood, chicken pieces, *chorizos* and vegetables. Valencian *paella* can include lobster, shrimps, prawns, clams and/or mussels. Castillian paella is likely to have only clams, but veal, beef or pork cubes may be added as well as chicken.
perdices estofadas	partridges braised in white wine with vegetables and garlic
pinchitos	Moroccan-style kebabs (Andalucía)
pollo a la chilindrón	sauteed chicken, with green and red peppers, tomato, serrano ham and green and black olives
pollo en pepitoria	casserole of chicken pieces braised in white wine with ground almonds, garlic and saffron
zarzuela de marisco	shellfish stew

Desserts

arroz con leche	rice pudding
bartolillos de madrid	small pastry fritters with custard filling
bizcocho borracho	squares of sponge cake soaked in a syrup of sweet wine and cinnamon
brazo de gitano	sponge cake roll with rum cream filling
buñuelos de viento	pastry fritters sprinkled with sugar and cinnamon
flan	creme caramel
helado	ice cream
leche frita	custard squares fried in olive oil and sprinkled with sugar and cinnamon

SPANISH

AT THE MARKET

Basics

bread	pan	pan
butter	man-te-*kihl*-yuh	*mantequilla*
cheese	*ke*-soh	*queso*
chocolate	choh-koh-*luh*-tay	*chocolate*
eggs	*hway*-vohs	*huevos*
flour	uh-*ree*-nuh	*harina*
margarine	mahr-gah-ree-nah	*margarina*
marmelade	mer-me-*la*-duh	*mermelada*
honey	mee-*el*	*miel*
milk	*le*-chay	*leche*
olive oil	a-*say*-tay day oh-*lee*-vuh	*aceite de oliva*
olives	a-say-*too*-nas	*aceitunas*
pasta	pah-stah	*pasta*
rice	uh-*rroth*	*arroz*
sugar	a-*soo*-kuh	*azúcar*
(mineral) water	*ag*-wuh (mee-ne-*ral*)	*agua (mineral)*
yogurt	yoh-*goor*	*yogur*

Meat & Poultry

beef	*ba*-kuh	*vaca*
chicken	*pohl*-yoh	*pollo*
(cured) ham	ha-*mohn* (se-*ruh*-noh)	*jamón (serrano)*
lamb	kor-*deh*-roh	*cordero*
meat	*kar*-nay	*carne*
pork	ser-doh	*cerdo*
pork sausage	sal-*chih*-chuh	*salchicha*
turkey	pa-voh	*pavo*
veal	ter-*neh*-rah	*ternera*

Vegetables

beetroot	re-moh-*la*-chuh	*remolacha*
cabbage	*ber*-sah	*berza*
carrot	za-na-o-ree-ah	*zanahoria*
capsicum	pih-mee-*en*-toh	*pimiento*
cauliflower	ko-lih-*flor*	*coliflor*
celery	a-*pee*-oh	*apio*
cucumber	pe-*pee*-noh	*pepino*
eggplant	be-ren-ke-nah	*berenjena*

AT THE MARKET

SPANISH

garlic	uh-khoh	ajo
green beans	hoo-dee-as ver-days	judías verdes
lettuce	le-choo-gah	lechuga
mushrooms	sham-pihn-yo-nes	des champiñones
onion	se-bol-yuh	cebolla
pea	gwee-san-tay	guisante
potato	pa-ta-tuh	patata
spinach	es-pee-na-ka	espinaca
tomato	to-ma-tay	tomate
vegetables	or-tuh-lee-thas	hortalizas
zucchini	ka-la-bah-sihn	calabacín

Seafood

fish	pes-kuh-doh	pescado
lobster	bo-gah-van-teh	bogavante
mussel	me-khil-yon	mejillón
oyster	os-trah	ostra
shrimp	gam-ba-roh	gámbaro

Pulses

broad bean	a-buh	haba
chickpea	gar-ban-thoh	garbanzo
kidney bean	hoo-dee-on	judión
lentils	len-te-kuh	lenteja

Fruit

apple	man-tha-nah	manzana
apricot	al-buh-rih-ko-ke	albaricoque
banana	pla-tuh-noh	plátano
fig	ee-goh	higo
fruit	froo-tuh	fruta
grapes	oo-vah	uva
kiwi fruit	kih-wee	kiwi
lemon	lih-mon	limón
orange	na-ran-kuh	naranja
peach	me-lo-ko-tohn	melocotón
pear	peh-ruh	pera
plum	sih-roo-e-lah	ciruela
strawberry	fre-suh	fresa

SPANISH

SHOPPING

bakery	la pa-nuh-deh-*ree*-uh	*la panadería*
bookshop	la lih-breh-*ree*-uh	*la librería*
camera shop	la tee-*en*-duh de foh-toh-gra-*fee*-uh	*la tienda de fotografía*
clothing store	la tee-*en*-duh de *rroh*-puh	*la tienda de ropa*
craft shop	la tee-*en*-duh de ar-te-suh-*nee*-uh	*la tienda de artesanía*
delicatessen	la char-koo-teh-*ree*-uh	*la charcutería*
department store	lohs *gran*-des al-muh-*seh*-nes	*los grandes almacenes*
general store	el al-muh-*sen*	*el almacén*
greengrocer	la vehr-doo-leh-*ree*-uh; froo-teh-*ree*-uh	*la verdulería; frutería*
launderette	la la-vuhn-deh-*ree*-uh	*la lavandería*
market	el mehr-*ka*-doh	*el mercado*
newsagency	el kee-*ohs*-koh	*el quiosco*
souvenir shop	la tee-*en*-duh de re-*kwer*-dohs	*la tienda de recuerdos*
supermarket	el soo-pehr-mer-*ka*-doh	*el supermercado*
travel agency	la a-*hen*-see-uh day bee-*a*-khes	*la agencia de viajes*

THEY MAY SAY ...

en kay *pwe*-doh ser-*veer*-le? kay de-*seh*-uh?	Can I help you?
al-goh mas?	Will that be all?
se loh en-*vwehl*-voh?	Would you like it wrapped?
lo see-*en*-toh, es el *oo*-nee-koh key te-*neh*-mohs	Sorry, this is the only one we have.
kwan-toh/s kee-*ehr*-e?	How much/many would you like?

SPANISH

How much is it?
   kwan-toh *kwes*-tuh?   *¿Cuánto cuesta?*
Do you accept credit cards?
   uh-*sep*-tan tar-*he*-tas   *¿Aceptan tarjetas de crédito?*
   day *creh*-dee-toh?
Can I have a receipt?
   poh-*dee*-uh *dar*-may oon   *¿Podría darme un recibo?*
   reh-*see*-boh?

Essential Groceries

I'd like (a) ...	kee-see-*eh*-ruh ...	*Quisiera ...*
batteries	*pee*-las	*pilas*
bread	pan	*pan*
butter	man-te-*kihl*-yuh	*mantequilla*
cheese	*ke*-soh	*queso*
chocolate	choh-koh-*luh*-tay	*chocolate*
eggs	*hway*-vohs	*huevos*
flour	uh-*ree*-nuh	*harina*
gas cylinder	sih-*lihn*-droh day gas	*cilindro de gas*
ham	ha-*mohn*	*jamón*
honey	mee-*el*	*miel*
matches	*fohs*-fer-ohs	*fósforos*
milk	*le*-chay	*leche*
olive oil	a-*say*-tay day ohl-ee-vuh	*aceite de oliva*
... olives	a-say-*too*-nas ...	*aceitunas ...*
black	*neg*-ras	*negras*
green	*ver*-days	*verdes*
shampoo	cham-*poo*	*champú*
soap	ha-*bohn*	*jabón*
sugar	a-*soo*-kuh	*azúcar*
toilet paper	puh-*pel* ee-hee-e-nih-koh	*papel higiénico*
toothpaste	*puhs*-tuh	*pasta dentífrica*
	den-*tee*-free-kuh	
washing	ha-*bohn* day luh-*var*	*jabón de lavar*
powder		
yogurt	yoh-*goor*	*yogur*

SPANISH

Souvenirs

fan	oon uh-ba-*nee*-koh	*un abanico*
castinets	kas-tuhn-*we*-luhs	*castañuelas*
embroidery	bor-*da*-doh	*bordado*
handicrafts	la ar-te-sa-*nee*-uh	*la artesanía*
jewellery	la hoy-e-*ree*-uh	*la joyería*
leather wine bottle	*oo*-nuh *boh*-tuh day vee-noh	*una bota de vino*
poster	oon *pohs*-tehr	*un póster*
pottery	la al-fuh-reh-*ree*-uh	*la alfarería*
silverware	la *pluh*-tuh	*la plata*
T-shirt	*oo*-nuh kuh-mee-*se*-tuh	*una camiseta*

Clothing

coat	oon uh-*bree*-goh	*un abrigo*
dress	oon ves-*tee*-doh	*un vestido*
jacket	*oo*-nuh chuh-*ke*-tuh	*una chaqueta*
jeans	lohs te-*kha*-nohs	*los tejanos*
jumper (sweater)	oon soo-e-tehr	*un suéter*
shirt	*oo*-nuh kuh-*mee*-suh	*una camisa*
shoes	lohs sa-*pa*-tohs	*los zapatos*
socks	lohs kal-seh-*tee*-nohs	*los calcetines*
swimsuit	oon ban-yuh-*dor*	*un bañador*
T-shirt	*oo*-nuh kuh-mee-*se*-tuh	*una camiseta*
umbrella	las puh-ruh-*gwas*	*las paraguas*
underpants (men's)	lohs kal-sohn-*seel*-yohs	*los calzoncillos*
(women's)	las *bruh*-gas	*las bragas*

Materials

ceramic	la say-*ra*-mee-kuh	*la cerámica*
cotton	el al-goh-*dohn*	*el algodón*
handmade	*eh*-choh a *ma*-noh	*hecho a mano*
glass	el vihd-*ree*-oh	*el vidrio*
leather	el *kwer*-oh	*el cuero*
of brass	day la-*tohn*	*de latón*

SPANISH

of gold	day *or*-oh	de oro
of silver	day *pluh*-tuh	de plata
silk	la *say*-duh	la seda
wool	la *la*-nuh	la lana
wood	la ma-*deh*-ruh	la madera

Colours

black	*neg*-roh/uh	negro/a
blue	a-*sool*	azul
brown	ma-*rohn*	marrón
green	*ver*-day	verde
orange	nuh-*ran*-huh	naranja
pink	*roh*-suh	rosa
red	*roh*-khoh/uh	rojo/a
white	*blan*-koh/uh	blanco/a
yellow	am-uh-*rihl*-yoh/uh	amarillo/a

Toiletries

comb	el *pay*-nay	el peine
dental floss	el *ee*-loh den-*tal*	el hilo dental
deodorant	el des-oh-dor-*an*-tay	el desodorante
hairbrush	el seh-*peel*-yoh	el cepillo
moisturiser	la *krem*-uh ee-druh-*tan*-tay	la crema hidratante
razor	la uh-fay-tuh-*dor*-uh	la afeitadora
razor blades	las koo-*chihl*-yas day uh-fay-*tar*	las cuchillas de afeitar
sanitary napkins	las kohm-*pre*-sas	las compresas
shaving cream	la es-*poo*-muh day uh-fay-*tar*	la espuma de afeitar
scissors	las tee-*her*-as	las tijeras
sunscreen	la *krem*-uh sohl-*uhr*	la crema solar
tampons	lohs tam-*poh*-nes	los tampones
tissues	lohs pan-*we*-lohs day puh-*pel*	los pañuelos de papel

SPANISH

Stationery & Publications

Do you have a copy of ...?
tee-*e*-nen el *lee*-broh ...?
¿Tienen el libro ...?

Is there a local entertainment guide?
tee-*e*-nen al-*goon*-ah *gee*-ah
del o-*see*-oh loh-*kal*?
¿Tienen alguna guía
del ocio local?

Do you sell ...?	*ven*-den ...?	¿Venden ...?
dictionaries	dihk-see-oh-*nuh*-ree-ohs	diccionarios
envelopes	*soh*-brays	sobres
magazines	las reh-*vees*-tas	las revistas
(English-language)	peh-ree-*oh*-dee-kohs	periódicos
newspapers	(en ihn-*glays*)	(en inglés)
paper	el puh-*pel*	el papel
pens	boh-*lee*-gruh-fohs	bolígrafos
postcards	poh-*sta*-les	postales
stamps	*sel*-yohs	sellos

... maps	*muh*-pas day ...	mapas de ...
city	luh see-oo-*dad*	la ciudad
regional	la *thoh*-nuh	la zona
road	kuh-re-*teh*-ras	carreteras

Photography

How much is it to process this film?
kwan-toh *kwes*-tuh rev-
ay-*luhr* es-*tay* kuh-*re*-tay?
¿Cuánto cuesta revelar
este carrete?

When will it be ready?
kwan-doh es-tuh-*ruh* lees-toh?
¿Cuándo estará listo?

I'd like a film for this camera.
kee-*er*-roh oon kuh-*re*-tay
puh-ruh es-tuh *kuh*-muh-ruh.
Quiero un carrete
para esta cámara.

I'd like to have some passport
photos taken.
may gus-tuh-*ree*-uh uh-*ser*-
may *foh*-tohs day puh-suh-*por*-tay
Me gustaría hacerme
fotos de pasaporte.

SPANISH

battery	la *pee*-luh	*la pila*
B&W	el *blan*-koh ih *neg*-roh	*el blanco y negro*
camera	la *kuh*-muh-ruh	*la cámara*
colour (film)	(pe-*lihk*-yoo-la) en koh-*lor*	*(película) en color*
film	el kuh-*re*-tay	*el carrete*
film speed	la sen-sih-*bih*-lee-dad	*la sensibilidad*
flash	la bohm-*bee*-yuh	*la bombilla*
lens	el ohb-he-*tee*-voh	*el objetivo*
slides	las dee-uh-poh-sih-*tee*-vohs	*las diapositivas*
video tape	la *sihn*-tuh day *vih*-day-oh	*la cinta de vídeo*

Smoking

A packet of cigarettes, please.
| oon puh-*ke*-tay day see-guh-*reel*-yohs, por fuh-*vor* | *Un paquete de cigarrillos, por favor.* |

Do you have a light?
| tee-*en*-ay *fway*-goh? | *¿Tiene fuego?* |

Do you mind if I smoke?
| lay ihm-*por*-tuh see *foo*-moh? | *¿Le importa si fumo?* |

Would you like one?
| kee-*ehr*-es *oo*-noh? | *¿Quieres uno?* |

cigarette papers	puh-*pel* day foo-*mar*	*papel de fumar*
cigarettes	lohs see-guh-*reel*-yohs	*los cigarrillos*
filter (with/ without)	(kohn/sihn) *fihl*-troh	*(con/sin) filtro*
lighter	el en-sen-deh-*dor*	*el encendedor*
matches	lohs *fohs*-fer-ohs	*los fósforos*
tobacco	el tuh-*ba*-koh	*el tabaco*

Sizes & Comparisons

also	tam-bee-*en*	*también*
big	*gran*-day	*grande*
enough	bas-*tan*-tay	*bastante*
few	*poh*-kos/ahs	*pocos/as*
less	*meh*-nohs	*menos*

SPANISH

a little bit	un *poh*-koh	*un poco*
a lot	*moo*-choh	*mucho*
many	*moo*-chohs	*muchos*
more	mas	*más*
small	peh-*ken*-yoh/uh	*pequeño/a*
some	al-goo-nohs/ahs	*algunos/as*
too much/many	deh-mas-ee-uh-doh/ohs	*demasiado/s*

HEALTH
Parts of the Body

My ... hurts.	may *dwe*-lay	*Me duele ...*
ankle	el toh-*bee*-yoh	*el tobillo*
arm	el *bruh*-thoh	*el brazo*
back	la es-*pal*-duh	*la espalda*
breast	el *peh*-choh	*el pecho*
chest	el *peh*-choh	*el pecho*
ear	la oh-*re*-khah	*la oreja*
eye	el *oh*-khoh	*el ojo*
finger	el *deh*-doh	*el dedo*
foot	el pee-*ay*	*el pie*
hand	la *ma*-noh	*la mano*
head	la kuh-*bay*-thuh	*la cabeza*
knee	la roh-*dihl*-yuh	*la rodilla*
leg	la pee-*er*-nah	*la pierna*
mouth	la *boh*-kah	*la boca*
muscle	el *moos*-koo-loh	*el músculo*
nose	la nuh-*reeth*	*la nariz*
ribs	las kohs-*teel*-yuhs	*las costillas*
shoulders	lohs *ohm*-brohs	*los hombros*
skin	la pee-*el*	*la piel*
spine	la koh-*loom*-nuh (ver-teh-bral)	*la columna (vertebral)*
stomach	el es-*toh*-muh-goh	*el estómago*
teeth	lohs dee-*en*-tays	*los dientes*
throat	la gar-*gan*-tuh	*la garganta*

SPANISH

Ailments

I'm (m/f) ill.	es-*toy* en-*fer*-moh/uh	*Estoy enfermo/a.*
I feel nauseous.	*ten*-goh *now*-see-as	*Tengo náuseas.*

I've been vomiting.
eh es-*tuh*-doh
voh-mee-*tan*-doh

He estado vomitando.

I feel ...	may see-*en*-toh ...	*Me siento ...*
dizzy	muh-ray-*uh*-doh/uh	*mareado/a*
weak	*day*-bihl	*débil*

I have (a/an) ...	*ten*-goh ...	*Tengo ...*
allergy	a-ler-*hee*-uh	*alergia*
burn	*oo*-nuh	*una*
	kay-muh-*doo*-ruh	*quemadura*
cold	oon res-free-*uh*-doh	*un resfriado*
constipation	es-tren-yee-mee-*en*-toh	*estreñimiento*
cough	tohs	*tos*
fever	fee-*eb*-ray	*fiebre*
hay fever	a-ler-*hee*-uh al *poh*-len	*alergia al polen*
headache	doh-*lor* day kuh-*bay*-thuh	*dolor de cabeza*
inflammation	*oo*-nuh ihn-fla-ma-see-*ohn*	*una inflamación*
lice	pee-*oh*-khohs	*piojos*
lump	oon *bul*-toh	*un bulto*
pain	doh-*lor*	*dolor*
rash	ih-rih-tuh-see-*ohn*	*irritación*
sore throat	doh-*lor* day gar-*gan*-tuh	*dolor de garganta*
sprain	*oo*-nuh tor-seh-*doo*-ruh	*una torcedura*
STD	*oo*-nuh en-fer-meh-*dad*	*una enfermedad*
	day trans-mih-see-*ohn*	*de transmisión*
	sex-oo-*al*	*sexual*
stomachache	doh-*lor* day	*dolor de estómago*
	es-*toh*-muh-goh	
sunburn	*oo*-nuh kay-muh-*doo*-ruh	*una quemadura*
	day sohl	*de sol*
travel sickness	muh-*ray*-oh	*mareo*
worms	lohm-*bree*-ses	*lombrices*

SPANISH

Useful Words & Phrases

Where's the	dohn-day es-tuh	¿Dónde está ...
nearest ...?	... mas sihr-kuh-noh?	más cercano?
chemist	la far-muh-see-uh	la farmacia
dentist	el den-tees-tuh	el dentista
doctor	el dohk-tohr	el doctor
hospital	el ohs-pee-tal	el hospital

At the Chemist

Where's the nearest all-night chemist?
>dohn-day es-tuh la far-muh-see-uh mas sihr-kuh-nuh? — ¿Dónde está la farmacia de guardia más cercana?

I need something for ...
>nes-seh-see-toh al-goh puh-ruh ... — Necesito algo para ...

Could I please	may poh-nay ...	¿Me pone ...
have ...?	por fuh-vor?	por favor?
antibiotics	an-tee-bee-oh-tih-kohs	antibióticos
contraceptives	lohs an-tee-kohn-sep-tee-vohs	los anticonceptivos
cough medicine	al-goh puh-ruh el ka-tuh-roh	algo para el catarro
painkillers	lohs an-al-hee-sih-kohs	los analgésicos

At the Dentist

I have a toothache.
>may dwe-lay oo-nuh mway-luh — Me duele una muela.

I've lost a filling.
>say may uh kai-ee-doh oon em-pas-tay — Se me ha caído un empaste.

My gums hurt.
>may dwe-len las en-see-as — Me duelen las encías.

I don't want it extracted.
>noh kee-eh-roh kay may loh uh-ran-kay — No quiero que me lo arranque.

SPANISH

TIME & DATES

Work starts in the morning around 9 am and goes through until about 2 pm. After a long lunch break, work resumes at about 5 pm and finishes at around 8 o'clock. It's common for the Spanish to go out after 10, especially on weekends.

Days

Monday	*loo*-nes	lunes
Tuesday	*mar*-tes	martes
Wednesday	mee-*er*-koh-les	miércoles
Thursday	*hwe*-ves	jueves
Friday	vee-*er*-nes	viernes
Saturday	suh-*buh*-doh	sábado
Sunday	doh-*mihn*-goh	domingo

Months

January	eh-*ner*-oh	enero
February	feb-*rer*-oh	febrero
March	*mar*-thoh	marzo
April	ab-*reel*	abril
May	*mai*-oh	mayo
June	*hoo*-nee-oh	junio
July	*hoo*-lee-oh	julio
August	uh-*gohs*-toh	agosto
September	set-ee-*em*-bray	se(p)tiembre
October	ohk-*too*-bray	octubre
November	noh-vee-*em*-bray	noviembre
December	dee-see-*em*-bray	diciembre

Seasons

spring	la pree-muh-*vehr*-uh	la primavera
summer	el ver-*uh*-noh	el verano
autumn	el oh-*tohn*-yoh	el otoño
winter	el ihn-vee-*er*-noh	el invierno

SPANISH

Present

right now	en *es*-tay moh-*men*-toh	en este momento
now	ow-*or*-uh	ahora
today	oy	hoy
this morning (daylight/ still dark)	*es*-tuh man-*yuh*-nuh/ mad-roo-*guh*-duh	esta mañana/ madrugada
this afternoon	*es*-tuh *tar*-day	esta tarde
tonight	*es*-tuh *noh*-chay	esta noche
this week	*es*-tuh seh-*man*-uh	esta semana
this month	*es*-tay mes	este mes
this year	*an*-yoh	este año

Past

yesterday	ai-*er*	ayer
day before yesterday	an-tay-ay-*er*	anteayer
yesterday morning (daylight/ still dark)	eye-*er* por la man-*yuh*-nuh/ mad-roo-*guh*-duh	ayer por la mañana/ madrugada
yesterday afternoon	eye-*er* por la *tar*-day	ayer por la tarde
last night	eye-*er* por la *noh*-chay	ayer por la noche
last night	uh-*noh*-chay	anoche
last week	la seh-*ma*-nuh puh-*suh*-duh	la semana pasada
last month	el mes puh-*suh*-doh	el mes pasado
last year	el *an*-yoh puh-*suh*-doh	el año pasado

Future

tomorrow	man-*yuh*-nuh	mañana
day after tomorrow	puh-*suh*-doh man-*yuh*-nuh	pasado mañana
tomorrow ...	man-*yuh*-nuh por la ...	mañana por la ...
morning	man-*yuh*-nuh	ma-ana
afternoon	*tar*-day	tarde
evening	*noh*-chay	noche

SPANISH

next ...	... kay vee-*en*-ay	... *que viene*
week	la seh-*ma*-nuh	*la semana*
month	el mes	*el mes*
year	el *an*-yoh	*el año*

During the Day

afternoon (3–8 pm)	day la *tar*-day	*de la tarde*
evening (9 pm–1 am)	day la *noh*-chay	*de la noche*
lunchtime	*or*-ruh day *koh*-mer	*hora de comer*
midnight	meh-dee-uh-*noh*-chay	*medianoche*
morning (6 am–1 pm)	day la man-*yuh*-nuh	*de la ma-ana*
noon	meh-dee-oh-*dee*-uh	*mediodía*
sunrise	uh-muh-neh-*ser*	*amanecer*
sunset	*pwes*-tuh del sohl	*puesta del sol*

NUMBERS & AMOUNTS

0	*say*-roh	*cero*	14	kuh-*tor*-say	*catorce*
1 (m)	*oon*-oh;	*uno;*	15	*kihn*-say	*quince*
(f)	*oo*-nuh	*una*	16	dee-e-thee-*says*	*dieciséis*
2	dohs	*dos*	17	dee-e-thee-see-*et*-ay	*diecisiete*
3	trays	*tres*	18	dee-e-thee-*oh*-choh	*dieciocho*
4	*kwat*-roh	*cuatro*	19	dee-e-thee-noo-*eh*-vay	*diecinueve*
5	*sihn*-koh	*cinco*	20	*vayn*-tay	*veinte*
6	says	*seis*	21	vayn-tee-*oo*-noh	*veintiuno*
7	see-*et*-ay	*siete*	22	vayn-tee-*dohs*	*veintidós*
8	*oh*-choh	*ocho*	23	vayn-tee-*trays*	*veintitrés*
9	noo-*eh*-vay	*nueve*	24	vayn-tee-*kwat*-roh	*veinticuatro*
10	dee-*eth*	*diez*	30	*trayn*-tuh	*treinta*
11	*ohn*-say	*once*	31	*trayn*-tuh ee *oo*-noh	*treinta y uno*
12	*doh*-say	*doce*	32	*trayn*-tuh ee dohs	*treinta y dos*
13	*tray*-say	*trece*	40	kwuh-*ren*-tuh	*cuarenta*

SPANISH

41	kwuh-*ren*-tuh ee *oo*-noh	*cuarenta y uno*
48	kwuh-*ren*-tuh ee *oh*-choh	*cuarenta y ocho*
50	sihn-*kwen*-tuh	*cincuenta*
51	sihn-*kwen*-tuh ee *oo*-noh	*cincuenta y uno*
60	seh-*sen*-tuh	*sesenta*
70	seh-*ten*-tuh	*setenta*
80	oh-*chen*-tuh	*ochenta*
90	noh-*ven*-tuh	*noventa*
100	see-*en*(-toh)	*cien(to)*
110	see-*en*-toh dee-*eth*	*ciento diez*
200	dohs-see-*en*-tohs	*doscientos*
1000	mihl	*mil*
2000	dohs mihl	*dos mil*
2200	dohs mihl dohs-see-*en*-tohs	*dos mil doscientos*
one million	oon mihl-*yohn*	*un millón*

ABBREVIATIONS

AVE	*tren de alta velocidad Español*	high-speed train
DNI	*documento nacional de identidad*	Spanish ID card
GR	*sendero de gran recorrido*	long-distance hiking path
I	*información*	information
IVA	*impuesto sobre el valor añadido*	value-added tax
PR	*sendero de pequeño recorrido*	footpath suited to day or weekend hikes
PVP	*precio de venta al público*	RRP, recommended retail price
REAJ	*red Española de albergues juveniles*	Spanish HI Youth Hostel network
s/m	*según mercardo*	according to market price (found on menus)
s/n	*sin numero*	without number (some times seen in street addresses)
Ud/Ud	*usted/ustedes*	you (pol, sg/pl)
v.o.	*version original*	foreign-language film subtitled in Spanish

SPANISH

EMERGENCIES

Help!	soh-*kor*-roh!	¡Socorro!
Look out!	oh-khoh!	¡Ojo!
Fire!	fway-goh!	¡Fuego!
Go away!	va-yuh-say!	¡Váyase!
Thief!	lad-*rohn*!	¡Ladrón!

Call the police!
    yuh-may a la poh-lee-*see*-uh!   ¡Llame a la policía!
Where's the police station?
    dohn-day es-*tuh* la   ¿Dónde está la
    koh-mih-suh-*ree*-oh?   comisaría?
Could you help me please?
    pwe-day ai-oo-*dar*-may,   ¿Puede ayudarme,
    por fuh-*vor*?   por favor?
Could I use the telephone?
    pwe-doh oo-*sar* el   ¿Puedo usar el teléfono?
    te-*le*-foh-noh?
There's been an accident!
    uh uh-*bee*-doh oon   ¡Ha habido un
    ak-see-*den*-tay!   accidente!

Call a ...!	*yuh*-may uh ...!	¡Llame a ...!
doctor	oon *meh*-dee-koh	un médico
an ambulance!	oo-nuh am-boo-*lan*-see-uh	una ambulancia

I'm ill.
    es-*toy* en-*fer*-moh/uh   Estoy enfermo/a.
I've (m/f) been raped.
    eh *see*-doh vee-oh-*luh*-doh/uh   He sido violado/a.
I have medical insurance.
    ten-goh seh-*goo*-roh *meh*-dee-koh   Tengo seguro médico.
I'm lost.
    es-*toy* per-*deed*-oh/uh   Estoy perdido/a.
Where are the toilets?
    dohn-day ke-dan lohs   ¿Dónde quedan los
    sehr-*vih*-see-ohs?   servicios?

SPANISH

Dealing with the Police

My ... was/were stolen.	may roh-bar-ohn mee(s) ...	*Me robaron mi(s) ...*
I've lost ...	eh per-*dee*-doh ... per-*dee* ...	*He perdido ... Perdí ...*
bags	mihs muh-*le*-tas	*mis maletas*
backpack	mih moh-*chee*-luh	*mi mochila*
handbag	mih *bohl*-soh	*mi bolso*
money	mih dih-*ne*-roh	*mi dinero*
passport	mih puh-suh-*por*-tay	*mi pasaporte*
travellers cheques	mihs *cheh*-kays day vee-*uh*-khay	*mis cheques de viaje*
wallet	mih kar-*te*-ruh	*mi cartera*

I apologise.
  dihs-*kul*-peh-may   *Discúlpeme.*

Is there someone here who speaks English?
  ai al-gee-*en* uh-*kee* kay   *¿Hay alguien aquí que*
  ab-lay ihn-*glays*?   *hable inglés?*

Do I have the right to make a call?
  ten-goh de-*reh*-choh a uh-*ser*   *¿Tengo derecho a hacer*
  al-*goo*-nuh yuh-*muh*-duh?   *alguna llamada?*

I want to contact my embassy/consulate.
  deh-*say*-oh koh-moo-nee-*kuhr*-may   *Deseo comunicarme con*
  kohn mee em-buh-*khuh*-duh/   *mi embajada/consulado.*
  kohn-soo-*luh*-doh

I'd like to see a duty solicitor (m/f).
  kee-*ehr*-oh ver a uhn/*uh*-nuh   *Quiero ver a una/un*
  uh-boh-*guh*-doh/uh day oh-*fih*-see-oh *abogado/a de oficio.*

TURKISH

QUICK REFERENCE

TURKISH

Hello!	mehr-hah-bah!	*Merhaba!*
Goodbye.	ahl-lah-hah	*Allaha ismarladik.*
(person leaving)	ihs-mahr-lah-dihk	
Goodbye.	goo-leh goo-leh	*Güle Güle.*
(person staying)		
Yes./No.	eh-veht/hah-yihr	*Evet./Hayir.*
Please.	loot-fehn	*Lütfen.*
Cheers!	sah-lih-ih-nih-zah!	*Sağliğinia!*
I want a	... beer bee-leht	... *bir bilet*
ticket to ...	ees-tee-yoh-room	*istiyorum.*
one way	ghee-deesh	*gidiş*
return	ghee-deesh-	*gidiş-*
	der-noosh	*dönüş*

Thank you.
   teh-shehk-kyoor   *Teşekkür*
   eh-deh-reem   *ederim.*
You're welcome.
   beer shehy deh-eel   *Bir şey değil.*
I don't understand.
   ahn-lah-mih-yoh-room   *Anlamiyorum.*
Do you speak English?
   een-ghee-leez-jeh   *Ingilizce*
   koh-noo-shoo-yohr   *konuşuyor*
   moo-soo-nooz?   *musunuz?*
Where's (the toilet)?
   (too-wah-leht) neh-reh-deh? *(Tuvalet) nerede?*
Go straight ahead.
   doh-roo ghee-deen   *Doğru gidin.*
On the left/right
   sohl-dah/sah-dah   *Solda./Sağda.*

1	beer	*bir*	6	ahl-tih	*alti*	
2	ee-kee	*iki*	7	yeh-dee	*yedi*	
3	oooch	*üç*	8	seh-keez	*sekiz*	
4	derrt	*dört*	9	doh-kooz	*dokuz*	
5	besh	*beş*	10	ohn	*on*	

Turkish is so different from other European languages that it can be bewildering at first. But it has advantages. There are no gender distinctions (he, she, it) and few articles (a, an, the). It also has a logical, if complex, structure. Context counts for a lot in Turkish, so you can say a few words and phrases to Turks and they'll pick up the rest easily.

The Turkish language is a member of the Ural-Altaic language family, which also includes lesser-known tongues such as Kyrgyz, Kazakh, Uyghur, Azerbaijani, Manchu, Chuvash, and Mongolian. Surprisingly, Korean and Japanese are also Ural-Altaic languages. When the Turks encountered Islam in AD 670, they adopted the Arabic alphabet, even though it was ill-suited to record the sounds of Turkish.

After the fall of the Ottoman empire, Kemal Atatürk, the founding-father and first president of modern Turkey, undertook to reform and 'purify' Turkish, to encourage literacy. He established the Turkish Language Society, in order with instructions for it to rid the Turkish language of Arabic and Persian words and grammatical constructions, and to replace them with revitalised Turkish ones. With the changes, Turks could say 'you', instead of 'your exalted personage' (Persian), and 'me', instead of 'your humble servant'.

In the interests of literacy, Atatürk ordered that the Arabic alphabet be abandoned in favour of a modified Latin one. On 1 November 1928, Parliament decreed that, after two months, no materials could be published in the Arabic script – only in the modern Turkish alphabet. Atatürk himself took blackboard and chalk to village squares and taught the new letters to the people.

Modern Turkish is spoken by the nearly 60 million citizens of the Turkish Republic and also by Turkish Cypriots and small communities of ethnic Turks in Greece. Ethnic Turkish minorities in Bulgaria and Yugoslavia speak dialects of Ottoman Turkish. If you can speak Turkish, you can make yourself understood from Yugoslavia to China.

PRONUNCIATION
Vowels

Each Turkish letter has a distinct pronunciation – there are no combinations of consonants, and there's only one silent letter, the ğ.

Turkish has two very different sounds represented by the letters *i* and *ı*. Notice that one, *i*, has a dot while the other, *ı*, does not. It's easy for the eye to ignore this difference when reading, so stay alert, because mispronunciation can cause confusion.

ısırır	ih-sih-rihr	*not*	eeh-seeh-reehr
ikinci	ee-keen-jee	*not*	ih-kihn-jih

Keep your eye out for the dot on the capital *İ*, as well:

Isparta	ihs-pahr-tah	*not*	ees-pahr-tah
İzmir	eez-meer	*not*	ihz-mihr

A, a	ah	as the 'a' in 'bar'
E, e	eh	as the 'e' in 'bed'
İ, i	ee	as the 'i' in 'marine'
I, ı	ih	as the 'i' in 'kiss'
O, o	oh	as the 'o' in 'low'
Ö, ö	er	as the 'e' in 'her'
U, u	oo	as the 'oo' in 'moo'
Ü, ü	ooo	shape your lips to say the 'oo' in 'too', but then say 'ee';
	yoo	sometimes as the word 'you'

Consonants

Most consonants are pronounced as in English. The most unusual exception is *c*, which is always pronounced like an English 'j'. The Turkish *h* is pronounced. Start saying 'hot', but stop with the 'h' – that's the sound. It's important to remember that *h* doesn't combine with other consonants.

ithal	eet-hahl	*not*	i-thahl
ıshal	ihs-hahl	*not*	ih-shahl

TURKISH

The Turkish *v* is soft, somewhere between an English 'v' and 'w', but closer to 'w'. When a Turk says 'very,' it sounds much like 'wery'.

Double consonants are held for a longer time.

dikkat	deek-kaht	*not*	dee-kaht
yollar	yohl-lahr	*not*	yoh-lahr

C, c	j	as the 'j' in 'joke'; never as the 'g' in 'gentle'
Ç, ç	ch	as the 'ch' in 'cheese'
G, g	g	as the 'g' in 'game'; never as the 'g' in 'gentle'
Ġ, ğ		silent – indicates that the preceding vowel should be lengthened
H, h	h	as the 'h' in 'hot'
J, j	zh	as the 's' in 'pleasure'
S, s	s	as the 's' in 'sin'; never as the 's' in 'pose'
Ş, ş	sh	as the 'sh' in 'shell'
V, v	v	usually as the 'v' in 'velvet';
	w	frequently as the 'w' in 'wet'
Y, y	y	as the 'y' in 'yes'

TURKISH

Stress

Stress is much less pronounced in Turkish than in English. Turkish spoken with little stress is considered the most correct and standard variety, therefore stress isn't indicated throughout this chapter.

PRONOUNS					
SG			**PL**		
I	behn	*ben*	we	beez	*biz*
you (inf)	sehn	*sen*	you	seez	*siz*
you (pol)	seez	*siz*	they	ohnlahr	*onlar*
he/she/it	oh	*o*			

GREETINGS & CIVILITIES

Hi./Hello!	mehr-hah-bah!	*Merhaba!*
Good night.	ee-yee geh-jeh-lehr	*İyi geceler.*
Goodbye. (person leaving)	ahl-lah-hah ihs-mahr-lah-dihk	*Allaha ısmarladık.*
Goodbye. (person staying)	goo-leh goo-leh	*Güle Güle.*
Yes./No.	eh-veht/hah-yihr	*Evet./Hayır.*
Please.	loot-fehn	*Lütfen.*

Thank you.
  teh-shehk-kyoor eh-deh-reem   *Teşekkür ederim.*
You're welcome.
  beer shehy deh-eel   *Bir şey değil.*
How are you?
  nah-sihl-sih-nihz?   *Nasılsınız?*
Very well, thank you.
  chohk ee-yee-yeem,   *Çok iyiyim, teşekkür*
  teh-shehk-kyoor eh-deh-reem   *ederim.*

Besides the normal everyday pleasantries such as 'hello' and 'thank you', on certain occasions Turks will automatically come out with a special phrase appropriate to the occasion. The giveaway in these phrases is the last word, *olsun*, meaning 'let it be that'. If you hear it, and the context seems right, just say sah ohl, 'thanks', in response.

May it contribute to your health!
  ah-fee-eht ohl-soon!   *Afiyet olsun!*
  (to someone sitting down to a meal)

May your life be spared!
  bah-shih-nihz sah ohl-soon!   *Başınız sağ olsun!*
  (to someone who's just
  experienced a death in the family)

May your soul be safe from harm!
  jah-nih-nihz sah ohl-soon!   *Canınız sağ olsun!*
  (to someone who's just
  accidentally broken something)

May it be in your past!
  gech-meesh ohl-soon!   *Geçmiş olsun!*
  (said to someone who's ill, injured
  or otherwise distressed)

May it last for hours!
  saht-lahr ohl-soon!   *Saatler olsun!*
  (to someone who's just emerged from
  a bath or shower, a shave or a hair cut.
  It's a corruption of *Sıhhatler olsun!*,
  'May it keep you healthy!')

Health to your hand!
  el-lee-nee-zeh sah-lihk!   *Elinize sağlık!*
  (to a cook who's prepared a delicious meal)

TURKISH

Forms of Address

The most common forms of address are *Bey*, 'Mr', and *Hanım*,
'Ms', preceded by a person's first name, as in *Mehmet Bey* or
Ayşe Hanım, or their job title. Just to use a person's name with
no title is very informal, and it's considered impolite if you don't
know the person well.

Mr Driver (taxi or bus)
  shoh-fer behy   *Şoför Bey*
Mr/Ms Doctor
  dohk-tohr behy/hahn-ihm   *Doktor Bey/Hanım*

TURKISH

SMALL TALK
Meeting People

What's your name?
   ees-mee-neez neh?   *İsminiz ne?*
My name's ...
   ees-meem ...   *İsmim ...*
Do you live here?
   boo-rah-dah mih   *Burada mı*
   oh-too-roo-yohr-soo-nooz?   *oturuyorsunuz?*
Where are you going?
   neh-reh-yeh   *Nereye*
   gee-dee-yohr-soo-nooz?   *gidiyorsunuz?*
What are you doing?
   neh yah-pih-yohr-soo-nooz?   *Ne yapıyorsunuz?*
What's this called?
   boo-noon ees-mee neh-deer?   *Bunun ismi nedir?*
Beautiful, isn't it!
   chohk goo-zehl deh-eel mee!   *Çok güzel, değil mi!*
We love it here.
   boo-rah-sih-nih   *Burasını*
   seh-vee-yoh-rooz   *seviyoruz.*
Are you waiting too?
   siz deh mee   *Siz de mi*
   beh-klee-yohr-soo-nooz?   *bekliyorsunuz?*
That's strange!
   oh too-hahf   *O tuhaf.*
That's funny. (amusing)
   oh koh-meek   *O komik.*
Can I take a photo of you ?
   rehs-mee-nee   *Resmini*
   che-keh-bee-leer mee-yeem?   *çekebilir miyim?*

Nationalities

If your country isn't listed here, try saying it in English – as many country names in Turkish are similar to those in English. Remember though that even if a word looks like the English equivalent, it will have a Turkish pronunciation.

Where are you from?
   neh-reh-lee-see-neez?   *Nerelisiniz?*

I'm ...

American	ah-meh-ree-kah-lih-yihm	*Amerikalıyım.*
Australian	ah-voo-strahl-yah-lih-yihm	*Avustralyalıyım.*
British	een-ghee-lee-zeem	*İngilizim.*
Canadian	kah-nah-dah-lih-yihm	*Kanadalıyım.*
English	een-ghee-lee-zeem	*İngilizim.*

Occupations

What do you do?
   neh eesh yah-pahr-sih-nihz?   *Ne iş yaparsınız?*

I'm a ...

businessman	eesh-ah-dah-mih-yihm	*İşadamıyım*
businesswoman	eesh-kah-dih-nih-yihm	*İşkadınıyım*
doctor	dohk-tohr-room	*Doktorum*
engineer	moo-hehn-dee-seem	*Mühendisim*
factory worker	eesh-chee-yeem	*İşçiyim*
journalist	gah-zeh-teh-jee-yeem	*Gazeteciyim*
musician (m/f)	myoo-zees-yeh-neem/	*Müzisyenim/*
	myoo-zeek-chee-yeem	*Müzikçiyim*
nurse	hem-shee-reh-yeem	*Hemşireyim*
student	er-rehn-jee-yeem	*Öğrenciyim*
teacher	er-reht-meh-neem	*Öğretmenim*

TURKISH

Religion

Are you a ...?   ... mih-sih-nihz?   *... mısınız?*

Christian	hrees-tee-yahn	*Hristiyan*
Buddhist	boo-deest	*Budist*
Catholic	kah-toh-leek	*Katolik*
Jew	moo-seh-vee	*Musevi*
Muslim	moos-loo-mahn	*Müslüman*
Protestant	proh-tehs-tahn	*Protestan*

Can I participate in this service/mass?
   boo ah-yee-neh/ee-bah-deh-teh   *Bu ayine/ibadete*
   kah-tih-lah-bee-leer mee-yeem?   *katılabilir miyim?*

TURKISH

Can I pray here?
boo-rah-dah doo-ah
eh-deh-bee-leer mee-yeem?
*Burada dua
edebilir miyim?*
Where can I pray/worship?
neh-reh-deh doo-ah
eh-deh-bee-lee-reem?
*Nerede dua
edebilirim?*

religious procession	deen-dahr ah-lah-yih	*dindar alayı*
sacraments	koot-sahl eesh-lehm-lehr	*kutsal işlemler*
shrine	tah-pih-nahk	*tapınak*

Family

Are you married?
ev-lee-mee-see-neez?
Evli misiniz?
I'm married/I'm not married.
ehv-lee-yeem/ehv-lee
deh-eel-eem
*Evliyim./Evli
değilim.*
Do you have children?
choh-jook vahr mih?
Çocuk var mı?
Do you have a (girlfriend)?
(kihz ahr-kah-dah-shih-nihz)
vahr mih?
*(Kız arkadaşınız)
var mı?*

boyfriend	ehr-kehk ahr-kah-dahsh	*erkek arkadaş*
brother	ehr-kehk kahr-dehsh	*erkek kardeş*
children	choh-jook-lahr	*çocuklar*
daughter	kihz	*kız*
family	ah-yee-leh/ah-krah-bah	*aile/akraba*
father	bah-bah	*baba*
girlfriend	kihz ahr-kah-dahsh	*kız arkadaş*
husband	koh-jah	*koca*
mother	ahn-neh	*anne*
older brother	ah-behy	*ağabey*
older sister	ah-blah	*abla*
sister	kihz kahr-dehsh	*kız kardeş*
son	oh-ool/oh-lahn	*oğul/oğlan*
wife	kah-rih	*karı*

Feelings

I'm tired.	yohr-goo-noom	*Yorgunum.*
I'm hungry.	ah-chihm	*Açım.*
I'm happy.	moot-loo-yoom	*Mutluyum.*
I'm angry.	kihz-gih-nihm	*Kızgınım.*
We're sorry.	ooz-goo-nooz	*Üzgünüz.*

Some feelings are expressed by idioms:

I'm sleepy.
　　ooy-koom gehl-dee　　*Uykum geldi.* (lit: my sleep has come)

TURKISH

Useful Phrases

Sure.	eh-meen	*Emin.*
Just a minute.	beer dah-kee-kah	*Bir dakika*
It's OK.	tah-mahm/	*Tamam/*
	peh-kee	*Peki.*
It's important.	er-nehm-lee	*Önemli.*
It's not important.	er-nehm-lee	*Önemli*
	deh-eel	*değil*
It's possible.	moom-kyoon	*Mümkün.*
It's not possible.	moom-kyoon	*Mümkün*
	deh-eel	*değil.*
Look!	bah-kihn!	*Bakın!*
Listen!	deen-leh-yeen	*Dinleyin!*
I'm ready.	hah-zih-rihm	*Hazırım.*
Are you ready?	hah-zihr mih-sih-nihz?	*Hazır mısınız?*
Good luck!	ee-yee shahns-lahr!	*İyi şanslar!*

BREAKING THE LANGUAGE BARRIER

Do you speak English?

   een-ghee-leez-jeh
koh-noo-shoo-yohr
moo-soo-nooz?   *İngilizce konuşuyor musunuz?*

Is there someone here who knows English?

   een-gee-leez-jeh bee-lehn
beer keem-seh vahr-mih?   *İngilizce bilen bir kimse var mi?*

Is there someone who knows English?

   een-gee-leez-jeh bee-lehn
beer keem-seh vahr-mih?   *İngilizce bilen bir kimse var mi?*

Do you understand?

   ahn-lih-yohr moo-soo-nooz?   *Anlıyor musunuz?*

Yes, I understand.

   eh-veht, ahn-lih-yoh-room   *Evet, anlıyorum.*

No, I don't understand.

   hah-yihr,
ahn-lah-mih-yoh-room   *Hayır, anlamıyorum.*

Could you repeat that?

   tehk-rahr
eh-dehr mee-see-neez?   *Tekrar eder misiniz?*

How do you say ...?

   ... nah-sihl sery-loo-yohr-soon?   *... nasıl söylüyorsun?*

What does ... mean?

   ... neh deh-mehk?   *... ne demek?*

TURKISH (vertical side tab)

BODY LANGUAGE

Turks indicate 'yes' by nodding the head once, forward and down. They may also say *var*, 'we have it' – more literally 'it exists', the same way. To indicate 'no', nod your head up and back, lifting your eyebrows at the same time (simply raising your eyebrows also signifies 'no'). Remember, when Turks seem to be giving you a mean look, they're often only saying 'no'. They may also make the sound 'tsk', which also means 'no'.

Wagging your head from side to side doesn't mean 'no' in Turkey, it means 'I don't understand'. So if a Turk asks you, 'Are you looking for the bus to Ankara?' and you shake your head, he or she will assume you don't understand English and will probably ask you the same question again, this time in German.

There are other body-language signs that can cause confusion, especially when you're out shopping. For instance, if you want to indicate length – 'I want a fish this big' – don't hold your hands apart at the desired length, rather hold out your arm and place a flat hand on it, measuring from your fingertips to the hand. Thus, if you want a pretty big fish, you must 'chop' your arm with your other hand at about the elbow.

Height is indicated by holding a flat hand the desired distance above the floor or some other flat surface such as a counter or table top.

Turks will invite you to follow them by waving one of their hands downward and toward themselves in a scooping motion. Some Turks, particularly women, will hold their hand in the same way, but flutter their fingers instead of scooping. Both signs mean 'follow me'. Wiggling an upright finger would never occur to a Turk, except perhaps as a vaguely obscene gesture.

TURKISH

SIGNS

AÇIK	OPEN
ÇIKIŞ	EXIT
GİRİLMEZ	NO ENTRY
GİRİŞ	ENTRANCE
KAPALI	CLOSED
SICAK	HOT
SİGARA İÇİLMEZ	NO SMOKING
SOĞAK	COLD
TUVALET(LER)/WC	TOILETS
YASAK(TIR)	PROHIBITED

TURKISH

PAPERWORK

adres	address
babanın adı	father's name
cinsiyet	sex
din	religion
doğum günü/yeri	date/place of birth
ehliyet	drivers licence
iş	business
isim/ad	name
kimlik	identification
meslek	occupation
pasaport numarası	passport number
uyruk milliyet	nationality
vize	visa
yaş	age
medeni hal	marital status
bekâr	single
boşanmış	divorced
dul kadın/erkek	widowed (w/f)
evli	married
seyahatın sebebi	reason for travel
ziyaretin sebebi	purpose of visit
tatil	holiday
akrabayı ziyaret etme	visiting relatives

THEY MAY SAY ...

You can go on foot.
yoo-roo-yeh-rehk
ghee-deh-bee-leer-see-neez

*Yürüyerek
gidebilirsiniz.*

GETTING AROUND
Directions

Where's a/the ...?
    ... neh-reh-deh?   *... nerede?*
Is it near/far?
    yah-kihn/oo-zahk mih?   *Yakın/Uzak mı?*
Go straight ahead.
    doh-roo ghee-deen   *Doğru gidin.*

on the left/right	sohl-dah/sah-dah	*solda/sağda*
here	boo-rah-dah	*burada*
there	shoo-rah-dah	*şurada*
over there	oh-rah-dah	*orada*
Cross the road	... yoh-loo kahr-shih-	*... yolu karşıya*
at the ...	yah gehch	*geç*
avenue	jahd-deh	*Cadde*
next corner	geh-leh-jehk	*Gelecek*
	ker-sheh-dehn	*köşeden*
road	soh-kahk	*Sokak*
square; town centre	mehy-dahn	*Meydan*
traffic light	trah-feek	*Trafik*
	ih-shih-ihn-dahn	*ışığından*
after	-dehn sohn-rah	*-den sonra*
behind	ahr-kah-sihn-dah/	*arkasında/*
	ahr-kah-sih-nah	*arkasına*
between	ah-rah-sihn-dah	*arasında*
far	-dehn oo-zahk	*-den uzak*
in front of	er-nyun-deh	*önünde*
near	yah-kihn/yah-kihn-dah	*yakın/yakında*
next to	-een yah-nihn-dah	*-in yanında*
opposite	kahr-shih	*karşı*
north	koo-zehy	*kuzey*
south	goo-nehy	*güney*
east	doh-oo	*doğu*
west	bah-tih	*batı*

TURKISH

TURKISH

Buying Tickets

Where's the ticket office?
bee-leht gee-sheh-see neh-reh-deh? — *Bilet gişesi nerede?*

I want a ticket to ...	... beer bee-leht ees-tee-yoh-room	*... bir bilet istiyorum.*
one way	ghee-deesh	*gidiş*
return	ghee-deesh-der-noosh	*gidiş-dönüş*
student (ticket)	er-rehn-jee/tah-leh-beh (bee-leh-tee)	*öğrenci/talebe (bileti)*
1st class	bee-reen-jee mehv-kee/ sih-nihf	*birinci mevki/ sınıf*
2nd class	ee-keen-jee mehv-kee/ sih-nihf	*ikinci mevki/ sınıf*
map	hah-ree-tah	*harita*
timetable	tah-ree-feh	*tarife*
ticket (office)	bee-leht (gee-sheh-see)	*bilet (gişesi)*
reserved seat	noo-mah-rah-lih yehr	*numaralı yer (lit: numbered place)*

Bus

Does this bus go to Izmir?
boo oh-toh-boos eez-mee-reh ghee-dehr mee? — *Bu otobüs İzmir'e gider mi?*

When does the bus to Ankara depart?
ahn-kah-rah-yah ghee-dehn oh-toh-boos neh zah-mahn kahl-kahr? — *Ankara'ya giden otobüs ne zaman kalkar?*

bus	oh-toh-boos	*otobüs*
bus station	oh-toh-gahr	*otogar*
direct	dee-rehkt	*direkt*
indirect	ahk-tahr-mah-lih	*aktarmalı*
minibus	dohl-moosh	*dolmuş*

Train

Where's the railway station?
gahr/ees-tahs-yohn
neh-reh-deh?

*Gar/istasyan
nerede?*

Does this train go to (Istanbul)?
boo trehn (ees-tahn-bool)
ghee-dehr mee?

*Bu tren (İstanbul)'e
gider mi?*

couchette	koo-sheht	*kuşet*
dining car	yeh-mehk-lee wah-gohn	*yemekli vagon*
non-smoking car	see-gah-rah ee-cheel-mee-yehn wah-gohn	*sigara içilmeyen vagon*
railway	deh-meer-yoh-loo	*demiryolu*
railway station	gahr/ees-tahs-yohn	*gar/istasyon*
sleeping car	yah-tahk-lih wah-gohn	*yataklı vagon*
train	trehn	*tren*

TURKISH

Taxi

Is this taxi available?
boo tahk-see
moo-sah-eet mee?

*Bu taksi
müsait mi?*

Please take me to (Sultanahmet).
loot-fehn beh-nee
(sool-tah-nah-meh)-teh
ger-too-roo-nooz

*Lütfen beni
(Sultanahmet)'e
götürünüz.*

How much does it cost to go to (Sultanahmet)?
(sool-tah-nah-meh)-teh
gheet-mehk neh kah-dahr
too-tahr?

*(Sultanahmet)'e
gitmek ne kadar
tutar?*

Do we pay extra for luggage?
bah-gahzh ee-cheen eks-trah
er-deh-yeh-jehk mee-yeez?

*Bagaj için ekstra
ödeyecek miyiz?*

Let's go!	ghee-deh-leem!	*Gidelim!*
Careful!	deek-kaht!	*Dikkat!*

I'm in a hurry.	ah-jeh-lehm vahr	*Acelem var.*
Slow down!	yah-vahsh ghee-deen!	*Yavaş gidin!*
Stop (here)!	(boo-rah-dah) doo-roon!	*(Burada) durun!*

Wait here!
boo-rah-dah bek-leh-yeen! *Burada bekleyin!*

Car

Where can I hire a car?
neh-reh-dehn ah-rah-bah *Nereden araba*
kee-rah-lah-yah-bee-lee-reem? *kiralayabilirim?*

How much is it for the day?
boo-toon goon neh kah-dahr? *Bütün gün ne kadar?*

We need a mechanic.
tah-meer-jee-yeh *Tamirciye*
ee-tee-yah-jih-mihz vahr *ihtiyacımız var.*

I have a flat tyre.
lahs-tee-yeem paht-lah-dih *Lastiğim patladı.*

I've lost my car keys.
ah-rah-bah-mihn *Arabamın*
ah-nahh-tah-rih-nih *anahtarını*
kahy-beht-teem *kaybettim.*

I've run out of petrol (gas).
behn-zee-neem beet-tee *Benzinim bitti.*

air	hah-vah	*hava*
brakes	frehnlehr	*frenler*
headlight	fahr	*far*
highways	kah-rah-yohl-lah-rih	*karayolları*
motorway	oh-toh-yohl	*otoyol*
oil	moh-tohr yah-ih	*motor yağı*
petrol (gasoline)	behn-zeen	*benzin*
regular	nohr-mahl	*normal*
super (extra)	soo-pehr	*süper*
road construction/	yohl yah-pih-mih/	*yol yapımı/*
repairs	oh-nah-rih-mih	*onarımı*

ACCOMMODATION
At the Hotel

Do you have any rooms available?
oh-dah-nihz vahr mih? *Odanız var mı?*

I want a ...	beer ... ees-tee-yoh-room	*Bir ... istiyorum.*
We want a ...	beer ... ees-tee-yoh-rooz	*Bir ... istiyoruz.*
room with one bed	tehk yah-tahk-lih oh-dah	*tek yataklı oda*
room with two beds	ee-kee yah-tahk-lih oh-dah	*iki yataklı oda*
double bed	ee-kee kee-shee-leek	*iki kişilik*
room with a bath	bahn-yoh-loo oh-dah	*banyolu oda*
quiet room	sah-keen beer oh-dah	*sakin bir oda*

TURKISH

How much per night?
beer geh-jeh-leek neh kah-dahr *Bir gecelik ne kadar?*

Can I/we sleep on the roof?
chah-tih-dah yah-tah-beer-leer mee-yeem/mee-yeez? *Çatıda yatabilir miyim/miyiz?*

Can I/we camp in the garden?
bah-cheh-deh kahmp yah-pah-bee-leer mee-yeem/mee-yeez? *Bahçede kamp yapabilir miyim/miyiz?*

TURKISH

I'll be staying ...	... kah-lah-jah-ihm	... kalacağım.
We'll be staying ...	... kah-lah-jah-ihz	... kalacağız.
one night	beer geh-jeh	bir gece
two nights	ee-kee geh-jeh	iki gece
a few nights	beer kahch geh-jeh	bir kaç gece
(at least) a week	(ehn ah-zihn-dahn)	(en azından)
	beer hahf-tah	bir hafta

Could I have the bill?
heh-sah-bihm loot-fehn   *Hesabım lütfen.*

(See also Camping, page 512.)

Requests & Complaints

Where's the toilet?
too-wah-leht neh-reh-deh?   *Tuvalet nerede?*
Is there a better (room)?
dah-hah ee-yee-see vahr mih?   *Daha iyisi var mı?*
Is there a cheaper room?
dah-hah oo-jooz-oo vahr mih?   *Daha ucuzu var mı?*
It's very noisy.
chohk goo-rool-too-loo   *Çok gürültülü.*
Can I leave my things with
you until tonight?
bah-gahzj-ih-mih   *Bagajımı*
ahk-kah-shah-mah kah-dahr   *akşama kadar*
see-zeen-leh bih-rah-kah-   *sizinle bırakabilir*
bee-leer mee-yeem?   *miyim?*

I WONDER ...

ah-jah-bah ...   *Acaba ...*   I wonder ...

This expression is used when you want to phrase a
question in a particularly polite manner.

poh-stah-neh neh-reh-deh, ah-jah-bah?
Postane nerede, acaba?
   Where's the post office, I wonder?

AROUND TOWN
At the Post Office

I'd like an airmail stamp for a postcard to (Australia).

(ah-voos trahl-yah)-yah oo-chahk-lah kahrt-pohs-tahl ee-cheen beer pool ree-jah eh-deh-reem

(Avustralya)'ya uçakla kartpostal için bir pul rica ederim.

Is there a letter for me in poste restante?

beh-neem-ee-chees behk-leh-yehn mek-toop vahr mih?

Benim için bekleyen mektup var mı?

aerogramme	hah-vah mek-too-boo	*hava mektubu*
air mail	oo-chahk-lah/ oo-chahk ee-leh	*uçakla/uçak ile*
customs	goom-rook	*gümrük*
express mail	ehks-press	*ekspres*
fax	eh-lek-troh-neek mehk-toop/fahks	*elektronik mektup/fax*
letter	mehk-toop	*mektup*
parcel	koh-lee/pah-keht	*koli/paket*
post office	pohs-tah-neh/ pohs-tah-hah-neh	*postane/ postahane*
postcard	kahrt-pohs-tahl	*kartpostal*
general delivery	gheh-nehl-dah-ih-tihm	*genel dağıtım*
registered mail	tah-ahh-hoot-loo	*taahhütlü*
stamp	pool	*pul*
telegram	peh-teh-teh	*PTT*

TURKISH

TURKISH

Telephone

Could I please use the telephone?
teh-leh-foh-noo kool-lah-nah-bee-leer mee-yeem?
Telefonu kullanabilir miyim?

I want to call ...
... teh-leh-fohn et-mehk ees-tee-yoh-room
... telefon etmek istiyorum.

I want to make a reverse-charge (collect) call.
er-deh-meh-lee teh-leh-fohn eht-mehk ees-tee-yoh-room
Ödemeli telefon etmek istiyorum.

What's the area code for ...?
... ah-lahn noo-mah-rah-sih neh-deer?
... alan numarası nedir?

The number is ...
... noo-mah-rah-sih
... numarası.

It's engaged/busy.	mehsh-gool	*Meşgul.*
I've been cut off.	kes-eel-dee	*Kesildi*
operator	oh-peh-rah-ter/ sahn-trahl	*operatör/ santral*
phone book	teh-leh-fohn reh-beh-ree	*telefon rehberi*
phone box	teh-leh-fohn koo-loo-beh-see	*telefon külübesi*
phonecard	teh-leh-fohn kahr-tih	*telefon kartı*
telephone	teh-leh-fohn	*telefon*
telephone debit card	teh-leh-kahrt	*telekart*
urgent	ah-jeel	*acil*

Internet

Is there a local Internet cafe?
jee-vahr-dah een-tehr-neht
kah-feh var mih?

*Civarda İnternet café
var mı?*

I want to connect to the Internet.
een-tehr-neh-teh
bah-lahn-mahk
ees-tee-yoh-room

*İnternet bağlanmak
istiyorum.*

I want to check my email.
ee-mahy-lee-meh
bahk-mahk
ees-tee-yoh-room

*E-mailime bakmak
istiyorum.*

At the Bank

Do you accept these
travellers cheques?
boo seh-yah-haht
chehk-leh-ree-nee kah-bool
eh-dehr mee-see-neez?

*Bu seyahat
çeklerini kabul
eder misiniz?*

Would you change this, please?
boo-noo boh-zahr
mih-sih-nihz?

*Bunu bozar
mısınız?*

cash	nah-keet	*nakit*
cashier	kah-sah/vehz-neh	*kasa/vezne*
cheque	chek	*çek*
coin(s)	mah-deh-nee pah-rah	*madeni para*
commission	koh-mees-yohn	*komisyon*
currency exchange	kahm-bee-yoh	*kambiyo*
exchange rate	koor	*kur*
foreign currency	der-veez	*döviz*
money	pah-rah	*para*
notes	kah-iht pah-rah	*kağıt para*
tax	vehr-ghee	*vergi*

INTERESTS & ENTERTAINMENT
Sightseeing

Where's the tourist information office?
too-reezm byoo-roh-soo neh-reh-deh?

Turizm bürosu nerede?

Do you have a local map?
sheh-heer plah-nih vahr mih?

Şehir planı var mı?

I'd like to see ...
... oo ger-mehk ees-tee-yoh-room

...'u görmek istiyorum.

What time does it open/close?
neh zah-mahn ah-chih-lah-jahk/ kah-pah-nah-jahk?

Ne zaman açılacak/kapanacak?

Can we take photographs?
foh-toh-raf che-keh-bee-leer mee-yeez?

Fotoğraf çekebilir miyiz?

Could you take a photograph of me?
rehs-mee-mee che-keh-bee-leer mee-see-neez?

Resmimi çekebilir misiniz?

What's that?
oh neh-deer?

O nedir?

What's happening/happened?
neh oh-loo-yohr/ohl-doo?

Ne oluyor/oldu?

It's beautiful here.
boo-rah-sih chohk goo-zehl

Burası çok güzel.

castle	kah-leh	*kale*
cathedral	kee-lee-seh	*kilise*
concert	kohn-sehr	*konser*
festival	bahy-rahm	*bayram*
fortress	kah-leh/hee-sahr	*kale/hisar*
historical	tah-ree-hee	*tarihi*
mosque	jah-mee	*cami*
museum	myoo-zeh	*müze*
park	pahrk	*park*
ruin(s)	hah-rah-beh(lehr)	*harabe(ler)*
statue	hehy-kehl	*heykel*
suburb	dihsh mah-hahl-leh	*dıs mahalle*
temple	tah-pih-nahk/mah-behd	*tapınak/mabed*
university	ooo-nee-vehr-see-teh	*üniversite*

TURKISH

Going Out

Where can we go dancing?
neh-reh-deh dahns
eh-deh-bee-lee-reez?
*Nerede dans
edebiliriz?*

I'm having a really good time.
chohk goo-zehl vah-keet
geh-chee-ree-yoh-room
*Çok güzel vakit
geçiriyorum.*

Shall we go someplace else?
bahsh-kah beer yeh-reh
ghee-deh-leem mee?
*Başka bir yere
gidelim mi?*

I don't like the music here.
boo-rah-dah-kee
myoo-zeek-tehn hohsh-
lahn-mih-yoh-room
*Buradaki müzikten
hoşlanmıyorum.*

I really like Reggae music.
reh-gehy myoo-zeek-tehn
gehr-chehk-tehn
hohsh-lah-nih-yoh-room
*Reggae müzikten
gerçekten
hoşlanıyorum.*

When shall we meet?
sah-aht kahch-tah
boo-loo-shah-lihm?
*Saat kaçta
buluralım?*

Where shall we meet?
neh-reh-deh boo-loo-shah-bee-lee-reez? — *Nerede buluṣabiliriz?*

See you then.
oh sah-aht-teh ger-roo-shoo-rooz — *O saatte görürüz.*

Sports & Interests

What do you do in your spare time?
bohsh zah-mahn-lah-rihn-dah neh yap-pahr-sihn? — *Boṣ zamanlarında ne yaparsın?*

Do you like sport?
spohr-dahn hohsh-lah-nihr mih-sih-nihz? — *Spordan hoṣlanır mısınız?*

I (don't) like ...	... dehn hohsh-lahn-(mah)-dihm	... 'den hoṣlan-(ma)dım.
art	sah-naht	*sanat*
basketball	bah-skeht-bohl	*basketbol*
football (soccer)	foot-bohl	*futbol*
cooking	pee-sheer-meh	*piṣirme*
dancing	dahns eht-meh	*dans etme*
film	see-neh-mah	*sinema*
going out	gehz-meh	*gezme*
music	myoo-zeek	*müzik*
photography	foh-toh-rahf-chih-lihk	*fotoğrafçılık*
reading	kee-tahp-lahr	*kitaplar*
	oh-koo-mah	*okuma*
shopping	ah-lihsh weh-reesh	*alış veriş*
skiing	skee	*ski*
surfing	serf	*sörf*
swimming	yooz-meh	*yüzme*
tennis	teh-nees	*tenis*
the theatre	tee-yah-troh	*tiyatro*
travelling	seh-yah-haht et-meh	*seyahat etme*
writing	yah-zih yahz-mah	*yazı yazma*

TURKISH

Festivals

Atatürk'ü Anma, Gençlik ve Spor Bayramı (19 May)
a festival with a combined purpose – to honour Atatürk, Modern Turkey's founder, and to celebrate youth and sport

Cumhuriyet Bayramı (29 October)
Turkish Republic Day Festival

Kurban Bayramı (Sacrifice Festival)
this festival occurs at a different time each year due to the difference between the Islamic and wester (Gregorian) calendars. Still, it always occurs two Islamic calendar months after *Ramazan*. This Festival has its origin in the biblical story of Abraham, Ishmael ('Isaac' in the Hebrew Bible) and the sacrificial lamb.

Ramazan Bayramı (also called *Şeker Bayramı)*
the 'sweets' festival marks the end of the Islamic fasting month of *Ramazan*. Like *Kurban*, *Ramazan* occurs at a different time each year, due to the difference between the Islamic and Gregorian calendars.

Ulusal Egemenlik ve Çocuk Bayramı (23 April)
National Independence and Children's Festival

Zafer Bayramı (Victory Festival, 30 August)
held to commemorate the Turkish War of Independence in 1922

Happy New Year!	ee-yee seh-neh-lehr!	*İyi Seneler!*
Enjoy the Festival!	ee-yee bahy-rahm-lahr!	*İyi Bayramlar!*
(said during the *Ramazan* and *Kurban* festivals)		

THEY MAY SAY ...

dih-shah-rih chih-kihp goo-zehl vah-keet geh-chee-reh-leem!

Let's go out and have a good time!

TURKISH

IN THE COUNTRY
Weather

What's the weather report?
  hah-vah rah-poh-roo nah-sihl?   *Hava raporu nasıl?*

The weather will be hot/cold.
  hah-vah sih-jahk/   *Hava sıcak/*
  soh-ook oh-lah-jahk   *soğuk olacak.*

It's going to rain/snow.
  yah-moor/kahr yah-ah-jahk   *Yağmur/kar yağacak.*

The weather's beautiful today!
  boo-goon hah-vah goo-zehl!   *Bugün hava güzel!*

cloudy	boo-loot-loo	*bulutlu*
extended summer	pahs-tihr-mah yah-zih	*pastırma yazı*
to freeze	dohn-mahk	*donmak*
ice	booz	*buz*
sun	goo-nesh	*güneş*
weather	hah-vah	*hava*
wind	rooz-gahr	*rüzgâr*

Camping

Is there somewhere to camp around here?
  boo-rah-lahr-dah beer kamp   *Buralarda bir kamp*
  yeh-ree vahr mih?   *yeri var mı?*

Can I/we camp here?
  boo-rah-dah kamp yah-pah-   *Burada kamp yapabilir*
  bee-leer mee-yeem/mee-yeez? *miyim/miyiz?*

Can you make a fire here?
  ah-tesh yahk-mahk   *Ateş yakmak*
  sehr-best mee?   *serbest mi?*

Where's the shower/toilet?
  doosh/too-wah-leht   *Duş/tuvalet*
  neh-reh-deh?   *nerede?*

campsite	kamp yeh-ree	*kamp yeri*
caravan (trailer)	kah-rah-vahn	*karavan*
tent	chah-dihr	*çadır*

FOOD

Turkish cuisine is based on vegetables, lamb and mutton. Beef and chicken are also readily available. Though strict Muslims don't touch pork, you can occasionally find pork products offered at the fancier city and resort restaurants.

Seafood is a Turkish specialty, and the Muslim prohibition against eating shellfish is ignored by many modern Turks. Fresh fruit and vegetables are a big part of the Turkish diet. In fact, the Turks have more than 40 ways of preparing eggplant – at least one of these is as a sweet dessert!

Bon apetit!	ah-fee-yeht ohl-soon!	*Afiyet olsun!*
breakfast	kah-vahl-tah	*kahvaltı*
lunch	ahk-shahm yeh-meh-ee	*öğle yemeği*
dinner	er-leh yeh-meh-ee	*akşam yemeği*

TURKISH

Vegetarian & Special Meals

Vegetarians should be aware that many Turkish soups and vegetable dishes are flavoured with small quantities of meat.

I can't eat ...	... yee-yeh-mee-yoh-room	... *yiyemiyorum.*
any meat	heech eht	*hiç et*
eggs	yoo-moor-tah	*yumurta*
spicy peppers	ah-jih bee-behr	*acı biber*

I only eat fruit and vegetables.
yahl-nihz mehy-veh veh   *Yalnız meyve ve sebze yiyorum.*
seb-zeh yee-yoh-room
I don't even eat meat juices.
eht soo-yoo bee-leh   *Et suyu bile yiyemiyorum.*
yee-yeh-mee-yoh-room
I eat chicken/fish.
tah-vook/bah-lihk   *Tavuk/balık yiyorum.*
yee-yoh-room

meatless dishes	eht-seez yeh-mehk-lehr	*etsiz yemekler*

TURKISH

Staple Foods & Condiments

brown lentils	merh-jee-mehk	mercimek
brown rice	ehs-mehr pee-reench	esmer pirinç
cinnamon	tahr-chihn	tarçın
fresh fish	tah-zeh bah-lihk	taze balık
fruit	mehy-vey	meyve
garlic	sah-rihm-sahk	sarımsak
gherkin	kohr-nee-shohn	kornişon
lamb	kuu-zuu	kuzu
mayonnaise	mah-yoh-nehs	mayonnes
mustard	hahr-dahl	hardal
olive oil	zehy-teen-yah-ih	zeytinyaği
salad	sah-lah-tah	salata
shish kebab	sheesh keh-bahp	şiş kebap
vegetables	sehb-zeh-lehr	sebzeler
yogurt	yoh-oort	yoğurt

PLACES TO EAT

aileye mahsustur	ahy-leh-yeh mah-soos-toor	a dining room reserved for couples and single women
büfe	boo-feh	a snack shop
fırın	fih-rihn	a bakery
kebapçı	keh-bahp-chih	a kebap (roast meat) shop
köfteci	kerf-teh-jee	a köfte (meatball) shop
lokanta	loh-kahn-tah	a simple restaurant with ready food
pastane	pahs-tah-neh	a pastry shop
pideci	pee-deh-jee	a Turkish-style pizza place
restoran	rehs-toh-rahn	fancier than a lokanta, usually serving alcohol

MENU DECODER

Soups

çorba	chohr-bah	soup
domates çorbasi	doh-mah-tehs chohr-bah-sih	tomato soup
düğün çorbasi	doo-oon chor-bah-sih chor-bah-sih	egg and lemon (wedding) soup
et suyu (yumurtali)	eht soo-yoo (yoo-moor-tah-lih)	mutton broth (with egg)
ezo gelin çorbasi	eh-zoh geh-leen chor-bah-sih	lentil and rice soup
işkembe çorbasi	eesh-kehm-beh chor-bah-sih	tripe soup
mercimek çorbasi	mehr-jee-mehk chor-bah-sih	lentil soup
paça	pah-chah	trotter soup
sebze çorbasi	sehb-zeh chor-bah-sih	vegetable soup
şehriye çorbasi	sheh-ree-yeh chor-bah-sih	vermicelli soup
tavuk çorbasi	tah-vook chor-bah-sih	chicken soup
yayla çorbasi	yay-lah chor-bah-sih	yogurt and barley soup

Kebabs

Kebap can refer to any roasted meat – generally lamb, mutton or chicken. Preparation, spices and extras like onions, peppers and *pide* (bread) make for the differences among *kebaps*. Meat may be served in chunks, or loaded onto a spit and roasted in front of a vertical grill, then sliced off. Or it may be ground and mixed with spices, then formed into meatballs and charcoal-grilled. Some *kebabs* can be ordered *yoğurtlu*, with a side-serving of yogurt.

adana kebap	ah-dah-nah keh-bahp	spicy-hot grilled *köfte*
bonfile	bohn-fee-leh	small fillet beefsteak
bursa kebap	boor-sah keh-bahp	*döner* with tomato sauce and browned butter
ciğer	jee-ehr	liver
dana rosto	dah-nah rohs-toh	roasted veal
döner kebap	der-nehr keh-bahp	slices of spit-roasted lamb

TURKISH

TURKISH

domuz eti	doh-mooz eh-tee	pork (forbidden to Muslims)
etli pide/etli ekmek	eht-lee pee-deh/ eht-lee ehk-mehk	flat bread topped with ground lamb and spices
güveç	gyoo-vech	meat and vegetable stew in a crock
karişik izgara	kah-rih-shihk ihz-gah-rah	mixed grill (lamb)
köfte	kerf-teh	grilled lamb meatballs with onion and spices
musakka	moo-sah-kah	eggplant and lamb pie
orman kebap	ohr-mahn keh-bahp	roasted lamb with onions
piliç kizartma	pee-leech kih-zahrt-mah	roasted chicken
pirzola	peer-zoh-lah	cutlet (usually lamb)
siğir eti	sih-ih eh-tee	beef
şiş kebap	sheesh keh-bahp	roasted lamb chunks on a skewer
tandir kebap	tahn-dihr keh-bahp	lamb roasted in an underground crock
tas kebap	tahs keh-bahp	lamb stew
tavuk	tah-vook	chicken

Appetisers

Meze (pronounced meh-zeh) – Turkey's answer to the Spanish tapas bar – serve drinks and small, delicious snacks. Turkish appetisers can include almost anything, and you can easily – and delightfully – make an entire meal of them. Often, you'll be brought a tray from which to choose from.

beyaz peynir	beh-yahz pehy-neer	sheep's milk cheese
börek	ber-rehk	flaky pastry filled with cheese or meat
cacik	jah-jihk	beaten yogurt with grated cucumber, garlic and mint
patlican salatasi	paht-lih-jahn sah-lah-tah-sih	eggplant puree

Salads & Vegetables

çoban salatasi	choh-bahn sah-lah-tah-sih	chopped tomato, cucumber and hot pepper
karişik salata	kah-rih-shihk sah-lah-tah	same as çoban salatasi
marul	mah-rool	lettuce
patlican salatasi	paht-lih-jahn sah-lah-tah-sih	roasted eggplant puree
söğüş	ser-oosh	sliced tomatoes and cucumbers
turşu	toor-shoo	pickled vegetables
yeşil salata	yeh-sheel sah-lah-tah	green salad
... dolma(si)	... dohl-mah(sih)	stuffed ...
kabak dolmasi	kah-bahk dohl-mah-sih	squash/marrow
lahana dolmasi	lah-hah-nah dohl-mah-sih	cabbage
yaprak dolmasi	yahp-rahk dohl-mah-sih	grape leaves

Desserts

Many Turkish baked desserts come swimming in sugar-syrup.
They're delicious, but very sweet.

baklava	bahk-lah-vah	flaky pastry with honey and nuts
dondurma	dohn-door-mah	ice cream
ekmek kadayif	ehk-mehk kah-dah-yihf	crumpet in syrup
firin sütlaç	fih-rihn soot-lahch	baked rice pudding (served cold)
komposto	kohm-pohs-toh	stewed fruit
krem	krehm	baked caramel
karamel	kah-rah-mehl	custard
pasta	pahs-tah	sweet pastry
sütlaç	sooot-lahch	rice pudding

Non-Alcoholic Drinks

The most popular drink in Turkey is certainly tea. If you want milk in your tea, you'll have to ask for it, causing neighbouring tea-drinkers to puzzle on the exotic preferences of foreigners.

A very popular alternative to regular tea is apple tea. In summer, try ayran, a tart, refreshing drink made by beating yogurt and mixing it with spring water and a little salt.

coffee	kah-veh	*kahve*
Turkish coffee	tooork kah-veh-see	*türk kahvesi*
without sugar	sah-deh	*sade*
with a little sugar	ahz	*az*
middling sweet	ohr-tah	*orta*
very sweet	chohk sheh-kehr-lee	*çok şekerli*
fruit juice	mehy-vah soo-yoo	*meyva suyu*
milk	sooot	*süt*
mineral water	soh-dah/mah-dehn	*soda/maden*
(carbonated)	soh-dah-sih	*sodası*
soft drink	mehsh-roo-baht	*meşrubat*
spring water	mehm-bah soo-yoo	*memba suyu*
(apple) tea	(ehl-mah) chahy	*(elma) çay*
water	dah-ha soo	*daha su*
yogurt drink	ahy-rahn	*ayran*

Alcoholic Drinks

Alcoholic drinks are usually referred to as *içki*. If a waiter says *İçecek?* or *Ne içeceksiniz?*, they're asking what you'd like to drink.

Alcohol is never served in traditional workers' restaurants, but in more upmarket restaurants a variety of beer and wine are served.

Cheers!	sah-lih-ih-nih-zah!	*Sağlığınıza!*
		(lit: to your (pl) health!)
In your honour!; To your health!		
	sheh-reh-fee-nee-zeh!	*Şerefinize!*

arrak (anise brandy)	rah-kih	*rakı*
light/dark beer	dee-eht/see-yahh	*diet/siyah*
	bee-rah	*bira*
rum	rohm	*rom*
whisky	wees-kee	*viski*
red/white wine	kihr-mih-zih/	*kırmızı/*
	beh-yahz shah-rahp	*beyaz şarap*
a small/big ...	beer koo-chook/	*bir küçük/*
	byoo-ook ...	*büyük ...*
bottle	shee-sheh	*şişe*
glass	bahr-dahk	*bardak*
jug	tehs-tee	*testi*

TURKISH

SHOPPING

barber	behr-behr	*berber*
bookshop	kee-tahp-chih	*kitapçı*
chemist (pharmacy)	ej-zah-neh	*eczane*
covered bazaar	kah-pah-lih chahr-shih	*kapalı çarşı*
market	mahr-keht	*market*
tailor	tehr-zee	*terzi*
shop	dook-kahn	*dükkan*
shopping district	ah-lish veh-reesh	*aliş veriş*
	mehr-keh-zee	*merkezi*
watch-repair shop	sah-aht-chee	*saatçi*

TURKISH

AT THE MARKET

Basics

bread	ehk-mehk	*ekmek*
butter	teh-reh-yah-ih	*tereyağı*
cereal	tah-hihl	*tahıl*
cheese	pehy-neer	*peynir*
chocolate	chee-koh-lah-tah	*çikolata*
eggs	yoo-moor-tah-lahr	*yumutalar*
flour	oon	*un*
honey	bahl	*bal*
margarine	mahr-ghah-reen	*margarin*
milk	soot	*süt*
mineral water	soh-dah/mah-dehn	*soda/maden*
olive oil	zehy-teen-yah-ih	*zeytinyağı*
rice	pee-reench	*pirin*
sugar	sheh-kehr	*şeker*
water	dah-ha soo	*daha su*
yogurt	yoh-oort	*yoğurt*

Meat & Poultry

beef	sih-ihr eh-tee	*sığır eti*
chicken	pee-leech	*piliç*
ham	zjahm-bohn	*jambon*
lamb	koo-zoo	*kuzu*
meat	eht	*et*
pork	doh-mooz eh-tee	*domuz eti*
salami	sah-lahm	*salam*
turkey	heen-dee	*hindi*
veal	dah-nah	*dana*

Vegetables

beans	fah-sool-yeh	*fasulye*
beetroot	pahn-jahr	*pancar*
cabbage	lah-hah-nah	*lahana*
capsicum	bee-behr	*biber*
carrot	hah-vooch	*havuç*
cauliflower	kahr-nah-bah-hahr	*karnabahar*
celery	sahp keh-reh-wee-zee	*sap kerevizi*
cucumber	sah-lah-tah-lihk	*salatalık*

AT THE MARKET

eggplant	paht-lih-jahn	*patlıcan*
garlic	sahr-mih-sahk	*sarmısak*
grapes	oo-zoom	*üzüm*
green beans	tah-zeh fah-sool-yeh	*taze fasulye*
leek	pih-rah-sah	*pırasa*
okra	bahm-yah	*bamya*
onions	soh-ahn	*soğan*
peas	beh-zehl-yeh	*bezelye*
potato	pah-tah-tehs	*patates*
spinach	ihs-pah-nahk	*ıspanak*
tomato	doh-mah-tehs	*domates*
vegetables	sehb-zeh-lehr	*sebzeler*
zucchini	sah-kihz-kah-bah-ih	*sakızkabağı*

Seafood

lobster	ihs-tah-kohz	*ıstakoz*
mussels	meed-yeh	*midye*
sardine	sahr-dahl-yah	*sardalya*
shrimp	kah-ree-dehs	*karides*
trout	ah-lah-bah-lihk	*alabalık*

Pulses

broad beans	bahk-lah	*bakla*
chickpeas	noh-hoot	*nohut*
kidney beans	bahr-boon-yah	*barbunya*

Fruit

apple	ehl-mah	*elma*
apricot	kah-yih-sih	*kayısı*
banana	mooz	*muz*
cherry	kee-rahz	*kiraz*
fig	een-jeer	*incir*
fruit	meh-weh	*meyve*
lemon	lee-mohn	*limon*
orange	pohr-tah-kahl	*portakal*
peach	shef-tah-lee	*şeftali*
pear	ahr-moot	*armut*
strawberries	chee-lehk	*çilek*
watermelon	kahr-pooz	*karpuz*

TURKISH

Essential Groceries

batteries	peel-lehr	*piller*
bottled water	shee-sheh-deh	*şişede*
	mem-bah soo-yoo	*memba suyu*
bread	ehk-mehk	*ekmek*
butter	teh-reh-ya-ih	*tereyağı*
cheese	pehy-neer	*peynir*
eggs	yoo-moor-tah-lahr	*yumurtalar*
flour	oon	*un*
gas cylinder	toop	*tüp*
ham	zhahm-bohn	*jambon*
honey	bahl	*bal*
matches	kee-breet	*kibrit*
milk	sooot	*süt*
pepper	bee-behr	*biber*
salt	tooz	*tuz*
soap	sah-boon	*sabun*
sugar	sheh-kehr	*şeker*
toilet paper	too-vah-leht kah-ih-dih	*tuvalet kağıdı*
toothpaste	deesh mah-joo-noo	*diş macunu*
washing detergent	deh-tehr-zhahn	*deterjan*

Souvenirs

carpet	hah-lih	*halı*
clothing	ehl-bee-seh/ghee-see	*elbise/giysi*
cloth	koo-mahsh	*kumaş*
handbag	chan-tah	*çanta*
jewellery	myoo-jehv-heh-raht	*mücevherat*
leather clothing	deh-ree ghee-yeem	*deri giyim*
old copperware	ehs-kee bah-kihr	*eski bakır*
porcelain	pohr-seh-lehn	*porselen*

Clothing

bag	chahn-tah	çanta
coat	pahl-toh	palto
dress	ehl-bee-seh	elbise
hat	shahp-kah	şapka
jeans	jeen	cin
jumper (sweater)	kah-zahk	kazak
scarves	eh-sharp-lahr	eşarplar
shirt	gherm-lehk	gömlek
shoes	ah-yah-kah-bih	ayakkabı
sunglasses	goo-nesh	güneş
	gerz-loo-oo	gözlülü
trousers	pahn-tah-lohn	pantolon
T-shirt	tee-sherrt	tişört

Materials

brass	toonch	tunç
copper	bah-kihr	bakır
gold	ahl-tihn	altın
leather	deh-ree	deri
silver	goo-moosh	gümüş
suede	soo-eht	süet

Colours

black	see-yahh	siyah
blue	mah-vee	mavi
brown	kah-veh-rehn-ghee	kahverengi
dark	koh-yoo	koyu
green	yeh-sheel	yeşil
light	ah-chihk	açık
orange	too-roon-joo	turuncu
pink	pehm-beh	pembe
red	kihr-mih-zih	kırmızı
white	beh-yahz	beyaz
yellow	sahr-rih	sarı

TURKISH

TURKISH

Toiletries

comb	tah-rahk	*tarak*
condom	preh-zehr-vah-teef	*prezervatif*
deodorant	deh-oh-doh-rahn	*deodoran*
moisturiser	ehl kreh-mee	*el kremi*
	lohs-yoh-noo	*losyonu*
mosquito repellent	see-vree-see-neh-eh	*sivrisineğe*
	kahr-shih ee-lahch	*karşı ilaç*
razor	oos-too-rah	*ustura*
sanitary napkins	hee-zheh-neek	*hijenik*
	kah-dihn bah-ih	*kadın bağı*
shampoo	sham-poo-ahn	*şampuan*
shaving cream	trahsh kreh-mee	*traş kremi*
sunscreen	goo-nesh ehn-geh-lee	*güneş*
		engeli
tampon	tahm-pohn	*tampon*
tissues	kah-iht mehn-dee-lee	*kağıt*
		mendili
toothbrush	deesh fihr-chah-sih	*diş fırçası*

Stationery & Publications

Do you sell ...?	... sah-tih-yohr moo-soon?	*... satıyor musun?*
dictionary	loo-gaht/serz-look	*lügat/sözlük*
envelopes	zahrf	*zarf*
English-language	een-gee-leez-jeh	*ingilizce bir*
newspaper	beer gah-zeh-teh	*gazete*
magazine	mej-moo-ah	*mecmua*
news stand	gah-zeh-teh	*gazete*
	koo-loo-beh-see	*kulübesi*
notebook	dehf-tehr	*defter*
paper	kah-iht	*kağıt*
pen	too-kehn-mehz	*tükenmez*
postcard	kahrt-pohs-tahl	*kartpostal*

Photography

How much would it cost
to print this film?
boo feel-mee bahs-tihr-mahk
kahch lee-rah?

*Bu filmi bastırmak
kaç lira?*

When will it be ready?
neh zah-mahn hah-zihr
oh-loor?

*Ne zaman hazır
olur?*

I'd like a film for this camera.
boo kah-meh-rah ee-cheen
fee-leem ees-tee-yoh-room

*Bu kamera için
filim istiyorum.*

battery	peel	*pil*
film	fee-leem	*filim*
flash	fee-lahsh	*filaş*
photo	foh-toh	*foto*
slide	slahyt	*slayt*
36-exposure	oh-tooz ahl-tih	*otuz altı*
	pohz-look	*pozluk*

TURKISH

Smoking

A packet of cigarettes, please.
beer pah-keht see-gah-rah,
loot-fehn

*Bir paket sigara,
lütfen.*

Are these cigarettes strong or mild?
boo see-gah-rah sehrt mee,
hah-feef mee?

*Bu sigara sert mi,
hafif mi?*

Do you have a light?
ah-teh-shee-neez vahr mih?

Ateşiniz var mı?

cigarettes	see-gah-rah-lahr	*sigaralar*
cigarette papers	see-gah-rah	*sigara*
	kah-ihd-lah-rih	*kağıdları*
filtered	feel-treh-lee see-gah-rah	*filtreli sigara*
lighter	chahk-mahk	*çakmak*
matches	kee-breet-lehr	*kibritler*
pipe	pee-poh	*pipo*
tobacco	too-toon	*tütün*

Sizes & Comparisons

also	dah-hee/beer deh	*dahi/bir de*
big	byoo-ook	*büyük*
enough	yeh-tehr-lee/kah-fee	*yeterli/kafi*
heavy	ah-ihr	*ağır*
light	hah-feef	*hafif*
little (amount)	ahz/bee-rahz	*az/biraz*
a little bit	koo-chook meek-tahr/ ah-zih-jihk	*küçük miktar/ azıcık*
many	chohk	*çok*
more	dah-hah	*daha*
small	koo-chook/oo-fahk	*küçük/ufak*
too much/many	fahz-lah	*fazla*

HEALTH
Parts of the Body

It hurts here.	boo-rah-sih ah-jih-yohr	*Burası acıyor.*
arm	koh-loom	*kolum*
back	sihr-tihm	*sırtım*
breast	meh-mehm	*memem*
chest	ger-ooo-sooom	*göğüsüm*
ear	koo-lah-ihm	*kulağım*
eye	ger-zoom	*gözüm*
finger	pahr-mah-ihm	*parmağım*
foot	ah-yah-ihm	*ayağım*
hand	eh-leem	*elim*
head	bah-shihm	*başım*
knee (cap)	deez (kah-pah-ih)	*diz (kapağı)*
leg	bah-jaah-ihm	*bacağım*
mouth	ah-ihz	*ağtz*
neck	bohy-noom	*boynum*
nose	boor-noom	*burnum*
stomach	kahr-nihm	*karnım*
throat	boh-ah-zihm	*boğazım*
tooth	dee-sheem	*dişim*

Ailments

My head's spinning./I'm dizzy.
    bah-shihm der-noo-yohr   *Başım dönüyor.*
I'm going to vomit.
    koo-sah-jah-ihm geh-lee-yohr   *Kusacağım geliyor.*

I have (a) ...	... vahr	... var.
cold	nehz-lehm	*nezlem*
constipation	ka-bihz-lih-ihm	*kabızlığım*
cough	erk-soo-roo-oom	*öksürüğüm*
diarrhoea	ees-hah-leem	*ishalim*
fever	ah-tehsh	*ateş*
hayfever	bah-hahr ah-lehr-zjee-see	*bahar alerjisi*
headache	bahsh ah-rihm	*baş ağrım*
pain	beer aah-rihm	*bir ağrım*
rash	der-koon-too	*döküntü*
stomachache	mee-deh ah-rihm	*mide ağrım*
sunburn	goo-nesh yah-nih-ih	*güneş yanığı*
venereal disease	zooh-reh-vee hah-stah-lihk	*zührevi hastalık*

TURKISH

At the Chemist

How many times a day?
    goon-deh kahch deh-fah?   *Günde kaç defa?*
Are there side effects?
    yahn eht-kee-see vahr mih?   *Yan etkisi var mı?*

antiseptic	ahn-tee-sehp-teek	*antiseptik*
aspirin	ahs-pee-reen	*aspirin*
bandage	sahr-gih	*sargı*
contraceptives	geh-beh-lee-ee ern-leh-yee-jee kohn-sehr-wah-teef	*gebelili önleyici konservatif*
laxatives	lahk-sah-teef	*laxsatif*
sleeping tablet	ooy-koo hah-pih	*uyku hapı*
sticking plaster	tihb-bee fih-lahs-tehr	*tıbbi filaster*

At the Dentist

I have a toothache.
dee-sheem ah-rih-yohr
Dişim ağrıyor.

I've lost a filling.
dohl-goom doosh-too
Dolgum düştü.

My gums hurt.
deesh eht-leh-reem
ah-rih-yohr
Diş etlerim ağrıyor.

Please give me an anaesthetic.
loot-fehn nahr-kohz
veh-reen
Lütfen narkoz verin.

TIME & DATES
Days

Monday	pah-zahr-teh-see	*pazartesi*
Tuesday	sah-lih	*salı*
Wednesday	chahr-shahm-bah	*çarşamba*
Thursday	pehr-shehm-beh	*perşembe*
Friday	joo-mah	*cuma*
Saturday	joo-mahr-teh-see	*cumartesi*
Sunday	pah-zahr	*pazar*

Months

January	oh-jahk	*ocak*
February	shoo-baht	*şubat*
March	mahrt	*mart*
April	nee-sahn	*nisan*
May	mah-yihs	*mayıs*
June	hah-zee-rahn	*haziran*
July	tehm-mooz	*temmuz*
August	ah-oos-tohs	*ağustos*
September	ehy-lool	*eylül*
October	eh-keem	*ekim*
November	kah-sihm	*kasım*
December	ah-rah-lihk	*aralık*

TURKISH

Seasons

spring	eelk-bah-hahr	*ilkbahar*
summer	yahz	*yaz*
autumn	sohn bah-hahr	*son bahar*
winter	kihsh	*kış*

Present

now	sheem-dee	*şimdi*
today	boo-goon	*bugün*
this week/month	boo hahf-tah/ahy	*bu hafta/ay*
early/late	ehr-kehn/gehch	*erken/geç*
in the morning	sah-bah-leh-yeen	*sabahleyin*
in the afternoon	er-leh-dehn sohn-rah	*öğleden sonra*
in the evening	ahk-shahm-dah	*akşamda*
at night	geh-jeh-leh-yeen	*geceleyin*

TURKISH

Past

(nine) hours	(doh-kooz)	*(dokuz)*
later	sah-aht-tahn sohn-rah	*saattan sonra*
yesterday	doon	*dün*
last week/month	geh-chen hahf-tah/ahy	*geçen hafta/ay*

Future

right away	heh-mehn	*hemen*
soon	yah-kihn-dah	*yakında*
tomorrow	yah-rihn	*yarın*
next week/	geh-leh-jehk	*gelecek*
month	hahf-tah/ahy	*hafta/ay*

During the Day

morning	sah-bah	*sabah*
afternoon	er-leh-dehn sohn-rah	*öğleden sonra*
evening	ahk-shahm	*akşam*
night	geh-jeh	*gece*
second	sah-nee-yeh	*saniye*
minute	dah-kee-kah/dahk-kah	*dakika/dakka*
hour	sah-aht	*saat*

NUMBERS & AMOUNTS

1	beer	*bir*	30	oh-tooz	*otuz*
2	ee-kee	*iki*	40	kihrk	*kırk*
3	oooch	*üç*	50	ehl-lee	*elli*
4	derrt	*dört*	60	ahlt-mihsh	*altmış*
5	besh	*beş*	70	yeht-meesh	*yetmiş*
6	ahl-tih	*altı*	80	sek-sehn	*seksen*
7	yeh-dee	*yedi*	90	dohk-sahn	*doksan*
8	seh-keez	*sekiz*	100	yooz	*yüz*
9	doh-kooz	*dokuz*	101	yooz beer	*yüz bir*
10	ohn	*on*	200	ee-kee yooz	*iki yüz*
11	ohn beer	*on bir*	1000	been	*bin*
12	ohn ee-kee	*on iki*	2000	ee-kee been	*iki bin*
13	ohn oooch	*on üç*	10,000	ohn been	*on bin*
20	yeer-mee	*yirmi*	a million	meel-yohn	*milyon*

ABBREVIATIONS

DDY	*Devlet Demiryolları*	Turkish state railway (same as TCDD)
PTT	*Posta, Telefon, Telğraf*	post, telephone & telegraph office
TCDD	*Türkiye Cumhuriyeti Devlet Demiryolları*	Turkish state railway (same as DDY)
TEM		Trans-European motorway
THY	*Türk Hava Yolları*	Turkish Airlines

EMERGENCIES

Help!	eem-daht!	*İmdat!*
Watch out!	deek-kaht!	*Dikkat!*
Thief!	hihr-sihz!	*Hırsız!*
Stop!	door!	*Dur!*
Go away!	gheet!	*Git!*
It's an emergency.	ah-jeel doo-room	*Acil durum.*
Fire!	yahn-gihn vahr!	*Yangın var!*

There's been an accident!
beer kah-zah ohl-doo!   *Bir kaza oldu!*

Call a(n) ...!	beer ... chah-ih-rihn!	*Bir ... çağırın!*
ambulance	ahm-boo-lahns	*ambulans*
doctor	dohk-tohr	*doktor*

Call the police!
poh-lees-seh
hah-behr veh-reen!   *Polise haber verin!*

Where's the police station?
poh-lees kah-rah-koh-loo
neh-reh-deh?   *Polis karakolu nerede?*

Could I please use the telephone?
teh-leh-foh-noo
kool-lah-nah-bee-leer
mee-yeem loot-fehn?   *Telefonu kullanabilir miyim lütfen?*

I've been raped/assaulted.
teh-jah-voo-zeh/
sahl-dih-rih-yah oo-rah-dihm   *Tecavüze/ Saldırıya uğradım.*

I've been robbed.
soh-yool-doom   *Soyuldum.*

I'm ill.
rah-haht-sih-zihm   *Rahatsızım.*

I have medical insurance.
sah-lihk see-gohr-tahm vahr   *Sağlık sigortam var.*

Where are the toilets?
too-wah-leht neh-reh-deh?   *Tuvalet nerede?*

TURKISH

Dealing with the Police

We want to report an offence.
sooch eeh-bahr eht-mehk	*Suç ihbar etmek*
ees-tee-yoh-rooz	*istiyoruz.*

My ... was/	beh-neem	*Benim*
were stolen.	... chah-lihn-dih	*... çalındı.*
backpack	sihrt chahn-tahm	*sırt çantam*
bags	bah-gah-zhihm	*bagajım*
camera	kah-meh-rahm	*kameram*
handbag	ehl chahn-tahm	*el çantam*
money	pah-rahm	*param*
travellers cheques	seh-yah-haht	*seyahat*
	chehk-leh-reem	*çeklerim*
passport	pah-sah-pohr-toom	*pasaportum*
wallet	jooz-dah-nihm	*cüzdanım*

I apologise.	er-zoor dee-leh-reem	*Özür dilerim.*

Can I call someone?
bee-ree-see-nee ah-rah-	*Birisini arayabilir*
yah-bee-leer mee-yeem?	*miyim?*

I want to contact my
embassy/consulate.
ehl-chee-lee-eem-leh/	*Elçiliğimle/*
kohn-soh-lohs-loo-oom-lah	*Konsolosluğumla*
teh-mah-sah gehch-mehk	*temasa geçmek*
ees-tee-yoh-room	*istiyorum.*

TURKISH

WELSH

QUICK REFERENCE

Hello.	shoo *mai*	Sut mae.
Goodbye.	hoo-eel *vowrr*	Hwyl fawr.
How are you?	sit *uh*-deekh khee?	Sut ydych chi?
(Very) well.	(dah) *yown*	(Da) iawn.
Yes./No.	oys/*nag* oys	Oes./Nac oes.
Excuse me.	ess-gi-*so*-dookh vee	Esgusodwch fi.
May I?	gah ee?	Ga i?
Please.	os *gwel*-ookh uhn thah	Os gwelwch yn dda
Thank you.	dee-*olkh*	Diolch.
You're welcome.	*krroy*-soh	Croeso.
Sorry.	main *thrroog* *guh*-da vee	Mae'n ddrwg gyda fi.
I'd like a (half) pint of ...	gah ee (*hann*-err oh) *baynt* oh ...	Ga i (hanner o) beint o ...
bitter	*khwe*-rroo	chwerw
cider	*say*-dirr	seidr
lager	*la*-gerr	lager

What's your name?
behth yoo uhkh *en*-oo khee?
Beth yw eich enw chi?

My name's ...
ne-noo ee *yoo* ...
Fy enw i yw ...

I'd like to introduce you to ...
gah ee guh-*vloo-ee*-noh ... ee khee
Ga i gyflwyno ... i chi.

Pleased to meet you.
main *thah* gen ee goorrth ah khee
Mae'n dda gen i gwrdd â chi.

0	dim	*dim*	5	pimp	*pump*
1	een	*un*	6	khwehkh	*chwech*
2	dai/doo-ee	*dau/dwy*	7	saith	*saith*
3	trree/tairr	*tri/tair*	8	oo-eeth	*wyth*
4	*ped*-wahrr/ *ped*-airr	*pedwar/ pedair*	9	now	*naw*
			10	dehg	*deg*

WELSH

WELSH

The Welsh language, *Gymraeg*, belongs to the Celtic branch of the Indo-European language family. Closely related to Breton and Cornish, and more distantly to Irish, Scottish and Manx, it is the strongest Celtic language both in terms of numbers of speakers (over 500,000) and place in society. It was once spoken throughout the island of Britain, south of a line between modern Glasgow and Edinburgh, but was gradually pushed westwards by the invading Angles and Saxons following the retreat of the Roman legions in the 5th century. Several thousand Welsh-speakers also live in the Welsh colony in Patagonia. Its earliest literature was written towards the end of the 6th century in what is now southern Scotland, when court poets Taliesin and Aneurin pioneered a literary tradition which continued for some 14 centuries.

By the early modern period, Welsh had lost its status as an official language. The Acts of Union with England (1536 and 1542) deprived the language of all administrative functions. However, translations of the *Book of Common Prayer* (1567) and the Bible (1588) into Welsh gave the language a renewed but limited public function. Up until the industrial revolution, most Welsh people spoke only Welsh, and some 50 percent still spoke Welsh in 1900. Thereafter the language retreated more rapidly, so that by 1961, only 26 percent were Welsh-speaking and there was general alarm that the language would disappear.

The Saunders Lewis lecture, *Tynged yr Iaith*, 'The Fate of the Language', in 1962 led to the creation of *Cymdeithas yr Iaith Gymraeg*, a protest movement in support of the language. It was spearheaded by university students and inspired by pop singers like Dafydd Iwan, and succeeded through campaigns of civil disobedience in winning equal recognition for Welsh in one domain of society after another. It now appears that the decline has been halted: the language is again part of the educational system; there's a Welsh-language TV channel; and in recent years the language has become a badge of national identity, particularly among the young.

PRONUNCIATION

All letters in Welsh are pronounced, and stress is usually placed on the second-last syllable.

Vowels

Vowels can be either long or short. Those marked with a circumflex (^) are always long and those with a grave accent (`) are short.

In words of one syllable, vowels that are followed by two consonants (remember that *ch, dd, ff, ng, ll, ph, rh,* and *th* count as single consonants in Welsh) are short:

| body | **korrf** | *corff* |

If a one-syllable word ends in *p, t, c, m* or *ng,* the vowel is short:

| ship | **hlong** | *llong* |

If it ends in one consonant which is *b, d, g, f, dd, ff, th, ch* or *s,* the vowel is long, as is any vowel ending a one-syllable word:

| boat | **bahd** | *bad* |
| plague | **plah** | *pla* |

In words of more than one syllable, all unstressed vowels are short. Stressed vowels can be long or short and in general follow the rules for vowels in monosyllables.

Short Vowels

a	a	as the 'a' in 'bat'
e	e	as the 'e' in 'bed'
i	i	as the 'i' in 'sin'
o	o	as the 'o' in 'hot'
u	i	as the 'i' in 'sin';
w	oo	short as the 'oo' in 'book'
y	i	short as the 'i' in 'sin';
	uh	sometimes as the 'u' in 'nut'

WELSH

Long Vowels

a	ah	as the 'a' in 'margin'
e	eh	as the 'ea' in 'pear';
	ee	as the 'ee' in 'see'
o	oh	as 'o' in 'bore'
u	ee	long as the 'ee' in 'meet'
w	oo	long as the 'oo' in 'spook'
y	ee	long as the 'ee' in 'see';
		sometimes as the 'a' in 'about', especially in common one-syllable words like *y*, *yr*, *fy*, *dy* and *yn*

Vowel Combinations

ae/ai/au	ai	as the 'y' in 'my'
aw	ow	as the 'ow' in 'cow'
ei/eu/ey	ay	as the 'ay' in 'day'
ew	e-oo	as short 'e' + the 'oo' in 'too'
iw/uw/yw	yoo	as the 'ew' in 'few'
oe/oi	oy	as 'oy' in 'boy'
ow	oe	as the 'ow' in 'row'
wy	oo-ee	as 'uey' as in 'chop suey'

WELSH

PRONOUNS					
SG			**PL**		
I	mi/fi	mee/vee	we	ni	nee
you (inf)	ti/di	tee/dee	you	chi	khee
you (pol)	chi	khee	they	nhw	noo
he	ef	ehv			
she	hi	hee			

Consonants

The consonants *ch*, *dd*, *ff*, *ng*, *ll*, *ph*, *rh* and *th* count as single consonants. Letters not described here are pronounced as in English.

c	k	as the 'c' in 'cat'; never as the 'c' in 'celery'
ch	kh	as the 'ch' in Scottish 'loch'
dd	th	as the 'th' in 'then'
f	v	as the 'v' in 'velvet'
ff	f	as the 'f' in 'fun'
g	g	gas the 'g' in 'game'; never as the 'g' in 'gentle'
ng	ng	as the 'ng' in 'sing'
ll	hl	as an aspirated 'l' – put the tongue in the position for 'l' and breathe out
ph	f	as the 'f' in 'fun'
r	rr	trilled
rh	hr	pronounced as 'hr'
s	ss	as the 's' in 'sin'; never as the 's' in 'busy' or in 'pleasure'
si	sh	as the 'sh' in 'shop'
th	th	as the 'th' in 'thin'

SOUND CHANGES

Sometimes the initial consonant of a word changes its sound to convey grammatical meaning. The consonant may change to become softer, nasal or aspirated.

GREETINGS & CIVILITIES
You Should Know

Hello.	shoo *mai*	Sut mae.
Good morning.	bo-rre *dah*	Bore da.
Good afternoon.	pruhn-*hown dah*	Prynhawn da.
Good evening.	noss-waith *thah*	Noswaith dda.
Goodbye.	hoo-eel *vowrr*	Hwyl fawr.
Goodnight.	nohss *dah*	Nos da.
See you (later).	*wel*-ah ee khee (*we*-din)	Wela i chi (wedyn).

WELSH

How are you?	sit *uh*-deekh khee?	Sut ydych chi?
(Very) well.	(dah) *yown*	(Da) iawn.
Yes./No.	oys/*nag* oys	Oes./Nac oes.
Excuse me.	ess-gi-*so*-dookh vee	Esgusodwch fi.
May I?	gah ee?	Ga i?
Please.	os *gwel*-ookh uhn thah	Os gwelwch yn dda.
Thank you.	dee-*olkh*	Diolch.
You're welcome.	*krroy*-soh	Croeso.
Don't mention it.	*pay*-dyookh ah *sohn*	Peidiwch â sôn.
Sorry.	main *thrroog* guh-da vee	Mae'n ddrwg gyda fi.

SMALL TALK
Meeting People

What's your name?
    behth yoo uhkh *en*-oo khee?   *Beth yw eich enw chi?*

My name's ...
    ne-noo ee *yoo* ...   *Fy enw i yw ...*

I'd like to introduce you to ...
    gah ee guh-*vloo-ee*-noh ... ee khee   *Ga i gyflwyno ... i chi.*

Pleased to meet you.
    main *thah* gen ee goorrth ah khee   *Mae'n dda gen i gwrdd â chi.*

Where do you live?
    bleh *uh*-deekh kheen *byoo*?   *Ble ydych chi'n byw?*

I live in (Darwin).
    doo een *byoo* uhn (Darwin)   *Dw i'n byw yn (Darwin).*

I don't understand.
    doo ee *thim* uhn *deh*-ahll   *Dw i ddim in deall.*

I don't know.
    oon ee *thim*   *Wn i ddim.*

WELSH

WELSH

Nationalities

Where are you from?	oh *ble uh*-deekh kheen *dohd*?	O ble ydych chi'n dod?
I'm from ...	doo een *dohd* oh ...	Dw i'n dod o ...
Australia	ow-*strra*-lee-ah	Awstralia
Canada	*gah*-nah-dah	Ganada
England	*loy*-gerr	Loegr
Ireland	ee-*werr*-thon	Iwerddon
New Zealand	se-land *neh*-with	Seland Newydd
Scotland	uhrr *al*-ban	Yr Alban
the USA	uhrr *in*-ol dah-*lay*-thee-ai	Yr Unol Daleithiau
Wales	*kuhm*-rri	Cymru

Occupations

What do you do?	behth *uh*-deekh kheen *nayd*?	Beth ydych chi'n wneud?
I'm (a/an) ...	doo een ...	Dw i'n ...
artist	arr-*lin*-ith	arlunydd
business person	ber-sson *biss*-ness	berson busnes
doctor	*veth*-ig	feddy
engineer	bayrr-*yan*-eeth	beiriannydd
musician	gerr-thorr	gerddor
nurse	nurrse	nyrs
office worker	gway-thyo meh-oon soo-*eeth*-vah	gweithio mewn swyddfa
retired	we-dee uhm-*theh*-ol	wedi ymddeol
scientist	wi-*thon*-eeth	wyddonydd
teacher (m)	ah-thrroh	athro
teacher (f)	ah-*thrrow*-ess	athrawes
unemployed	uhn *thee* waith	yn ddi-waith
waiter	*way*-neeth	weinydd

Religion

What's your religion?
pah *grreh*-vith *uh*-deekh khee?   *Pa grefydd ydych chi?*

I'm not religious.
doo i *thim* uhn grreh-*vuh*-thol   *Dw i ddim yn grefyddol.*

I'm a(n) ...	doo een ...	Dw i'n ...
atheist	an-*fuh*-thyoorr	*Anffyddiwr*
Buddhist	voo-deeth	*Fwdydd*
Catholic	*bah*-beeth	*Babydd*
Christian	*grrist*-yon	*Gristion*
Hindu	*hin*-doo	*Hind*
Muslim	*vooss*-lim	*Fwslim*
pagan	*ba*-gan	*Bagan*
Sikh	seek	*Sîc*

Family

Do you have a partner?
oyss *parrt*-nerr *gen*-eekh khee?   *Oes partner gennych chi?*

Do you have a girlfriend/boyfriend?
oyss *karr*-yad *gen*-eekh khee?   *Oes cariad gennych chi?*

How many children do you have?
vaint oh *blant* see   *Faint o blant sy*
gen-eekh khee?   *gennych chi?*

I'm ...	doo een ...	Dw i'n ...
married	*brree*-od	*briod*
separated	doo ee we-dee	*dw i wedi*
	gwa-*han*-ee	*gwahanu*
single	*seng*-el	*sengl*
a widow	*oorraig weth*-oo	*wraig weddw*
a widower	oorr *gweth*-oo	*ŵr gweddw*

AROUND TOWN
Placenames

The Welsh and English names of a town can be quite different.

Holyhead	*Caergybi*	kairr-*guh*-bee
Newport	*Casnewydd*	kass-*ne*-with
Swansea	*Abertawe*	ab-err-*tow*-eh

Placenames are often built on words that describe a feature of the countryside.

aber	*ab*-berr	estuary/confluence
afon	*a*-von	river
bach	bahkh	small
bro	broh	vale
bryn	brrin	hill
caer	kairr	fort
cwm	koom	valley
dinas	*dee*-nass	hill fortress
eglwys	*eg*-loo-eess	church
fach	vahkh	small
fawr	vowrr	big
isa	*iss*-a	lower
llan	hlan	church/enclosure
llyn	hlin	lake
maes	maiss	field
mawr	mowrr	big
mynydd	*muh*-neeth	mountain
pen	pen	head/top/end
uchaf	*ikh*-av	upper
ynys	*uh*-niss	island/watermeadow

WELSH

INTERESTS & ENTERTAINMENT

What do you do in your spare time?
behth *uh*-deekh kheen *nayd* uhn uhkh *am*-sserr *ham*-then?	Beth ydych chi'n wneud yn eich amser hamdden?

Do you like sport?
uh-deekh kheen *hof*-ee khwa-*rray*-on?	Ydych chi'n hoffi chwaraeon?

Yes, very much.
uh-*doo*, uhn *vowrr yown*	Ydw, yn fawr iawn.

No, not at all.
nag uh-doo, *dim* oh goo-*bool*	Nac ydw, dim o gwbl.

Sightseeing

What are the main attractions?
behth yoorr *prreev* a-tuhn-*ya*-dai?	Beth yw'r prif atyniadau?

ancient	huh-*nav*-ol	*hynafol*
archaeological	ar-khay-o-*le*-gol	*archaeolegol*
beach	trraith	*traeth*
building	a-*day*-lad	*adeilad*
castle	*kah*-stelh	*castell*
cathedral	eg-*loo*-eess gah-*dayrr*-yol	*eglwys gadeiriol*
chapel	*kah*-pel	*capel*
church	eg-*loo*-eess	*eglwys*
concert hall	*nay*-ath guhng-*herr*-thai	*neuadd gyngherddau*
library	*hluh*-vuhrr-gehl	*llyfrgell*
monastery	muhn-*akh*-lohg	*mynachlog*
monument	kohv-*gol*-ovon	*cofgolofn*
opera house	tee *op*-err-ah	*t opera*
palace	*pah*-lass	*palas*
ruins	ad-*vayl*-yon	*adfeilion*
statue	*del*-wai	*delwau*
tower	translit	*twr*
university	prreev-*uhss*-gol	*prifysgol*

WELSH

Going Out

What are you doing
this evening?

    behth *uh*-deekh kheen
    nayd *hen*-oh?
        *Beth ydych chi'n
        wneud heno?*

Nothing special.

    dim beed arr-*ben*-ig
        Dim byd arbennig.

I feel like going to ...

    mai gen ee *ow*-eeth
    mind ee ...
        *Mae gen i awydd
        mynd i ...*

Would you like to go out for
a (drink/meal)?

    ho-fekh khee vind *ahl*-an
    am (*thee*-od/brreed oh
    voo-eed)?
        *Hoffech chi fynd allan
        am (ddiod/bryd o
        fwyd)?*

Yes, that'd be great.

    oyss, *buh*-dheh *huh*-neen
    weekh
        *Oes, byddai hynny'n
        wych.*

I'm sorry, I can't.

    main *thrroog* gen ee,
    ahl-ah ee thim
        *Mae'n ddrwg gen i,
        alla i ddim.*

I'll buy.	veh *dah*-lah *ee*	*Fe dala i.*
OK.	iown	*Iawn.*

SIGNS

ALLANFA	EXIT
AR AGOR	OPEN
AR GAU	CLOSED
DIM MYNEDIAD	NO ENTRY
DYNION	MEN
HEDDLU	POLICE
MERCHED	WOMEN
MYNEDFA	ENTRANCE

Arranging to Meet

What time shall we meet?
    am *vaint* ohrr *glokh* wnown   Am faint o'r gloch wnawn
    nee guh-*vahrr*-vod?   ni gyfarfod?
Where shall we meet?
    bleh wnown nee   Ble wnawn ni
    guh-*vahrr*-vod?   gyfarfod?
Let's meet at (eight o'clock)
in St Mary Street.
    behth am guh-*vahrr*-vod   Beth am gyfarfod
    am (*oo-eeth* ohrr *glokh*) uhn   am (wyth o'r gloch) yn
    heh-ool uh *sant*-ess *vairr*   Heol y Santes Fair.
OK. I'll see you then.
    yown *we*-lah ee khee   Iawn. Wela i chi
    brreed huh-nee   bryd hynny.

Afterwards

It was nice talking to you.
    rroyth heen *brrahv*   Roedd hi'n braf
    sha-rrad ah khee   siarad â chi.
I have to get going now.
    hrraid *i*-mee *vind* nowrr   Rhaid imi fynd nawr.
I had a great day/evening.
    kehss ee thee-*yoorr*-nod   Ces i ddiwrnod gwych/
    gweekh/*noss*-on *weekh*   noson wych.
Hope to see you again soon.
    go-*bay*-thyo uhkh *gweld*   Gobeithio eich gweld
    khee *eh*-toh uhn *vee*-an   chi eto yn fuan.

WELSH

Festivals

Wales holds many local, regional and national competitive arts festivals, called *eisteddfodau*, where people compete in literary, music and art competitions. The old traditions of folk poets competing in *ymryson y beirdd*, traditional Welsh meter, and *cerdd dant*, the setting of poetry to harp music, are still very much alive.

Dydd Calan   deeth *ka*-lan
New Year's Day. Traditionally, children would go from house-to-house singing special new year songs and asking for a gift.

Dydd Gwyl Dewi   deeth goo-eel *de*-wee
St David's Day, 1 March. St David is the patron saint of Wales.

Eisteddfod Genedlaethol   ay-*steth*-vod gen-ed-*lay*-thol
competitive arts festival held in the first week of August

Santes Dwynwen   *sant*-ess *doo-een*-wen
St Dwynwen is the Welsh patron saint of lovers and her feast-day is on 25 January.

WEATHER

What's the weather like?
shoot *behh* yoorr *tuh*-with?   Sut beth yw'r tywydd?
Will it stop raining?
veeth uh glow uhn *pay*-dyoh?   Fydd y glaw yn peidio?
Will it snow?
veeth heen *boo*-rroo *ay*-rrah?   Fydd hi'n bwrw eira?

The weather's ...	mai heen ...	Mae hi'n ...
today.	*heh*-thyoo	heddiw.
Will it be ...	veeth heen ...	Fydd hi'n ...
tomorrow?	uh-*vorr*-ee?	yfory?
cloudy	guh-*muh*-log	gymylog
cold	oyrr	oer
fine	brrahv	braf
foggy	nyoo-log	niwlog
hot	boyth	boeth
windy	win-tog	wyntog

WELSH

FOOD
Traditional Dishes

bara brith *bah-*rra *brreeth*
rich, fruited tea-loaf

bara lawr *bah-*rra *lowrr*
laver seaweed boiled and mixed with oatmeal and
traditionally served with bacon for breakfast

cawl cowl
broth of meat and vegetables

caws caerffili cows kairr-*fil*-ee
Caerphilly cheese, a crumbly, salty cheese that used to be
popular with miners

ffagots a pys *fa*-gots a *peess*
seasoned balls of chopped pork and liver in gravy served
with peas

lobsgows lobs-*goess*
a Northwalian version of *cawl*

pice ar y maen *pi*-keh arr uh *mahn*
(lit: cakes on the griddlestone) small, scone-like griddle cakes
containing fruit, known also as 'Welsh cakes'

WELSH

Drinks

I'd like a (half)	gah ee (*hann*-err	*Ga i (hanner o)*
pint of ...	oh) *baynt* oh ...	*beint o ...*
bitter	*khwe*-rroo	*chwerw*
cider	*say*-dirr	*seidr*
lager	*la*-gerr	*lager*
orange juice	*seeth oh*-ren	*sudd oren*
water	doorr	*dŵr*

TIME & DATES
Days

Monday	deeth *hleen*	dydd Llun
Tuesday	deeth *mowrrth*	dydd Mawrth
Wednesday	deeth *merr*-kherr	dydd Mercher
Thursday	deeth *yai*	dydd Iau
Friday	deeth *gwen*-err	dydd Gwener
Saturday	deeth *sad*-oorrn	dydd Sadwrn
Sunday	deeth *seel*	dydd Sul

Months

Some names for months are borrowed from Latin. Others are native Welsh.

January	*yon*-owrr	Ionawr
February	*khwe*-vrrohrr	Chwefror
March	mowrrth	Mawrth
April	*eh*-brrihl	Ebrill
May	mai	Mai
June	me-*he*-vin	Mehefin (lit: middle of summer)
July	gorr-*fen*-ahv	Gorffennaf (lit: end of summer)
August	owst	Awst
September	*med*-dee	Medi (lit: reaping)
October	huh-drrev	Hydref (the rutting season, lit: stag-roaring)
November	*tahkh*-weth	Tachwedd (the time for slaughtering animals before winter, lit: slaughter)
December	*hrrag*-virr	Rhagfyr (the shortest day, lit: before short)

WELSH

NUMBERS

0	dim	*dim*
1	een	*un*
2	dai/doo-ee	*dau/dwy*
3	trree/tairr	*tri/tair*
4	*ped*-wahrr/*ped*-airr	*pedwar/pedair*
5	pimp	*pump*
6	khwehkh	*chwech*
7	saith	*saith*
8	oo-eeth	*wyth*
9	now	*naw*
10	dehg	*deg*

The Celts used to count in twenties, and this ancient way of counting is still used in Welsh and Gaelic today. This system, known as the 'vegisimal' system, is also used by the French, who inherited it from the Gauls.

	VEGISIMAL SYSTEM	DECIMAL SYSTEM
11	*een*-ahrr-thehg	een dehg-*een*
	unarddeg	*un deg un*
12	*day*-thehg	een dehg *dai*
	deuddeg	*un deg dau*
13	*trree*-ahrr-*thehg*	een dehg *trree*
	tri ar ddeg	*un deg tri*
14	*ped*-wahrr-ahrr-*thehg*	een dehg *ped*-wahrr
	pedwar ar ddeg	*un deg pedwar*
15	*puhm*-thehg	een dehg *pimp*
	pymtheg	*un deg pump*
16	*een*-ahrr-*buhm*-thehg	een dehg *khwehkh*
	un ar bymtheg	*un deg chwech*
17	*dai*-ahrr-*buhm*-thehg	een dehg *saith*
	dau ar bymtheg	*un deg saith*
18	*day*-now	een dehg *oo-eeth*
	deunaw	*un deg wyth*
19	*ped*-wahrr-ahrr-*buhm*-thehg	een dehg *now*
	pedwar ar bymtheg	*un deg naw*

WELSH

WELSH

20	*ig-ain*	dai thehg
	ugain	*dau ddeg*
21	*een-ahrr-hig-ain*	dai thehg *een*
	un ar hugain	*dau ddeg un*
22	*dai-ahrr-hig-ain*	dai thehg *dai*
	dau ar hugain	*dau ddeg dau*
23	*trree-ahrr-hig-ain*	dai thehg *trree*
	tri ar hugain	*dau ddeg tri*
30	*dehg-ahrr-hig-ain*	*trree dehg*
	deg ar hugain	*tri deg*
40	*day-gain*	*ped-wahrr dehg*
	deugain	*pedwar deg*
50	*hann-err* kant	*pim dehg*
	hannar cant	*pum deg*
60	*trri-gain*	khwe dehg
	trigain	*chwe deg*
70	dehg-ah-*thrri*-gain	saith dehg
	deg a thrigain	*saith deg*
80	*ped-wahrr ig-ain*	oo-eeth dehg
	pedwar ugain	*wyth deg*
90	*dehg-ah-fed-wahrr ig-ain*	now dehg
	deg a phedwar ugain	*naw deg*
99	*ped-wahrr ahrr buhm*	now dehg now-*thehg*
	pedwar ar bymthgeg	*naw deg naw*
100	cant	kant
1000	mil	*meel*

GERMAN 161

LONELY PLANET

Series Description

travel guidebooks	in depth coverage with backgournd and recommendations download selected guidebook Upgrades at www.lonelyplanet.com
shoestring guides	for travellers with more time than money
condensed guides	highlights the best a destination has to offer
citySync	digital city guides for Palm TM OS
outdoor guides	walking, cycling, diving and watching wildlife
phrasebooks	don't just stand there, say something!
city maps and road atlases	essential navigation tools
world food	for people who live to eat, drink and travel
out to eat	a city's best places to eat and drink
read this first	invaluable pre-departure guides
healthy travel	practical advice for staying well on the road
journeys	travel stories for armchair explorers
pictorials	lavishly illustrated pictorial books
eKno	low cost international phonecard with e-services
TV series and videos	on the road docos
web site	for chat, Upgrades and destination facts
lonely planet images	on line photo library

LONELY PLANET OFFICES

Australia
Locked Bag 1, Footscray,
Victoria 3011
☎ 03 8379 8000
fax 03 8379 8111
email: talk2us@lonelyplanet.com.au

USA
150 Linden St, Oakland,
CA 94607
☎ 510 893 8555
TOLL FREE: 800 275 8555
fax 510 893 8572
email: info@lonelyplanet.com

UK
10a Spring Place,
London NW5 3BH
☎ 020 7428 4800
fax 020 7428 4828
email: go@lonelyplanet.co.uk

France
1 rue du Dahomey,
75011 Paris
☎ 01 55 25 33 00
fax 01 55 25 33 01
email: bip@lonelyplanet.fr
website: www.lonelyplanet.fr

**World Wide Web: www.lonelyplanet.com *or* AOL keyword: lp
Lonely Planet Images: lpi@lonelyplanet.com.au**